American Architecture

AN ILLUSTRATED ENCYCLOPEDIA

American Architecture

AN ILLUSTRATED ENCYCLOPEDIA

CYRIL M. HARRIS

W · W · NORTON & COMPANY · NEW YORK · LONDON

Printed in the United States of America
The text of this book is composed in Caledonia with the display set in Kabel
Composition and production by Ken Gross
Manufacturing by Hamilton Printing
Book design by Antonia Krass

Library of Congress Cataloging-in-Publication Data

Harris, Cyril M.
    American architecture : an illustrated encylopedia / Cyril M. Harris.
        p.   cm.
    ISBN 0-393-73029-8
    1. Architecture—United States—Encyclopedias. I. Title.
NA705.H36 1998   98-10793
720'.973—dc21   CIP

ISBN 0-393-73029-8

W. W. Norton & Company, Inc., 500 Fifth Avenue, New York, N.Y. 10110
http://www.wwnorton.com

W. W. Norton & Company Ltd., 10 Coptic Street, London WC1A 1PU

0 9 8 7 6 5 4 3 2 1

TO ANN

PREFACE

This book spans the full range of the built environment in America from precolonial times through the present. It has been written to be comprehensive in scope, reliable in fact, informative in substance, and succinct in presentation. In defining and illustrating all those terms that provide the basic language of American architecture, the intention is to provide readers not only with precise information about the various types of local dwellings, houses, civic and commercial buildings, and houses of worship illustrative of American architectural design, and the techniques and materials used in building them, but also to set this information in a context that recognizes the multiple influences which have shaped that design. Constructed by a nation of immigrants, beginning with the earliest Spaniards who arrived among the indigenous peoples of Florida to settle Saint Augustine in 1565, America's architecture, like its culture, has been configured in important ways by the traditions, customs, and religious practices of the lands from which these immigrant tides came, by the varied physical landscapes in which they settled, by the peoples whom they found on their arrival, and by the process of Americanization itself.

Thus, the entries contain historical as well as descriptive detail. Construction materials and methods, decorative terms, technical processes, and practical devices are all included. Entries place special emphasis not only on important characteristics that distinguish built structures in appearance—their plans, façades, doors, windows, roofs, chimneys, decorative elements—but on the ways in which they were physically and functionally adapted to their settings.

Where specific buildings are dated, the dates signify the year of completion; when construction took place over a number of years, both the starting and completion dates are given. Dates of styles and modes of architecture are necessarily approximate, not only because with rare exceptions these forms appeared over a period of time, but because they tended to become prominent in one area of the country and to spread only gradually to more interior or distant regions.

Special emphasis has been given to architectural styles. Vital though these classifications are, there has been no general agreement among architectural historians as to the precise meaning of such commonly used descriptors as *style, substyle, mode,* and *type,* which tend to be used variously and often interchangeably in the literature, though frequently they are not synonymous. A style of architecture may be defined differently from one text to another. Confusing the picture further, significantly different names may be used to describe the same style. An example is the term *Classical Revival Style,* popular in America from about 1770 to 1830, which in various sources is called *Early Classical Revival, Neoclassical Revival, Roman Classicism, Roman Revival,* or *Jeffersonian Classicism.*

Because this variant terminology is often imprecise or confusing, this book bases the terms identified as styles of American architecture on the following explicit definition of *architectural style*:

> A classification characterizing buildings that share many common attributes, including similarity in general appearance, in the arrangement of major design elements, in ornamentation, in the use of materials, and in form, scale, and structure. Architectural styles are often related to a particular period of time, geographical region, country of origin, or religious tradition, or to the architecture of an earlier period.

Based on these criteria, readers will recognize that many an architectural term that includes the word *style* in its name does not necessarily qualify as a style. For example, there is no such thing as "Victorian style"; Victorian describes an *era,* which did in fact encompass a specific exuberant, ornate, and highly decorative group of styles, such as Victorian Romanesque.

In many instances what is called a style is actually an *architectural mode,* defined as:

> An inexact classification for buildings that share selected architectural features but, unlike an architectural style, may not share consistency of design, form, or ornamentation with other buildings similarly classified.

Many forms of Revival architecture are properly architectural modes, especially when such buildings emulate earlier prototypes. Thus *Colonial Revival* is in general an architectural mode rather than an architectural style because details intrinsic to the prototype may have been omitted or exaggerated in size or importance; design elements, such as a type of dormer, chimney, or windows that never existed in the prototype may have been added; or materials may have been used that did not exist at the time of the prototype.

To describe architectural styles accurately, this book presents them in a uniform format: a general description that sets them in a historical or social context, followed by a standard group of classifications to highlight their distinctive features: **façade and exterior wall treatments, roof treatments, window treatments,** and **doorway treatments.** This format will enable readers not only to distinguish among different styles but to make valid comparisons between them. Detailed illustrations also enhance these distinctions.

The drawings that accompany the entries range from plans and elevations to renderings of entire buildings; from utilitarian objects such as locks to such exotica as sun disks; from dogtrot cabin to skyscraper, from covered bridge to Crystal Palace (the New York one), from impost to pilaster to Richardsonian Romanesque. Taken together, the text and illustrations are intended to be a standard resource for professionals and lay readers alike. Architects, students of architecture, architectural historians, art historians, archaeologists, designers, conservators, preservationists, restorationists, landscape architects, and curators should find this book a valuable reference and research tool. For nonspecialists, whether they are architecture buffs or simply curious, these pages may offer a fresh understanding of the world around them: the landscapes, buildings, roadways, skylines, and structures they see in their neighborhoods or on their travels that have much to tell them about their country's past and present.

ACKNOWLEDGMENTS

I extend special appreciation to a long-time friend and professional colleague, Adolf K. Placzek, Avery Librarian Emeritus of Columbia University, for his comments, insights, and substantive suggestions during the preparation of this book. He has been generous with his time, his knowledgeability, and the very great pleasure of his company.

The Avery Architectural and Fine Arts Library at Columbia University, which Professor Placzek directed for many years, also deserves special thanks. This library, founded in 1890, contains the world's largest collection of books on architecture, an unrivaled record of architectural thought and design. Housed in the School of Architecture, Planning and Preservation's Avery Hall designed by McKim, Mead & White, its magnificent collection includes the first printed book on architecture, Alberti's *De Re Aedificatoria* of 1485, the first printed edition of Vitruvius's *De Architectura* of 1486; and the first printed book to contain architectural illustrations, Francesco Colonna's *Hypnerotomachia* of 1499. Avery Library was an invaluable resource, and I am grateful to its director, Angela Giral, her associates Katherine R. Chibnik and William O'Malley, and others on the staff for their help and support.

Numerous other libraries were also generous in providing information and assistance; I express my appreciation to them all, and want to thank in particular the library of the American Philosophical Society, founded in Philadelphia in 1743 by Benjamin Franklin, its librarian, Edward C. Carter, II, and his associate Roy E. Goodman; the library of The Athenaeum of Philadelphia; the library of the Winterthur Museum and Gardens in Winterthur, Delaware; the library of the Colonial Williamsburg Foundation in Williamsburg, Virginia; and the library of the Historic American Buildings Survey (HABS) in the Library of Congress in Washington, D.C.

Finally, I thank Nancy N. Green, my editor at W. W. Norton & Company, for her professionalism, commitment, and unwavering support.

With few exceptions, I have chosen to use drawings rather than photographs to illustrate the entries in this book because relevant features are easier to discern in line drawings. A number of them have been taken from my own collection gathered in the preparation for two of my prior books: *Illustrated Dictionary of Historic Architecture* and the *Dictionary of Architecture and*

Construction. The extensive collection of trade catalogs in the Avery Library was a valuable source of illustrations, as was the extensive collection of HABS.

James Matthew Brown prepared drawings on those occasions when a suitable illustration could not be found or where an existing drawing in the public domain required computer enhancement to display certain architectural features.

Permission to reproduce drawings from other copyrighted sources, listed below, has been granted for use only in this book by their copyright owners:

Avery Architectural and Fine Arts Library, Columbia University in the City of New York, for Franklin stove, from *Catalog of Unsurpassed Stoves and Ranges,* Isaac A. Sheppard & Co., Philadelphia, 1890; spandrel,2, from *Auditorium*, Exhibit Publishing Co., Chicago, 1890; and Sullivanesque, from *Forms and Fantasies* by Louis H. Sullivan, Chicago, 1898.

Chelsea Green Publishing Company, for straw bale house, reprinted from *The Straw Bale House,* copyright © 1994 by Atena Swentzell Steen, Bill Steen, and David Bainbridge. With permission from Chelsea Green Publishing Company, White River Junction, Vermont.

Claitor's Law Books and Publications/J. Desmond, for columbage, from *Antebellum Architecture* by John Desmond, 1970.

Mary Mix Foley, for glass house, from *The American House,* Harper & Row, Publishers, Inc., 1980.

Frank O. Gehry & Associates, for Deconstructivist architecture.

Geoscience Publications, Louisiana State University, for bousillage, briquette entre poteaux, Cajun cottage, Creole house, plaunch debout entre terre, poteaux-sur-solle house, and umbrella roof, from *Louisiana's Remarkable French Vernacular Architecture 1700–1900* by Dr. Jay D. Edwards.

Johns Hopkins University Press, for Gothic Revival (a), from *Gothic Revival & American Church Architecture* by Phoebe B. Stanton, 1968, and for forebay barn and pent roof,1, from *The Pennsylvania Barn* by R. F. Ensminger, 1992.

Office of Philip C. Johnson, for Post-Modern architecture.

F. B. Kniffen Cultural Resources Laboratory, Louisiana State University, for Cajun cottage.

Randell L. Makinson, for U-plan, from *Greene and Greene,* Gibbs Smith, Publisher.

The Metropolitan Museum of Art, for stained glass window (b) tryptych (1912), courtesy of The Metropolitan Museum of Art; purchase, 1967, E. C. Moore, Jr. Gift and Edgar J. Kaufmann Charitable Foundation Gift (67.231.1-3).

Missouri Historical Society, St. Louis, for Steamboat Gothic.

Mount Vernon Estate & Gardens, for treading barn.

The New-York Historical Society, for theater, © Collection of The New-York Historical Society.

Allen Noble and Richard K. Cleek, for bank barn, bent frame, continuous house, crib barn, jacal,1, potato barn, tobacco barn, and zigzag fence, from *The Old Barn Book,* Rutgers University Press,1995.

W. W. Norton & Company, Inc., for window, from *Residential Windows,* © 1996 by John Carmody, Stephen Selkowitz, and Lisa Heschong.

The Octagon, for Châteauesque style, the Astor House in New York City, by Richard Morris Hunt, Architect, from The Prints and Drawings Collection, The Octagon Museum, The American Architectural Foundation.

Oklahoma Historical Society, for sod house,1 (a), from *Of the Earth* by H. L. and M. E. Meredith.

Oxford University Press, for earthlodge, hogan, ki, and wigwam, from *Native American Architecture* by Peter Nabokov and Robert Easton. Copyright © 1989 by Peter Nabokov and Robert Easton. Used by permission of Oxford University Press, Inc.

William A Pierson, photographer, for Round Arch style, Bowdoin College Chapel, Brunswick, Me., Richard Upjohn, Architect.

Reader's Digest, for bark house,1, bent-frame construction,1, iglu, kiva, longhouse, pit house,2, plank house (b), sod dwelling, tipi, and winter house,1. Reproduced from *America's Fascinating Indian Heritage* © 1978 The Reader's Digest Association, Inc. Used by permission.

Shelter Publications, for grass house,1, excerpted from *Shelter* © 1973 by Shelter Publications, Inc., P. O. B. 279, Bolinas, Ca. 94924. Drawing by Bob Easton. Distributed in bookstores by Random House. Reprinted by permission.

St. Augustine Historical Society, for arbor, balcony, palma hut (b), reja, Saint Augustine house and plan, Spanish Colonial architecture of Florida, wattle-and-daub, well curb, and wicket, from from *The Houses of St. Augustine* by Albert Manucy, 1962, reproduced with permission.

Mimi Sloane, for sawpit, from *American Barns and Covered Bridges* by Eric Sloane, published by Funk and Wagnalls.

Society of Architectural Historians, for plank house (a), from *Buildings of Alaska* by Alison K. Hoagland, Buildings of America Series of the Society of Architectural Historians, Oxford University Press, 1993.

Southern Methodist University Press, for zaguán, from *Taos Adobes* by Bainbridge Bunting, published by Southern Methodist University and the Museum of New Mexico Press.

Janann Strand, for angled bay window, knee brace, and stepped windows, from *Greene & Greene Guide,* 1974.

Charles E. Tuttle & Company, Inc., for folly and octagon house (b), from *Architectural Follies in America* by Clay Lancaster, 1960.

University of Illinois, for distyle in antis, from *Architecture in Old Kentucky.* Copyright 1981 by Rexford Newcomb and Margaret A. Larson. Used with the permission of the University of Illinois Press.

University of Oklahoma Press, for sweathouse (b), from *The Indian Tipi: Its History, Construction, & Use* by Reginald Laubin, Gladys Laubin, and Stanley Vestal. Copyright © 1957.

University of Pittsburgh Press, for double chimney,1, double stair, lintel (b), random ashlar, ribbon window, semicircular window, and tollhouse, from *The Early Architecture of Western Pennsylvania* by Charles Morse Stotz, © 1936. Reprinted by permission of the University of Pittsburgh Press.

Sally B. Woodbridge, for blockhouse, dogtrot, and Sunday house, from *The Cabin, The Temple, The Trailer* by Charles W. Moore and Sally Woodbridge, drawings by Diana Woodbridge.

Winterthur, for rauchkammer, from *Winterthur Portfolio,* vol. 21, 1986, by William Ways Weaver.

Frank Lloyd Wright Foundation, for Wrightian: Fallingwater and Robie House. Frank Lloyd Wright drawings are Copyright © 1998 The Frank Lloyd Wright Foundation, Scottsdale, AZ.

American Architecture
AN ILLUSTRATED ENCYCLOPEDIA

abacus The uppermost member of the **capital** of a column, especially of a capital of the **Doric order**; often a simple square slab, but sometimes molded or otherwise enriched.

abacus

abat-vent In the **French Vernacular architecture** of New Orleans, an extension of a roof over a sidewalk.

abutment A masonry mass that receives the thrust of an arch, vault, or strut.

Acadian cottage Same as **Cajun cottage.**

acanthus A common plant of the Mediterranean, whose leaves, stylized, are used as a characteristic decoration on capitals of the **Corinthian order** and **Composite order.**

acanthus

acorn A small ornament in the shape of a nut of the oak tree; sometimes used in American Colonial architecture as a finial, pendant, or decorative element within a broken pediment or as a decoration on a carved panel.

acorn: ornament on a baluster, Le Prêtre Mansion, New Orleans, La.

acroterion 1. A pedestal at a corner or peak of a roof; usually supports an ornament or statue. 2. The ornament itself.

acroterion: Brooklyn Institute of Arts and Science (1897), Brooklyn, N.Y.

active solar-energy system In a **solar house,** a system by which energy from the sun is collected and stored, then distributed throughout the house primarily by mechanical equipment (such as fans and pumps) powered by energy not derived from solar radiation. Compare with **passive solar-energy system.**

acute arch Same as **lancet arch.**

Adamesque style An imprecise term implying a derivation from the **Adam style** but with possible differences depending on the time and place of application.

Adam Revival *See* **Colonial Revival**.

Adam style A style developed in the late 18th century, based on the work of Robert Adam (1728–1792), assisted by his three brothers; his architectural firm had the most extensive practice in England and Scotland. Born in Scotland and educated at the University of Edinburgh, Robert Adam was architect to the king from 1762 to 1768, when he was succeeded by his brother James. Adam style is characterized by clarity of form, elegance and lightness, use of color, subtle detailing, and unified schemes of interior design; often-employed design motifs included honeysuckle and fan ornaments, festoons, urns, wreaths, and small round or oval ornaments decorated with leaves, petals, and the like. The Adam style was so strongly influential in the colonies, being largely the basis for the **Federal style,** that some architectural historians in America use these two terms more or less interchangeably. This is not surprising since the interior decorative elements of the two styles are almost identical. For example, the ceiling of George Washington's home at Mount Vernon and many mantelpieces in elegant homes in the colonies are excellent illustrations of the Adam style. However, the exteriors of American buildings in the Federal style generally differ from English buildings in the Adam style, particularly with respect to scale, entrances, and fenestration.

added lean-to Same as **integral lean-to.**

Adirondack Rustic style *See* **Rustic style.**

adobe A heavy soil, composed largely of clay and silt, especially used in making adobe bricks and adobe plaster; it contains sufficient quantities of clay and silt to form a matrix in which sand particles are firmly embedded. To this mixture, straw, manure, and fragments of tile may be added to provide increased mechanical strength and cohesion. The proper amount of water needed for making adobe bricks varies with the clay content of the soil but is often between 15 and 30 percent. To form *adobe bricks,* the mixture is shaped by hand, usually in a wooden mold; then it is sun-dried, rather than burnt in a kiln (*see* **brick**). An 18th-century publication provides the following instructions on how to make adobe bricks on a large scale: "(a) Remove the top surface of the earth. (b) Plow the clay and silt below the surface layer; then flood it. (c) Scatter a 'binder' such as straw, reeds, sedge grass, or manure over the flooded area. (d) Ensure that the area is well trodden

Adam style: fireplace at
George Washington's Headquarters, Rocky Hill, N.J.

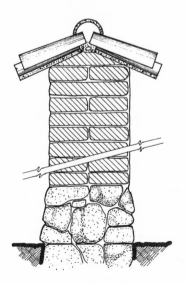

adobe brick wall
tile capped (c. 1834), Monterey, Calif.

by a beast of burden until the binders are thoroughly worked into the wet earth. (e) Pour the mixture of wet earth and binder into wood boxes that serve as molds, usually about 18 inches long, 12 inches wide, and 6 inches deep. (f) Leave to dry until fairly well hardened; when the brick dries, the addition of the binder increases its structural strength."

Adobe was widely used in the American Southwest long before the coming of the Spaniards, but it was the Spaniards who introduced the use of bricks made of adobe. They usually built their walls on foundations, in contrast to the native inhabitants who poured their first course of **puddled adobe construction** directly on the ground. The use of foundations substantially reduces the tendency of an adobe wall to erode at its base. Even so, unless an adobe wall is lime-plastered, it will usually erode beyond repair in about 25 years. To reduce such erosion and to improve its resistance to weather, a stabilizing agent such as **slaked lime, whitewash,** cactus juice, or fresh animal blood sometimes was added to the adobe mixture before it was molded

into bricks or before it was applied as a surface coating of adobe plaster. Adobe brick was especially used in **Mission architecture, pueblo architecture, Spanish Colonial architecture.**

adobe quemado An adobe brick that has been kiln-dried at a temperature not sufficiently high to produce a **hard-burnt brick**; usually it is deep in color, relatively soft, and rough in texture; once used in some areas of the American Southwest.

A-frame house A house, usually constructed of wood, with a roof that extends steeply downward from both sides of a central ridge, almost to the building foundation. The roof is supported by a rigid structural framework in the shape of the upright capital letter **A**. One or both of the end walls of the house are usually almost completely glazed. Much of the living area on the ground floor is open to the underside of the roof; the bedrooms are frequently located on a balcony directly under the roof. There is often an exterior deck at one end of the house. *See also* **rafter house**.

adobe arch: unplastered, Mission San Miguel Arcángel (1797), Paso Robles, Calif.

A-frame house

aggregate An inert granular material, such as sand, crushed stone, or gravel, which is mixed with a cement binder to form concrete, mortar, plaster, or the like. In early colonial America, broken bits of clam, mussel, or oyster shells were sometimes used as an aggregate.

airplane bungalow A **Craftsman style** bungalow having a **gable** whose face is parallel to the main ridge of the roof; has a single room on the second floor.

air-supported structure *See* **pneumatic structure.**

Alamo A Franciscan mission in San Antonio, Texas, founded in 1718, originally named "San Antonio de Valero." Construction of the first stone church structure at the mission was started in 1744 but never completed. It was replaced by a second church, which was begun in 1756. The remains of this structure have undergone modifications. The present façade contains an elaborately carved portal with an arched doorway, two pairs of spirally fluted columns flanking the doorway, and niches at the side of the columns. The mission was secularized in 1793. During the Texas War of Independence in 1836, the Alamo was the site of a famous siege, when it was defended by Davy Crockett and Colonel James Bowie and became a symbol of heroic resistance for the Texans. Several legends explain how the mission came to be called the *Alamo* (Spanish for cottonwood tree). Of these, the most widely accepted is that the structure was renamed after a Spanish cavalry unit from the Mexican town of El Alamo de Parras, which was stationed in the abandoned mission in the early 1800s.

ale house A village tavern licensed to sell alcoholic beverages in an early American community.

alicatado Work that is executed with colorful, glazed, patterned earthenware tiles called **azulejos;** especially found in **Spanish Colonial architecture** of the American Southwest; used to decorate pavements and walls, as in patios.

almshouse A building in which charity was distributed to the poor; found in some early American cities or settlements, for example, in Philadelphia in the 1760s. *See also* **poorhouse.**

American basement In houses in cities such as New York after about 1880, a basement story that is situated at or just below ground level and contains the kitchen, pantry, and other functional rooms; the living room, dining room, library, and the like are on the floor above. Access to the house is provided by a short outside stair down to an entrance vestibule at basement level. Also called a walk-out basement.

American bond Same as **common bond.**

airplane bungalow

Alamo (1756)
San Antonio, Tex.

almshouse
Society of Friends (1729), Philadelphia, Pa.

American Bracketed style A term occasionally used for the **Italianate style**.

American Châteauesque style *See* **Châteauesque style.**

American Colonial architecture A broad, sometimes confusing term, most often applied to buildings constructed in America by English immigrants to the New World; but also often classified according to time period, country of origin of the settlers (*see* **Dutch Colonial architecture, French Colonial architecture, German Colonial architecture**, and **Spanish Colonial architecture**), or region in America. When the earliest arrivals landed in America from England (at Jamestown, Virginia, in 1607 and at Plymouth, Massachusetts, in 1620), their first priority was to construct some type of basic shelter in which to live and to store food supplies. During this *settlement phase*, when the colonists were engaged in tasks essential to their survival, such as the clearing of land and the planting of crops, most of their dwellings were relatively primitive, for example, dugouts, huts, or modified indigenous dwellings. Within a few years, these temporary structures were replaced by more substantial one- or two-story houses, one room deep, similar to those the colonists were familiar with in their countries of origin. Methods of building construction were adapted to prevailing local conditions. Various historians refer to architecture during the period following the settlement phase with terms such as: *Early English Colonial architecture, Early Colonial architecture, American Colonial architecture, Pre-Revolutionary architecture,* or *First Period Colonial architecture.* Less often, the term *Post-Medieval* is used to describe dwellings that exhibited many of the characteristics of timber-framed medieval houses, with steeply pitched roofs, very large fireplaces, large chimney stacks, small casement windows, and other characteristics described in the following two entries.

Architecture in colonial America exhibited significant differences in appearance, depending on the local materials available for construction. For example, compare **American Colonial architecture of early New England** with **American Colonial architecture of the early South**, from which it differed considerably, as can be seen in the two entries that follow.

American Colonial architecture of early New England Architecture of the English colonies in New England, from the period following the initial settle-ment of the English in Massachusetts in 1620 to the emergence of Georgian-style architecture around 1700. The typical house was timber-framed, using heavy timbers of readily available hardwood, such as oak, with hewn-and-pegged joints, following the tradition of English medieval construction and emphasizing practicality and simplicity. Many of the earliest houses consisted of only a single room with a loft space above (*see* **one-room plan**). Houses of the more prosperous settlers were one, one-and-a-half, or two stories high and one room deep and were usually built on the **hall-and-parlor plan,** with one room on each side of an interior wall containing a massive, centrally located fireplace and large, high chimney. One of the rooms served as the kitchen, sewing room, and general living area for the family; the room on the other side of the wall served as a parlor and usually as the parents' bedroom. With the passage of time, many such houses were enlarged, often becoming two rooms deep. A common addition in New England was a lean-to at the rear of the house that served primarily as a kitchen. If the roof of the lean-to continued the slope of the main roof, the long sloping contour that resulted gave the house a shape similar to that of a box then used for holding salt; hence the term **saltbox house**. Other expansions were achieved by adding windows to the loft space under the roof so that it became a reasonably comfortable living area

American Colonial architecture of early New England:
(a) Peak House (1670), Medfield, Mass.

and/or by the addition of a front porch with a bedroom above it. *See also* **Cape Cod house, stone-ender, whale house.**

Early New England Colonial architecture varies considerably from region to region in the Northeast and with chronology; nevertheless, buildings in this category usually exhibit many of the following characteristics:

Façade and exterior wall treatments: A timber-framed house with the space between the timber-framing members usually filled with mud, plaster, or **wattle-and-daub;** the exterior walls were sometimes covered with a coat of hard plaster, then clad with oak clapboard (pine clapboard was not used until later in the colonial period) or with unpainted wood shingles. Frequently the second story overhung the first floor along the façade and occasionally on the sides as well. Carved ornaments called **pendants** or **drops** were often suspended from the front overhang at the corners of house and were also hung on each side of the entry door, usually serving as the only decorations on the façade.

Roof treatments: In many of the earliest homes, a **gable roof** and a **side gable** that was steeply pitched and **thatched** to shed water quickly. Later the thatching was replaced with hand-split wood shingles, which were much less of a fire hazard and more durable. The steep pitch was often retained in order to shed the heavy New England snows more easily. **Hipped roofs** were also popular. The eaves had no significant overhang.

Window treatments: In the early settlements, medieval-type **casement windows,** in wood frames on wrought-iron hinges. Usually the windows were few in number and small in size because of the high cost of glass; the **sashes** contained small, diamond-shaped panes (called **quarrels**) set in grooved cast-lead strips **(cames).** If an additional half-story was added to the house, casement windows would often be set in the gable ends. Windows in the homes of less prosperous settlers often had no glazing; the openings were closed either with solid wood shutters or with frames covered with oiled paper or oiled cloth.

Doorway treatments: Usually, heavy **battened doors** constructed of vertical boards or planks held together by horizontal boards on the interior side of the door.

American Colonial architecture of early
New England: (b) Manton House
(c. 1680), Manton, R.I.

American Colonial architecture of early New England:
(c) Col. Wentworth House (1701), Stafford, N.Y.

American Colonial architecture of the early South Architecture in the pre-Revolutionary colonial South, as well as the colonies along the mid-Atlantic coast, from the initial settlement of the English in Jamestown, Virginia, in 1607 to the emergence of Georgian-style architecture in about 1700. The single-room houses of the earliest settlers in Virginia were somewhat similar to those of the earliest settlers in Massachusetts (*see* **one-room plan**), although they used lighter-weight oak beams and posts. Later, as the houses became larger, the arrangement of the rooms usually followed a **hall-and-parlor plan** or a **center-hall plan.**

Buildings in this category usually exhibit many of the following characteristics:

Façade and exterior wall treatments: After about 1630, brick exterior walls were laid with lime mortar made from oyster shells. The brick patterns most popular in early Maryland and Virginia were **Flemish bond** and **English bond.** The brickwork included **relieving arches,** flat arches, a molded brick **belt course,** and a brick **water table** that prevented water from running down the face of the lower part of the wall; often, a narrow, projecting gabled-fronted pavilion; occasionally, a **chimney pent,** especially in Maryland.

Roof treatments: Hand-split shingles, which replaced the thatching of the very earliest dwellings after about 1630. In many of the earliest homes, the chimney framework was constructed of wood and then fire-protected by a clay, lime, or mud plaster. Later a massive decorative brick or stone exterior chimney, with **corbeled chimney caps,** was built at one or both gabled end walls. Often there was a side-gabled and steeply pitched roof with no significant eaves overhang, occasionally with roof dormers. Pent roofs were common in the mid-Atlantic area.

Window treatments: In many of the earliest colonial dwellings in the South, window openings covered with oiled paper or oiled cloth, protected by solid-wood shutters. After the middle of the 17th century, these were replaced by narrow casement windows having small, diamond-shaped glass panes (**quarrels**) set in grooved strips of cast lead (**cames**); windows were few in number because of the high cost of glass.

Doorway treatments: Commonly, **battened doors,** constructed of vertical boards held together by horizontal battens on the interior side of the door; the front door was usually located at the center of the façade, providing access to the rooms on the ground floor via a central hall. In small houses without a central hall, the front door opened directly into one of the rooms.

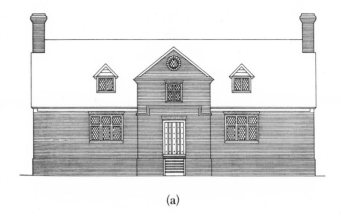

(a)

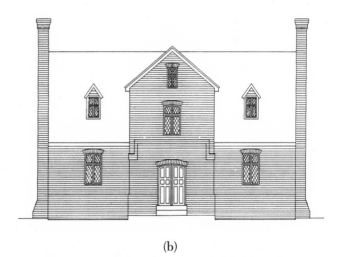

(b)

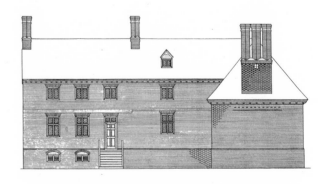

(c)

American Colonial architecture of the early South: (a) Foster's Castle (c. 1690), New Kent County, Va.; (b) Criss Cross (1690–1710), New Kent County, Va.; (c) Fairfield (1692), Gloucester County, Va.

American Colonial Revival *See* **Colonial Revival.**

American Eskimo dwellings *See* **barabara, iglu, pole house, sod dwelling, winter house.**

American four-square house 1. A one- or two-story house having a square **floor plan** consisting of four rooms, one in each corner, a steeply pitched **hipped roof** or **pyramidal roof,** occasionally with hipped dormers facing the street, an off-center entry door on the front façade, and often a kitchen attached to one of the rooms; popularized by **pattern books** from about 1905 to 1915 and beyond; also called a four-square house. 2. A **Prairie box** having a low-pitched hipped roof, a symmetrical façade, and a front entry, primarily from 1900 to 1920.

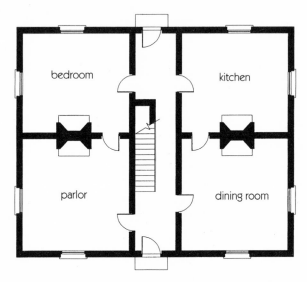

American four-square house: plan, Nauvoo, Ill.

American Georgian style *See* **Georgian style.**

American Indian dwellings *See* **bark house, bent-frame construction,1, big house,1, brush house, cavate lodge, chickee, earthlodge, grass house, hogan, ki, kiva, longhouse, mat house, mud house,1, palma hut, pit house,1, plank house, pueblo architecture, ramada,2, roundhouse,1, sweathouse, tipi, wigwam, wikiup, winter house.**

American Institute of Architects (AIA) In 1837 a group of architects established a professional organization called the American Institution of Architects, which lasted only briefly despite the fact that its members represented the leaders in the architectural profession throughout the country. Another attempt to form a professional organization was made by Richard Upjohn (1802–1878) in mid-February of 1857. The first regular meeting of the new organization, following its incorporation as the "American Institute of Architects," was held on May 5, 1857. Its purposes were, and remain, the establishment and promotion of professionalism and accountability on the part of its members and the promotion of design excellence. Address: 1735 New York Avenue NW, Washington, DC 20006.

American International style *See* **Contemporary style and International style.**

American Mansard style A seldom-used synonym for **Second Empire style.** *See also* **Mansard style.**

American Renaissance Revival A term occasionally used for **Italian Renaissance Revival.**

American Rundbogenstil Same as **Round Arch style.**

American Society of Landscape Architects (ASLA) The professional organization of **landscape architects** in America, founded in 1899. Address: 4401 Connecticut Avenue NW, Washington, DC 20008.

American Society for Testing and Materials (ASTM) An organization that establishes voluntary test standards for materials and products in the United States, including those used in building construction. These standards are widely used by the architectural and engineering professions and by the construction industry. Address: 1916 Race Street, Philadelphia, PA 19103.

American style A seldom-used term for **Italianate style.**

American Tudor style *See* **Tudor Revival.**

anchor, anchor iron A wrought-iron clamp on the exterior side of a brick building wall that is connected to the opposite wall by a steel tie rod so as to prevent the walls from spreading apart; of Flemish origin, and used on many houses in New Amsterdam (now New York City). These wall clamps were often in the shape of numerals indicating the year of construction, letters representing the owner's initials, or simply fanciful designs. Also called a wall stay.

anchor beam In a typical **Dutch barn,** a massive horizontal timber that runs from one gable end to the other; usually located about 12 feet (366 cm) above the threshing floor.

ancillary A term descriptive of a building that provides an auxiliary service to a larger principal building; *see also* **dependency.**

ancon A scrolled or decorative bracket that supports a cornice or **entablature** over a door, mantel, or window.

ancon

angle bead A molding used to protect the exterior angle between two intersecting surfaces, such as two walls.

angle brace A piece of wood or other material that is fixed at an angle between two members of a frame, usually to provide increased rigidity.

angle capital The **capital** of a corner column, especially an Ionic capital where the four **volutes** project equally on a diagonal toward the corner.

angle capital

angled bay window A **bay window** that is triangular in plan and protrudes outward from a wall.

angled bay window: Bowen House (1905), Pasadena, Calif.; Greene and Greene, Architects

angled chimney stacks *See* **diagonal chimney stacks.**

angle fireplace A fireplace across one corner of a room; for example, *see* **fogón.**

angle modillion A **modillion** located at a corner of a cornice.

angle rafter Same as **hip rafter.**

angle tie Same as **dragon tie.**

Anglo-Italian Villa style A term occasionally used for the **Italianate style.**

angular pediment A **pediment** having a horizontal cornice and slanting sides that meet in a point so as to form a triangle. Also called a triangular pediment.

annex A subsidiary structure adjoining a larger principal building.

anta (*pl.* **antae**) A **pilaster** or a rectangular **pier** formed by a thickening at the end of a wall, usually projecting into the façade or portico; its capital and base usually differ from those on columns within the portico. Antae usually occur in pairs, one on each side of the portico; columns within the portico, between the antae, are said to be in antis. Found in the **Greek Revival style.** *See also* **distyle in antis.**

antebellum Dating before or existing before the United States Civil War (1861–1865).

antefix In **Classical architecture** and derivatives, a decorated upright ornament at the eaves, at the ends of the ridge of the tiled roof, or at the peak of a triangular gable.

antefix

antepagment The stone or stucco decorative dressing enriching the jambs and head of a doorway or window; same as **architrave,1.**

anthemion A common Greek decoration suggestive of honeysuckle or palmette, an ornament derived from a palm leaf; used singly or as a **running ornament,** for example, in the **Greek Revival style.**

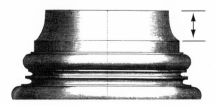

anthemions: used as a running ornament: Bowery Savings Bank (1895), New York City

apartment A room or group of rooms designed as a self-contained dwelling; usually one of many such units in the same building.

apex stone Same as **saddle stone.**

apophyge 1. That part of a column where the shaft of the column springs from its base or where the shaft terminates at its capital; usually molded into a concave sweep; also called a scape or congé. 2. The hollow (i.e., **scotia**) beneath the **echinus** of some classical capitals.

apophyge,1: at the base of a column

appentice 1. Same as **pentice.** 2. Same as **pent,2.**

applied molding Same as **laid-on molding.**

applied trim Supplementary and separate decorative strips of wood or moldings affixed to the face or sides of a door or window frame or the like.

appliqué 1. An accessory decorative feature applied to an object or structure. 2. In ornamental work, one material affixed to another.

apse A semicircular (or nearly semicircular) or semi-polygonal recess that terminates an axis of a church having a **cruciform plan;** usually houses an altar.

apteral A term descriptive of a classical building having columns and a portico at one or both ends but no columns along the sides.

araeostyle Same as **areostyle.** *See* **intercolumniation.**

arbor 1. A light, open structure having a lattice framework, usually supporting intertwined vines or flowers. 2. A shaded, leafy recess usually formed by tree branches; also called a bower.

arbor

arcade 1. A covered walk with a line of arches along one or both sides. 2. A covered walk or passageway that is lined with shops or offices on one or more levels.

arch A construction that spans an opening; usually curved; often consists of wedge-shaped blocks (called *voussoirs*) having their narrower ends toward the opening. Arches vary greatly in shape, from those that have little or no curvature to those that are acutely pointed. For additional definitions and illustrations of particular types of arches, *see* **acute arch, basket-handle arch, blind arch, camber arch, compound arch, discharging arch, Dutch arch, elliptical arch, equilateral arch, flat arch, French arch, garden arch, gauged arch, Gothic arch, horseshoe arch, jack arch, keystone arch, lancet arch, memorial arch, miter arch, Moorish arch, ogee arch, pointed arch, Queen Anne arch, relieving arch, round arch, rowlock arch, segmental arch, semicircular arch, semielliptical arch, shouldered arch, stepped arch, straight arch, street arch, three-centered arch, trefoil arch, triangular arch, Tudor arch, two-centered arch.**

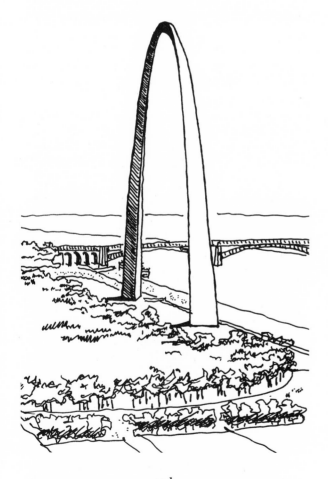

arch
Jefferson National Expansion Memorial (1964),
St. Louis, Mo.; Eero Saarinen, Architect

arch bar A curved wrought-iron or steel bar used as a **lintel** to carry the weight of the masonry above a fireplace opening.

arch brick A wedge-shaped brick used in arch or circular construction; its two large faces are inclined toward each other. Also called a radius brick.

arched dormer A dormer having a semicylindrical (or approximately semicylindrical) roof; the head of the upper sash may be either round-topped or flat-topped; especially found in the **Beaux-Arts style, Second Empire style, French Eclectic architecture.**

arched dormer

architect A person who is trained and experienced in the design of buildings and in the coordination and supervision of all aspects of the construction of buildings; contemporary architects are also responsible for meeting all legal requirements to which the buildings may be subject. The earliest important designer of buildings in the American colonies was Peter Harrison (1716–1775), for whom architecture was an avocation; his designs included Redwood Library (1750) in Newport, King's Chapel (1754) in Boston, Christ Church (1761) in Cambridge, and Touro Synagogue (1763) in Newport. Other important early architects in America included Charles Bulfinch (1763–1844), Benjamin Henry Latrobe (1764–1820), who emigrated from England to Philadelphia in 1796; and Latrobe's outstanding pupils William Strickland (1788–1854) and Robert Mills (1781–1855). Before about 1860, little distinction was made between an architect and an engineer; a single individual usually carried out the functions of both professions. The first school to provide formal training in architecture in the United States was founded at the Massachusetts Institute of Technology in 1865; before that time, architects received their training through apprenticeships. In 1897 Illinois became the first state to establish formal licensing requirements for the practice of architecture. *See also* **American Institute of Architects.**

architectonic Related or conforming to technical architectural principles.

architectural 1. Pertaining to architecture: its features, characteristics, design, and/or details. 2. Pertaining to materials used to build or ornament a structure.

architectural details The relatively small elements of design and finish of a building.

architectural mode An inexact classification for buildings that share selected architectural features but, unlike an **architectural style**, may not share consistency of design, form, or ornamentation with other buildings similarly classified. When such buildings emulate an earlier prototype, architectural details that characterize the prototype often are omitted or exaggerated in size or importance; other design elements (such as a type of dormer, chimney, or window that never existed in the prototype) may be added; or characteristic building materials of the prototype may be replaced with newer types of materials. For example, Colonial Revival buildings are usually poor emulations of their colonial prototypes; as a result, such buildings may be appropriately classified as belonging to an architectural mode rather than an architectural style.

architectural style A classification characterizing buildings that share many common attributes, including similarity in general appearance, in the arrangement of major design elements, in ornamentation, in the use of materials, and in form, scale, and structure. Architectural styles are often related to a particular period of time, geographical region, country of origin, or religious tradition, or to the architecture of an earlier period. In order to describe architectural styles accurately and to facilitate comparisons among styles, this book uses a uniform group of categories in such entries to highlight the distinctive features of each style. These categories are: *façade and exterior wall treatments, roof treatments, window treatments,* and *doorway treatments.* This format makes it evident that certain terms that customarily include the word *style* do not actually qualify as architectural styles. In some cases the terms themselves have been altered to reflect this distinction; for example, *Eastlake style* is identified as *Eastlake ornamentation.* It will also be evident that some types of Revival architecture are **architectural modes** rather than styles. The word *style* is attached to terms for Revival architecture only when such architecture is similar in appearance to and

displays a consistency of design, form, ornamentation, and choice of materials with the style of architecture it seeks to emulate, as for example, Classical Revival style, Greek Revival style, Italianate style, or Neoclassical style.

For descriptions of architectural styles and architectural modes that are often called styles, *see* **Adamesque style, Adam style, Adirondack Rustic style, American Bracketed style, American Châteauesque style, American Georgian style, American International style, American Mansard style, American Renaissance Revival, American Rundbogenstil, American style, American Tudor style, Anglo-Italian Villa style, Art Deco, Art Moderne, Art Nouveau, Beaux-Arts style, Bracketed style, Brutalism, Builders' Shed style, California Mission Revival, Carpenter Gothic, Châteauesque style, Chicago Commercial style, Churrigueresque style, Classical Revival style, Classic Revival, Collegiate Gothic, Colonial Georgian style, Commercial Italianate style, Commercial style, Contemporary style, Corporate style, Craftsman style, Early Gothic Revival, Eastern Stick style, Elizabethan Manor style, English Revival, Federal style, Franco-Italianate style, French Revival, French Second Empire style, General Grant style, Georgian Revival, Georgian style, Gothic Revival, Gothic survival, Greek Revival style, High Victorian Gothic, High Victorian Italianate, International Revival, International style, Italianate style, Italian Villa style, Jacobethan style, Jeffersonian Classicism, Jeffersonian style, Late Georgian style, Late Gothic Revival, Lombard style, Mansard style, Mediterranean Revival, Mission Revival, Mission style, Modernistic style, Modern style, Monterey style, National style, Neo-Adamesque, Neoclasssical style, Neoclassicism, Neo-Gothic, Neo-Grec, Neo-Tudor, Neo-Victorian, New England Federal style, New Shingle style, Period Revival, Picturesque Gothic, Plateresque architecture, Prairie style, Pueblo Revival, Pueblo style, Queen Anne Style, Regency Revival, Regency style, Renaissance Revival, Richardsonian Romanesque style, Rococo, Romanesque Revival, Romanesque style, Romantic style, Round Arch style, Rundbogenstil, Ruskinian Gothic, Rustic style, Santa Fe style, Second Classical Revival style, Second Empire style, Second Renaissance Revival, Shed style, Shingle style, Spanish Colonial Revival, Spanish Mission Revival, Spanish Mission style, Steamboat Gothic, Stick style, Streamline Moderne, Style Moderne, Symmetrical**

Victorian style, Transitional style, Tudor Revival, Tudor style, Tuscan Villa style, Victorian Romanesque, Villa style, Western Stick style.

See also **American Colonial architecture, American Colonial Revival, Arts and Crafts movement, Baroque, Cajun cabin, Cajun cottage, Chinese Chippendale, Classical architecture, Colonial architecture, Colonial Revival, Deconstructivist architecture, Dutch Colonial architecture, Dutch Colonial Revival, Early Colonial architecture, Early English Colonial architecture, Eastlake ornamentation, Eclectic architecture, Egyptian Revival, Elizabethan architecture, English Colonial architecture, English Regency, Federal Revival, First Period Colonial architecture, Flemish Colonial architecture, folk architecture, Folk Victorian architecture, French-Canadian architecture, French Colonial architecture, French Eclectic architecture, French Vernacular architecture, German Colonial architecture, Gingerbread folk architecture, Gothic architecture, High-Tech architecture, High Victorian architecture, Hispanic Colonial architecture, Jacobean architecture, Louisiana Vernacular architecture, Medieval architecture, Mid-Colonial architecture, Mission architecture, Modern architecture, Moorish Revival, Neo-Colonial architecture, Neo-Eclectic architecture, Neo-Federal style, Neo-French architecture, Neo-Georgian, Neo–Greek Revival, Organic architecture, Oriental Revival, Picturesque movement, Pointed style, Post-Modern architecture, pueblo architecture, PWA Moderne, Renaissance architecture, Revival architecture, Shaker architecture, Spanish Colonial architecture, Spanish Eclectic architecture, Spanish Pueblo Revival, Swiss Cottage architecture, Territorial style, Tuscan Revival, Victorian architecture, Victorian Gothic, Victorian Queen Anne style.**

architectural terra-cotta A glazed or unglazed clay unit that has been burnt in a kiln at a high temperature; finer in texture than brick and usually larger in size than brick or **facing** tile; may be glazed in vibrant colors. It was used as a facing on buildings in America primarily from the middle of the 19th century until the 1930s. *See also* **terra-cotta.**

architecture 1. The art and science of designing and building structures or groups of structures, in keeping with aesthetic and functional criteria. 2. Structures built in accordance with such principles.

architrave 1. An ornamental molding or decorative band around or above an opening such as a door or window, or around a panel; *see also* **double architrave.** 2. In the Classical orders, the lowest member of an **entablature**, i.e., the beam that spans from column to column, resting directly upon the capitals of the columns.

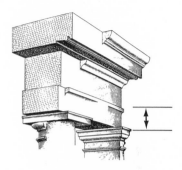

architrave,2

architrave cornice In Classical architecture and derivatives, an **entablature** having a cornice that rests directly on the architrave, the **frieze** being omitted.

archivolt An ornamental border, molding, or decorative band on the face of an arch; it follows the contour of the exterior surface of the arch, as around the curved opening of masonry arches used in the **Richardsonian Romanesque** style.

archivolt
entrance to Ames Memorial Library (1879), North Easton, Mass.; H. H. Richardson, Architect

arch stone A wedge-shaped masonry unit in a curved arch. Also called a voussoir.

arch street A street carrying vehicular traffic that passes through a building, for example, the arch street designed by the architect Charles Bulfinch (1763–1844) as part of Franklin Place and Tontine Crescent (1804) in Boston, Massachusetts.

arch surround A seldom-used term for a decorative border around an **arch;** same as **archivolt.**

areostyle *See* **intercolumniation.**

armory, arsenal A building used for military training, for the storage of weapons and military equipment, or as a weapons-manufacturing plant.

arris An external angular intersection between two planar faces or two curved faces, for example, as between two flutes on a Doric column.

Art Deco A decorative style stimulated by the Paris *Exposition International des Arts Décoratifs et Industrielles Modernes* of 1925; usually characterized by angular, zigzag, or other geometric ornamentation in low relief on building façades. It was much used in American architecture of the 1930s, primarily in the design of skyscrapers and apartment houses; an outstanding example, the Chrysler Building (1930) in New York City, by William Van Alen, was the tallest building in the world (1,046 feet) at the time of its completion. Another excellent example is the old McGraw-Hill Building (1930) on West 34th Street in New York City, designed by Raymond Hood. Miami Beach has many apartment houses in the Art Deco style, sometimes referred to as **Style Moderne.**

art glass A type of colored glass used in windows in America during the late 19th and early 20th centuries; characterized by combinations of hues and special effects in transparency and opaqueness.

artifact *See* **building artifact.**

Art Moderne An architectural style found principally in houses constructed in the 1930s following the earlier Art Deco; usually characterized by smooth stuccoed wall surfaces, flat roofs, architectural details that emphasize the horizontal appearance of the building, rounded exterior corners, **ribbon windows** that may continue around a corner, glass blocks, most often, an asymmetrical façade. The jagged version of this style is also called Zigzag Moderne. *See also* **Art Deco, PWA Moderne,** and **Streamline Moderne.**

arch street: Tontine Crescent (1794), Boston, Mass.;
Charles Bulfinch, Architect

Art Deco
tower of the Chrysler Building (1930), New York City

Art Nouveau A style of decoration in architecture and applied art developed principally in France and Belgium toward the end of the 19th century; characterized by organic and dynamic forms, curving design, and whiplash lines. Such embellishments were somewhat similar to the continuous foliated motifs employed by Louis Sullivan in America (*see* illustration under **Sullivanesque**). Louis Comfort Tiffany (1848–1933) was particularly influential in the application of Art Nouveau in the United States, especially with regard to his work in **stained glass.**

Arts and Crafts movement The emphasis by a group of artisans on craftsmanship and high standards in all architectural details; beginning in the late 19th century and greatly influenced by the Craft movement of William Morris (1834–1896) and his company of artists near London, who had in turn been primarily inspired by John Ruskin (1819–1900). In the early 20th century, the Arts and Crafts movement had a significant impact on the **Prairie Style**, with its low-pitched roofs and widely overhanging eaves. Also, it significantly influenced American domestic architecture, particularly through the efforts of Gustav Stickley (1858–1942); in the early 20th century, it had a further impact on both the **Craftsman style** and the **Prairie style.** The emphasis on craftsmanship espoused by the Arts and Crafts movement was especially embodied in the designs of the southern California architects Charles Sumner Greene (1868–1957) and his brother Henry Mather Greene (1870–1954), in whose work architectural details were carried to a high art.

art window A term sometimes applied to a window in which the upper and lower sashes are of different size and the upper sash contains a number of small panes of colored glass.

ash house In colonial America, a small **dependency** for the storage of ashes used primarily in the making of soap.

ashlar, ashlar masonry Masonry composed of rectangular blocks of stone or the like, generally larger in size than a brick; the blocks are sawed or dressed so they are square on all faces. *See also* **nidged ashlar** and **random ashlar.**

ashpit A small chamber built into the base of a chimney in which ashes are collected for removal; a cast-iron access door usually closes off the chamber.

asistencia Same as **contributing chapel.**

astragal A **bead,** usually half-round, with a **fillet** on one or both sides; may be plain, although the term often describes a small convex molding decorated with a string of beads or bead-and-reel shapes.

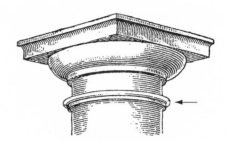

astragal

astylar A term descriptive of a façade without columns or pilasters.

atrio In **Mission architecture** of the American Southwest, the walled forecourt of a **mission**; often used for mass on Sundays and feast days.

attached house A house that is joined to an adjacent house by a common wall.

attic A garret or loft space beneath a roof and above the uppermost floor of a house.

Attic base The base of a column of the **Ionic order** consisting of an upper and a lower **torus,** with a **scotia** and two narrow fillets between them. *See also* illustration under **base,2.**

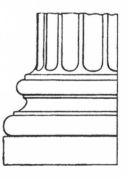

Attic base

attic story In **Classical architecture** and its derivatives, the story of a building that is above the cornice of a wall.

awning window A rectangular window that opens outward on a frame that turns about a horizontal axis along its upper edge.

axed brick Brick that has been shaped with an ax; requires thicker mortar joints when laid than brick manufactured to close tolerances does.

axed work A hand-dressed stone surface showing toolmarks made by an ax, pick, or bushhammer

azotea In **Spanish Colonial architecture**, a terrace or flat platform on the roof of a house. Occasionally this term refers to a type of house built in the vicinity of Saint Augustine, Florida, in the early 18th century, that was characterized by a flat roof drained by waterspouts (**canales**).

azulejo In **Spanish Colonial architecture,** glazed earthenware tile, usually painted in richly colored patterns that often have a metallic luster.

B

back hearth That part of a **hearth** contained within a fireplace. Also called an inner hearth.

back house, back building 1. A privy or outhouse. 2. A structure that stands behind a building to which it is a subsidiary.

baguette A small, convex **molding.**

bake house A small subsidiary structure with one or more ovens used exclusively for the baking of breads and pastries; relatively common before the mid-19th century in religious communities and on plantations; usually located away from the principal dwelling to reduce the risk of setting it on fire.

bake oven An oven constructed of bricks, usually having a circular or oval dome. Often located within the inner hearth of the principal fireplace of a colonial house, two to three feet (61–91cm) above the floor, bake ovens became an integral part of chimney construction primarily after the middle of the 17th century. Many bake ovens had a small hearth of their own and a small flue connected to the main flue; others were heated by glowing charcoal or embers that were swept out before the unbaked loaves were inserted and the iron oven door closed. The backs of some bake ovens projected beyond the exterior wall of the house and were protected from the weather by a covering of stucco. Bake ovens were widely used in Dutch Colonial houses. Also called a beehive oven, bread oven, brick oven, or Dutch oven.

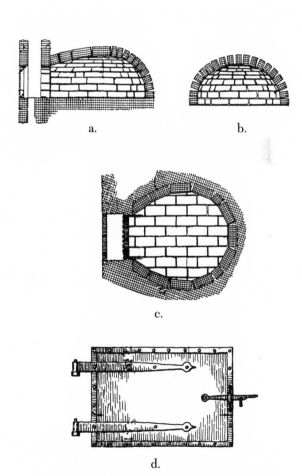

bake oven: at Coeyman House, Belleville, N.J.:
(a) longitudinal section; (b) cross section; (c) plan;
(d) wrought-iron door to oven

balconet In front of a window, a balustrade or railing that is suggestive of a balcony.

balconet

balcony A projecting platform on a building that is either supported from below or cantilevered from the structure; enclosed with a railing or balustrade.

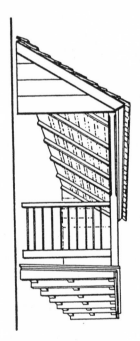

balcony
Spanish Colonial home (18th cent.),
St. Augustine, Fla.

bale house 1. *See* **straw bale house**. 2. An obsolete term for a warehouse.

balk A squared timber used in building construction.

balloon framing A system of **framing** in a building in which all vertical structural elements of the exterior **load-bearing walls** consist of studs that extend the full height of the building frame; all floor joists are usually attached to these studs, and the framing is sometimes covered by a brick veneer facing. This system of framing contrasts with **platform framing,** in which each floor is framed separately. The development of balloon framing in the 1830s, together with the commercial availability of lumber in uniform sizes and mass-produced nails of good quality, made possible the construction of inexpensive houses in America. It also made possible dwellings in shapes that could not have been constructed using earlier types of essentially medieval framing systems. *See also* **braced framing.**

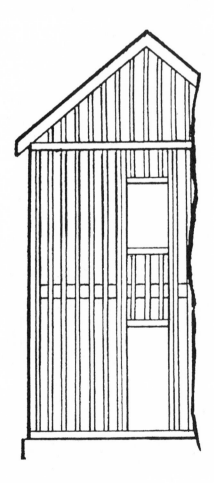

balloon framing

baluster 1. One of a number of short vertical structural members, often circular or square in cross section, used to support a stair handrail or the like. Before about 1730 balusters were commonly carved by hand; after that date they were usually turned on a lathe and tended to be taller and more slender than earlier ones. On a stair there were often two or three balusters per step, each of which would therefore be of a different height. 2. The roll forming the side of an **Ionic capital.**

balustrade An entire railing system, as along the edge of a porch, balcony, or roof deck; includes a top rail and its **balusters,** and often a bottom rail.

banco In **Spanish Colonial architecture** of the American Southwest, a built-in seat.

band, band molding Any horizontal flat molding, rectangular or slightly convex in profile, that projects slightly from a surface; used as a decorative element.

bandage A strap, ring, chain, or band placed around a structure to secure and hold its parts together, as around a silo or the springing of a dome.

band course Same as **belt course,1.**

baluster,1: King's Chapel (1754), Boston, Mass.

baluster,2.

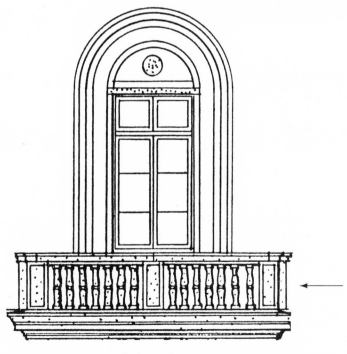

balustrade

banded A term descriptive of masonry having adjacent courses of stones of two different sizes or types; if the courses alternate in color, for example, brownstone alternating with light-colored limestone, this term or the adjective **polychromed** may be used; sometimes found in the **Queen Anne style** and **High Victorian Gothic.**

banded column A column with **drums** that alternate in size or color or degree of ornamentation.

banded column

banded surround A decorative architectural element around a doorway or window that is **banded;** usually the adjacent masonry blocks are of two different sizes. *See* **door surround, Gibbs surround, window surround.**

band window One of a horizontal series of three windows or more, separated only by **mullions,** that form a horizontal band across the façade of a building; for example, *see* **frieze-band window.** Most commonly found in buildings erected after 1900. Also called a ribbon window.

bank barn A two-story barn usually built into the slope of a hill so as to provide some protection against the prevailing wind. An inclined driveway leads to a large sliding door on the upper floor, which contains an area set aside for threshing grain, storing grain, and storing animal feed. The lower level of the barn provides housing for horses and cattle and is entered at ground level from an enclosed yard. Sometimes called a German barn, Pennsylvania barn, or Pennsylvania Dutch barn because of its popularity among German-speaking immigrants who settled in that state in the late 18th century and beyond. This type of barn was also common in the adjacent mid-Atlantic states. *See also* **barn, forebay barn, Swiss barn, Yankee barn.**

bank barn

bank house *See* **German Colonial architecture.**

banquette 1. A long, built-in upholstered seat against a wall. 2. A raised, narrow walk along a roadway. 3. A term once used in some parts of the American South for a sidewalk.

banquette cottage In New Orleans in the early 19th century, a Creole town house flush against a sidewalk; usually consisted of four rooms in a square array.

bar 1. *See* **door bar.** 2. One of a number of thin strips of wood or metal forming the several divisions of a window sash or a wood-paneled door. 3. Same as an iron **mantel,3.**

barabara 1. A **sod house.** 2. A partially underground communal dwelling of inhabitants of the Aleutian Islands of Alaska; its barrel-vault-like structural framework was constructed of driftwood or whalebone and then covered with thatch and with a layer of sod or turf. It was usually about 100 feet (30m) long and 30 to 40 feet (9–12m) wide; light was provided by the two entryways at ground level, from which ladders descended to the dwelling below.

barbed-wire fence, barbwire fence A fence fabricated of small pieces of heavy wire that are sharply pointed and twisted together at short intervals and strung between vertical posts. Patented in 1868, it was not widely used until a practical machine was developed for its manufacture more than ten years later. Because this type of fence was efficient, cheap, and durable, it played an important role in domesticating the West, effectively leading to the demise of the open range for grazing animals.

bargeboard A board that hangs from the projecting edge of a sloping gable roof; sometimes carved and elaborately ornamented. Highly decorated bargeboards are found, for example, in **Gothic Revival** and **Tudor Revival** houses in America. Also called a gableboard or vergeboard.

bar iron A strong, malleable iron, available in the form of bars, which can be beaten into shape by blacksmiths to form tools, horseshoes, hardware, and highly decorative ironwork. *See* **wrought iron.**

bark house 1. A dwelling, once used by some Indian tribes as far west as California; had a conical shape, or a rectangular shape with rounded corners, formed by a framework of wood poles lashed together and covered with overlapping slabs of bark. 2. A rectangular dwelling of the 18th-century Iroquois of upstate New York and Canadian territory to the north; had a barrel-shaped or gable roof covered with overlapping slabs of bark. 3. A shed used to store bark prior to its processing in a **bark mill.**

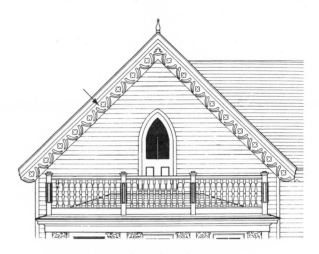

bargeboard
J. D. Roberts House, Carson City, Nev.

(a)

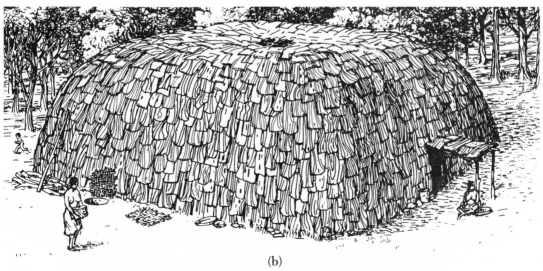

(b)

bark house,1: (a) conical; (b) rectangular, with rounded corners

bark mill In American colonial days and beyond, a mill used for processing bark used in dying and tanning.

barn A building, most often rectangular (but occasionally circular or polygonal), for housing farm animals, storing farm equipment, threshing grain, and storing grain, hay, and other agricultural produce. The barns constructed by the colonists in America depended on such factors as the type of barn used in their country of origin, the local climate, the building materials available, the skills and time required for construction, and the cost. Thus, stone or brick barns were built less frequently because they usually took more time, required greater skill, and were more expensive. German barns usually had masonry walls up to the second (threshing) floor and were of wood construction above. In brick barns the mortar between some of the vertical joints of adjacent bricks was sometimes deliberately omitted, leaving the space between them to ventilate the barn and to form a decorative pattern. Polygonal barns, while uncommon, have had a long history in America; they date back to George Washington, who designed a 16-sided **treading barn** for his estate. Barn types are frequently identified by their usage, their wall materials, their shape and structure, the materials used in the foundation and roof, or the type of doors, dormers, roofs, ventilators, or window openings. *See* **bank barn, basement barn, circular barn, connected barn, Connecticut barn, crib barn, double-decker barn,** **Dutch barn, English barn, forebay barn, four-crib barn, German barn, hex barn, New England connected barn, octagon barn, Pennsylvania barn, Pennsylvania Dutch barn, potato barn, raised barn, round barn, side-hill barn, Sweizter barn, Swiss barn, three-bay threshing barn, tobacco barn, treading barn, Yankee barn.**

barn raising In many parts of pre-20th-century America, a cooperative effort in which the framework of a large barn was assembled and then lifted in position in sections. The walls were supported by sections of a massive timber framework, called **bent frames** (one for each bay of the barn), that were designed to carry both lateral and vertical loads. The first step in building a large barn of **wood-frame construction** was to dig the cellar and lay the barn floor. Next, the bent frames were assembled on the ground adjacent to the barn by fitting the various components of the frame together and fastening them with wood pegs driven into previously drilled holes. Finally, at the appropriate locations, each bent frame was raised into an upright position with metal-tipped poles and then secured (*see* the illustration under **bent frame**). Since the bent frames were much too heavy for any one family to raise into position, the assistance of neighbors was required. This collaborative effort, known as a *barn raising* or *raising bee*, was a festive occasion with an ample supply of food and drink. Similar efforts, known as *house raisings,* helped in erecting large timber-framed houses.

barn

Baroque A European style of architecture and decoration that developed in 17th-century Italy from late Renaissance forms; usually characterized by the intersection of oval spaces and curved surfaces and by the conspicuous use of decoration, sculpture, and color. Decorative elements of its latter phase, called **Rococo,** characterized by profuse, often semiabstract ornamentation, were used in the late 19th century by many major American architects, for example, in the work of McKim, Mead & White. Compare with **Renaissance architecture.**

barreaux Wood bars forming a latticework between wall posts in **French Vernacular architecture** of Louisiana and environs; provided a structural support for an **infilling** (called **bousillage**) fitted between wood posts to receive them. *See* illustration under **bousillage.**

barrel roof 1. A roof of semicylindrical cross section; capable of spanning long distances parallel to the axis of the cylinder. 2. A **barrel vault.**

barrel vault A masonry **vault** of semicylindrical cross section supported by parallel walls or arcades; encloses an elongated rectangular space.

barrel vault: Bates Hall, Boston Public Library (1895), Boston, Mass.

base 1. The lowest and often widest visible part of a building, frequently distinctively treated; usually distinguished from a foundation or footing in being visible rather than buried. 2. The lower part of a column or pier that rests on a **pedestal, plinth,** or **stylobate.**

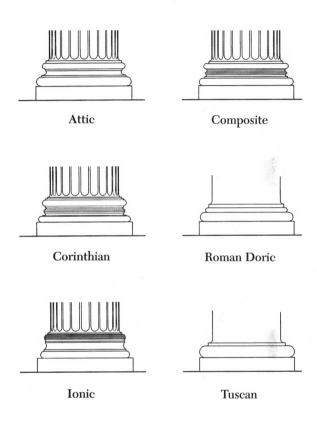

Attic   Composite

Corinthian   Roman Doric

Ionic   Tuscan

base,2
for different orders in Classical architecture

baseboard A relatively narrow board at the foot of an interior wall to protect the wall from damage. Also called a mopboard, skirt board, or washboard.

base course The lowest **course** of masonry units in a wall; may serve as a **foundation** or **footing.**

basement Usually the lowest story of a building, either partly or entirely below ground level at the outer walls of the building; same as a **cellar.** *See also* **American basement** and **raised basement.**

basement barn A term sometimes used for **bank barn.**

basket-handle arch, basket arch A flattened arch whose elliptical shape is determined by three arcs that are interconnected, each arc being drawn from a different center of curvature. In American architecture it is found in the **Beaux-Arts style, Châteauesque style,** and the **Italianate style.** Also called a semielliptical arch or an elliptical arch.

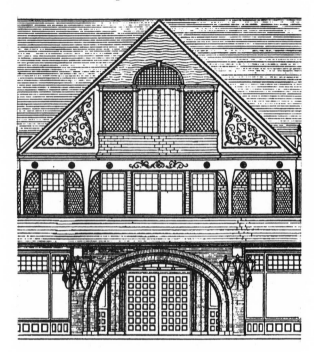

basket-handle arch: Casino (1881), Newport, R.I.; McKim, Mead & White, Architects

basket newel A series of balusters that supports one end of a handrail at the bottom of a flight of stairs and has the general conformation of a tall cylindrical basket.

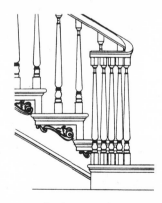

basket newel:
Cooleemee Plantation, near Macksville, N.C.

basket-weave bond An arrangement of bricks that forms a checkerboard pattern.

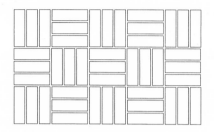

basket-weave bond

bas-relief Sculptured work, carving, or embossing that protrudes slightly from the plane of its background. Also called low relief.

bastion A projection from the outer wall of a **fort,** principally to defend the adjacent perimeter. *See also* **rampart.**

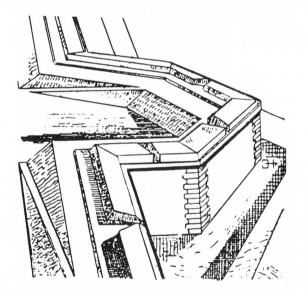

bastion

batten 1. A narrow strip of wood used to cover a joint between the edges of two adjacent boards in the same plane, as in **board-and-batten construction.** 2. A board fastened across two or more parallel boards to hold them together and/or to stiffen them, as in doors, panels, and window shutters. 3. A flat strip of wood attached to a wall as a base for **lath** or the like; also called a furring strip.

battened door, batten door A wood door constructed of vertical planks or boards held together by horizontal **battens,2** that are usually nailed to the interior side of the door. On some colonial doors, decorative nail heads were used to form an ornamental pattern. Doors of this type were usually carried on very long **strap hinges** fastened to the door frame. Over time the strap hinges were largely replaced by lighter-weight hinges, such as **H**-hinges. Exterior battened doors were usually of double thickness; in contrast, interior doors were usually only a single layer thick. Often found in **American Colonial architecture of early New England, Craftsman style, Pueblo Revival, Spanish Colonial architecture, Tudor Revival.** Also called a board-and-batten door, ledged door, or unframed door. *See also* **ledged-and-braced door** and **Z-braced battened door.**

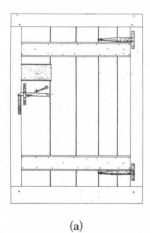

(a)

(b)

battened door: (a) showing exterior face, with a decorative nail-head pattern; (b) interior face

battened shutter Usually, one of a pair of solid window shutters similar in construction to a small **battened door;** used by the earliest American colonists to cover window openings. Because of the high cost of glass, such openings were often unglazed and covered instead with oiled cloth or oiled paper.

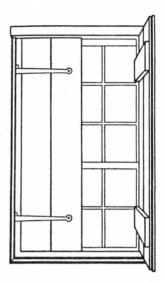

battened shutter

battered A term descriptive of a surface that is inclined or tilted with respect to the vertical, for example, a battered wall.

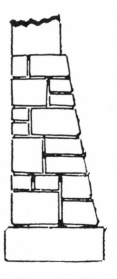

battered wall

battlement 1. A parapet with alternating solid parts (**merlons**) and openings (**crenels**) that is used for defense on fortifications; also called an embattlement. 2. A decorative motif having the general shape of **battlement,1;** sometimes used in **Gothic Revival** architecture in America.

Bauhaus A school of architectural design established by Walter Gropius (1883–1969) in Germany in 1919, characterized by emphasis on functional design in architecture and the applied arts, and having as guiding structural principles the use of a repetitive interval between members of the framework of a building and the maintenance of purely geometric forms. As a result major building components such as bays, doors, and windows are placed to coincide with this repetitive interval, although the building itself may be asymmetrical. The Bauhaus influence in America increased further when Gropius became professor and chairman of the department of architecture at Harvard University's Graduate School of Design in 1936 and Ludwig Mies van der Rohe (1886–1969), who was the director of the Bauhaus in the early 1930s, came to the Illinois Institute of Technology as Director of Architecture that same year.

bawn A 17th-century colonial American house designed to serve as a fort in the event of an enemy attack; its stone walls were usually massive. *See also* **garrison house.**

bay 1. Within a structure, a regularly repeated spatial element defined by beams or ribs and their supports. 2. A regularly repeated subdivision in a façade, particularly applied to houses; for example, a three-bay house has three windows evenly spaced across the upper floors; on the ground floor, because the entry door is tallied as one of the windows, this floor has two windows plus the door. 3. In a barn, the distance between **bent frames.**

bay window A window or series of windows that protrude from a wall; usually bowed, canted, polygonal, segmental, semicircular, or square-sided in plan; typically one story in height, although sometimes higher; sometimes corbeled out from the face of the wall, as an **oriel.** Commonly found in America in **Gothic Revival** and the **Queen Anne style.** *See also* **angled bay window, bow window, cant window.**

beacon house Same as **lighthouse.**

battlement,1

bay,2

bead A small, convex **molding** of semicircular (or greater) profile.

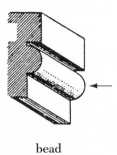

bead

bead-and-butt Descriptive of a wood-framed panel that is flush with its framing; has a **bead** that runs along two edges of the panel, the other two edges being left unbeaded.

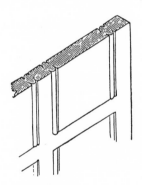

bead-and-butt

bead-and-reel molding A semiround convex **molding** decorated with a pattern of disks alternating with round or elongated **beads.**

bead-and-reel molding

beaded clapboard *See* **clapboards.**

bead molding 1. Same as **bead.** 2. Same as **paternoster.**

beam A horizontal structural member, such as a joist or girder, whose chief function is to carry loads perpendicular to its length. The term *beam* may be modified by an adjective indicating its location; as, for example, an *end beam* or *side beam. See also* **anchor beam, binding beam, breastsummer, camber beam, ceiling joist, collar beam, cross beam, dragon beam, ground beam, hammer beam, summerbeam, tie beam, wind beam.**

beam anchor A metal tie used to fasten a beam or joist to a wall, or to tie a floor securely to a wall.

beam infilling *See* **infilling.**

bearer One of a number of horizontal structural members that supports a load. In a colonial timber-framed house, the term *bearer* describes a horizontal timber that is usually smaller in cross section than a **girt** but performs a similar function. The term may be modified by a word (such as *end, front,* or *rear*) that indicates its location; for example, an *end bearer* runs horizontally across one end of the house; a *cross bearer* runs between joists.

bearing wall A wall capable of supporting an imposed load by transferring it to the foundation. Also called a structural wall or load-bearing wall.

Beaux-Arts architecture Elaborate, historic, and eclectic architecture, designed on a monumental scale, as taught at (and associated with) the École des Beaux Arts in Paris in the 19th century; freely adapting features of French architecture of the 16th, 17th, and 18th centuries and having considerable influence on American architecture. Usually characterized by formalism in design, symmetrical plans, mansard roofs, heavily rusticated arched masonry, sculptured figures, arched dormers, banded columns, cantons, cartouches, engaged columns, floral patterns, garlands, ornamented keystones, paired columns, roofline balustrades, and quoins. The first American to graduate from the *École* was Richard Morris Hunt (1827–1895), designer of The Breakers (1892) at Newport, R.I.; others who followed and later achieved distinction as architects included William Robert Ware (1832–1915), Charles Follen McKim (1847–1909), Louis H. Sullivan (1856–1924), Ernest Flagg (1857–1947), and Julia Morgan (1872–1957), the first woman graduate of the *École.*

Beaux-Arts style, Beaux-Arts Classicism A grandiose style of architecture, widely applied in America from about 1880 to 1930 to public buildings such as courthouses, libraries, museums, and railroad terminals, as well as some elaborate and pretentious residences, for example, Rosecliff (1902) designed by McKim, Mead & White in Newport, R.I.; based on the design principles of **Beaux-Arts architecture.** Compare with **Châteauesque style, Second Empire style, French Eclectic architecture.**

Buildings in this style usually exhibit many of the following characteristics:

Façade and exterior wall treatments: A massive symmetrical façade, frequently with a projecting central **pavilion;** often, a monumental **attic story;** commonly decorated with dentils; enriched **entablatures;** monumental flights of stairs; classical columns (especially Corinthian or Ionic) often set in close pairs; coupled pilasters; highly decorated pilastered parapets; balconies; ashlar stone walls with rusticated stonework, usually light colored, especially on the ground floor and raised basement levels; sculptured spandrels; decorative brackets with elaborate detailing; sculptured figures; cartouches, egg-and-dart moldings, escutcheons, floral patterns, garlands, Greek key designs, ornamental keystones, leaf decorations, medallions; elaborately decorated panels; quoins, swags, wreaths, and the like.

Roof treatments: A flat roof, a low-pitched hipped roof, or a mansard roof; occasionally, a balustrade at the roof line; often, domes and rotundas.

Window treatments: Rectangular windows, often one pane in the upper sash and one in the lower sash (1/1), symmetrically disposed, with lintels overhead; arched windows, balustraded windows, pedimented windows, or windows with balconets.

Doorway treatments: Paneled doors; often, a glass-paneled canopy over the primary entryway, flanked by columns or pilasters; a wrought-iron grille on the exterior side of the entry door.

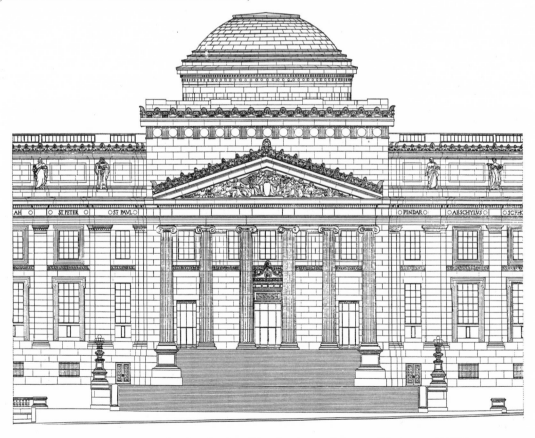

Beaux-Arts style: façade, Brooklyn Institute of Arts and Sciences (1897), Brooklyn, N.Y.; McKim, Mead & White, Architects

bed molding 1. A molding or group of moldings on the cornice of an **entablature**; located below the **corona** of a cornice and above the frieze. 2. Any molding directly below the projecting underside of a cornice or the like.

bed place An alcove into which a bed is built; found, for example, in many Dutch Colonial houses in America.

bed sill A horizontal timber at the base of a **timber-framed building**; the timber rests on, or is set into, the ground; same as **groundsill,2.**

beehive oven Same as **bake oven.**

belfry That part of a steeple or top of a tower in which one or more bells are hung. Also called a bell tower or campanario.

bell The body of a Corinthian capital or a Composite capital, with the foliage removed.

bellcast eaves Same as **flared eaves.**

bellcast roof Same as a **bell roof.**

bell cote A small belfry astride the ridge of a church roof, often crowned with a small spire.

bellflower A bell-shaped floral ornament; often, one of a string of such decorative elements.

bell gable A **wall gable** having one or more openings for bells.

bell pull A device once used to summon servants in an elegant home. In each room a small handle was connected to a wire that was mechanically connected in turn to a bell in the servants' quarters. A pull on the handle rang a bell in the servants' quarters; each bell produced a sound of a different pitch, so that the servants could identify the room calling for service.

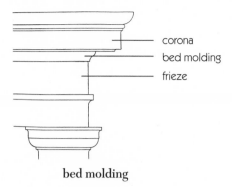

bed molding

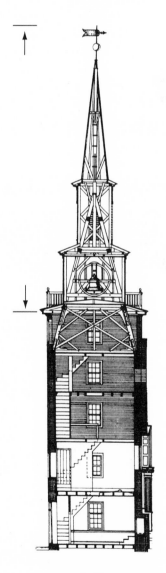

belfry
cross section of Trinity Church (1784),
Swedesboro, N.J.

bell pull

bell roof A roof having a cross section similar to that of a bell, flaring out at its lower edge.

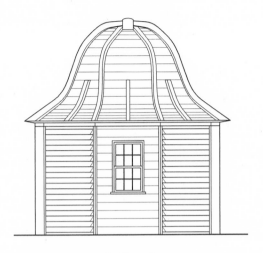

bell roof

bell tower A tall structure supporting one or more bells; may be part of a building or an independent structure. *See also* **belfry.**

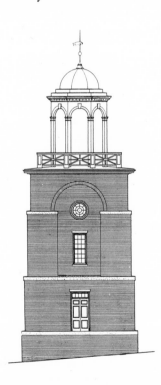

bell tower (1824):
Richmond, Va.

belt course 1. A horizontal band of masonry extending horizontally across the façade of a building and occasionally encircling the entire perimeter; usually projects beyond the face of the building and may be molded or richly carved; also called a stringcourse or band course; called a **sill course** if set at windowsill level. 2. A horizontal board across or around a building, often having a molding.

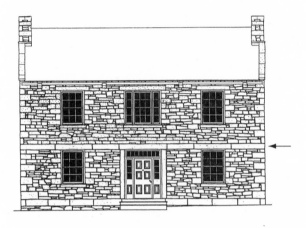

belt course

belvedere 1. A rooftop pavilion from which a view can be enjoyed. 2. Same as **gazebo**. 3. Same as **mirador.**

bent frame, bent A section of a timber framework that is transverse to the length of a large house or barn of timber-frame construction; usually designed to carry both lateral and vertical loads. Before the 20th century in America, such a framework was usually constructed on the ground and then raised to its upright position with the assistance of neighbors in a **barn raising.**

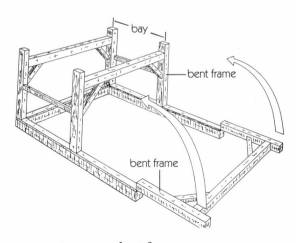

bent frame

bent-frame construction 1. A type of construction used by American Indians for dwellings such as **brush houses**, **grass houses, wikiups**, and some types of **wigwams**. First, a series of saplings was inserted in the ground, usually in the shape of a circle or oval; then the saplings were bent over and lashed together at the top with bark ties to form a domelike framework that was covered with bark, hide, reed matting, or thatch. 2. Any type of construction employing a **bent frame**, as in some barns and in some Dutch Colonial buildings.

bent-frame construction, 1.

berm 1. A continuous bank of earth alongside a road; also called a shoulder. 2. A narrow terrace built into an embankment, or the like, that breaks the continuity of an otherwise long slope. 3. A continuous bank of earth piled against a masonry wall.

béton brut *See* **Brutalism**.

bettering house An archaic term for **almshouse** or **poorhouse**.

bevel The angle that one surface makes with another surface when they are not at right angles. *See also* **chamfer**.

bevel siding *See* **clapboards**.

bezant An ornament shaped like a coin or disk, occasionally used in decorative moldings on the **archivolt** of an arch in the **Richardsonian Romanesque style**.

big house 1. A large multifamily dwelling of the Delaware Indians, usually used for tribal rituals. 2. In the South, a synonym for **great house**.

binding beam 1. Any timber that serves to tie together components of a **timber-framed building**. 2. *See* **summerbeam**.

binding joist In a colonial **timber-framed building**, a transverse horizontal beam that joins two vertical posts.

black diapering Same as **diaperwork**.

blacksmith shop A shop where iron bars are forged into objects such as tools, and where horses are fitted with horseshoes. Blacksmith shops, once an essential facility in early American towns, may still be found in some communities of Amish farmers in **Pennsylvania Dutch** country.

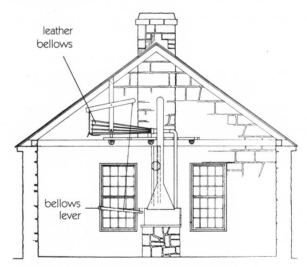

blacksmith shop: Chesterfield, N.H.

blade 1. One of the **principal rafters** of a roof. 2. Same as **cruck**.

blank door, blind door 1. A recess in a wall having, or suggesting, the appearance of a door; usually used to provide symmetry in the design of the wall. 2. A door that has been sealed off but is still visible.

blank wall, blind wall A wall whose whole surface is unbroken by a window, door, or other opening.

blank window, blind window A recess in an external wall having, or suggesting, the appearance of a window. Also called a false window.

blind arcade An ornamental row of **blind arches** on a wall that serves as a decorative element; may be found, for example, in **Richardsonian Romanesque style.**

blind arch An arch in which the opening is permanently closed by a wall construction.

blind floor Same as **subfloor.**

blindstory A floor level without exterior windows.

blind wall Same as **blank wall.**

blockhouse A fortified structure, often built by early American settlers to furnish protection against enemy attack at a location of strategic importance, such as a bend in a river; usually square or polygonal in plan; in frontier areas, usually constructed of hewn timbers with dovetailed notches at the corners to provide rigid joints; commonly, an overhanging upper story; often, masonry walls on the ground story with log construction above; frequently, a **pyramidal roof**; windows, small in size and few in number, with heavy shutters; **loophole** openings through the walls to permit the firing of guns in different directions over a wide range of angles. Compare with **garrison house.**

blocking course 1. A plain finishing course of masonry directly above a cornice. 2. Same as **belt course.**

block modillion *See* **modillion.**

bluffland house An Anglo-French Creole house characterized by a gable roof, overhanging cornices supported by brackets, pedimented front dormers, exterior chimneys, and tall windows; especially found in the area around Baton Rouge, Louisiana; said to be the final phase of **French Vernacular architecture.**

board-and-batten construction Wall construction for a timber-framed house in which the exterior covering consists of closely spaced boards set vertically, with narrow wood strips covering the joints between the boards.

board-and-batten door *See* **battened door.**

boarded wall An exterior wall of a building of **wood-frame construction** having boards usually applied horizontally, although vertically positioned boards are occasionally found.

blockhouse
Parker, Tex.

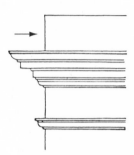

blocking course

board-and-batten construction
Yosemite Chapel (1887), Yosemite, Calif.

board fence A **fence** constructed of boards that are spaced horizontally and fastened to square lumber posts; once widely used in the American countryside, but now found primarily in upscale rural communities because of their relatively high cost.

board fence

board house 1. A house of **board-and-batten construction, board-on-board construction**, or the like. 2. A one-room cottage in Saint Augustine, Florida, during the late 16th century when Florida was a Spanish colony; had a timber frame sheathed with vertical cypress boards, battened doors, a dirt floor, and a gable roof of thatched palm leaves with a hole along the ridge that permitted smoke to escape from a fireplace directly below it.

boardinghouse A house that rents furnished rooms to and provides meals for its boarders for the payment of a weekly or monthly fee. Boardinghouses provided important facilities for unmarried workers and transients, especially in mill towns of the 19th and early 20th centuries. Compare with **lodging house.**

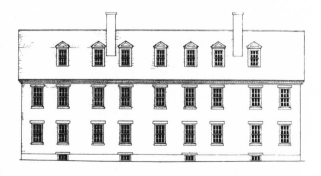

boardinghouse
Cheshire textile mill, Harrisville, N.J.

boarding joist A **joist** to which floor boarding is nailed.

board-on-board construction Wall construction for a timber-framed house having an exterior covering consisting of a double layer of vertical boards of approximately the same width. The boards in the second layer are positioned so as to cover the joints between the boards in the first layer.

boasted work A stone surface having a series of parallel grooves hand-cut across its face with a chisel.

bog house A synonym for **outhouse.**

boiserie Carved wood **panels** on the interior walls of a house, usually floor to ceiling, that are often enriched by gilding, painting, or with inlay. *See also* **wainscot.**

bolection molding A decorative molding that projects outward from a wood surface; used to conceal a joint between wood surfaces at different levels, for example, between a door panel and a surrounding framework.

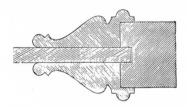

bolection molding

bolster 1. A horizontal piece of wood or a timber that caps a column, pillar, or post in order to provide greater bearing area to support a load imposed from above; often highly decorated, such as a **zapata** in Spanish Colonial architecture. 2. One of the rolls forming the sides of an **Ionic capital**, joining the **volutes** of the front and rear faces.

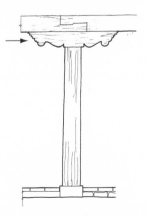

bolster,1: Spanish Colonial architecture

bolting mill An early American structure in which flour was sifted.

bond An arrangement of brick **headers** and **stretchers** in a pattern that provides a brick wall with strength, stability, and in some cases, decorativeness, depending on the pattern in which the bricks are laid. For descriptions of various masonry bonds, *see* **American bond, basket-weave bond, common bond, Dutch bond, English bond, English cross bond, Flemish bond, header bond, running bond, stack bond, stretcher bond**. The most widely used brick patterns in the American colonies were English bond and Flemish bond.

bond course In brickwork, same as **belt course,1.**

bond header, bondstone In stone masonry, a stone set with its longest dimension perpendicular to the face of a wall. Its ends are exposed on both faces of the wall. Also called a bonder.

bond timber A horizontal timber built into a brick or stone wall, either to strengthen the wall or to tie it together during construction.

bonnet A covering over an exterior door or window to provide shelter and/or a decorative element.

bonnet roof In **French Vernacular architecture**, particularly in the Mississippi Valley, a roof having a double slope on all four sides, the lower slope being less steep than the upper slope. When it extends over an open-sided raised porch, such a roof provides excellent shade for the house and protection against rain.

book matching The assembling of wood veneers from the same log so that successive sheets are alternately face-up and face-down. In wood with a visible grain or burl, sheets laid side by side show a symmetrical mirror image along the joint.

boot scraper A horizontal metal plate set in a small frame and usually located near the front steps of a building; used to clear dirt or mud from the bottoms of shoes or boots before entering the building; common in America before the advent of paved streets. Also called a foot scraper.

borning room In colonial New England houses, a small room in which women gave birth and where babies were sometimes kept during infancy; usually adjacent to the warm kitchen or the **keeping room.**

bottlery In colonial American houses, a room in which bottled goods such as beer and ale were stored.

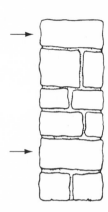

bond header: shown in the cross section of a wall

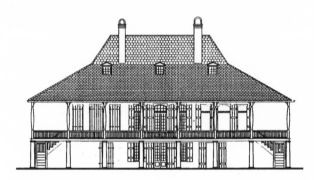

bonnet roof
Destrehan Plantation (1787), Destrehan, La.

book matching

boot scraper

bottom rail 1. The lowest horizontal structural member of the frame of a door or window that interconnects its vertical members. 2. The lower rail in a **balustrade.**

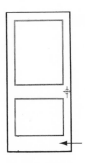

bottom rail,1

bottom stone Same as **footing stone.**

bousillage A mixture of clay and Spanish moss or clay and grass; used as a plaster to fill the space between cypress timbers acting as structural framing in *bousillage entre poteaux;* particularly found in **French Vernacular architecture** of Louisiana of the early 1700s. A series of wood bars (*barreaux*) were set between the posts to aid in holding this plaster in place. The *bousillage* increased the thermal insulation and greatly improved structural rigidity. When molded and used in brick form as an infilling between posts, it is referred to as **briquette-entre-poteaux.** *See also* **pierrotage.** Also spelled bouzillage.

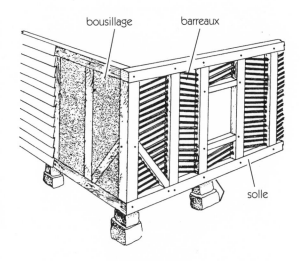

bousillage: between posts in a *poteaux-sur-solle* house

bowed roof Same as **segmental roof.**

bower Same as **arbor,2** or **garden arch.**

bow window A rounded **bay window** projecting from the face of a wall; in plan it forms the segment of a circle. Occasionally this term is used for any type of bay window.

box-and-strip construction, box construction In some areas of the American Midwest and South (for example, in the Ozarks) in the late 1800s, a relatively simple, economical wall construction used for small houses and dependencies. The **sillplates** are secured on a foundation consisting of flat stones. The walls are composed of closely spaced upright boards, approximately one foot (30 cm) wide and one inch (2.5 cm) thick; the cracks between the boards are covered with vertical battens only on the exterior surface of the boards so that the construction is relatively thin and requires a minimum of wood. The exterior appearance is similar to that of **board-and-batten construction.**

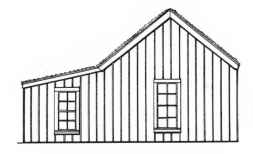

box-and-strip construction
elevation of end wall, Scurry, Tex.

boxed cornice, box cornice A **cornice** enclosed by boards and/or moldings so that the lower ends of the **rafters** are not visible. Also called a closed cornice.

boxed cornice

boxed eaves That part of a roof that projects beyond the exterior wall (i.e., the eaves) and that is enclosed by boards and/or moldings so that the **rafters** are not visible. Also called closed eaves.

box garden A somewhat formal garden that uses hedges of boxwood to separate various sections of the garden.

box gutter A rectangular wood **gutter**, usually lead-lined, that is set into and partially below the lower edge of a roof.

box house A house with **gables** on its end walls; usually two or three rooms wide and two rooms deep.

boxing shutter, boxed shutter One of a pair of window **shutters** that can be folded into a recess at the side of the window. Also called a folding shutter.

box lock A metal **door lock** that is mounted on the interior surface of a door. The lock mechanism is commonly encased in a flat rectangular box often fabricated of brass, but in early colonial America, occasionally encased in oak; much used in **Georgian style** and **Federal style** houses.

box stair An interior staircase constructed with a **closed string** on both sides, often enclosed by adjacent walls.

boxwinder A staircase that is concealed behind a door next to a fireplace; sometimes architecturally balanced by a pantry door on the opposite side of the fireplace; often found in elegant American homes in the 18th and 19th centuries.

brace A wood or metal component used to stiffen or support a frame.

braced framing In a **timber-framed house** in colonial America, a system of timber framing in which diagonal braces are placed between huge horizontal **girts** and vertical posts; used to provide considerable rigidity against wind pressure acting on the house. The sill was laid on the foundation wall, and the joists were tenoned into mortises in the sill. Opposite common rafters were joined by collar beams to prevent the rafters from spreading and provide for increased rigidity. In New England, sheathing (to which clapboards were fastened) was provided to increase the thermal insulation of the walls; in contrast, in the South, sheathing was usually omitted. By 1850 this type of construction was largely supplanted by less expensive **balloon framing** usually constructed of wood two-by-fours.

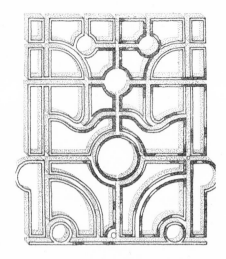

box garden
Greenwood Plantation (1830), Bains, La.

box lock (1694)
Annapolis, Md.

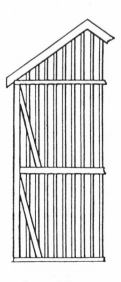

braced framing

bracket Any support that sustains, or helps to sustain, the weight of an overhanging member, such as a cornice, eaves, or a shelf projecting from a wall. *See also* **eaves bracket, stair bracket, step bracket, wall bracket.**

bracket capital Same as **bolster,1.**

bracketed cornice A deep **cornice** supported by decorative brackets, often in pairs; found, for example, in American architecture of the **Italianate style, Prairie style, and Second Empire style.**

bracketed eaves *See* **eaves bracket.**

bracketed hood A projecting surface above a door or window that provides shelter or serves as ornamentation; supported by brackets.

bracketed stair An **open-string** stair having decorative **brackets** on the exposed outer string.

Bracketed style A term occasionally used for the **Italianate style**; has deeply overhanging eaves supported by a series of **brackets.**

brass A ductile copper alloy having zinc as the principal alloying element, often mixed with small quantities of other elements. Imported from England to the American colonies as early as the 1600s and widely used for ornamentation, hardware, and the like.

brattishing Same as **cresting.**

breakfast nook A small recessed area, often in a kitchen or an adjunct to a kitchen, where light meals may be eaten; usually has a built-in table and seating; came into use in America in the early part of the 20th century.

breast 1. A projecting part of a wall; for example, *see* **chimney breast.** 2. That portion of a wall between the floor and a window directly above it.

breastsummer, breast beam A horizontal beam that spans a wide opening in an wall.

breastwork 1. Masonry work for a **chimney breast.** 2. The **parapet** of a building. 3. A **retaining wall.** 4. A defensive wall, usually hastily constructed, about breast-high.

breezeway A covered passageway, open to the outdoors, connecting two parts of a cabin or house, or connecting two structures, as, for example, between a house and a garage; sometimes serves as an outdoor sitting area. Also called a dogtrot. *See* illustration under **dogtrot cabin.**

bracket: fabricated of cast iron,
Kinsman House, Warren, Ohio

bracketed hood
Arnold Homestead (1814), Charlestown, Mass.

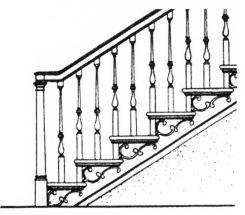

bracketed stair
Philosophical Hall (1887–1889), Philadelphia, Penna.

brick A solid masonry unit, usually of clay, molded into a rectangular shape while plastic, and then placed in a kiln at an elevated temperature to harden it, to give it mechanical strength, and to provide it with resistance to moisture; after being removed from the kiln, the brick is said to be *burnt, hard-burnt, kiln-burnt, fired,* or *hard-fired*. Bricks laid lengthwise in a wall are called **stretchers**; bricks laid crosswise in a wall are called **headers**. Bricks were produced in the New England colonies by the middle of the 17th century. In the northern colonies, brick construction was limited because it was considerably more expensive and took more time than wood construction did; furthermore, lime mortar used in laying bricks was not abundant. Therefore the use of brick was restricted primarily to chimney construction and to the homes of well-to-do settlers. In the southern colonies, there was a good supply of clay for bricks and lime for mortar, so that brick construction was much more widespread. Bricks were handmade from colonial days until the second half of the 19th century, when efficient mechanical processes were developed for their manufacture.

The current American brick is typically about 8 inches long, 3¾ inches wide, and 2¼ inches (20 x 9.5 x 5.7cm) thick. In contrast, in colonial America, the size of most bricks fell within the following dimensions: 7¾ to 8½ inches (19.6–21.5cm) long, 4 to 4½ inches wide, and 2 to 2½ (10.2–11.4cm) inches thick; mortar joints were usually about ¼ to ½ inch (0.6–1.3cm) thick. Colonial bricks varied in color, ranging from dark red to rose and salmon, and pink to blue-black and purple, depending on the type of clay that was available and on the temperature of the kiln in which they were hard-burnt. Often one end of the brick was glazed, giving it a bluish black color. Distinctive designs were obtained by laying bricks so their glazed surfaces were exposed on the **gable end wall** of the houses, particularly along the mid-Atlantic coast and in the South. Various types of patterns common in laying bricks are listed under **bond**. For specific types of brick, *see* **adobe quemado, arch brick, axed brick, burnt brick, dog-tooth course, Dutch brick, firebrick, fired brick, flooring brick, gauged brick, glass brick, glazed brick, hardburnt brick, kiln-fired brick, molded brick, mortar brick, mud brick, pug-mill brick, radius brick, roughaxed brick, rubbed brick, sailor, salmon brick, soldier, stock brick, twin brick, unburnt brick**. *See also* **adobe** for a description of sun-dried brick.

brick filling In **half-timbering**, brick laid between the heavy structural timbers to provide the wall so formed with thermal insulation and fire resistance.

brick nogging *See* **nogging**.

brick oven Same as **bake oven**.

brick tumbling *See* **tumbling course**.

brick veneer A **facing** of brick that is laid against an exterior wall but is not bonded to it; provides a decorative, durable wall surface. Bricks typically are laid lengthwise, so this construction is relatively thin, economical, and easy to lay.

brickwork Masonry consisting of **bricks** and **mortar**. *See also* **bond** and **patterned brickwork**.

bridging A brace, or a system of braces, placed between joists (or the like) to stiffen them, to hold them in place, and/or to help distribute a superimposed load.

briquette-entre-poteaux In **French Vernacular architecture** of Louisiana, a relatively inexpensive, porous brick *(briquette)* that was used to fill the spaces between upright posts *(poteaux)* and diagonal braces in a home of timber-framed construction; often found in **poteaux-en-terre houses**. Usually the entire brick-filled exterior surface was finished with a coat of lime plaster and often covered with clapboard. Many two-story town houses and houses of well-to-do planters had a brick basement and upper walls of *briquette-entre-poteaux*. *See also* **bousillage**.

briquette-entre-poteaux construction

broach 1. An octagonal spire surmounting a square tower, the transition between being made without any intermediate architectural feature, such as a parapet. 2. Any pointed ornamental structure.

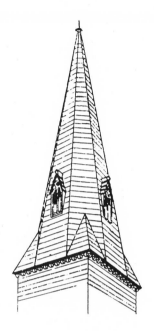

broach,1

broached spire Same as **broach,1.**

broad glass Same as **cylinder glass.**

broken gable A vertical surface at the end of a building having a **broken-pitch roof**; extends from the level of the cornice to the ridge of the roof.

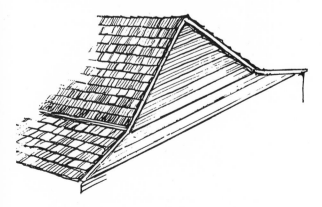

broken gable

broken pediment A **pediment** whose sloping or curving sides terminate before reaching the pediment's highest point, resulting in an opening that is often filled with an urn, cartouche, or other ornament. Found, for example, in the **Georgian style, Queen Anne style, Neoclassical style,** and **Colonial Revival** buildings. Sometimes called an open pediment or split pediment.

broken pediment
Wentworth-Gardner House (1760), Portsmouth, N.H.

broken-pitch roof A roof having more than one pitch on each side of a central ridge.

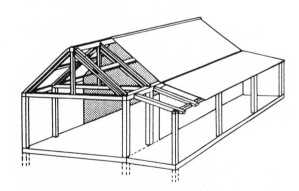

broken-pitch roof: early Creole house in Louisiana;
galeries on each side of the house

broken rangework Stone masonry laid in horizontal courses of different heights; any single course may be broken at intervals into two or more courses.

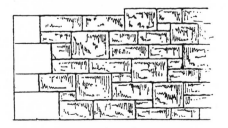

broken rangework

broken-scroll pediment Same as **swan's-neck pediment.**

brownstone 1. A dark brown or reddish brown sandstone, quarried and used extensively for buildings in the eastern United States from the middle of the 19th century to the early 20th century. 2. A dwelling faced with brownstone, often a **row house.**

brush house A multifamily dwelling of the Pomo and Yokut Indians of central California; usually rectangular, oval, or circular in plan. Poles were fixed in the ground and bent over and lashed together at their tops to form a rigid framework; then overlaid with reeds, rushes, thatching, or the like to provide a water-resistant covering. Also called a reed house. *See also* **bent-frame construction.**

Brutalism, New Brutalism A mode of modern architecture, primarily employed in the 1960s, emphasizing heavy, monumental, stark concrete forms and raw surfaces; may show patterns of rough wooden formwork used in casting the concrete (*béton brut*). Brutalist buildings are often suggestive of massive sculptures. An outstanding example is the Art and Architecture Building (1963) at Yale University by Paul Rudolph (1918–1997).

bucranium A sculptured ornament that represents the head or skull of an ox in relief, often draped with garlands; occasionally used as a decorative element in early American architecture, particularly in the South.

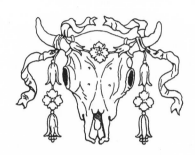

bucranium
Jockey Club (late 18th cent.), Alexandria, Va.

builders' guide, builders' handbook, builders' manual *See* **pattern book.**

Builders' Shed style Same as **Shed style.**

building artifact An element in a building that is demonstrative of human workmanship, such as a carving, bas-relief, or stained-glass window.

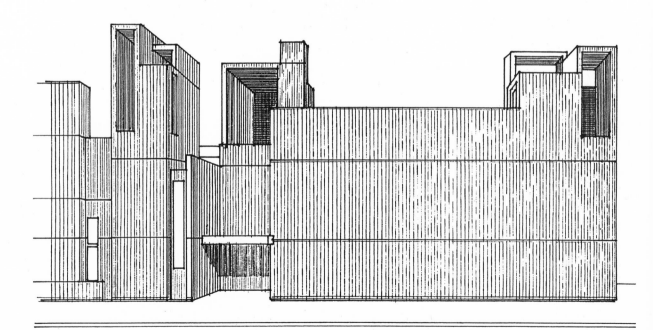

Brutalism: Christian Science Student Center (1965), Urbana, Ill.;
Paul Rudolph, Architect

building code, building regulation 1. A legal instrument adopted by a political jurisdiction, such as a city or state, that prescribes the minimum acceptable levels of design, construction, installation, and performance of materials, components, devices, items of equipment, and appliances used in a building or in building systems and/or subsystems. 2. A published body of rules and regulations for building practices, materials, and installations designed to protect the health, welfare, and safety of the public. The first building code in America in this sense of the term was enacted in New York City in 1867.

building conservation Management of a building directed toward preventing its decay, destruction, misuse, or neglect; may include recording the history of the building and conservation measures applied to it.

building preservation The process of applying physical measures to maintain and sustain the existing materials, integrity, and form of a building, including its structure and building artifacts.

building restoration The accurate reestablishment of the form and details of a building, its artifacts, and the site on which it is located, usually as it appeared at a particular time. The restoration may require the reconstruction of earlier work on the building that had been removed or had deteriorated, or it may require the removal of inappropriate work added at a later date.

building stone Any stone used in building construction, such as granite, limestone, marble, or sandstone.

building survey A detailed report of the present condition of a building, including its appearance and structural integrity; may include details of the building's history, illustrations of the façade and other walls, as well as analyses of the condition of the masonry, roofing, windows, and other elements.

built environment The aggregate of the physical surroundings and conditions constructed by human beings, in contrast to those conditions and surroundings resulting from the natural environment.

built-up roofing A continuous roof covering made up of laminations or plies of coated roofing felts alternating with layers of asphalt or coal-tar pitch; usually finished with a layer of gravel or sand; in the 19th century, usually made up of layers of felt or cloth that were saturated with asphalt or pitch and nailed to the roof, at that time called composition roofing.

bulkhead 1. An inclined or horizontal door giving access from the outside of a building to its cellar. 2. Same as **hatch.**

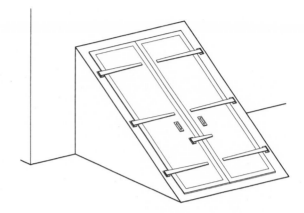

bulkhead,1

bull-nosed A term descriptive of a structural member or architectural trim having a rounded edge, for example, the overhanging rounded edge of a stair step.

bull's-eye 1. A **bull's-eye window.** 2. An ornamental glass disk comprising raised concentric circular bands; *see also* **crown glass.**

bull's-eye window A round or oval aperture, usually glazed but also may be open or louvered; most often used in doors, gables, or pediments. Found, for example, in the **Beaux-Arts style.** Also called an oculus, oeil-de-boeuf, or oxeye window.

bull's-eye window

bungalow A small one-story or one-and-a-half-story house, usually having a low profile and of wood-frame construction; popular in the early part of the 20th century, especially in the western United States. Such houses were particularly adaptable in meeting housing requirements in different geographical areas. They were relatively low in cost because they could be built according to plans taken from available **pattern books** or could be purchased as early as 1908 as precut boards and timbers ready for assembly (for example, from Sears, Roebuck). They continue to be popular in some areas of the country. Sometimes called a California bungalow or a bungaloid-style house. *See also* **prefabricated house.**

bungalow court A group of three or more detached, essentially identical one-story single-family dwellings, with building utilities and services usually under common ownership.

bungalow sash The upper **sash** of a **double-hung window** that has been divided by secondary members into a number of long vertical panes.

bungalow siding A wood finish material that covers the exterior wall of a house of wood-frame construction. The siding is applied horizontally and usually has a minimum width of eight inches (20 cm). *See also* **siding.**

bunker fill roof In adobe construction of the American Southwest, a flat roof supported by roof beams of heavy logs stripped of their bark; wood **sheathing** is laid on the roof beams, which are covered with building paper, earth fill, a second layer of building paper, asphalt, and gravel.

burnt brick Brick that has been treated in a kiln at an elevated temperature to harden it, give it mechanical strength, and improve its resistance to moisture. Compare with **unburnt brick.**

butler's pantry A small service room, situated between a kitchen and dining room, usually equipped with a sink and cupboards, a small stove, and often with a supplementary refrigerator and appliances.

butterfly hinge A decorative hinge having the general outline of a butterfly. Hand-wrought iron hinges of this type were widely used for interior applications in America before 1750. Also called a dovetail hinge.

bungalow
available from Sears, Roebuck and Company in 1908
for $999

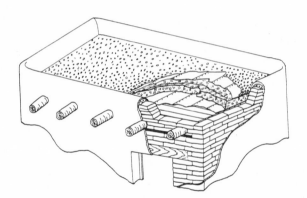

bunker fill roof

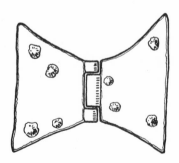

butterfly hinge (1669)
hand wrought, Connecticut

butterfly roof A roof shape that has two surfaces that rise from the roof's centerline to the eaves; has a **valley** along the centerline; the contour of the roof is suggestive of the wings of a butterfly. In areas where water is scarce, the water drained from the valley may be carried off to a **cistern.**

buttery In colonial America, a term once used to denote any room that served as a storage area for food, liquor, and/or utensils for the preparation of food or beverages; could apply, for example, to a pantry or wine cellar.

butt hinge A door or window hinge consisting of two rectangular metal plates that are joined with a pin; usually fastened against butting surfaces, such as the face of a door jamb and an edge of the door.

butt joint A plain, square joint between two members, in which the contact surfaces are cut at right angles to the faces of the two members; they are fitted squarely against each other and do not overlap.

buttress An exterior mass of masonry set against, or built into, an external masonry wall to strengthen or support it.

buttress
St. Thomas's Episcopal Church, Glassboro, N.J.

C

cabanne A primitive one-room dwelling used by the early French pioneers in the Mississippi Valley as a temporary shelter; had a framework consisting of poles with branches woven between them; the steeply pitched gable roof was thatched with palmetto fronds or bark attached to a wood framework. Similar to the **palma hut** of the Seminoles of Florida.

cabin A simple one-story cottage or hut, often of relatively crude construction. *See* **central-hall cabin, continental cabin, dog-run cabin, dogtrot cabin, double-pen cabin, log cabin, possum-trot cabin, saddlebag cabin, single-pen cabin, stone cabin, tourist cabin, vertical log cabin, Virginia cabin.**

cable molding, cabling An ornament or molding that has the appearance of a cable, showing twisted strands. Also called a rope molding.

caisson A sunken panel, especially in a vaulted or coffered ceiling or the inside of a **cupola.**

Cajun cottage, Cajun cabin A simple dwelling built by immigrants to the Louisiana Territory who left their native Acadia (a region in what is now Canada's Maritime Provinces) after it was ceded by France to England in 1713. From about 1760 to 1790, the Acadians who came to America settled largely in the bayou districts of southern Louisiana, where their descendants are usually referred to as *Cajuns.* In the early 1800s, the typical Cajun cottage was built on **groundsills,** supported on cypress-block piers (called *dés*) or on brick piers to prevent the groundsills from rotting. Cajun cottages were characterized by: a moderately steep end-gabled roof covered with cypress or oak shingles; hand-riven clapboards, ceiling boards, and floorboards; rooms often in a relatively straight line from front to back; French doors at the front and rear of the house to promote the flow of air through the house; a porch (**galerie**) across the front, commonly without a railing; usually, a steep stairway at one end of the porch leading to a loft above, where the young male members of the family slept (the young females usually slept in a room adjacent to the parents' bedroom, with no external access); battened doors; battened shutters on the windows; often, a **clay-and-sticks chimney** having a fire-retardant coating of mud; commonly, a kitchen at the rear of the cottage.

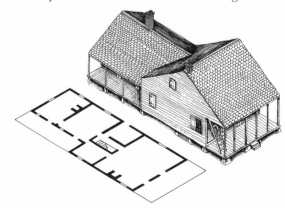

Cajun cottage (c. 1810–1815): Lafourche Parish, La.

California bungalow, California Craftsman A loosely used term, applied to a small one-story or one-and-a-half-story wood **bungalow**; widely found in California from about 1880 to 1900, but also popular in other areas of the United States.

California Mission Revival *See* **Mission Revival.**

California ranch house *See* **ranch house.**

camber arch An arch that is essentially flat but has a slight upward curve toward its midpoint.

camber beam A convex-shaped beam, arched slightly upward toward its midpoint so as to reduce the sag at its center when a load is imposed on it.

camber window A window that has a slight arch at its top.

camber window

cames Slender strips of cast lead, usually with a groove on each side, into which small panes of glass are set. *See* **quarrel.**

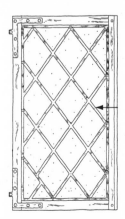

cames: small panes of glass are set in grooves in the cames

campanario Literally, the Spanish word for *bell tower*. In **Mission architecture** of the American Southwest, usually indicative of a **belfry** or a pierced wall that serves as a belfry, with a bell usually hung in an arched opening.

campanario
Mission San Antonio de Pala (1816), Pala, Calif.

canale In **Spanish Colonial architecture** and derivatives, a **waterspout** used to drain rainwater from an essentially flat roof. It projects through, and beyond, the face of the parapet so that the discharged rainwater falls clear of the wall, to minimize erosion of the wall.

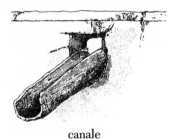

canale

cancela In **Spanish Colonial architecture**, a wood gate, usually decorated with **spindlework** or a **lattice** grille.

candle-snuffer roof Same as **conical roof.**

canopy roof A roof, often over a balcony or porch, that is suggestive of the curvature of a suspended cloth canopy.

canted A term descriptive of a line or surface angled with respect to another line or surface, for example, a wall that is slanted with respect to the vertical, or a molding that is slanted rather than horizontal or vertical.

cantilever 1. A beam, girder, structural member, truss, or surface that projects horizontally beyond its vertical support, such as a wall or column. 2. A projecting bracket used for carrying the cornice or extended eaves of a building.

cantilevered window Same as **oriel.**

canton An exterior corner of a building that is decorated with a projecting masonry course, one or more pilasters, engaged columns, or similar features.

cant window, cant-bay window A bay window whose sides are angled in plan. *See also* **angled bay window.**

cant window

cap The uppermost crowning member of any architectural element, such as a cornice or lintel above a door or window; usually acts as a protective cover or decorative feature.

Cape Ann house A rectangular house, commonly one or one-and-a-half stories high, that is similar to a **Cape Cod house** but has a shingled **mansard roof** instead of a **gable roof.**

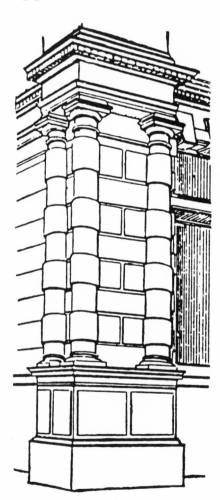

canton

a modern Cape Ann house

Cape Cod house A house having a style developed on Cape Cod, Massachusetts, primarily in the 1700s; typically, a one-and-a-half-story rectangular house of wood-frame construction usually having the following characteristics: a massive central chimney that served all fireplaces and that pierced a pitched, gable roof; commonly without dormers (except for such houses of modern construction); a roof covering and exterior wall covering of long, hand-split wood shingles, left unpainted to weather to a gray color; double-hung windows on the first story and often on the gable-end walls; paneled doors; a partial basement. Cape Cod houses are of three types: **full Cape house** (also called a *double house*), which has two windows on each side of the front door; **three-quarter Cape house** (also called a *three-quarter house* or a *house-and-a-half*), which has two windows on one side of the front door and a single window on the other side; and **half Cape house** (also called a *house*), which has two windows on one side of the front door and none on the other. The name *Cape Cod house* was not used until 1800; modern adaptations, usually with dormers, are still being constructed on Cape Cod and elsewhere.

Cape house A term used in some parts of New England for a **Cape Cod house.**

capital The topmost structural member of a column, pilaster, anta, or the like, often decorated; may support an **architrave** or may be surmounted by an **impost.** *See* **angle capital, bracket capital, Composite capital, Corinthian capital, corner capital, cushion capital, Doric capital, Ionic capital, lotus capital, palm capital,** and illustrations under the various **orders.**

capping Any architectural member serving as a **cap**; for example, a **coping.**

capstone 1. A stone placed at the top of a stone arch. 2. Same as **coping stone.**

captain's house In colonial New England, a house having a truncated **hipped roof** and chimneys at both gable ends; has a **widow's walk** and/or a cupola on the roof.

captain's walk Same as **widow's walk.**

caracole Same as **spiral stair.**

carcass, carcase The **frame** of a building structure before the installation of the exterior wall covering or exterior finish.

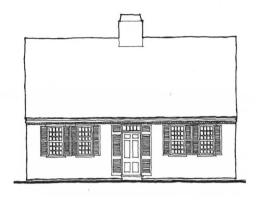

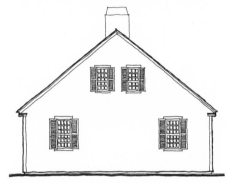

Cape Cod house

a modern Cape Cod house

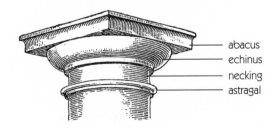

abacus
echinus
necking
astragal

capital: nomenclature

Carpenter Gothic, Carpenter Gothic Revival
A style of architecture used primarily in mid-19th-century America in which highly decorative woodwork, **gingerbread,** and Gothic motifs were applied to otherwise simple homes or churches; usually designed and constructed by carpenters and builders; often asymmetrical in plan. Architects prominent in promoting this style were Alexander Jackson Davis (1803–1892) and Andrew Jackson Downing (1815–1852). Occasionally termed Carpenter's Gothic. *See also* **Steamboat Gothic** and **Gothic Revival.**

Buildings in Carpenter Gothic style usually exhibit many of the following characteristics:

Façade and exterior wall treatments: Walls that sometimes extend into the gables without interruption; pointed arches that extend into the gables to promote a vertical emphasis; Gothic motifs such as foliated ornaments, pinnacles with battlements, crockets, decorative brackets, label moldings, quatrefoils, towers, trefoils, turrets, and wall dormers; often, an entry porch having a flattened Gothic or Tudor arch; sometimes a full-width porch.

Roof treatments: A steeply pitched **gable roof**, often with a gable at the center of the façade or with intersecting gables; lacy, highly ornate bargeboards and finials decorating the gables and dormers that suggest Gothic architecture; projecting eaves; boxed eaves; decorative shingle patterns on the roof; high, ornamental chimney stacks; often, clusters of chimney pots.

Window treatments: **Bay windows,** casement windows with diamond-shaped or rectangular panes, lancet windows, ogee arch windows, oriel windows, stained glass windows, triangular arch windows often with mullions and relatively thin **tracery,** including foils; **label moldings**, particularly over ground-floor windows.

Doorway treatments: An elaborately paneled entry door, often glazed or partially glazed in a Gothic motif or in a rectangular or diamond-shaped pattern; a wood-paneled door or a battened door suggestive of the medieval period (sometimes within a recessed porch or under a doorhood), occasionally bordered with **sidelights**; often a **label molding** terminated with label stops above the doorway.

Carpenter Gothic

carpenters' guides, carpenters' handbooks
See **pattern book.**

carpet bedding Beds of small annual plants with ornamental foliage or flowers, sometimes interspersed with gravel-filled sections; usually arranged in patterns intended to be seen from a higher elevation.

carreau 1. A small square or diamond-shaped tile used in decorative flooring. 2. A small square or diamond-shaped pane of glass used in ornamental glazing.

carriage, carriage piece An inclined beam that adds support for the steps in a wood stair; usually centered between the wall and the **outer string.**

carriage house Often, a synonym for **coach house.**

carriage-mounting steps Same as **coach-mounting steps.**

carriage porch Same as **porte cochère.**

carriage shed A rough structure, with one or more open sides, once used as a temporary shelter for horse-drawn carriages; found, for example, in the yard of a church.

cart house An enclosure, such as a shed, once used for sheltering two-wheeled horse-drawn vehicles.

cartouche An ornamental tablet, often slightly convex and decorated or inscribed; frequently framed with an elaborate scroll-like carving; found, for example, in the **Beaux-Arts style.**

cartouche: over window at the New York Public Library (1911), New York City

casa del campo In **Spanish Colonial architecture** of the American Southwest, a one-story farmhouse usually built around a patio, constructed primarily of adobe and wood; usually had a **mission tile** roof having a central ridge, or a shed roof having a single shallow pitch, usually with considerable overhang to provide shade.

casa del pueblo, casa del poblador In **Spanish Colonial architecture** of the 18th and 19th centuries in the Southwest, a house in a village or town usually constructed of adobe brick that has been plastered and whitewashed. The mission tile or shed roof was typically supported by beams (**vigas**) that penetrated the walls and were visible on the exterior; the house had wood-framed casement windows, with those facing the street protected by grilles or gratings (**rejas**).

casa del rancho In **Spanish Colonial architecture** of the American Southwest in the 18th and 19th centuries, the main dwelling of a ranch that usually included a large courtyard (**placita**) entered by way of a massive wooden gate (**zaguán**); a corral; an enclosed or partially enclosed patio; living quarters for all members and servants of the household; housing for domestic animals; and associated storage spaces. This compound was usually designed to provide defense against attack by marauders.

casa de tablas Same as **tabla house.**

case lock A surface-mounted lock, such as a **box lock.**

casemate A chamber or room in a rampart of a fort, with **embrasures** through which to fire artillery. Such rooms were in widest use in America during the Civil War.

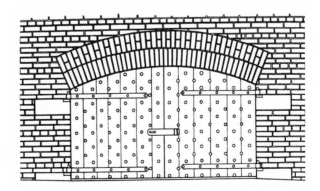

entrance to a casemate
Fort McHenry (1803), Baltimore, Md.

casement door *See* **French door.**

casement sash, casement A rectangular window **sash**, usually oriented and hinged vertically, that swings open along its entire length, usually in an outward direction. Modern casement sashes are usually composed of a single pane (light) or several panes. In casement sashes of 17th-century colonial America, small **diamond lights** were set into the grooves in slender strips of lead called **cames.** This diamond-shaped pattern emulated grillwork in English medieval windows. Often such sashes were stiffened by **saddle bars** or **guard bars.**

casement window A window composed of one or more **casement sashes.** In colonial America casement windows set with diamond lights were popular until about 1700, when they gradually began to be replaced by **double-hung windows**; by the 1740s this replacement was largely complete. More recently, casement windows have been used in **Art Deco, Art Moderne, International style, Prairie style, Spanish Colonial architecture,** and **Tudor Revival.**

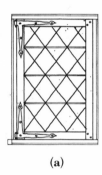 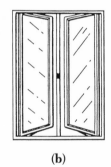

(a)   (b)

casement window: (a) early American; (b) modern

casing 1. The exposed framing, lining, or trim molding around a door or window; may either be flat or molded. 2. Finished millwork of uniform profile that encases a structural member, such as a post or beam.

castellated A term descriptive of ornamentation having a battlement-like pattern or a crenellated pattern; found in **Gothic Revival** and occasionally in **Tudor Revival** buildings in America.

cast iron An iron alloy, usually including 2 to 4 percent carbon and a small amount of silicon, that has a high compressive strength, a low tensile strength, cannot be welded or wrought, and is so brittle that it may fracture on impact. Building products made of

this material are formed by pouring the molten alloy (pig iron) into sand molds and then machining the resulting casting. The development of this process made it possible to produce cast-iron building components in large quantities and at a relatively low cost, as compared with similar components in wrought iron, beaten into shape by hand.

cast-iron architecture By the 1850s ornamental cast iron was popular in many American cities, especially New York, New Orleans, Saint Louis, and Charleston. In building construction cast iron (used in compression) in combination with wrought iron (used in tension) came into use in America for the **framing** of commercial buildings and for the components of cast-iron fronts (described below) from about 1850 until the advent of **steel-frame construction** around 1875. The **Crystal Palace** in New York City was a dramatic

cast-iron architecture: (a) cast-iron front from the 1865 sales catalogue of Daniel Badger's Architectural Iron Works of New York

early use of cast iron in building construction. It had a wide variety of other uses as well, such as shop fronts, auditoriums (*see* illustration under **pendentive**), and church windows (*see* illustration under **tracery**).

James Bogardus (1800–1874), who obtained a patent in 1850 on a complete building system of iron components (including beams, columns, and panels), is generally regarded in America as the major innovator of cast-iron construction. Among the many foundries that produced cast-iron architecture during this period was Daniel Badger's Architectural Iron Works of New York, which opened in 1846 and became well known for its own designs, described in *Badger's Illustrated Catalogue of Cast-Iron Architecture* (1865). Methods of mass production fostered the use of *cast-iron façades* or *cast-iron fronts,* which were load-bearing and consisted of prefabricated cast-iron components. They were characterized by repetitive modules and large windows, in contrast to earlier masonry façades, in which large windows were impractical because they weakened the wall into which they were set. Some cast-iron façades exhibit a strong influence of other styles, such as the **Italianate style, Round Arch style, Second Empire style,** or combinations of these and other styles.

cast-iron architecture
(b) detail of cast-iron front

cast-iron lacework Mass-produced **ironwork** of intricate ornamental design, formed by the casting process and therefore relatively inexpensive compared with similar wrought-iron work.

cast-iron lacework

cast-iron stove *See* **Franklin stove.**

catslide 1. A term sometimes used in the South for a **saltbox house**. 2. The long sloping roof at the rear of such a house.

catslide

caulicole, cauliculus Any one of the ornamental stalks rising between the leaves of a Corinthian capital, from which the **volutes** spring. *See* illustration under **Corinthian capital.**

cavate lodge A very early American Indian dwelling that is partly or wholly excavated in a cliff or the side of a steep mountain.

cavetto A hollow member or round concave molding usually containing at least a quadrant of a circle. Also called a gorge.

cavetto

cavetto cornice Same as **Egyptian gorge.**

cavity wall A wall, usually of masonry, consisting of an outer leaf and an inner leaf that are separated by a continuous air space. For walls above a specified height, building codes usually require that the two leaves be interconnected by wire or sheet-metal ties.

cedero In **Spanish Colonial architecture** of the American Southwest, one of many unsplit, peeled, relatively straight saplings supported by **vigas**; used in ceiling construction.

ceiling The overhead surface of a room, often decoratively treated, which conceals the joists of the floor above, an overhead roof, or building services such as ductwork or wiring.

ceiling joist, ceiling beam A **joist** or overhead beam from which the ceiling of a room is hung.

ceiling medallion, ceiling ornament, ceiling rose A ceiling ornament, usually cast in plaster; often a luminaire or chandelier is hung from its center. *See* **medallion,2.**

cellar 1. A room (or several rooms or an entire floor) of a building that is partially or entirely underground; often used in the past as a storage place for dairy products, vegetables, and some bulk foods since it was relatively cool in the summer and above freezing in the winter. In colonial New England, most homes had a cellar with a dirt floor under the entire house; it provided storage space and some thermal insulation resulting from the air space between the dirt floor and the wood flooring above. Today's uses are many, from the location of heaters to additional storage space. 2. That part of a building having at least half of its clear height below grade. *See also* **storm cellar** and **basement.**

cellar bulkhead, cellar cap Same as **bulkhead,1.**

cellar sash A window **sash** set into the foundation wall of a building, usually just below the horizontal member or surface that provides bearing and anchorage for the wall above.

cement A calcined combination of limestone and clay, combined with an **aggregate**, such as gravel, that reacts chemically when water is added; after this reaction occurs, the mixture hardens in place as it dries, resulting in a stonelike material. The ancient Romans developed a cement that could harden under water (called *hydraulic cement*), but there was little information in modern times on how to produce such a cement until 1756, when John Smeaton in England carried out experiments that led to the development of a cement in 1796 that could set in 10 to 20 minutes, in or out of water. *See also* **portland cement** and **Roman cement.**

center-gabled pediment A **pediment** on a gable located at the center of a façade; may be flush with the front wall or project forward from it.

center-hall plan In **American Colonial architecture**, the **floor plan** of a house usually having two rooms symmetrically situated on each side of a centrally located hallway extending from the front to the rear of the house. The rooms on one side of the house served as the family living area, functioning as the kitchen, sewing room, dining area, and general workroom; the rooms on the other side served as a parlor or as a combination of a parlor and bedroom. A stair in the hallway led to the loft space above. *See also* **hall-and-parlor plan.**

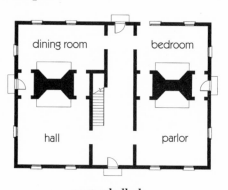

center-hall plan

centerline A line representing an axis of symmetry of a **plan**; usually shown on architectural drawings as a broken line.

centerpiece An ornament placed in the middle of a surface; for example, a decoration at the center of the ceiling.

center-to-center, on center The distance between the centerline of one building component (such as stud or joist) and the centerline of the next.

central-hall cabin A cabin having two rooms that are separated by a hallway; often there is an **exterior chimney** on each end wall. Compare with **dogtrot cabin** and **saddlebag cabin.**

central-hall plan, central-passage plan Same as **center-hall plan.**

centrally located chimney An **interior chimney** located near the middle of a house; often massive in size and situated so as to keep the entire house warm during the winter; widely used in colonial New England.

central pavilion A prominent projection from the façade of a monumental public building or stately home; often two stories high, domed, or with other distinguishing architectural features; in general, seldom appeared in America before 1750.

central pavilion
Rosalie (1820), Natchez, Miss.

ceramic veneer An **architectural terra-cotta** having a ceramic glazed surface. The dimensions of its face are usually large compared with its thickness; the back-side is either scored or ribbed to assist in its attachment to a wall or other surface.

chaff house A subsidiary building used on a farm to store fodder, such as corn husks, cut hay, and the like.

chain-link fence A fence made of heavy steel wire that has been interwoven so as to produce a continuous diamond-shaped mesh fabric without ties or knots except at the top and bottom edges of the fence; usually the wire fabric is stretched between metal posts.

chair rail, chair board A horizontal strip, usually of wood and often decorated, affixed to a wall at a height that prevents the backs of chairs from marring the wall surface; first appeared in American colonial houses in the 18th century.

chalet *See* **Swiss cottage architecture.**

chamber A term once used for bedroom.

chamfer An oblique surface or a bevel along the edge of a beam, timber, or between two intersecting surfaces; one of the few decorative architectural elements found in very early New England colonial houses.

chamfer

chancel That part of a church reserved for the clergy and church officials; often includes the choir.

channeling A series of deep decorative grooves in an architectural member, such as a column. *See also* **fluting.**

channeling
shown on cross section of a column

chapel 1. A building or room designated for religious worship within the complex of a college, school, hospital, or other large institution. 2. A small area within a larger Christian church that contains an altar and is intended primarily for private prayer. 3. A small building devoted to worship or special services.

Charleston house Either of two distinctive types of 18th- and early-19th-century town houses in Charleston, South Carolina; usually Georgian or Greek Revival in style, two stories in height, with the first story often set well above ground level; had double-hung windows, generally with shutters; and a two-tiered colonnaded porch. The more common type, called a **single house,** was long and narrow (only a single room deep), was built with its long side perpendicular to the street, and faced a garden. The entrance was at the street end of the house, by way of a flight of stairs leading up to the porch, which ran along the long side of the house, with all the rooms opening onto it. The second type of Charleston house, called a **double house**, much less common, was two rooms deep, more boxlike in shape, conventionally oriented so that it faced the street; typically, it had a portico with a classical two-tiered porch at the middle of the façade. Some houses also had a two-tiered porch at the rear, a feature often found in other types of more elegant homes in the South.

Châteauesque style, Château style, Châteauesque Revival An opulent style of architecture loosely based on the monumental French châteaus and castles of the 16th century; some elegant mansions in this style were built in America from about 1880 to 1910 and beyond. The style was popularized by Richard Morris Hunt (1827–1895), who was the first American to study at the Ecole des Beaux Arts in Paris. Compare with **Beaux-Arts style** and **Second Empire style.**

Buildings in the Châteauesque style usually exhibit many of the following characteristics:

Façade and exterior wall treatments: Masonry walls, usually smoothed and squared limestone or brick; an attic story; single or continuous balconies; prominent use of vertical elements such as pilasters, crockets, pinnacles, finials, and hip knobs; basket-handled arches; wall dormers with gables (often pinnacled) that may break the roof line; cross gables; a

chapel,1
Capilla Real de San Carlos, Monterey, Calif.

Charleston house: a single house (1825)

balustraded terrace; a belt course; often, a façade ornamented with gargoyles, griffins, or with shallow ornamental relief; occasionally, a **porte cochère**.

Roof treatments: An ornate **hipped roof** that is either steeply pitched to a ridge or truncated by a horizontal surface; often, a railing or cast-iron cresting on the roof; through-the-cornice wall dormers; roof dormers with pedimented parapets, pinnacles, and spires; a cylindrical corner turret having a conical roof, sometimes corbeled out from the second floor; tall, decorative chimneys and ornamental chimney caps.

Window treatments: Windows, frequently in pairs, usually divided by heavy stone mullions or set in **basket-handle arches**; oriels; semicircular bay windows; occasionally, **hood moldings** or **label moldings** with label stops over the windows with stone window tracery.

Doorway treatments: Exterior doors usually set in semicircular arches or in basket-handle arches; often, a canopy over the entry door to provide some shelter.

Châteauesque style
Astor House (1895), New York City; Richard M. Hunt, Architect

checkerwork 1. An arrangement of masonry units, on floors or pavements, laid so as to produce a pattern resembling a checkerboard. 2. A pattern on a brick wall, produced by glazed brick laid in a **Flemish bond** pattern.

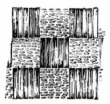

checkerwork,1

cheek One of two narrow upright surfaces on opposite sides of a structural member, or forming both sides of an opening; for example, a **chimney cheek.**

chevron pattern A V-shaped zigzag pattern, used singly or in groups for ornamental purposes; found, for example, in 17th-century Maryland brickwork.

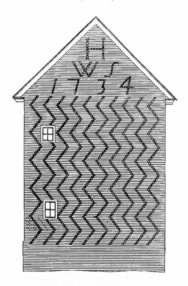

chevron pattern: Hancock House (1734), Salem, N.J.

Chicago Commercial style *See* **Commercial style.**

Chicago cottage A small, narrow, inexpensive, quickly built **cottage** set on a brick foundation with its lower story partially below ground level; characterized by **balloon framing**, clapboard exterior walls, an exterior stair between the street and a second-story entrance, an attic above the second story; developed in Chicago for speculative construction in the mid- to late 1800s.

Chicago School A group of highly influential architects and their followers in Chicago in the latter part of the 19th century to 1920, including partners Dankmar Adler (1844–1900) and Louis H. Sullivan (1856–1924); Daniel Hudson Burnham (1846–1912) and John Wellborn Root (1850–1891); William Holabird (1854–1923) and Martin Roche (1853–1927); and William Le Baron Jenney (1832–1907). The school's philosophy was based on the precept that design should be of its time rather than based on the past. This group initially applied its philosophy to both skyscrapers and homes, but its greatest and most lasting influence was in the design of **skyscrapers**, and its greatest achievements may have been structural. *See also* **Chicago window.**

Chicago window In commercial buildings, a large, fixed, plate-glass window with a narrow operable window on each side of it to provide ventilation. Because of its large size, this three-part window provided much more daylight within than earlier window arrangements; particularly popular in Chicago during the last two decades of the 19th century.

chickee A small, transportable single-family dwelling of the Seminoles of Florida primarily before the arrival of the Spaniards in the early 16th century. Cypress or palmetto posts were driven into the ground and interconnected at their tops with notched beams. This framework, fastened together with rope made from palmetto fibers, formed a rectangular structure that supported a floor about 20 feet (6m) long, 10 feet (3m) wide, and 3 (.9m) feet above the ground; the floor itself was made of palmetto logs that had been split in half, with the flat side facing upward. The gabled roof was thatched, usually with palmetto fronds, providing protection against the sun and rain. *See also* **palma hut.**

chickee: typical dwelling of the Seminole Indians

chicken house *See* **poultry house.**

chimney An incombustible, hollow vertical structure containing one or more flues to provide a draft for a fireplace and to carry off gaseous products of combustion to the outside air; usually constructed of brick, stone, or some combination thereof. Early American settlers and frontiersmen built chimneys of clay and sticks with an interior coating of clay or mud for fireproofing; despite the fact that such chimneys constituted a fire hazard, they were common where brick, stone, and lime mortar were not available. A chimney is sometimes classified according to its location, i.e., **interior chimney** or **exterior chimney**. In the warmer southern colonies, exterior chimneys located at the ends of the house were widely used, since in hot weather these locations reduced the discomfort from heat generated by cooking in the fireplace. Some Georgian-style houses had double chimneys, i.e., a pair of exterior chimneys at one end or at both ends of the house. Chimneys were an especially important design element, not only in **American Colonial architecture** of early New England and of the early South, but also in the architecture of the **French Eclectic style, Italianate style, Queen Anne style,** and **Tudor Revival.** *See also* **centrally located chimney, clay-and-sticks chimney, double chimney, double-shouldered chimney, end chimney, flush chimney, mud-and-sticks chimney, outside chimney, pilastered chimney, sloped offset chimney, stepped-back chimney, sticks-and-clay chimney, fireplace.**

chimneyback Same as **fireback.**

chimney bar A wrought-iron or steel horizontal member, supported by the sides of a fireplace, that carries the weight of the masonry above a fireplace opening; if the member is curved, it is known as an **arch bar.**

chimney breast That part of a fireplace wall which projects into a room.

chimney cap 1. A cornice forming the crowning termination of a chimney; *see also* **corbeled chimney cap.** 2. Same as **chimney hood.**

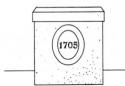

chimney cap,1

chimney cheeks The sides of a fireplace opening that support the **mantelpiece.**

chimney corner An area outside a fireplace, but adjacent to the hearth, on one or both sides of a fireplace; sometimes provided with seating. Also called an inglenook.

chimney corner: Craftsman style

chimney crook Same as **trammel.**

chimney flue An incombustible, heat-resistant enclosed passage in a chimney to control and carry away products of combustion from a fireplace to the outside air. In early America it was common practice to connect several fireplaces within a home to a single large flue, although it was also not unusual to carry up a flue for each fireplace.

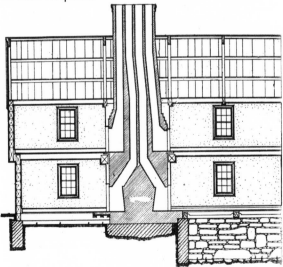

chimney flues: carried up from several fireplaces, McIntire Garrison House, York County, Maine

chimney foundation In an early New England colonial house, the substructure that supported the load of the massive **centrally located chimney** and transmitted this load to the earth or rock below. The foundation for the fireplace and chimney varied considerably in size and design from one house to another but was necessarily immense because of the heavy load of the fireplace above it. Usually rectangular in shape and five to ten feet (1.5–3m) on a side, a foundation was constructed of brick, stone, fieldstone, stone rubble, or some combination thereof; it often had heavy supporting timbers at the ceiling, known as *cradles*. An additional fireplace or **bake oven** was occasionally built into the chimney foundation.

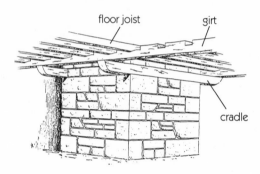

chimney foundation
Butler House, West Hartford, Conn.

chimney girt In American Colonial architecture, a structural framing timber that acts as a main horizontal support between **chimney posts.**

chimney hood A covering that shelters the opening at the top of a chimney from rain and snow but permits gaseous products to escape. A flat horizontal flagstone, elevated several inches above the top of the chimney shaft, often serves as a hood, although more complicated configurations are also common, such as a brick semicircular arch or a double arch. Occasionally the hood is of more fanciful design.

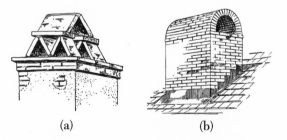

(a)   (b)

chimney hood: (a) Mission (founded 1776), San Juan Capistrano, Calif.; (b) an arched chimney hood

chimney pent A small area, covered by a small, narrow sloping roof, built flush between two exterior brick chimneys on an end wall of a house at the level of the ground-floor ceiling. It buttresses the chimneys. On the interior of the house, it provides additional floor space, which is usually used for storage; often referred to as a *single chimney pent*. If a similar addition is also built between the outer edge of each chimney and the corner of the house, this configuration is referred to as a *triple chimney pent*. Chimney pents were relatively common in Maryland, and to a lesser extent in Virginia, during the 17th and 18th centuries.

chimney pent (single)

chimney pent (triple)

chimneypiece An ornamental construction above and/or around a fireplace opening and decorative superstructure, often projecting from the wall.

chimney post In a **timber-framed house** of early New England, one of the wood **posts** providing the main vertical structural supports on the sides of a chimney. One pair of posts was located at each side of the chimney at the front of the chimney; another pair was located on each side at the rear.

chimney pot A cylindrical pipe, often of terra-cotta and decoratively shaped, placed atop a chimney to extend its height and thereby increase the draft through the chimney; sometimes used as a decorative element, as in **Gothic Revival.**

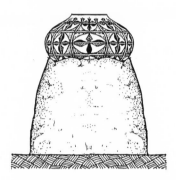

chimney pot
Pueblo Indians, Acoma, N.M.

chimney shaft That part of a chimney that rises above the roof of a building, often corbeled out at its top as a form of decoration, as illustrated under **corbeled chimney cap.**

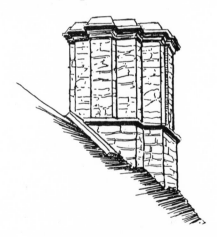

chimney shafts (late 17th cent.): pilastered to provide
additional strength, Rhode Island

chimney stack A number of chimneys or flues grouped together.

chimney throat That portion of a chimney directly above a fireplace, between the fireplace and the flue, where the opening narrows to increase the upward draft through the chimney; i.e., the upward flow of air and gaseous products through the **chimney flue.** Also called a fireplace throat.

Chinese Chippendale Descriptive of a design, suggestive of Chinese motifs, by Thomas Chippendale (1718–1779), England's most widely known furniture maker of his time. His book, *The Gentleman and Cabinet Maker's Director*, published in London in 1754, was also popular in America. Chinese Chippendale lattice patterns, especially used in railing systems, were a combination of horizontal, vertical, and diagonal lines forming geometric patterns, usually within a rectangular frame.

Chinese Chippendale: design for a Georgian gateway
at Cowles House, Farmington, Conn.

chinking The material used to fill chinks (i.e., long cracks, openings, or fissures), especially between logs that form the exterior walls of a **log cabin.** Where the cracks are small, the filling material is often mud or plaster; where the cracks are large, the filling often includes wood chips, pebbles, straw, or small sticks.

chinking

chinking board A board used to cover the **chinking** in an exterior wall.

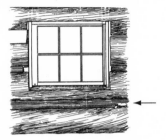

chinking board

chisel pattern On a roof, a pattern of **shingles** or **tiles** having their bottom corners angled at each end; suggestive of the shape of a chisel.

choir That part of a church usually reserved for the singers.

chord 1. A principal structural member that extends from one end of a **truss** to the other. 2. The **span** of an arch.

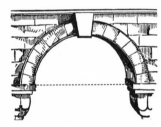

chord,2: shown as a horizontal dashed line

Christian door The paneled front door of an early colonial New England house in which the stiles and rails of the door form a pattern suggestive of a cross; the two bottom panels are usually vaguely suggestive of an open book that some colonists interpreted as representing the Bible. Also called a cross-and-Bible door.

Christian door

church An edifice or place of assembly specifically set apart for Christian worship. In colonial New England, Protestant denominations that had left the established Church of England often used the term **meeting house** instead, reserving the term *church* for the congregation itself.

Churrigueresque style A Spanish colonial decorative style, often used in the late 17th century and the first half of the 18th century, characterized by elaborate and lavish **Baroque** ornamentation and detailing; named after the Spanish architect José Benito de Churriguera (1665–1725). *See also* **Mission architecture, Plateresque architecture, Spanish Colonial architecture.**

Churrigueresque style
Mission San Xavier del Bac (1784–1797), Tucson, Ariz.

cimborio In **Spanish Colonial architecture** and derivatives, a cupola or lantern above the high altar of a church.

cincture A circular molding or fillet, or a ring of moldings, around the top or bottom of the shaft of a classical column, separating the shaft from its capital or from its base.

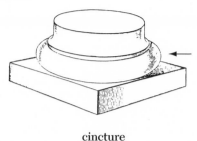

cincture

cinquefoil In an opening, a pattern having five lobes divided by **cusps**; particularly found in **Gothic Revival**. *See* **foil.**

cinquefoil

circular arch An arch whose **intrados** is cylindrical.

circular arch
(c. 1800)

circular barn A barn having a circular plan; requires less building material than a rectangular barn enclosing the same volume, although it usually costs somewhat more to construct. The first barn of this type, built by the Shakers in Hancock, Massachusetts, in 1826, had stone walls 30 inches thick and a diameter of 90 feet. In 1889 F. H. King, the developer of circular silos, was asked to design the optimal barn to house 80 cows, 10 horses, and their feeding facilities. A year later, the first circular barn constructed of wood was erected following his design. From then until 1910, many such barns were built in the Midwest, especially in Indiana. Their popularity diminished thereafter, because of their higher cost and because carpenters skilled in their construction had become scarce. Also called a cylindrical barn or a round barn.

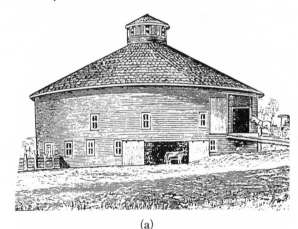

(a)

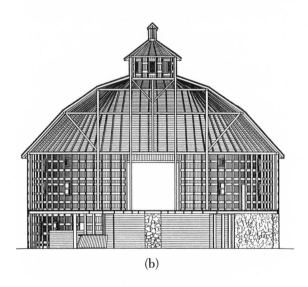

(b)

circular barn: Delaware County, Ind.
(a) barn exterior; (b) barn interior

circular stair Same as **spiral stair.**

circular window A large window having the shape of a full circle, often with decorative elements within the circle disposed in a radial manner.

circular window
St. Peter's Church, Philadelphia, Pa.

cistern An artificial reservoir or a tank for storing water, such as rainwater collected from a roof.

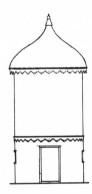

cistern
Uncle Sam Plantation, St. James Parish, La.

city plan A large-scale comprehensive map of a city that delineates streets, important buildings, and other urban features compatible with the scale of the map.

city planning *See* **community planning.**

civic center An area of a city where municipal buildings are grouped; often includes the city hall, courthouse, public library, and other public buildings such as a concert hall, municipal auditorium, or museum.

cladding 1. A nonstructural material, or the surface formed by such a material, used as the exterior covering for the **carcass** or framework of a building. 2. The surface on which shingles, tiles, or clapboards are fastened. *See also* **siding** and **veneer,2.**

clairvoyée In colonial America, an open fence or an ironwork screen through which a vista could be enjoyed.

clapboard house A term occasionally used for a **Virginia house.**

clapboards An exterior covering of wood boards over a building usually of wood-frame construction. In early colonial America, the boards were usually hand-split, about five inches (12.7cm) wide and five feet (1.5m) long, and applied horizontally with the grain running lengthwise. At that time clapboards were of more or less constant thickness and were usually applied with a one-inch (2.5cm) vertical overlap. In the later 17th century, clapboards were usually wedge-shaped, thicker along the lower edge than along the upper edge. After 1700 some clapboards were sawn and nailed to the building studs and painted white; later they were nailed over **cladding,2** which provided greatly increased thermal insulation. In the South, clapboards were often decorated with a horizontal bead molding. Also called bevel siding or lap siding. *See also* **weatherboards,** which are similar to, but thicker than, clapboards.

clapboards

Classical architecture The architecture of Hellenic Greece and Imperial Rome on which the Italian Renaissance and subsequent styles such as the Classical Revival style and Neoclassical style based their development. The five Classical **orders** are a characteristic feature. *See* illustrations under **order**.

Classical order *See* **order**.

Classical Revival style A style of American architecture, most popular from about 1770 to 1830, typified by simplicity, dignity, monumentality, and purity of design; based primarily on the use of Roman forms of classical antiquity, although later examples exhibit some characteristics of the **Greek Revival style** which followed. Typically symmetrical in form and sometimes similar to a classical temple, including a dome; often used in major public buildings. In domestic architecture, houses in this style were usually rectangular in plan and two rooms deep; the long side of the house commonly faced the street. Such houses were also front-gabled, with a wing on each side.

The Classical Revival stye of architecture is also called **Jeffersonian Classicism** because it is closely associated with the work of Thomas Jefferson (1743–1826). Notable examples of Jefferson's own designs include his home, Monticello, and the Virginia State Capitol (1791), especially significant because it was the first building in America whose design was directly based on an ancient temple (the Maison-Carrée at Nîmes, France).

After a 65-year hiatus, Classical Revival architecture reemerged in popularity from about 1895 to 1940, with modifications described under **Neoclassical style**. Uniform terminology has not always been used in the literature to describe these earlier and later forms of Classical architecture in America. Thus, for example, Classical Revival style sometimes has been called Early Classical Revival or Neoclassical or Roman Classicism, which can be a source of confusion.

Buildings in the Classical Revival style usually exhibit many of the following characteristics:

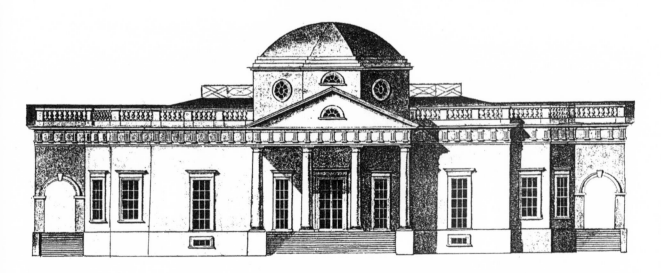

(a)

Classical Revival style
(a) Monticello (reconstruction 1796–1809), near Charlottesville, Va.

Façade and exterior wall treatments: A symmetrical façade, usually two stories high, commonly with one- or two-story wings; walls of brick, stucco, stone, or wood construction; often, a two-story monumental portico, painted white, with a triangular **pediment**, frequently with a semicircular window set within its **tympanum**; the pediment roof is usually supported by four columns—but very occasionally by six—on square bases; the columns are usually of the Roman Doric or Tuscan order, although columns of the Roman Ionic, Corinthian, or Composite order are also found. The **entablature** above the columns is sometimes bracketed and decorated with dentils, heavy modillions, and triglyphs, but it may also be relatively plain.

Roof treatments: Commonly, a low **hipped roof**, occasionally partially hidden by balustrades.

Window treatments: Usually a five-**ranked** façade (i.e., five windows across the upper floor and four on the ground floor plus the entry door), with the windows aligned both vertically and horizontally; polygonal bay windows; oval windows.

Doorway treatments: Typically, a paneled door, often with a semicircular or semielliptical fanlight above the door.

(b)

Classical Revival style
(b) Andrews-Taylor House (1843), Harrison County, Tex.

classic box A term sometimes used to describe a **Colonial Revival** house having a hipped roof and a full-width front porch.

classicism In architecture, the principles that emphasize the correct use of the Roman and Greek **orders**.

Classic Revival A term often used as a synonym for the **Classical Revival style.**

clay A fine-grained, cohesive, natural earthy material; plastic when sufficiently wet; rigid when dry; vitrified when heated to a sufficiently high temperature; used in making brick and tile, as wall **infilling**, and as **daub** in wattle-and-daub.

clay-and-hair mortar A plastic mixture of clay and water to which animal hair is added to improve the mechanical strength of the resulting mortar after it has dried; widely used in construction in colonial America.

clay-and-sticks chimney A chimney usually constructed of clay or mud and sticks or planks and then coated on the interior with clay, mud, or plaster to provide some protection against setting the chimney on fire. Such chimneys were often used in homes of the earliest American settlers (and later in frontier houses) because they did not require bricks, stone, or lime mortar for their construction, which were often unavailable.

clay-and-sticks chimney: on a log cabin

clay tile A **tile** made of clay that has been burnt in a kiln at a high temperature; formed in individual units that are primarily used for roofing. *See also* **structural clay tile.**

clerestory, clearstory That part of a building which rises above the adjoining roof and is pierced with a series of windows both to admit light and often to ventilate the loft room below it. Found, for example, in Spanish Colonial missions.

clipped gable Same as **jerkinhead roof.**

cloister A covered walk surrounding a courtyard; for example, a covered walk linking a church to other buildings of a monastery.

cloister
Abbey of Gethsemane (1866), Nelson County, Ky.

close A courtyard that is enclosed except for one or two narrow entrances.

close-boarded A term descriptive of a surface that is covered with square-edge boards, laid in the same plane and in close contact with each other; often used as **sheathing** on the roof or walls of a house.

closed cornice Same as **boxed cornice.**

closed eaves Same as **boxed eaves.**

closed newel The central shaft of a spiral stair constructed within a cylindrical wall; has no stairwell.

closed string An inclined board, parallel to the average slope of a stair, that supports the ends of the steps; conceals the profile of the steps so that the stair treads are not visible when viewed from the side. Compare with **open string.**

closer The last brick, block, stone, or tile at the end of a horizontal **course** of masonry units; usually such a unit is trimmed to the appropriate size on the site, to finish the course.

coach house A subsidiary building primarily for housing carriages and occasionally horses. Also called a carriage house.

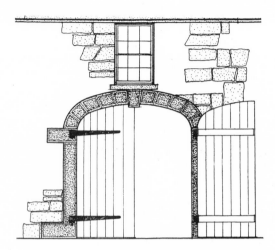

coach house: entrance, Hurst House,
Lorain County, Ohio

coach-mounting steps A small elevated platform on which a person would step when mounting or dismounting from a coach or carriage; often set near the entryway of a house.

coach-mounting steps

coal house A subsidiary building for the storage of coal; in colonial times, especially one connected to a blacksmith's shop.

cob A mixture of clay and chopped straw, often with the addition of gravel; sometimes used in wall construction in colonial America.

cobblestone A naturally rounded stone used in paving, wall construction, and foundations.

cobblestone house A house whose rubble masonry walls are surfaced with **cobblestone.**

cochlea 1. A tower for a spiral staircase. 2. Same as **spiral stair.**

cocina A kitchen in a Spanish Colonial dwelling.

cockleshell cupboard Same as **shell-headed cupboard.**

cockle stair Same as **spiral stair.**

cockloft A small garret or loft under a roof and above the uppermost floor.

code *See* **building code.**

coffer One of a number of deeply recessed panels in a ceiling; often square or octagonal and sometimes highly ornamented; especially used in buildings in the **Classical Revival style.**

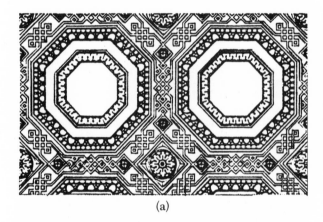

(a)

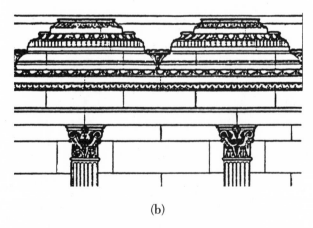

(b)

coffer: (a) partial reflected ceiling plan
showing two coffers in a ceiling;
(b) section through the ceiling

cold cellar A **cellar,** or portion thereof, that is used during the winter to store root crops at a temperature usually slightly above freezing.

collar beam In a **timber-framed house** having a roof with a steep pitch on each side of a central ridge, a horizontal structural member that ties together (and stiffens) two opposite **common rafters**, usually at a point about halfway up the rafters between the apex and the eaves.

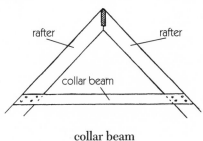

collar beam

collar-beam roof A roof supported by common rafters tied together by **collar beams**.

Collegiate Gothic The secular version of **Gothic architecture**, characteristic of many of the older colleges of Oxford and Cambridge, as adapted in the late 19th and early 20th centuries at a number of colleges in America, such as Bryn Mawr, Princeton University, Duke University, and the Graduate College and Divinity School at Yale University. Leading architects who designed outstanding buildings in this style include Ralph Adams Cram (1863–1942), Richard Morris Hunt (1827–1895), and John Russell Pope (1874–1937). *See also* **Late Gothic Revival.**

colonette, colonnete A small column, usually decorative.

Colonial architecture *See* **American Colonial architecture, Dutch Colonial architecture, English Colonial architecture, French Colonial architecture, German Colonial architecture, Spanish Colonial architecture.** Compare with **Colonial Revival.**

Colonial Georgian style *See* **Georgian style.**

colonial joint Same as **tooled joint.**

Colonial New England architecture *See* **American Colonial architecture.**

Collegiate Gothic: John Russell Pope's 1919 plan for
Library Court, Yale University, New Haven, Conn.

Colonial Revival Architecture that reuses aspects of earlier colonial prototypes; found from around 1870 onward. For descriptions of architecture imitative of Dutch, French, and Spanish prototypes, *see* **Dutch Colonial Revival, Châteauesque style, French Eclectic architecture, Spanish Colonial Revival, Mission Revival, Pueblo Revival.** When this term is used without reference to a country of origin (simply as *Colonial Revival*), it usually refers to architecture based on prototypes in the English colonies in America. Of these prototypes, the **Georgian style** and the **Federal style** (*Adam style*) are the most widely imitated, giving rise to the terms **Georgian Revival** and **Federal Revival** (*Adam Revival*). Colonial Revival houses are usually the result of a rather free interpretation of their prototypes; they tend to be larger, may differ significantly from the houses they seek to emulate, and often exaggerate architectural details. *See also* **Neo-Colonial architecture, garrison house,** and **Cape Cod house.**

Colonial Revival architecture usually exhibits many of the following characteristics:

Façade and exterior wall treatments: A façade featuring an extension of the pediment above the entrance, or a prominent portico covering the full width of the building; commonly, a classical cornice; a cupola; a **widow's walk;** occasionally, a balcony; colonial detailing; bevel siding or a smooth brick wall finish with fine joints, with brickwork often set in a **Flemish bond** pattern; splayed lintels. Colonial Revival may also include treatments of the façade that were not present or were rarely found in their colonial prototypes, such as an asymmetrical façade, wall dormers, brick veneer, and/or broken pediments.

Roof treatments: A hipped, gabled, or (less frequently) gambrel roof; a roof covering of slate tiles or wood shingles; often, a **boxed cornice**. Colonial Revival may also include roof treatments never found in their colonial prototypes, such as a balustrade at the roof line or exposed rafters supporting the roof.

Window treatments: Double-hung, rectangular sash windows with multiple panes in both the upper and lower sashes; symmetrically arrayed windows in the façade; often, adjacent pairs of windows (or three adjacent windows) treated as single architectural unit; a **fanlight** over the main entry door and sidelights on each side of door; louvered shutters. Colonial Revival may also include window treatments usually not found in their colonial prototypes, such as multiple panes in the upper sash and a single pane in the lower sash, bay windows in adjacent pairs, a **three-part window,** or a **Palladian window.**

Doorway treatments: A front door commonly crowned by a pediment supported by **pilasters** that may extend forward and be supported on columns so as to form an entry porch; often, an overhead fanlight. Colonial Revival may also include doorway treatments usually not found in their colonial prototypes: for example, a glass-paneled entry door, pedimented doors without pilasters, sidelights without fanlights, and heavily ornamented entrance doors.

Colonial Revival

colonial siding Wide, square-edged boards (as opposed to tapered boards) used extensively as the exterior covering of early colonial American buildings of wood-frame construction; each upper board overlaps the board below. *See also* **weatherboards.**

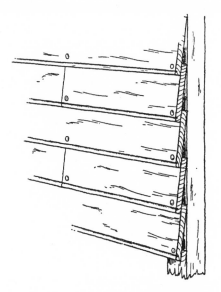

colonial siding

colonnade A series of columns placed at regular intervals (*see* **intercolumniation**), supporting an **entablature** and often one side of a roof that provides a covered walkway.

colonnade

colonnette *See* **colonette.**

colossal column A column that is more than one story in height.

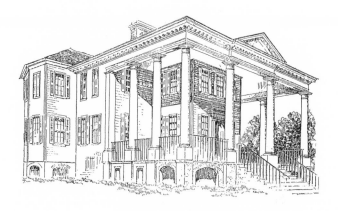

colossal columns

colossal order In Classical architecture, an **order** in which the columns rise more than one story, most commonly two or three stories. Also called a giant order.

columbage In French Vernacular architecture of Louisiana, **timber-framed buildings** with diagonal bracing of the framework; the space between the structural timbers was usually filled with **bousillage** or **pierrotage.**

columbage
Rouge House, Natchitoches, La.

column 1. A relatively long, vertical, slender structural compression member such as a pillar or post that supports a load acting in the direction of its longitudinal axis. 2. In **Classical architecture**, a cylindrical vertical support consisting of a capital, a shaft, and a base (except for the Greek Doric, which has no base); the shaft may be either monolithic or built up of a number of cylinders or **drums**. 3. A pillar standing alone as a monument.

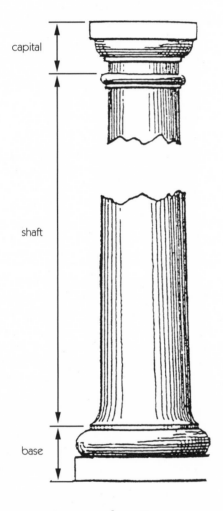

column,2

comb board A board at the ridge of a roof that has notches along its upper edge.

comedor A dining room in a Spanish Colonial house.

Commercial Italianate style *See* **Italianate style**.

Commercial style An American style of commercial architecture employed by the **Chicago School**, applied primarily to multistory office buildings and mercantile buildings constructed from about 1875 to 1930; often associated with the work of Louis H. Sullivan (1856–1924). Usually characterized by a **tripartite scheme** consisting of: a *base* one to four stories high; a *shaft* many stories high that tends to emphasize the steel-frame construction; and a *cap,* usually one to four stories high, which tops the structure. Buildings in this style have a flat roof; an overhanging cornice; unadorned fenestration, most often with large rectangular windows (for example, *see* **Chicago window**); bay windows with decorative **spandrels,1.** Sometimes called Chicago Commercial style because it was widely applied in that city after the Great Fire of 1871.

Commercial style
The Bank of Commerce (1898), Chicago, Ill.

common In colonial New England, a large plot of grassy, fenced-in, publicly owned land, generally at the center of a village or town; its use was shared by the townspeople, often as a pasture. A well-known urban example is Boston Common. The **meeting house**, as well as the homes of prominent members of the community and the minister, frequently faced this plot of land. Commons are still found in many old New England towns.

common bond A pattern of brickwork in which every third, fifth, sixth, or seventh course consists of **headers** (i.e., bricks laid horizontally with their lengths perpendicular to the face of the wall), and the other courses consist of **stretchers** (i.e., bricks laid horizontally so that their lengths are parallel to the face of the wall). This pattern is widely used because it can be laid relatively quickly. Also called American bond.

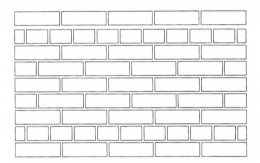

common bond

common house A term sometimes applied to a one-room cottage in **Spanish Colonial architecture of Florida,** primarily in the first half of the 18th century. Its walls were often constructed of **tabby,** which was usually whitewashed. It had a hipped roof, thatched with palmetto fronds, and a smoke hole at the ridge of the roof. *See also* **Saint Augustine house.**

common joist One of a series of parallel horizontal beams on which **floorboards** are laid; supports ceiling loads, but neither supports nor is supported by another joist.

common purlin In timber-framed construction, one of a number of horizontal timbers that are parallel to the ridge of the roof and are joined to the **principal rafters,** into which they are seated. The upper surfaces of the common purlins and the principal rafters are in the same plane.

common rafter In wood-frame construction, one of a number of slanting structural members, extending from the **ridgeboard** down to the **eaves,** that support the roof. Usually the common rafters are all of the same size and are evenly spaced along the length of the roof ridge.

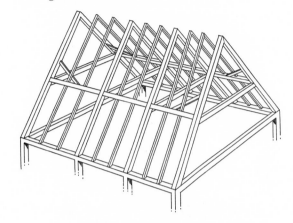

common rafter (ridgeboard not shown)

common wall Same as **party wall.**

community plan *See* **city plan** and **town plan.**

community planning The process of planning a future community, or the guidance and shaping of the expansion of a current community, in an organized manner and with an organized layout, taking into account such considerations as convenience for its inhabitants, environmental conditions, social requirements, recreational facilities, aesthetic design, and economic feasibility. Such planning includes a study of present requirements and conditions as well as projections for the future and often includes proposals for implementation of the plan.

company town A community whose inhabitants depend predominantly on a single business organization for their work and personal needs. A well-known early example is Pullman, Illinois, now part of Chicago, where an entire community was built in 1880 around a plant for assembling railroad passenger cars. The town provided housing, schools, shopping facilities, recreational facilities, and church and library facilities for its workers and their families, all owned by the Pullman Company. Pullman became famous (or infamous) in 1894 when, as a result of a bitter labor dispute, President Grover Cleveland dispatched federal troops there to break the strike.

compass roof A convex-shaped roof formed either by curved **rafters** or by a combination of rafters, beams, and braces in the shape of a segment of a circle. Also called a compass-headed roof.

compass window 1. A rounded **bay window** that projects from the face of a wall; in plan, it forms the segment of a circle. 2. A semicircular **oriel** window. 3. A window having a rounded, usually semicircular, upper member.

Composite capital The topmost member of a column of the **Composite order;** a Roman adaptation of a Corinthian capital, being much more elaborate; consists of volutes and an ovolo between them, somewhat similar to the Ionic capital; has a circle of acanthus leaves applied to the lower part of the bell used in the Corinthian capital.

Composite order In Classical architecture, one of the five Classical **orders**; combines characteristics of both the Corinthian and Ionic orders; similar to the Corinthian order, but much more embellished. The capital consists of **volutes** borrowed, with modifications, from the Ionic capital; the circle of acanthus leaves applied to the capital is borrowed from the **Corinthian capital.** *See also* illustrations under **base** and **entablature.**

compound arch An elaborate arch formed by arches set within one another.

concave joint A recessed masonry joint, formed in mortar by the use of a steel tool, that gives the joint a concave shape, making it highly effective in resisting the penetration of rain; especially used in regions subject to heavy rainfall and high winds.

concha In **Spanish Colonial architecture,** a decorative element in the form of the inside of a sea scallop; *see* **shell-headed.**

concrete A composite stonelike material formed by mixing an **aggregate** (such as stones or crushed rocks) with **cement** (which acts as the binding material) and water, then allowing the mixture to harden. In colonial America the aggregate was often coarse rubble or broken seashells and the binding medium was usually lime mortar. The **portland cement** now used in making concrete was not developed until the 19th century. *See also* **reinforced concrete.**

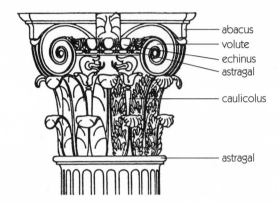

Composite capital

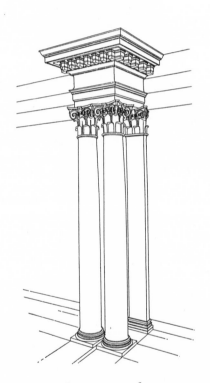

Composite order

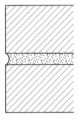

concave joint

concrete block A hollow or solid concrete masonry unit molded into the shape of a rectangular block, consisting of portland cement and a suitable aggregate often combined with lime, fly ash, and a material (called an *admixture*) that is added in small quantities to produce a desired change in the physical properties of the concrete. Such blocks were commonly used in the early 20th century in **Prairie style** homes. An interesting example of the decorative use of concrete block is illustrated under **Wrightian.**

concrete slab A flat, rectangular, reinforced-concrete structural member; often acts as the foundation for a building.

conductor Same as **leader.**

conductor head Same as **leader head.**

conduit A channel, pipe, or tube commonly used for carrying water, electrical cables, or other utilities.

congé 1. A base molding flush at the top with the wall above, but with a fillet between the cove and the floor; any molding of similar profile. 2. Same as **apophyge,1.**

conical roof A roof in the shape of an inverted cone atop a cylindrical tower; similar in shape to a candle snuffer; especially found in the **Châteauesque style** and **Queen Anne style.** Also called a candle-snuffer roof or a witch's hat.

connected barn *See* **continuous house.**

Connecticut barn Same as **Yankee barn.**

conservation The overseeing of a building to prevent or arrest its decay or destruction, usually by applying a variety of measures. *See also* **building conservation** and **building preservation.**

conservatory A structure, attached to a dwelling, chiefly used for growing flowers, plants, and out-of-season fruits and vegetables under protected conditions. It serves the same purpose as a **greenhouse,** but a greenhouse is usually separated from a dwelling and is located in a garden or field. *See also* **hothouse** and **orangery.**

console A decorative bracket, usually in the form of an upright scroll, that projects from a wall to support a cornice, **doorhead**, **window head**, or the like. Also called an ancon.

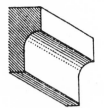

congé,1

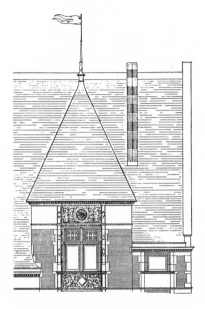

conical roof

console
Independence Hall (1732–1748), Philadelphia, Pa.

Contemporary style A loose term applied to any of a number of types of domestic architecture popular in America from the 1940s through the 1970s and beyond; sometimes included under the term *modern architecture*. One type is characterized by a façade and flat roof somewhat similar to that of the **International style** and is therefore sometimes called the *American International style*; it differs significantly in that its wall construction is usually a combination of wood, stone, and brick, rather than the stucco commonly used in the International style. It may have a balcony with an overhanging sunscreen, roof decks, and a patio that may serve as an extension of the living area. Another type is characterized by a low-pitched roof with widely overhanging eaves, exposed roof beams, and front-facing gables with heavy piers that support the gables, somewhat suggestive of houses of the **Prairie style** or the **Craftsman style.**

contextualism The design of a building so that it is in harmony with surrounding buildings, especially in terms of scale, form, mass, and color.

continental cabin A one-and-one-half-story **log house** attributed to German-speaking immigrants to colonial America; usually consisted of a large room at the front of the house, a bedroom behind it, and a long narrow kitchen. A sizable stove in the kitchen was used both for cooking and for heating the adjacent large room.

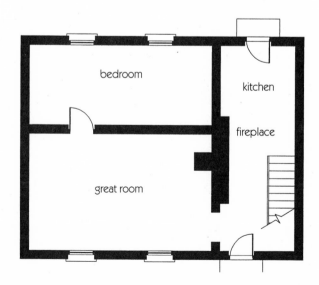

continental cabin: plan

continuous house A house that is interconnected with several other ancillary facilities such as a barn, privy, shed, and/or stable; still found in areas having a cold winter climate because it permits the residents to use these dependencies without going outdoors. *See also* **telescope house.**

continuous house

contrevents In **French Vernacular architecture** of Louisiana, wood shutters.

contributing chapel In **Spanish Colonial architecture** of the American Southwest, a chapel usually having no permanent padre to officiate at religious ceremonies, relying instead on the part-time assistance of visiting priests. Also called an asistencia or visitá.

convento In **Spanish Colonial architecture**, a convent or monastery usually having living quarters, workrooms, storerooms, a balcony, and patio.

cook house Same as **outkitchen.**

coping A protective cap that covers the top of a wall, parapet, pilaster, or the like; provides shelter against the penetration of rainwater; usually constructed of brick, stone, terra-cotta, tile, concrete, metal, or wood; commonly sloping, double-beveled, or convex in shape, so as to shed water effectively. *See also* **feather-edge coping.**

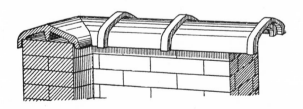

coping: fabricated of terra-cotta

coping stone Any stone that forms a **coping.**

copper roofing A flexible metal roof covering made of copper sheets joined by waterproof seams. As the copper oxidizes, it develops a green coating on its surface called a **patina.**

coquina A soft limestone formed of broken shells and coral; cut into blocks and used in the construction of Spanish Colonial dwellings in early Florida settlements. The chips, produced when this material was cut into blocks, were used as an aggregate in making a concretelike material.

corbel 1. In masonry, a projection or one of a series of projections, each stepped progressively outward with increasing height, and usually projecting from a wall or chimney; serves as a support for an overhanging member or course above or as a purely decorative. 2. A projecting stone that supports a superincumbent weight. 3. A heavy bracket, often decorated, that is set into an adobe wall to act as a bearing surface to support a roof beam (**viga**); especially found in **Mission architecture** and **Spanish Colonial architecture.**

corbel course A horizontal course or series of courses of masonry that acts, or appears to act, as a **corbel.**

corbeled chimney cap The crowning termination of a chimney in which successive courses of bricks step outward with increasing height.

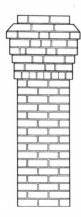

corbeled chimney cap
The Old Mansion, Bowling Green, Va.

corbel table A projecting course of masonry, supported by a row of **corbels**, often located just below the eaves of a roof.

corbiestep gable, corbie gable Same as **stepped gable.**

Corinthian capital The topmost member of a column of the **Corinthian order;** characterized by acanthus leaves and relatively small **volutes.**

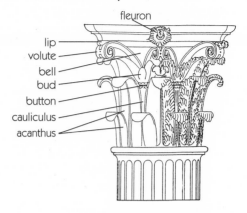

Corinthian capital (Roman)

Corinthian order In Classical architecture, the slenderest and most ornate of the three original Greek **orders**; commonly has an elaborate cornice and a fluted shaft. For an illustration of a Corinthian base, *see* **base.**

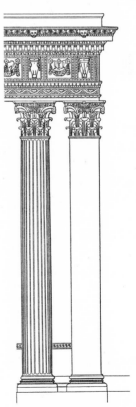

Corinthian order

corncrib, corn house A structure used since colonial times in America for storing unhusked ears of corn; designed to provide adequate air circulation to ensure that the freshly picked corn dries more or less uniformly so as to minimize spoilage. Found in a wide variety of sizes and shapes, but most often the sides slope inward so that the area is smaller at the bottom of the crib than at the top. Also called a corn loft.

corncrib

corner bead A vertical molding, plain or filleted, used to protect the external angle of two intersecting walls.

corner block A square, relatively flat wood block, often decoratively carved, placed at the upper corners on each side of the wood framing around a door. Also called a trim block.

corner block

corner board A vertical board, usually one of a pair, that is used as trim on the external corner of a house of wood-frame construction and against which the ends of the **siding** are fitted; first used in the New England colonies in the 18th century.

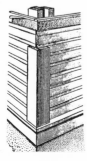

corner board

corner brace In a **timber-framed house**, a diagonal brace to reinforce the corners and stiffen the structure.

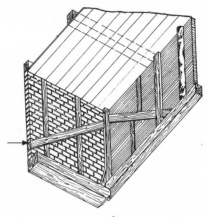

corner brace

corner capital Same as **angle capital.**

corner chimney A chimney placed so that its face forms an angle with the side walls of a room; *see also* **fogón.** Occasionally called an angle chimney.

corner drop A hand-carved or hand-turned wood ornament that is suspended from the corners of an overhanging second story of an early colonial American house. *See also* **pendant,1** and **turned drop.**

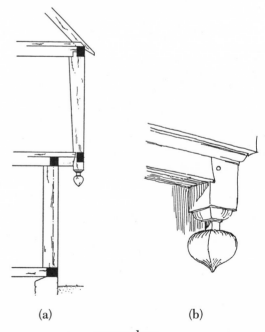

(a)   (b)

corner drop
(a) suspended from a framed overhang;
(b) detail

corner notch At a corner of a log cabin or log house, any one of several types of **notches** cut near an end of an exterior timber to form a rigid joint when mated with another appropriately notched timber set at right angles to it. *See* **double-saddle notch, dovetail notch, half-cut notch, half-dovetail notch, halved-and-lapped notch, round notch, saddle notch, single notch, single-saddle notch, V-notch.**

corner pilaster An engaged pier or pillar, often with a capital and base, located at the corner of a building or colonnade.

corner pilaster

corner post In a **timber-framed house,** a heavy **post** that is placed at the intersection of two exterior walls to act as an important structural member of the framing system; provides a nailing surface for the wall construction. In modern wood-frame construction, a similar post at the corner is often built up from two or more two-by-four (4x9cm) timbers.

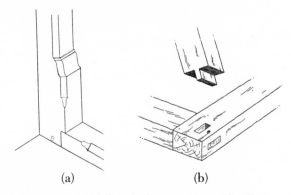

(a)   (b)

corner post: (a) detail of connection with sill;
(b) detail of connection with sill at foundation level

cornerstone A ceremonial stone, prominently situated at one corner and near the base of a building; often encloses or caps a sealed box containing contemporary memorabilia and information concerning the dedicatory ceremonies. Also called a foundation stone.

cornerstone: Freylinghusen Parsonage (1751),
Washington Place, N.J.

corn house *See* **corncrib.**

cornice 1. Any molded horizontal projection that crowns or finishes the top of a wall where it meets the edge of the roof; sometimes ornamented. 2. The exterior trim of a structure where the wall and roof meet. 3. The third or uppermost division of an **entablature,** resting on the frieze. 4. An ornamental molding that forms the top member of a door or window frame, usually of wood or plaster. 5. An ornamental molding that usually extends around the walls of a room just below the ceiling. For special types, *see* **architrave cornice, boxed cornice, bracketed cornice, cavetto cornice, closed cornice, eaves cornice, modillion cornice, open cornice.**

cornice,1

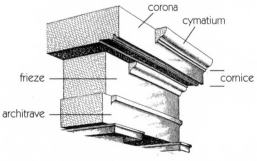

cornice,3

cornice return The continuation of a **cornice,1** in a changed direction, as at the gable end of a house.

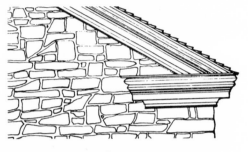

cornice return

corona In **Classical architecture,** the overhanging vertical member of a **cornice,1** supported by the **bed moldings** and crowned with the **cymatium**; usually intended to throw rainwater clear of the building.

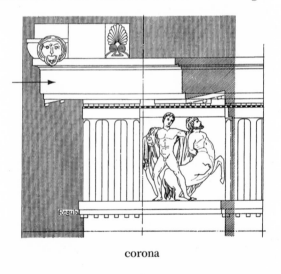

corona

coronet A pediment or other decorative element, in relief, on a wall above a door or window.

Corporate style The austere style of industrial buildings used in New England during the early part of the 19th century; characterized by red brick walls in combination with white stone lintels; often gracefully proportioned.

corredor A long, narrow porch or arcade that often covers the entire front and/or one or more sides of a Spanish colonial house in the American Southwest.

corridor A long interior passageway in a building that connects the areas at both ends and may also provide access to, and egress from, the rooms adjoining it.

corrugated metal Sheet metal having parallel ridges and furrows that provide the sheet with additional mechanical resistance to bending in a direction at right angles to the parallel ridges. This metal, commonly fabricated of tin, was widely used in America in the mid-19th century for roofing; now such roofing is usually fabricated of corrugated aluminum or galvanized sheet metal.

cortina In **Spanish Colonial architecture**, corbeled stonework directly below a balcony or windowsill.

cottage 1. A relatively small house in a village, in the countryside, in a suburb, or at the seashore. Certain imposing houses (as in Newport, Rhode Island) are also called cottages, perhaps in some form of reverse snobbery. 2. A small vacation house. 3. In early colonial America, a dwelling, often temporary, providing only basic shelter. *See also* **banquette cottage, Cajun cottage, Chicago cottage, Normandy cottage, one-and-one-half-bay cottage, one-bay cottage, one-room cottage, palma hut, prairie cottage, raised house, Tidewater cottage, two-bay cottage.**

cottage orné A small, picturesque house in a rural or country setting, primarily in the 19th century, the modifier *picturesque* permitting wide latitude in interpretation. Thus, some cottages were considered to be in this category because straight tree trunks were used as columns and selected parts of tree branches as brackets; others were so classified merely because their ornamentation was said to create a picturesque effect.

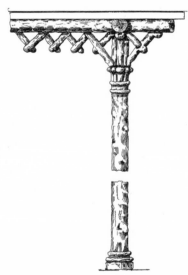

cottage orné: detail of a post and beam

Cottage style house 1. A style of domestic architecture, usually of wood construction, popularized in the 19th century primarily by the **pattern books** of architects Andrew Jackson Downing (1815–1852) and Alexander Jackson Davis (1803–1892). Usually included many of the following characteristics: an asymmetric plan, walls of **board-and-batten construction**, balconies, decorative chimneys, steeply pitched roofs, and bay windows. 2. A loose term infrequently applied to a **bungalow.**

Cottage style house
Andrew Jackson Downing, Architect

cottage window A **double-hung window** having its upper sash smaller than the lower sash; the upper pane is often decorated.

counterfloor Same as **subfloor.**

counterscarp The face of a ditch of a fortress sloping toward the defender.

country seat A rural residence of some importance.

counterwall A wall of a building that is adjacent to, but separated from, the wall of another building on the other side of the property line. Compare with **party wall.**

couple A pair of opposite rafters that are joined at their upper ends and interconnected by a **collar beam** or **tie beam**, usually near their midpoints.

coupled brackets Two closely spaced brackets that form a pair.

coupled columns Two closely spaced columns that form a pair.

coupled columns:
Brockenbrough House (1818), later "The White House of the Confederacy," Richmond, Va.

course 1. A layer of masonry units, bonded with mortar, that runs horizontally in a wall or, much less commonly, that is curved over an arch. 2. A continuous row of units, such as shingles, tiles, or the like. For specific types, *see* **band course, base course, belt course, blocking course, bond course, corbel course, dogtooth course, masonry course, random course, sill course, stringcourse, tumbling course.**

coursed ashlar, coursed masonry Stone masonry in which the stones *within* each course are identical in height, although the courses themselves need not be the same height.

coursed pattern A pattern formed by shingles that are laid in regular horizontal rows of equal height, each row overlapping the row below, with the vertical joints of one row usually falling approximately midway between those of adjacent rows.

coursed rubble Masonry construction in which roughly dressed stones of random size are used to build up **courses**; the interstices between the stones are filled with much smaller pieces of stone and/or with mortar.

coursed rubble

courthouse A building where justice is administered and judicial affairs are transacted; often the most prominent structure in many small towns in 19th-century America.

courtyard An open area that is partially or fully enclosed by one or more buildings and/or by walls. Courtyards that are enclosed or partially enclosed by walls are sometimes referred to as patios. *See also* **placita**.

coussinet 1. The stone that is placed on the impost of a pier to receive the first stone of an arch. 2. That part of the front of an Ionic capital between the **abacus** and **echinus**.

cove A concave molding, especially placed at the transition from a wall to the ceiling or from a wall to the floor.

coved ceiling A ceiling having a **cove** at its intersection with the wall.

coved eaves The **eaves** of a building that are covered with a concave surface so that the rafters are not visible.

covered bridge A bridge, usually constructed of heavy timbers and trusses, enclosed or partially enclosed on its sides, whose roadway is protected by a roof; especially found in regions with heavy snowfall. In early bridges of this type, the timbers were usually cut from a nearby stand of trees, the abutment stones were taken from adjacent fields, and the metal used in their construction was often taken from broken-down carriages and/or from farm machinery no longer in working condition. The structural members were generally precut and assembled in a nearby field to ensure that all parts would fit. Then they were numbered, taken apart, and reassembled over the stream to be bridged. Many such covered bridges were erected in America in the 19th century. The first long covered bridge was constructed over the Schuylkill River at Philadelphia in 1806.

cow barn, cow house, cow shed A dependency used to house cattle.

coyn Obsolete term for **quoin**.

cradle roof Same as **barrel roof,1**.

cradle vault Same as **barrel vault**.

cradle *See* **chimney foundation**.

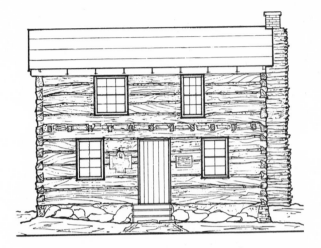

courthouse: Decatur, Ill. (1829), where
Abraham Lincoln practiced law

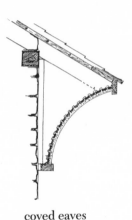

coved eaves

covered bridge
Johnson's Mill Bridge (1866), Susquehanna River, Pa.

Craftsman style A style of house most popular from about 1900 to 1920, greatly influenced by the **Arts and Crafts movement** and popularized by Gustav Stickley (1858–1942) in his magazine, *The Craftsman*, published from 1901 to 1916. Stickley also made construction drawings of such houses, in many sizes and configurations, available at a reasonable price. Complete precut components for the houses were available for purchase by catalogue from mail-order companies such as Sears, Roebuck and Company and were shipped by railroad to destinations throughout the nation. As a result, this style of house became the most popular small dwelling in the nation. The interior typically featured a high wainscot that was integrated with the door and windows as part of the structural decoration. The stairway from the living room to the floor above was often an important feature. *See also* **Arts and Crafts movement.**

Craftsman-style houses usually exhibit a number of the following characteristics:

Façade and exterior wall treatments: A nonsymmetrical façade, typically sheathed with stucco, wood clapboards, or wood shingles, and less often with board-and-batten, brick, concrete block, or stone; often, masonry walls on the first story and clapboard or wood shingles on the second story; occasionally, a **battered** foundation; a partial-width or full-width gabled porch facing the street, with square columns or tapered square columns (often rising from wide pedestals or from ground level) that support the porch roof; commonly, structural members of the porch are exposed. Frequently, a **recessed porch** or a trellised porch (sometimes screened, and separately gabled), often with a **porte cochère** at one side of the porch.

Roof treatments: Usually, a low- to moderate-pitched front-gabled roof; occasionally, a cross-gabled, side-gabled, or hipped roof; wide overhanging eaves. Along the eaves, exposed roof rafters, beams, false beams, or triangular knee braces inserted as decorative elements under the gables; gabled dormers or **shed dormers** with exposed beams; frequently, exterior chimneys of stone construction.

Window treatments: Commonly, **double-hung windows**, each with multiple panes in the upper sash and a single pane in the lower sash; often, heavily framed **casement windows.**

Doorway treatments: Commonly, a **battened door** with wrought-iron strap hinges of the type used in the early American colonies.

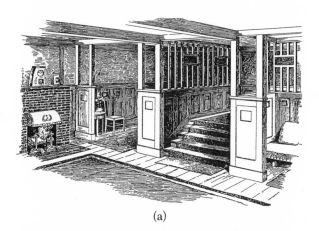

(a)

(b)

(c)

Craftsman style: (a) interior of a typical house; (b) windows and doors are part of the structural decoration; (c) newel-post lamp

cramp A **U**-shaped metal fastener used to hold adjacent units of masonry together, as in a **parapet** on a wall; usually set into holes cut in the stone and then filled with mortar.

crane *See* **fireplace crane.**

cratchet In a dwelling of the earliest settlers in America, an upright tree trunk having a natural fork; the **Y** of the fork was used to support the **ridgepole** of the roof.

crenel An open space between the **merlons** of a parapet used for defense on a fortification.

crenellation An alternating series of **crenels** and **merlons**; *see* **battlement.** Often found in **Gothic Revival** and **Collegiate Gothic** architecture.

Creole house Although there are a variety of meanings for the term, in the context of its relevance to **French Vernacular architecture,** a *Creole* is usually considered to be a person of European ancestry born in the Mississippi Valley, along the Gulf Coast, or in the West Indies, or the descendant of such a person, raised in an American tropical environment, often speaking a French patois. The Creole house, which had its origins in the West Indies and Brazil in the 16th and 17th centuries, was developed by the Creoles along the Gulf Coast, particularly in the southern Louisiana countryside, in the early 18th century to provide maximum comfort under the local conditions of high humidity

cramp

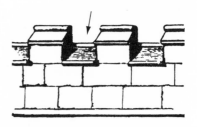

crenel

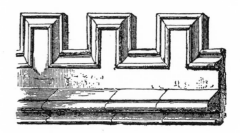

crenellation

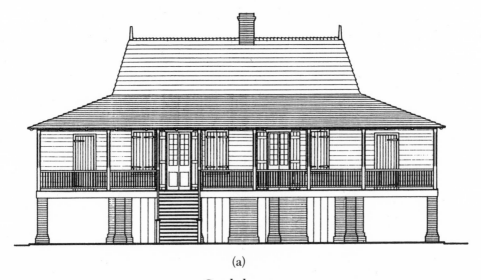

(a)

Creole house
(a) Holoden House (18th cent.), Rougon, La.; broken-pitch roof with a *galerie*, rafters at the front, and large loggia at the rear;

and temperature. It was usually rectangular in plan, with one or two rooms, a garret overhead; windows with battened shutters; and a **bonnet roof** or a roof having a single slope on each side of a central ridge. From this modest beginning developed a series of logical expansions and changes culminating in more complex **raised houses** of many rooms, surrounded, or partially surrounded, by **galeries.** The architectural historian Jay D. Edwards has shown that Creole houses may be grouped into three closely related classes consisting of various combinations of a central core of rooms, surrounded by full-length porches (called **galeries**) along one or both sides of the house, with different types of pitched roofs. In addition, there were dependencies, usually including a kitchen. The floor on which the family lived was raised well above ground level, often by as much as a full story, to provide improved air circulation that was further enhanced by the use of French doors, as described under **raised house, galerie house,** and **plantation house.** Compare with **Cajun cottage.**

(b)

Creole house
(b) town house, Rougon, La.

crescent A building or series of buildings whose façades follow a concave arc of a circle or ellipse. An early example is the Tontine Crescent (1793) in Boston, Massachusetts, by Charles Bulfinch (1763–1844).

cresting A decorative board or metal strip along the ridge of a roof, coping, cornice, or parapet; generally highly ornamented, rhythmic, and often perforated. Found, for example, in the **Châteauesque style, Queen Anne style,** and **Second Empire style.** Also called brattishing.

cresting
Boston Public Library (1895), Boston, Mass.

crib A partial enclosure for storing hay, corn, or the like. *See also* **corncrib.**

crib barn A crudely constructed barn once used to house animals or to store agricultural products; usually timber-framed, but sometimes built of logs; most commonly found in Kentucky and Tennessee. If constructed with one storage space, it was called a *single-crib barn*; if constructed with two storage spaces, a *double-crib barn;* if constructed with four storage spaces, a *four-crib barn.*

crib barn: four cribs

crocket An ornament of medieval origin, often plantlike in form, usually placed at regularly spaced intervals along the edge of a sloping supporting surface of spires or pinnacles or the like, curving up and away from the surface. Found in America primarily in **Gothic Revival** and **Collegiate Gothic** architecture.

crockets: Hartford College, Hartford, Conn.

cross-and-Bible door Same as **Christian door.**

cross bar A seldom-used term for **door bar.**

cross beam 1. A large structural beam between two opposite walls; also called a girder. 2. A horizontal beam that is perpendicular to the centerline of a structure. 3. Same as **wind beam.**

cross-brace Same as **X-brace.**

crossette A decorative embellishment, such as a molding around a door, window, or fireplace opening, that somewhat resembles a squared-off ear; especially popular in America during latter half of the 18th century. Also called a dog's ear or an ear.

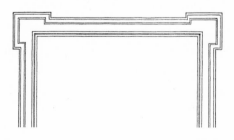

crossette

cross gable A **gable** whose face is parallel to the main ridge of the roof.

cross house, cross-plan house A brick house having a **cruciform plan**, suggestive of the shape of a cross; especially found in colonial Maryland and Virginia. At the front of the house, entry was through a door in a two-story extension in the transverse direction of the cross; at the rear of this extension was an enclosed porch on the ground floor containing a small, steep stair leading to a room above. Cooking was usually done in an **outkitchen** close to the house.

cross section A representation of a building, or portion thereof, drawn as if it were cut vertically to show its interior or internal structure; often taken at right angles to the longitudinal axis of a building.

crowfooted gable Same as **stepped gable.**

crown 1. Any decorative upper termination, such as the keystone of an arch, a doorhood, or the top of a window frame. 2. The central area of any convex surface. 3. The projecting part of a cornice.

crown glass A hand-made **glass** of soda-lime composition, often used in early colonial America for windows. It was the highest-quality glass then available, being clearer than **cylinder glass**, and was imported from England to the colonies at a considerable cost. In the early 19th century, crown glass was manufactured in New England by a now-obsolete process in which a hollow sphere of hot glass was blown, then spun to form a large, nearly flat circular disk usually about four to five feet (1.2–1.5m) in diameter. At the center of the spun disk, ripple lines formed during the spinning process produced a pattern of concentric circles; this central area was used in a **bull's eye,2.** *See also* **glass.**

crown molding Any molding that forms the upper termination of a structure.

crown plate 1. Same as **bolster,1**. 2. A longitudinal structural member at the apex of a roof that supports the upper ends of the rafters.

crown post Any vertical structural member in a roof **truss**, especially a **king post.**

crown tile Same as **ridge tile.**

crowstep gable Same as **stepped gable.**

crowstone The top horizontal stone of a **stepped gable.**

cross gables
Spring Villa House (1867), Lee County, Ala.

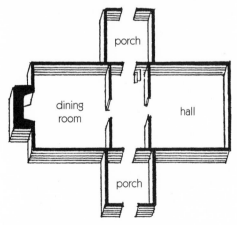

cross house: (above) New Kent County, Va.;
(below) plan for ground floor of cross house

cruciform plan A **floor plan** of a building in the shape of a cross; the characteristic plan for many large churches formed by the intersection of nave, chancel, and apse (the long axis of the cross) with the transept (the short axis of the cross).

cruck One of a pair of naturally curved timbers that rise from the outer walls to support the ridge beam of a timber-framed house or farm building, each cruck also called a *blade;* joined at the top and connected by one or two tie beams, the resulting arched frame forming one unit of framework of the structure.

Crystal Palace A large exhibition building constructed largely of prefabricated iron components for framing, glass walls, and wood floors. The first building of its kind was built in London in 1851. The second such structure, a huge arcade 451 feet (137.5m) long, was built at 42nd Street and Sixth Avenue in New York City for the 1853 Exhibition. Shortly after its opening,

cruck

Crystal Palace (1853),
New York City: (a) exterior

Horace Greeley gave this description of the Crystal Palace:

> The building is two stories high. The first is in the form of an octagon, the second in the form of a Greek cross. The centre of this is a dome, one hundred and forty-eight feet high. The four corners of the octagon are furnished each with two towers, seventy feet high. These towers support flag-staffs, adding to the lightness of their appearance. The construction is similar to that of the original in London, so far as the connection of iron columns, girders, and so forth, go; but the principal parts of the rest, the dome included, were fashioned by the architects, Messrs. George Carstensen and Charles Gildmeister, who devised the plan of the whole structure as well as the details. The main building covers 173,000 square feet . . . there are twelve stairways . . . [placed] at each point of the compass, on the sides and under the dome. The great circular windows, facing at four points, add much to the charm of the effect. The cast-iron weighs 1,200 tons; the wrought, 300 [tons]. . . . The prevailing style of the architecture is Moorish and Byzantine in its decorations. The ceilings are painted blue, white, red, and cream color. The single fault we find with the other portions of the building is that the supporting pillars are the same color with the other solid works, while if they were bronzed, a certain sameness would be avoided, and the impression of the character for strength would be distinctly conveyed.

Since the building was built entirely of iron and glass—except for the wood floors—it was considered fireproof. When a major fire did occur in 1858, the entire structure collapsed within fifteen minutes. Nevertheless, the Crystal Palace represented a milestone in the history of building construction in the United States because it demonstrated the practicality of using iron as an important architectural material.

**Crystal Palace (1853),
New York City: (b) interior**

Cumberland house A one-story **folk house** primarily in Tennessee; usually had a gable on one or both ends of the house and a front porch that often served as the center of family activity.

cupola A structure on a roof or dome, often set on a circular or polygonal base at the ridge of a roof or set on pillars; may serve as a belfry, **belvedere**, or **lantern**; often glazed to provide light in the space below or louvered to provide ventilation in that space. Especially found in elegant buildings in America in the **Federal style, Greek Revival style, Italianate style, Second Empire style.**

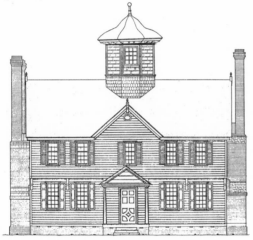

cupola: Cupola House (1758), Edenton, N.C.

curb roof A roof, symmetric about the ridge, that slants away from the ridge in two successive planes of differing slope; where the roof changes slope, there is a raised horizontal rim.

curb roof: Trinity Church (1735), Boston, Mass.

curtail A spirallike, scroll-shaped termination of any architectural member, for example, at the lower end of a stair rail.

curtail plate A **plate** that acts as a support for a **gambrel roof** where the roof changes pitch.

curtail step A step, usually lowest in a flight of steps, in which one or both ends are rounded in a spiral or scroll shape that projects beyond the post that supports the lower end of the handrail.

curtain wall A non-load-bearing exterior wall of a building, usually relatively lightweight, lacking any structural function. In modern buildings such walls are usually relatively large prefabricated panels designed for assembly at the building site.

curtilage The land occupied by a house, its outbuildings, and a yard; often enclosed by a fence.

curved pediment Same as **segmental pediment.**

curvilinear gable Same as **multicurved gable.**

curvilinear parapet A **parapet** whose outline usually consists of a combination of several curved and straight lines, as, for example, in a **mission parapet.**

cushion capital A **capital** resembling a cushion that is pressed down as if there were weight on it; found in America, for example, in the **Richardsonian Romanesque style** of architecture.

cushion capital

cushion frieze A **frieze** that bulges outward at its sides, as found in the convex profile of the frieze in some Classical **orders.**

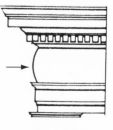

cushion frieze

cusp In **tracery**, the intersection of two arcs or lobes. *See* **foil** and illustration under **cinquefoil.**

cut nail A wedge-shaped nail manufactured from a sheet of iron or steel by slicing the sheet so that the nail thus formed is tapered on only two of its four sides; such iron nails were first produced in quantity in the 1790s. Cut nails are still used today in building construction for special purposes. Compare with **wrought nail** and **wire nail.**

cut-work *See* **gingerbread.**

cuzine, cuisine In **French Vernacular architecture** of Louisiana, a kitchen.

cyclone cellar Same as **storm cellar.**

cyclopean concrete Concrete in which large stones, each weighing 100 pounds or more, are embedded.

cylinder glass A type of relatively poor quality **glass,** made by blowing a cylinder of molten glass, dividing it lengthwise and rolling these sheets flat while the glass was still hot. This type of glass was widely used in colonial America because it was much cheaper than the higher quality **crown glass**; both were imported from England before Independence. Also called sheet glass.

cylinder lock A lock having its keyhole-and-tumbler mechanism in a cylinder that is removable from the lock case; intended for installation in the cylindrical hole in a door. *See also* **lock.**

cylindrical barn Same as **circular barn.**

cylindrical stair Same as **spiral stair.**

cyma A molding having a profile of double curvature, so that its section is **S**-shaped.

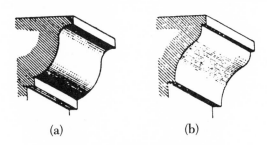

(a)   (b)

cyma: (a) cyma recta; (b) cyma reversa

cymatium The molding crowning a classical **cornice**, especially one having a double curvature profile.

cymatium

D

dado 1. The middle portion of a **pedestal** between the base (plinth) and the cap (the cornice, entablement, or surbase); also called a die. 2. A rectangular groove cut across the full width of a piece of wood to receive the end of another piece. 3. The middle part (or sometimes all parts) of protective ornamental paneling applied to the lower walls of a room above the baseboard.

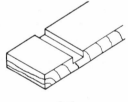

dado

dado cap A chair rail or cornice along the top of a **dado,3**.

dado joint A wood joint formed by a **dado,2** and a piece of wood that is inserted in the groove.

dado rail Same as **chair rail.**

dairy *See* **milk house.**

damper A pivoted metal plate set just above the **chimney throat** of a fireplace; used to regulate the flow of air (draft) through the chimney.

dancette A zigzag pattern used for ornamental purposes.

date stone A stone, embedded in the walls of many colonial buildings, that was carved with the date of completion of the structure.

date stone

daub A material such as clay, mortar, mud, or plaster (often mixed with straw), used as **infilling** between logs, as a coating over walls, or as plaster in **wattle-and-daub.**

dead A term descriptive of a door or window that is fixed in its frame so that it cannot be opened.

deadlight 1. A window, glazed in a fixed frame, that does not open. 2. A window that has been permanently closed with an opaque material.

dead wall A wall whose entire surface is unbroken by a door, window, or other opening.

dead window A recess in an external wall that has the contours of a window.

decastyle A term descriptive of a building having a **portico** with ten columns in front.

deck dormer A **hipped dormer** that has been truncated so that it has a flat, horizontal roof.

deck roof, deck-on-hip roof A **hipped roof** that has been truncated to form a flat top.

Deconstructivist architecture Architecture in the late 20th century that seeks to arrive at new forms of expression by turning away from structural restraints and functional and thematic hierarchies, often toward nonrectangular, fantastic, and seemingly disjointed designs. Such work represents an application of the philosophical theories of Jacques Derrida in France, who sought to arrive at new insights in literature by breaking apart literary texts into their contradictory and hidden components of meaning. This same philosophy was then applied to architectural structures by Frank Gehry (1929–), Peter Eisenman (1932–), Bernard Tschumi (1944–), and others. This form of architecture was the subject of a 1987 exhibit at the Museum of Modern Art in New York City.

deck dormer

deck roof: Anthony Benezet House (before 1818), Philadelphia, Pa.; drawn by William Strickland

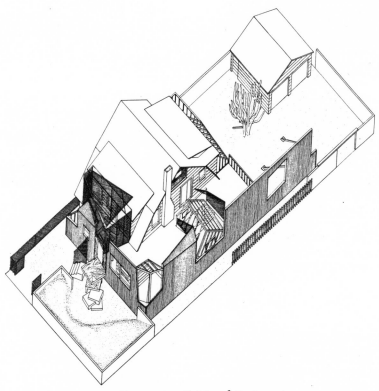

Deconstructivist architecture
Gehry House (1978), Santa Monica, Calif.; Frank Gehry, Architect; often cited as an early example of
Deconstructivist architecture in America

decorative half-timbering Same as **false half-timbering.**

decorative pendant *See* pendant, 1.

dentil One of a series of small, square, toothlike blocks that form part of the characteristic ornamentation of the Ionic, Composite, Corinthian, and sometimes the Doric **orders.** Found, for example, in the **Classical Revival style, Federal style, French Eclectic architecture, Georgian style, Greek Revival style.**

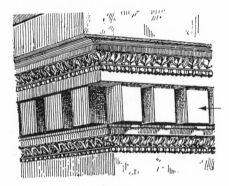

dentil

dentil band A plain, uncarved band occupying the position in a cornice where **dentils** would normally occur in Classical architecture.

dependency 1. A subsidiary building near or adjoining a principal structure, including now-obsolete auxiliary structures such as a **bake house, outkitchen, spinning house, wagon shed,** and **wash house.** 2. Any subsidiary building connected to the main house.

detached house A house that stands completely alone, not connected to any other structure.

detached house

details The relatively small elements of design and finish of a building.

diagonal chimney stacks An array of brick **chimney stacks** (often three in number) that are square in cross section and oriented so that diagonals through them form a straight line; usually corbeled and joined at their tops. Occasionally found in **Tudor Revival.**

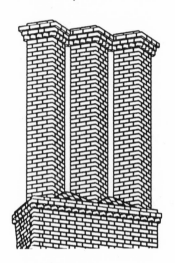

diagonal chimney stacks
Winona (late 17th cent.), Northampton County, Va.

diamond-bond pattern Same as **diaperwork.**

diamond light, diamond pane A small pane of glass, either diamond-shaped or square-shaped, set diagonally in lead **cames** in casement windows.

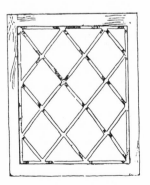

diamond light

diamond notch Same as **V-notch.**

diamond pattern On a roof, a pattern of shingles or tiles having **V**-shaped bottoms.

diaperwork, diaper pattern A decorative masonry pattern formed by brick **headers** having a dark glazed finish on one end; often laid in the gables of some colonial houses in a repeated pattern of diamonds, crisscrossed lines, inverted **V**s, or chevrons. Found particularly in the gable end of 17th-century Maryland houses and in some Dutch Colonial houses. Also called black diapering.

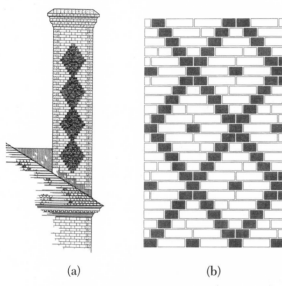

(a)   (b)

diaperwork
(a) on chimney of Brooke's Bank (1734), Essex County, Va.; (b) on side of colonial house

diastyle *See* **intercolumniation.**

die The middle portion of a **pedestal** between the base and its cap. Also called a dado.

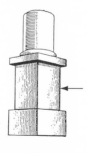

die

dingle An obsolete term for a temporary enclosure constructed at the entrance to a building as protection against the weather.

dirt-and-sticks chimney, dirt chimney Same as **clay-and-sticks chimney.**

discharging arch A **segmental arch**, i.e., having the shape of an arc of a circle, that is filled in with bricks; located within a brick wall, above the **lintel** over an opening in the wall, to transfer the weight of the wall directly above to each side of the lintel.

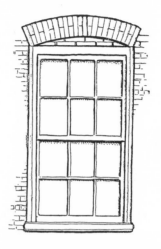

discharging arch: above window

distyle A term descriptive of a **portico** having two columns in front.

distyle
Greek Revival style, South Congregational Church (1829), Middletown, Conn.

distyle in antis A term descriptive of a **portico** having two columns in front that are placed between **antae**, forming a recessed portal.

distyle in antis
Bank of Louisville, Louisville, Ky.

divided door Same as **Dutch door.**

divided light Glass in a window or glazed door that is divided into smaller panes by secondary framing members; *see* **muntin,1.**

docked gable Same as **jerkinhead roof.**

dogleg stair A stair composed of successive flights that make a 180-degree turn at the landing between the flights; there is no **wellhole** between successive flights.

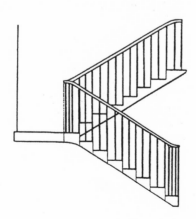

dogleg stair

dog nail In early American construction, a **wrought nail** used for fastening door hinges.

dog-run cabin Same as **dogtrot cabin.**

dog's ear Same as **crossette.**

dog-tooth course A horizontal band of bricks (a **course**) that is laid diagonally; each brick is set so that one corner usually projects from the face of the wall at an angle of about 45 degrees. Also called a dog's-tooth course.

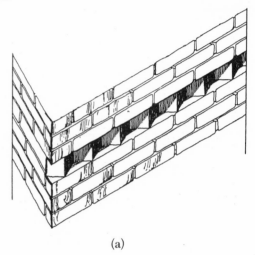

(a)

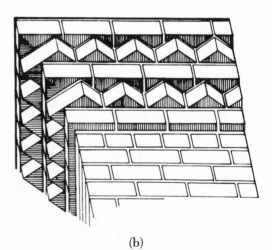

(b)

dog-tooth course
(a) on wall; (b) dog-tooth cornices,
which are corbeled out

dogtrot The covered passageway, with its sides open to the outdoors, that connects two separate cabins or two rooms of a house. Same as **breezeway.**

dogtrot cabin A dwelling, often of log construction, consisting of two single-room cabins separated from each other by a covered open-air passageway (**dogtrot**); a common wood-shingled pitched roof typically covers both cabins, and each cabin has a chimney at its gable end. The dogtrot not only serves to link the cabins, but also provides an outdoor sitting area. Each cabin has its own entrance. Also called a double-pen cabin.

dome A roof structure whose base is usually circular in plan but may be polygonal; often the roof is in the shape of a hemisphere or some portion thereof; occasionally it may be slightly pointed or bulbous. *See also* **geodesic dome** and **saucer dome**.

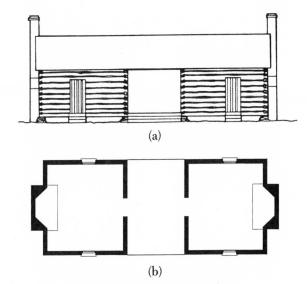

(a)

(b)

dogtrot cabin: (a) façade; (b) plan

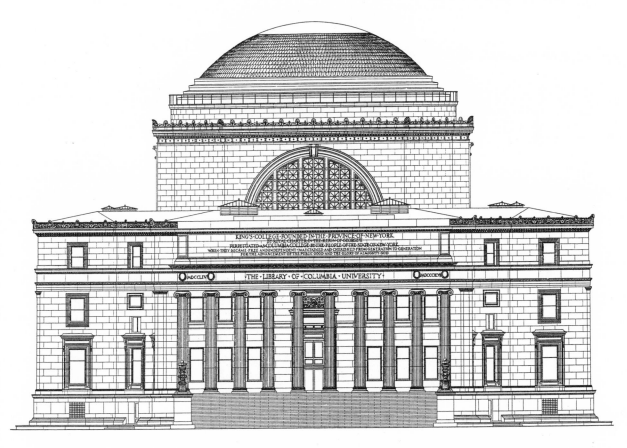

dome:
Columbia University Library (1893), New York City;
McKim, Mead & White, Architects

dome light A **skylight** having the shape of a shallow **dome**. It is often fabricated of glass or plastic and may be placed in the roof above the principal staircase, or elsewhere, to provide supplementary daylighting.

door A barrier (usually solid) that swings, slides, or tilts to close an opening in an entranceway, cabinet, or the like. In early-17th-century colonial America, **battened doors** were the first type of exterior door to appear; later in the century **paneled doors** were introduced, becoming elaborate in the **Georgian style** after about 1700. Around 1750, interior doorways also became more elaborate, with the head of the door often being topped with a frieze and cornice. **Double doors** were incorporated in American architecture in the 18th century. For additional definitions and illustrations of specific types, *see* **battened door, blank door, blind door, board-and-batten door, Christian door, cross-and-Bible door, divided door, double-acting door, double door, Dutch door, Egyptian door, false door, flush door, folding door, French door, jib door, ledged-and-braced door, ledged door, Palladian door, paneled door, pocket door, revolving door, roll-up door, single-acting door, sliding door, storm door, swinging door, unframed door, vertical plank door, weather door, witch door.**

door bar A heavy bar across a door that prevents it from being opened. In colonial America the bar was usually a heavy oak plank dropped between wrought-iron holders on each side of the door frame, providing a means of protection not unlike similar safety devices used in many large cities today. Sliding iron bolts and **box locks** were also used in colonial days to prevent entry.

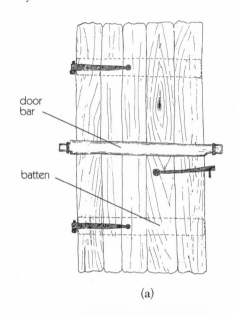

(a)

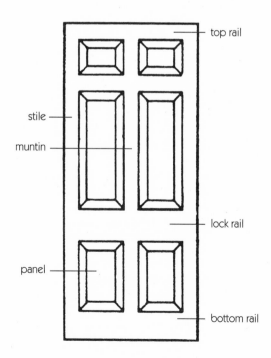

door: nomenclature

(b)

door bar: (a) of oak wood, secures a 17th-cent. battened door; (b) for a metal-framed door, bar near top made of iron, bar near middle of door made of wood; Greenwich, N.J.

door case, door casing The finished frame surrounding a door, i.e., the visible frame.

doorcap The wall area or decorative element directly above a doorway, often ornamented.

door frame A framework, built or set into a wall, consisting of two upright members (called **jambs**) and a transverse member (**door head**) that enclose a doorway and provide support from which to hang the door. This term is sometimes applied to the molded trim or framing around the door.

door head The uppermost transverse member of a door frame.

doorhood A covering over an external door to provide shelter from rain or snow.

doorhood: Meeting House, Mount Lebanon, N.Y.; unusual in that the doorhood covers three door entrances rather than a single one

doorjamb The vertical structural member on each side of a door frame. This is in contrast to a vertical structural member of the door itself, called a door stile.

door knocker *See* **knocker.**

doorlatch *See* **latch.**

door lock A device that prevents a door from being opened except with a key. In Georgian-style and Federal-style houses, **box locks** or **case locks**, fabricated of brass, were common. *See* **lock.**

door post In colonial days, a heavy **post** that framed one side of a doorway; doors were sometimes hinged directly to this post instead of to a door frame.

door rail One of the horizontal cross-members that forms a part of the framework of a door; connects the **hinge stile** to the **lock stile**, and may be exposed (as in paneled doors) or concealed (as in flush doors).

doorsill The horizontal board or metal plate on the floor beneath a door; covers the joint where two types of floor material meet. Also called a saddle or threshold.

door stile A vertical structural member of the door itself; this is in contrast to a vertical structural member of the **door frame**, called a **jamb**. The inner stile, i.e., the one nearest the axis about which the door swings, is called the **hinge stile**; the outer stile is called the **lock stile**. *See* illustration under **door.**

door surround A decorative element or structure around a doorway; for example, *see* **Gibbs surround.** Often found in the **Federal style, Georgian style, Greek Revival style.**

door surround

Doric capital The topmost member of a column or pilaster of the **Doric order.**

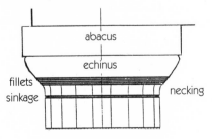

Doric capital

Doric order In Classical architecture and derivatives, the column and entablature developed by the Dorian Greeks. Characterized by sturdy proportions, a simple capital, a **frieze** usually having regularly spaced triglyphs and metopes, and mutules in the cornice; plainer than the **Corinthian order** or the **Ionic order**, although the **Tuscan order** (later introduced by the Romans) was even plainer. The Roman Doric column is usually not fluted but has a base (see illustration under **base**); in contrast, the Greek Doric column is usually fluted but has no base. *See also* illustration under **entablature.** Compare with **Tuscan order.**

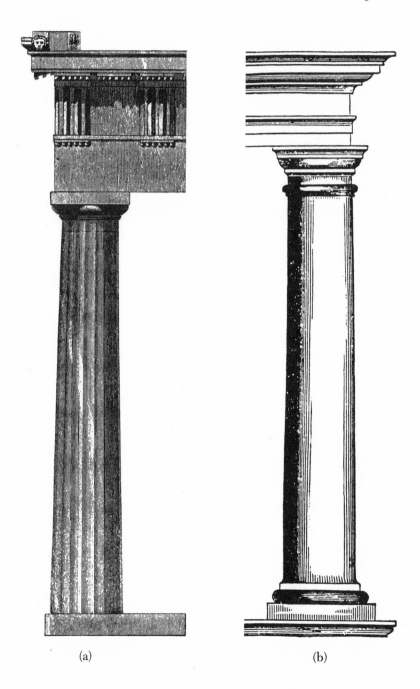

(a)   (b)

Doric order: (a) Greek; (b) Roman

dormant, dormant tree In a **timber-framed house**, a large horizontal beam that supports beams of a lesser size.

dormant window Same as **dormer**.

dormer, dormer window A structure projecting from a sloping roof, usually housing a vertical window or louvers. It is not part of the roof structure but is framed separately, and often provides daylight and ventilation for a bedroom located in a garret or loft space. Dormers were a rarity in New England in the 1600s; where they do appear in homes of that period, they are often later additions. In general, before the year 1750, dormers had rectangular windows; after that date, some dormers had arched or segmental windows. In the South the ratio of the height of the dormer to its width was usually greater than that in the North. For definitions and illustrations of specific types, *see* **arched dormer, deck dormer, eyebrow dormer, flat-head dormer, gable dormer, hipped dormer, inset dormer, mission dormer, Palladian dormer, pitched-roof dormer, pointed dormer, recessed dormer, round dormer, segmental dormer, shed dormer, through-the-cornice wall dormer, triangular dormer, wall dormer, watershed dormer.**

double-acting door *See* **swinging door**.

double architrave An **architrave,1** having two decorative bands around an opening, such as a door or window, in a wall of a building, instead of a single band; usually the bands are in different planes, separated by an ornamental molding.

double-bellied baluster A **baluster** whose profile is the same at both its upper and lower halves.

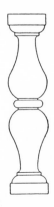

double-bellied baluster

double chimney 1. A pair of exterior chimneys, of approximately the same size, at a **gable end** of a house. 2. The chimney for two fireplaces that open back to back, serving two different rooms; commonly has two flues.

double chimney,1

double decker A house that provides living quarters for two families; it has two stories, with one apartment on each floor; there are separate entrances for each family.

double-decker barn A barn (with a loft above) having three levels that is built into the slope of a steep hillside.

double-decker porch *See* **two-tiered porch**.

double door A door consisting of two **leaves**, hinged on opposite jambs.

double door: The Old Meeting House, Sandown, N.H.

double-entry stair Same as **double stair.**

double-gable roof Same as **M-roof.**

double-hipped roof A **hipped roof** having a double slope. *See also* **bonnet roof.**

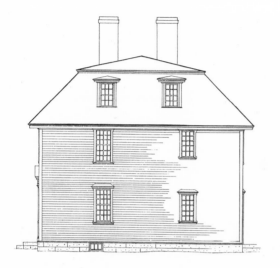

double-hipped roof

double house 1. A pair of **semidetached houses** having a plan that is symmetric on both sides of a centerline; each of the two units has its own entry; especially popular in America during the mid-19th century. 2. Same as **full Cape house.** 3. *See* **Charleston house.**

double house
New Kent County, Va., mid-19th cent.

double-hung window A window having two vertically sliding **sashes**, each designed to close a different half of the window. First developed in England, these windows were introduced in the American colonies at the turn of the 18th century, when they were sometimes called *up-and-down windows*. At that time the upper sash was usually fixed; only the lower sash moved. Later a method was developed for counterbalancing the weight of both sashes for ease of opening and closing; this led to the use of counterweights connected by a sash cord over a pulley. By about 1740 double-hung windows had largely replaced **casement windows.** In the earliest double-hung windows, the **muntins** that held the panes were relatively thick; by the late 18th century, they had become thinner and more delicate. Often the upper part of the window frame, in which the sashes were set, was decorated by a **crossette.**

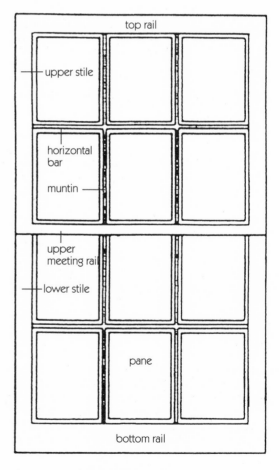

double-hung window
terminology

double lancet window A window having **mullions** shaped so as to form two **lancet windows** that are side by side; often found in **Carpenter Gothic, Châteauesque style, Collegiate Gothic, French Eclectic architecture, Gothic Revival,** and **Tudor Revival.** *See also* illustration under **lozenge.**

double lancet window: St. Peter's Episcopal Church (1867), Carson City, Nev.

double log-house Same as **dogtrot cabin.**

double-L stair A stair having two intermediate landings, one near the top of the stair and one near the bottom, with a 90-degree change of direction at each landing.

double-pen cabin A **log cabin** having two adjacent rooms under a common roof; usually with a chimney at each end of the cabin. It is often formed by the addition of a second room to a **single-pen cabin**; often a porch spans the full width of the two rooms. *See also* **central-hall cabin, dogtrot cabin, saddlebag cabin.**

double-pile house A house that is two rooms deep and any number of rooms wide. *See also* **pile,2** and **single-pile house.**

double-pitched roof A roof having two flat slopes on each side of a central ridge; for example, *see* **gambrel roof.**

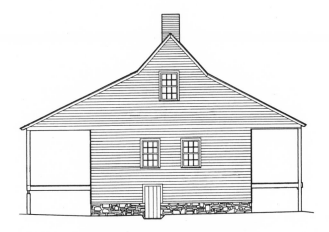

double-pitched roof
Amorous House, Ste. Genevieve, Mo.

double porch A **two-tiered porch** in which the porches on the first and second stories appear to be virtually identical in design.

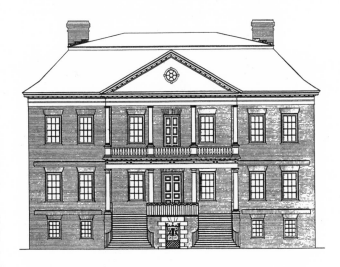

double porch
Drayton Hall (1738–1742), on Ashley River, S.C.

double-raised panel *See* **raised panel.**

double-return stair A stair having a single flight from the main floor to an intermediate landing and then two side flights from that landing to the floor above; for example, *see* **good-morning stair.**

double-saddle notch In log cabin construction, at a corner, one of a pair of rounded notches cut on opposite sides of a horizontal log near one end; it forms a corner joint with a round unnotched log set between such a pair of notched logs. Sometimes simply called a saddle notch. *See also* **notch.**

double-shouldered chimney Same as **stepped-back chimney.**

double stair An **open stair** having a pair of staircases leading down from a landing; usually designed primarily to be impressive. Compare with **double-return stair.**

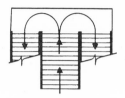

double-return stair

double-saddle notch: chinking between the logs

double stair
Greek Revival style, Playford House, Brownsville, Pa.

double-tiered porch Same as **two-tiered porch.**

dovecote A structure that houses pigeons or doves; usually square, hexagonal, octagonal, or round in plan and one-and-a-half or two stories high; often topped with a finial. The interior contains pigeon roosts and is usually honeycombed with niches for the birds to nest. Dovecotes were popular in colonial America because the birds provided a tasty source of fresh meat. Also called a pigeon house or pigeonnier.

dovecote
Angelina Plantation, near Mt. Airy, La.

dovetail A **tenon** shaped like a dove's tail, broader at its end than at its base; fits into a correspondingly shaped **mortise.**

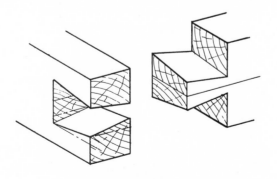

dovetail

dovetail hinge Same as **butterfly hinge.**

dovetail notch At a corner of a log house, a **notch** in the shape of a **dovetail** at the end of a rectangular exterior timber; forms a strong, interlocking, rigid joint when mated with an appropriately notched hewn timber at right angles to it. Compare with **half-dovetail notch.**

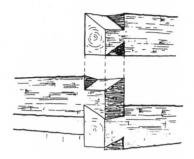

dovetail notch

dowel A cylindrical wood or metal rod; often used to secure two pieces of wood by inserting it into a hole drilled through the two pieces.

downspout Same as **leader.**

dragon beam A horizontal piece of timber between two perpendicular **wall plates** that intersect at a corner of a timber-framed house and is in the same plane as the wall plates; it usually bisects the angles between them and is connected to them at their point of intersection. The other end of the dragon beam is usually supported by a **dragon tie** or occasionally by a **summerbeam.**

dragon tie An **angle brace** between (and in the same plane as) two intersecting wall plates; supports one end of a **dragon beam.** Also called a dragon piece or an angle tie.

drawing room A formal reception room, usually in a prominent location of a large home, mansion, or manor house, often next to the dining room.

drip cap, drip molding An external horizontal molding over an opening, such as a door frame or window frame; its function is to discharge rainwater from the face of the wall surface; usually decorative in appearance.

dripstone A **drip cap** made of stone.

drop 1. Same as **pendant;** *see also* **corner drop.**
2. Same as **turned drop.**

drop handle A door handle that hangs vertically when not in use; in colonial America, usually fabricated of wrought iron.

drop-head window A **double-hung window** whose lower sash can drop through the window sill into a pocket below the sill.

dropped roof The roof of an addition to a house; usually has a flat surface of single pitch, with its upper edge attached to the house, below the eaves.

drop siding An exterior wall **cladding** of horizontal wood boards that are tongued-and-grooved so that the lower edge of each board interlocks with the board immediately below it; introduced in the late 19th century. Also called matched siding, novelty siding, rustic siding.

drum 1. One of the stone cylinders that form a column that is not monolithic. 2. A cylindrical or polygonal wall below a dome, often pierced with windows.

dry wall 1. A stone wall constructed without mortar. 2. An interior wall that is constructed of a material having a dry finish, such as gypsum board or plywood, that does not require the application of wet plaster.

dual-pitched roof A roof having a double slope on both sides of a central ridge; for example, a **gambrel roof.**

dugout A primitive, usually miserable, shelter, often windowless, used by some early colonists in America and later by homesteaders on the Great Plains (the region between the Mississippi River and the Rocky Mountains, from Canada to Texas); often consists of an excavation in a bank of sloping terrain that is roofed over with bark and/or straw laid over a pole framework and then covered with sod; has a crude front door and a stovepipe to serve as a chimney. Also called a pit house. *See also* **half-dugout.**

dumbbell tenement A multiple-dwelling substandard apartment house, usually built in Atlantic coast cities primarily in the 19th century, that commonly is four or five stories high and has relatively long and narrow apartments within it, with windows only at the front and rear of the apartment. Shafts, located on one or both sides of the exterior walls of the apartments, provide air and a little light in the rooms that do not face the front or rear of the building. The **floor plan** of each floor resembles the outline of a dumbbell. A single apartment in a dumbbell tenement is called a railroad flat.

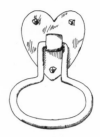

drop handle: hand-forged

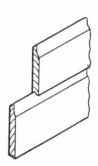

drop siding

drum,1

dugout

dumbwaiter A hoisting mechanism incorporating a small platform that moves vertically in a shaft; used exclusively for carrying small items from one floor of a building to another. For his home, Monticello, Thomas Jefferson designed a hand-operated dumbwaiter to hoist food from the serving area in the basement to the dining room on the floor above. Such mechanisms became fashionable installations in prosperous American houses in the 19th century.

dumbwaiter

duplex house Same as **double house,1.**

Dutch arch Same as **flat arch.**

Dutch barn 1. A distinctive type of front-gabled barn erected by early Dutch settlers in America, particularly in the Hudson River Valley of New York and in New Jersey, primarily during the 17th and 18th centuries, and later in southwestern Michigan. These barns were approximately square in plan, usually about 36 to 40 feet (11–12m) high, and were built on stone piers one to two feet (30–61cm) high; they had a steeply pitched roof forming an angle of about 70 to 90 degrees between opposite rafters at their intersection and were often sheathed with planks overlapped and beveled to shed water readily. A unique feature of the barn was its **curtain wall** construction; the barn's weight and live load were carried by the **plates**, anchor beam posts, and piers, so the outer wall sheathing could be removed temporarily for maintenance of the barn framework. There was often a small **pent roof** directly over the entryway for wagons; **owl holes** near the peaks of the gables provided ventilation and access to the barn for mouse-eating birds. 2. Same as **bank barn.** 3. Same as **hay barrack.**

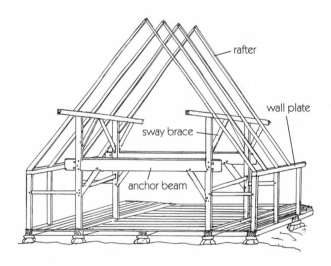

Dutch barn: framing system

Dutch bond Same as **Flemish bond.**

Dutch brick A hard yellow brick often used in the interior of Dutch Colonial houses; commonly laid in the floor of the fireplace hearth that extended into the room. Occasionally this term refers to a brick having a thickness of only about 1½ inches (3.8cm).

Dutch Colonial architecture A broad term describing the architecture prevalent in the Dutch-settled parts of North America during the early part of the 17th century, particularly in areas of the Hudson River Valley of New York, western Long Island, and northern New Jersey; first developed by settlers who emigrated to the new world from Holland, the Flemish regions of Belgium, and northern France to establish New Amsterdam, later renamed New York. When the earliest Dutch settlers arrived in America, they lived in primitive shelters such as **dugouts** while they engaged in tasks essential to their survival, such as clearing land and planting crops; then they built improved housing in the form of simple one-story, single-room dwellings. Finally, the settlers constructed permanent homes whose characteristics depended largely on the architecture of the region from which they originated and on the availability of local building materials. Although Peter Stuyvesant surrendered Dutch territory to the British in 1664, the Dutch influence in architecture continued until the Great Fire of 1776 that destroyed most of the old section of New York City. There were significant differences between Dutch Colonial houses in the countryside and those in the principal cities, as described in the next two entries.

Dutch Colonial architecture, rural A term descriptive of most Dutch Colonial rural houses that shared certain common characteristics such as interior chimneys, **bake ovens**, and heavy plank floors. Other major characteristics (including the type of walls, type of roof, and type of gable) depended on geographical location and on the date of the house's construction.

Typical characteristics of Dutch Colonial rural houses include:

Façade and exterior wall treatments: In the Hudson River Valley and northern New Jersey, stone was relatively abundant, so in these areas rural homes were usually constructed of stone walls as much as three feet (.9m) thick, with a mortar consisting of a mixture of lime, clay, and straw or hair. Lime for the mortar was usually obtained by heating oyster shells or made from New Jersey limestone. Some houses had **shed dormers** or **gabled dormers,** and a chimney at a gable end or gambrel end of the house. Rural houses in the northern Hudson River Valley (for example, in the areas near Rensselaer, Schenectady, and Fort Orange—now called Albany) were often of brick laid in a Flemish bond pattern. **Straight-line gables** with a **mouse-tooth pattern** were widely used on these houses because this brick construction is usually leakproof at the roofline. In contrast, rural homes in western Long Island, where timber was plentiful, were primarily of wood construction with wide **weatherboards** as **siding,** although some homes on Long Island had stone walls for the first story and weatherboards above.

Roof treatments: A roof covering of wood shingles or tiles; steeply pitched gables with parapets; brick chimneys. Dutch gambrel roofs having **flared eaves** and a

(a)

(b)

Dutch Colonial rural architecture
Samuel Demarest House, New Milford, N.J., (a) exterior; (b) interior

considerable overhang were probably of Flemish origin and did not come into popular use until after the beginning of the 18th century. The chimneys were located in the exterior walls.

Window treatments: Outward-swinging **casement windows** with small panes and **battened shutters**; windows in gable-end walls and in gambrel-end walls. The double-hung sash windows found in most surviving rural Dutch Colonial houses are replacements of the original casement windows.

Doorway treatments: Commonly, a **Dutch door** having two separate leaves, one above the other.

Dutch Colonial architecture, urban A term descriptive of Dutch colonial houses in New Amsterdam (now New York City) and Fort Orange (now Albany). Houses used solely as residences were typically two-and-a-half or three-and-a-half stories high. Houses in which the owners conducted a business on the ground floor and lived in the floors above were typically four or five stories high, including a garret that was used for storage; block and tackle, hung from a projecting beam above the garret, served as a means for hoisting supplies and goods from street level up to the garret and in through battened doors. The face of some houses of this type slanted slightly outward with increasing height; this prevented goods from scraping against the building while being hoisted. Since these buildings were derivatives of their prototypes in Holland, New Amsterdam had the appearance of a miniature Dutch city.

Typical characteristics of Dutch Colonial urban houses include:

Façade and exterior wall treatments: Thick exterior walls usually having a rough timber structure faced with a yellow or red brick veneer, often laid in a Flemish bond pattern with glazed blue-black brick **headers** providing a decorative element. The brickwork was secured to the timber framing by decorative wrought-iron **anchors**. In areas where wood was plentiful, wide weatherboarding was often used as siding instead of brick facing; alternatively, where stone was readily available, it was used. A parapeted gable-end wall often faced the street.

Roof treatments: Initially, a steep roof covered with wood shingles; later, **pantiles** were more common; typically, **stepped gables** or steeply pitched **straight-line gables** emulating those in Holland; often, a gambrel roof with **flared eaves**; usually, a brick

chimney within the exterior walls, topped with a chimney cap.

Window treatments: In the earliest houses, outward-swinging **casement windows** with small diamond-shaped glass panes or square-shaped panes set diagonally; battened shutters; often, one or more windows in the end walls. Later double-hung windows replaced the casement windows.

Doorway treatments: Typically, a **Dutch door** having two separate leaves, one above the other; or a paneled double door, often with a **transom light** above the door. Usually a **stoop.**

Dutch Colonial urban architecture
New Amsterdam

Dutch Colonial Revival Revival architecture from the late 19th century onward, usually very loosely based on the Dutch Colonial prototypes described above, including a **gambrel roof**, **flared eaves**, and multipaned double-hung windows. Revival houses often retain many of the characteristics of their prototypes, but differ significantly from them as a result of modern introductions such as dormers in the gambrel roof, wood shutters with decorative designs cut through the shutters, and cross gambrels, and occasionally a front-facing **gambrel end**.

Dutch door A door consisting of two separate **leaves**, one above the other, in the same opening; the leaves may operate independently or together; occasionally, a **transom light** above the upper leaf.

Dutch Colonial Revival

(a)

(b)

Dutch door
(a) exterior view, Sickles House, Pearl River, N.Y.; (b) interior view, Georgian-period door

Dutch gable 1. Same as **Flemish gable.** 2. A stepped gable.

Dutch gambrel roof A type of **gambrel roof** that has two flat surfaces on each side of the ridge of the roof, each at a different pitch. Initially the downward slope from the ridge of the roof is at an angle of about 22 degrees; then the slope becomes much steeper, at an angle of about 45 degrees. Near the eaves, there is a pronounced flare, somewhat similar to that of a flaring bell. Also called a Flemish gambrel roof.

Dutch oven Same as **bake oven.**

Dutch roof A term occasionally used in the past for a **Dutch gambrel roof.**

Dutch tile A flat, square, decorative tile imported from Holland primarily for fireplace facings; different colors were popular at different times, but the Delft tiles were among the most widely used tiles in colonial America.

D-window 1. Same as **semicircular fanlight.** 2. Same as **semicircular window, 2.**

Dymaxion House An unconventional lightweight house conceived by R. Buckminster Fuller (1895–1983), who applied for a patent on it in 1928; his Dymaxion (*Dynamic plus maximum efficiency*) house, octagonal or circular in plan, was supported by a massive central shaft that housed all building services, such as electrical and waste disposal facilities. Originally called the "4D house," it was redesigned at the close of World War II for manufacture at the Beech Aircraft Company, where a prototype was built in 1946. Although it was never put into mass production, Fuller's work was influential in stimulating subsequent prefabricated housing designs by others.

Dutch gambrel roof

E

ear Same as **crossette.**

Early Classical Revival A term occasionally used as a synonym for the **Classical Revival style,** popular from about 1770 to 1830; the addition of the adjective *Early* is intended to differentiate this style from **Neoclassical style**, a later reuse of Classical architecture between about 1895 and 1940.

Early Colonial architecture *See* **American Colonial architecture.**

Early English Colonial architecture *See* **American Colonial architecture.**

Early Gothic Revival *See* **Gothic Revival.**

earth berm *See* **berm.**

earth cellar A **cellar** that is excavated in the face of a steep slope of ground so that its floor is at approximately the same **elevation,2** as the ground at the entrance door. Because the surrounding earth keeps the interior of the cellar cool, it provides effective storage for food. Compare with **root cellar.**

earthfast A term descriptive of a timber-framed structure that is supported by posts sunk in the ground, rather than being supported by a foundation. *See also* **post-in-the-ground construction** and **poteaux-en-terre house.**

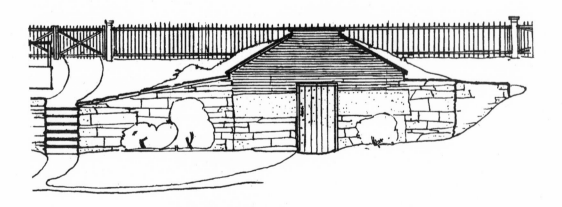

earth cellar: Miller House (1858), Valhalla, N.Y.

earth floor In many types of primitive dwellings, a floor that provided a reasonably durable walking surface; usually composed of a compacted mixture of materials such as packed earth or some combination of ashes, clay, lime, pebbles, straw, or the like. In some parts of the country (for example, New Mexico), adding animal blood to the mixture was said to improve its stability. *See also* **rammed earth.**

earthlodge A large American Indian domelike dwelling; found in such diverse locations as the Great Plains, New Mexico and other parts of the Southwest, and the Northwest. Although the construction of such dwellings varied with time, with the tribe, and with geographical location, all these structures had certain common characteristics. Twelve posts were arrayed in a circle usually from 40 to 60 feet (12–18m) in diameter, with cross beams across their tops providing supports for the walls and for as many as 100 rafters that radiated from a central opening above the firepit in the lodge floor to these posts. Further support for the rafters came from a central post-and-beam array of four heavy beams, linked by cross beams, set between the firepit and the outside walls. This construction produced a domelike framework, which was covered with branches, bark, prairie grass, and then with a heavy outer layer of sod; a smokehole was left open at the center of the dome directly above the firepit.

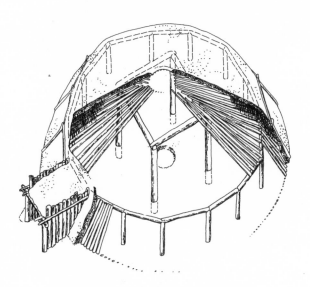

earthlodge: Hidatsa tribe in the Dakotas, 40 feet (12m) in diameter

earth roof *See* **sod roof.**

earth table The lowest **course** of a building that is visible above the ground, especially a projecting course or **plinth** resting directly upon a foundation. Also called a ground table.

earth-wall dwelling *See* **earthlodge, jacal,2, kiva, pueblo, sod house.**

Eastern Stick style Same as **Stick style.** *See also* **Western Stick style.**

Eastlake ornamentation A style of ornamentation rather than a style of architecture; associated with the English designer Charles Locke Eastlake (1836–1906), internationally known for his book *Hints on Household Taste,* published in London in 1868. Decorative elements included: spindlework (especially balusters or posts turned on a lathe), perforated bargeboards and pediments, carved panels, large ornamental fanlike brackets, highly ornamental moldings, and decorative cast-hardware fittings such as door knobs and locks. Especially found in the **Queen Anne style** and in **High Victorian Gothic** architecture.

Eastlake ornamentation: parquet flooring

eaves That part of a roof that projects beyond the exterior wall; usually the lower edge of a sloped roof. *See also* **bellcast eaves, boxed eaves, bracketed eaves, closed eaves, coved eaves, flared eaves, Flemish eaves, open eaves.**

eaves bracket A **bracket** that supports the eaves; usually one of many, often in pairs.

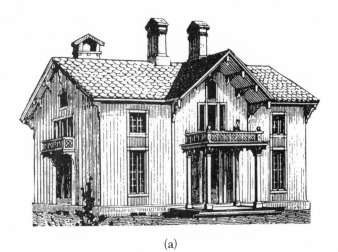

(a)

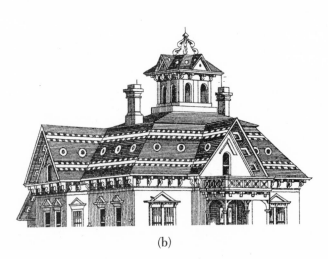

(b)

eaves brackets
(a) supporting widely overhanging eaves;
(b) as a decorative element

eaves cornice A **cornice** at the eaves of a roof.

eaves fascia, eaves board Same as **fascia board.**

eaves trough Same as **gutter.**

echinus The convex projecting molding supporting the abacus of a Doric capital or a Tuscan capital; hence, the corresponding feature in capitals of other orders, which often had an **egg-and-dart molding,** an **ovolo molding**; also any other molding similar in profile or decoration.

echinus: Doric capital

eclectic architecture Architecture that combines elements and characteristics of a wide range of historical styles. *See* **Exotic Revival, French Eclectic architecture, Neo-Eclectic architecture, Spanish Eclectic architecture.**

egg-and-dart molding A decorative molding consisting of egg-shaped ornaments alternating with dart-like ornaments.

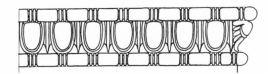

egg-and-dart molding

Egyptian door A door whose frame is narrower at the top than at the bottom, with **doorjambs** that are inclined with respect to the vertical; occasionally found in America in **Egyptian Revival** architecture.

Egyptian gorge A cornice that consists of a large concave molding, often decorated with vertical leaves and a roll molding below; found in America only in **Egyptian Revival** architecture. Also called cavetto cornice.

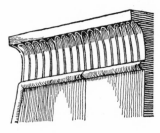

Egyptian gorge

Egyptian Revival A style of **Exotic Revival** architecture suggestive of the architecture of ancient Egypt; used in America from about 1830 to 1850 and then again, although rarely, from about 1920 to 1930. Such architecture usually exhibits some of the following characteristics and/or decorative elements: ashlar-finished exterior walls that are tilted inward at their tops with respect to the vertical; window frames that are narrower at the top than at the bottom; lotus capitals; columns that bulge or that imitate papyrus stalks bundled by bands at the top and bottom of the columns; an **Egyptian gorge**; winged **sun disks** often used as decorative emblems; an entrance portal flanked by a monumental gateway having slanting side walls.

(a)

(b)

Egyptian Revival
(a) cemetery entrance gateway (1848), New Haven, Conn.;
(b) Mt. Auburn Cemetery, Cambridge, Mass.

electrical rod Obsolete term for **lightning rod.**

elevation 1. A drawing showing the vertical elements of a building, either exterior or interior, as a direct projection onto a vertical plane. 2. The vertical distance above or below some established reference level.

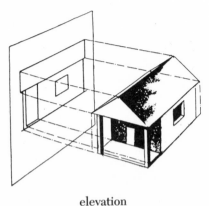

elevation

Elizabethan architecture The transitional style between Gothic architecture and Renaissance architecture in England; named after Elizabeth I, who reigned from 1558 to 1603, and applied primarily to country houses; the characteristics of such architecture include large mullioned windows and **strapwork** ornamentation. For American adaptations suggestive of Elizabethan architecture, *see* **Queen Anne style**, **Tudor Revival**, and **Neo-Tudor.** Compare with **Jacobethan style.**

Elizabethan Manor style *See* **Tudor Revival.**

ell A secondary wing or extension of a building, usually at right angles to the building's principal dimension. *See also* **wing.**

elliptical arch An **arch** having the shape of half an ellipse. In its construction the ellipse is often approximated by three adjoining circular arcs, as in a **basket-handle arch.**

elliptical fanlight A **fanlight** that has the shape of half an ellipse, often placed over a door; rods or bars radiating from the center are suggestive of the shape of an open fan; frequently used in the **Federal style** of architecture.

embarrado In **Spanish Colonial architecture** and derivatives, a term descriptive of a surface that is roughly plastered with adobe or mud.

embattlement Same as **battlement.**

embrasure A widening of an opening on the interior face of a wall, formed by splaying the sides of the opening so that it is wider at the inner face of the wall than at the exterior face; especially used in blockhouses, bastions, and forts to provide the defenders with a greater angle of coverage when firing through the opening.

encarpus A sculptured festoon of fruit and flowers.

encaustic tile A decorative tile in which the pattern is inlaid with colored clays and then fired in a kiln at a high temperature.

end beam *See* **beam.**

end board A wood board that closes off the end of a **cornice** when there is no **cornice return.**

end board: at cornice

end chimney 1. A chimney located on an end wall of a house that has a gable at each end; may be either an **interior chimney,** in which the outer surface is flush with an exterior wall. 2. An **exterior chimney,** in which the chimney projects from the exterior wall.

end gable A **gable** at the end wall of a house.

end gable

end girt A heavy timber that acts as a main horizontal support for the second floor in an early American **timber-framed house**. It is located along one end of the house, for example, between a center post and each of the corner posts, and serves to tie together various components of the frame. *See also* illustration under **timber-framed house.**

end girt

end house A house having one of its two ends facing the street. *See,* for example, the *single house* illustrated under **Charleston house.**

engaged Attached (or apparently attached) to a wall by being partly embedded or bonded to it; for example, an engaged column.

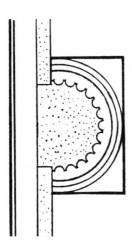

engaged: cross-section of a fluted engaged column, showing attachment to wall

engaged porch Same as **integral porch.**

English barn 1. A barn in New England, usually of timber-framed construction, either separate from the house or connected to it by a passageway. 2. Same as **Yankee barn.**

English basement The lowest floor of a residential building that is partly below but mostly above **grade**; the principal entrance to the building is at the level of the floor above.

English bond A brickwork pattern in which courses of **headers** and courses of **stretchers** alternate; strong and easy to lay; popular in colonial America prior to the Revolution.

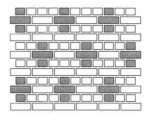

English bond

English Colonial architecture *See* **American Colonial architecture.**

English cross bond Similar to **English bond** except that the stretchers, in alternating courses, have their joints displaced by half the length of a stretcher.

English frame house In colonial America, particularly along the mid-Atlantic coast in the middle and latter part of the 17th century, a **timber-framed house** whose construction followed the then-current traditional framing techniques used in England, such as the use of massive timbers; well constructed, with very strong joints.

English frame house

English gambrel roof Same as **New England gambrel roof.**

English log house A one-room **log house**, square in plan, having an exterior gable-end chimney; one exterior door is centered on the façade of the house and another door is centered on the rear wall.

English Regency *See* **Regency Revival** and **Regency style.**

English Revival, English Tudor style *See* **Tudor Revival** and **Neo-Tudor.**

enlucido In **Spanish Colonial architecture**, a term descriptive of a surface that is plastered.

entablature 1. In Classical architecture and its derivatives, an elaborate horizontal band and molding supported by columns; horizontally divided into three basic elements: **architrave** (the lowest member); **frieze** (the middle member), and **cornice** (the uppermost member). The proportions and detailing of an entablature are different for each **order** and are strictly prescribed. 2. Any similar construction that crowns a wall, window, or doorway.

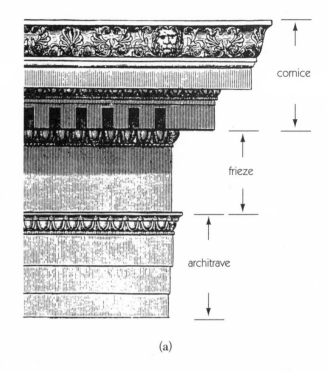

(a)

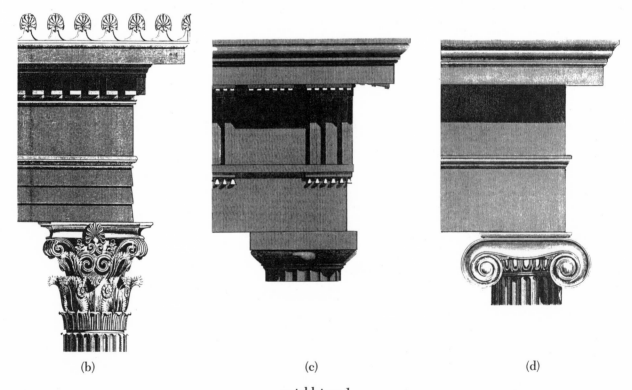

(b)   (c)   (d)

entablature,1
(a) components of an entablature; (b) Composite order; (c) Doric order; (d) Ionic order

entasis The intentional slight convex curving of the vertical profile of a tapered column in the **Classical Revival style** or **Neoclassical style**; used to overcome the optical illusion of concavity that characterizes tall straight-sided columns.

entrance hall A large vestibule or hall at the main entryway to a **Georgian style** home. It is usually high-ceilinged and well lighted and often has an **elliptical arch** that subdivides this area into two rooms: a *reception hall*, and a *stair hall* that contains an elaborate **open-string** staircase, often with highly decorative step brackets and ornamental balusters.

entrance hall
Carter's Grove (1750–1753), Charles City County, Va.

equilateral arch A **two-centered arch** whose radius of curvature (*R*) is equal to the **span** (*S*) of the arch.

equilateral arch

escutcheon A protective plate or ornamental cover, for example, over a keyhole.

escutcheon

Eskimo dwellings *See* **barabara, iglu, pole house, sod dwelling, winter house.**

espadaña In **Mission architecture** of the American Southwest, a decorative **gable end** of a church having a multicurved **mission parapet**; the gable end usually has a false front, designed to be impressive. Unlike a campanario, it usually does not pierce the wall or house a bell.

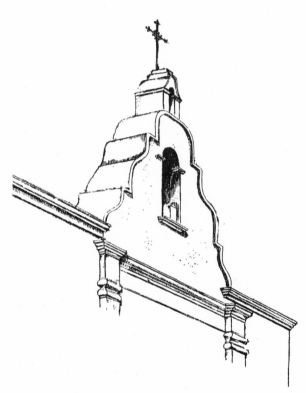

espadaña
Mission San Luis Rey de Francia, California

eustyle in classical **intercolumniation**, having columns uniformly spaced so that the columns have a clear space of 2¼ column diameters between them at their base.

excess joint In brickwork, a joint in which more mortar is applied in laying the joint than is required for a satisfactory masonry bond. As a result, some of the mortar projects beyond the face of the wall, producing an irregular appearance and creating relatively poor weather protection for the brickwork.

Exotic Revival, Exotic Eclectic A term descriptive of architecture in America based loosely on exotic prototypes, of limited popularity primarily from about 1835 to 1890. *See* **Egyptian Revival, Moorish Revival, Oriental Revival, Swiss Cottage architecture.**

expanded-metal lath A metal lath used as a base on which to apply plaster; commonly fabricated by slitting sheet metal and then pulling it apart to form openings through which plaster is troweled, thereby holding the plaster coat in place.

exterior chimney, **external chimney** A chimney located outside, and usually attached to, an exterior wall of a house at the gable end, gambrel end, or mansard end, or located outside the house along the eaves. In the American southern colonies, exterior chimneys were widely used because, in hot summer weather, they reduced the discomfort from heat radiated by the chimney when the fireplace was used for cooking.

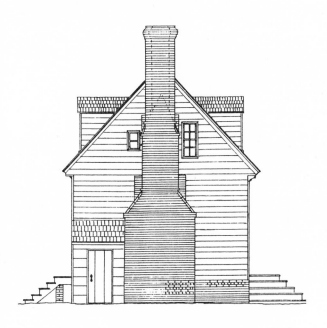

exterior chimney

extrados The exterior surface of an arch. Compare with **intrados.**

eyebrow dormer A low **dormer** that has no sides, the roofing being carried over the dormer in a wavy line.

eyebrow dormer

eyebrow eave On a shingled roof, an eave that is carried over a door entry in a wavy line.

eyebrow eave

eyebrow lintel A **lintel** above a window, carried over the window in a wavy line.

eyebrow lintel

eyebrow window 1. A bottom-hinged, inward-opening **sash** in the uppermost level of a house, usually under the front eaves; used occasionally after 1800; often one of a series of windows in the frieze of a **Greek Revival style** building. 2. A window in an **eyebrow dormer.**

eye-catcher Same as a **folly.**

eye-house *See* **I-house.**

F

fabric The basic structure (i.e., the framework or **carcass**) of a building without its finishing materials or decorations.

façade The exterior face of a building that is considered to be the architectural front, sometimes distinguished from the other faces by more elaborate architectural and/or ornamental details.

façade gable A **wall gable** on the architectural front of a building.

face 1. The exposed **facing** of any surface such as a wall, panel, masonry unit, or sheet of material. 2. Same as **fascia**. 3. The **façade** of a building.

face string An inclined board, parallel to the slope of a stair, that is located at the end of the steps away from the wall; the upper edge of the board is cut to the profile of the treads and risers of the stair, and the treads project beyond the face of the board and are visible. The inclined board is usually of better material or finish than the rough string that it covers; it may be part of the actual construction or applied to the face of the supporting member. Also called a finish string.

face string

facework *See* **facing**.

fachwerk The term used by German-speaking immigrants to America in the 18th and 19th centuries for **half-timbering**, i.e., the medieval system of braced timber-framing of a house in which the space between the structural timbers is usually filled either with brick or with a **nogging** consisting of clay (often taken from the cellar excavation) mixed with chopped straw to provide additional rigidity and improved thermal insulation. The timbers were usually left exposed, although in some 19th-century houses, they were also coated with plaster to protect the nogging. Wisconsin has the greatest concentration of *fachwerk* in America, commonly with timbers hewn of elm, white oak, or local pine.

facia Same as **fascia**.

facing A veneer of material such as brick, masonry, metal, plaster, stone, stucco, terra-cotta, or decorative wood; used to finish the surface of a rougher or less attractive material. Also called facework.

falling wainscot In 18th-century America, a movable partition that served to separate two adjacent rooms; it was hinged along its upper edge, at ceiling level, so that it could be swung up to the ceiling, thereby joining the two rooms into one.

false door Same as **blank door,1**.

false ellipse A curve that approximates an ellipse but is actually made up of several adjoining circular segments.

false front A front wall that extends above the roof and/or beyond the sides of a building to create a more imposing façade; most often placed on commercial buildings.

false front
Lundberg Bakery (1876), Austin, Tex.

false half-timbering A wall that appears to be of **half-timbered construction** but whose woodwork is merely decorative and serves no structural function, for example, boards applied over a material such as stucco on lath. Also called decorative half-timbering.

false half-timbering

false overhang Same as **hewn overhang**.

false plate *See* **wall plate**.

false window Same as **blank window**.

false woodgraining Simulating a wood grain by painting a surface with a translucent stain and then working the stain into suitable patterns with graining brushes, combs, and rags to produce the appearance of wood; employed in **French Vernacular architecture** of Louisiana for a short period after 1800, where locally available cypress was made to look like a number of other exotic woods. Also called faux bois.

fanlight A semicircular or semielliptical window over a door; commonly with radiating rods or bars suggestive of an open fan. The door below is often flanked by **sidelights**. Although usually associated with American Colonial architecture and used as early as the mid-18th century, such windows were not in common use until after the American Revolution. Often found in **Federal style, Classical Revival style,** and **Colonial Revival** houses; occasionally found in opulent **French Colonial architecture.** Also called a sunburst light.

fanlight: above door

fascia 1. Any flat horizontal member or molding having little projection, as the bands into which the **architraves** of Ionic or Corinthian **entablatures** are divided. 2. Any relatively narrow vertical surface that is projected or cantilevered or supported on columns or elements other than a wall below.

fascia board A broad, flat board that is nailed across the lower ends of roof rafters; sometimes supports a gutter.

faux bois In **French Vernacular architecture** of Louisiana, same as **false woodgraining.**

faux marbre In **French Vernacular architecture** of Louisiana after 1800, the hand-painting of wood columns, usually of cypress, to make them appear to be marble.

fayre house Early nomenclature for a **timber-framed house.**

featheredge board A horizontal board that tapers away in thickness at its upper edge; usually overlapped by a similar board above it.

featheredge coping A **coping** that slopes primarily in one direction, being thicker on one side of the wall than the other. Also called a wedge coping.

Federal Revival A loose term describing architecture, primarily from about 1870 to 1970, that reuses aspects of the earlier **Federal style.**

Federal style A style of architecture in the post-colonial era in America, from about 1780 to 1820 and beyond. Compared with the **Georgian style** that preceded it, the Federal style is noted for its clarity of form, simplicity, restraint, and subtle use of color, as well as its delicacy and lightness in detailing; exemplified, for instance, in the work of Charles Bulfinch (1763–1844) and Benjamin Latrobe (1764–1820). It was greatly influenced by the work of Robert Adam—so much so that many architectural historians make little or no distinction between the term **Adam style** as applied in the American colonies and the term Federal style. While the interior decorative elements of the two styles are largely identical, the exteriors of buildings in the American Federal style and the English Adam style may differ, particularly with respect to scale, entrances, and fenestration. Houses in the Federal style are typically rectangular or square in plan, two

Federal style: (a) Sabine Hall (c. 1730), Rappahannock River, Va.

rooms deep with four rooms on the first floor, and usually two or three stories high. An excellent example of the Federal style is Homewood (1801) in Baltimore, Maryland. This style was also widely used for row houses in cities along the Atlantic coast.

Buildings in the Federal style usually exhibit a number of the following characteristics:

Façade and exterior wall treatments: A symmetric façade, often with a giant entrance portico, sometimes domed; commonly, brick construction with a Flemish bond pattern and thin mortar joints, or **clapboards** over timber framing with corner boards; often a **belt course** separating the first and second stories; occasionally, a cornice with moldings, friezes, pilasters, quoins; classical decorative elements such as festoons, garlands, modillions, urns, and swags, as well as dentils and egg-and-dart moldings. Row houses in the Federal style commonly had brick or brownstone façades.

Roof treatments: Usually, a side-gabled, center-gabled, or hipped roof having a moderate pitch, often enclosed or partially enclosed with a balustrade at the line of the cornice. In the northern states, **centrally located chimneys** were common because they pro-

vided additional heating within the house during the cold winters; in the southern states, **exterior chimneys** at the ends of the house were common because during the warm summers they reduced discomfort from the heat generated by fireplaces used for cooking. The roofs of row houses usually had two dormers and boxed eaves with little overhang.

Window treatments: By the time the Federal style became popular, glass was manufactured in the United States at a much lower cost than glass previously imported from England, so windows were much larger than they had been. Double-hung windows on upper floors were directly over those on the main floor, commonly with six panes in the upper sash over six panes in the lower sash (6/6), although (9/9) and (12/12) were also common, usually with relatively thin **muntins**. In early Federal-style homes, the windows often had plain stone **lintels** of marble or brownstone; later, more decorative splayed lintels or lintels ornamented with a keystone became popular, often with elaborate window crowns. Frequently, louvered window shutters; occasionally, a **Palladian window**, a half-round window, or a three-part window with an ornate arch above.

Federal style: (b) Deming House (1790), Litchfield, Conn.

Doorway treatments: Often, elegantly elaborate main doorways, especially in the latter part of the Federal period; decorative elements as well as ornamental structural elements such as relatively thin columns in the Ionic order, full-height **pilasters**, or framing to form a small entry porch or a **portico**; an elliptical or semicircular **fanlight** over a paneled front door or a row of rectangular panes above the door, often with **sidelights** on each side of the door; often, a short flight of stairs between the street and the door to the parlor floor above, usually set well above ground level.

Federal style: door

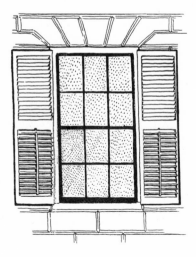

Federal style: window

fence A barrier that defines a property line or encloses or borders a field, a yard, or the like. For illustrations and definitions of specific types, *see* **barbed-wire fence, board fence, chain-link fence, picket fence, plank fence, post-and-rail fence, rail fence, split-rail fence, sunk fence, Virginia rail fence, worm fence, zigzag fence.**

fenestration The design and arrangement of windows in a building.

festoon A festive decoration of suspended flowers, foliage, fruit, leaves, ribbons, or the like; especially found in the **Beaux-Arts style, Colonial Revival,** and **Federal style**. Same as **swag.** Also called a garland.

festoon

fiber house Same as **brush house.**

field 1. The central portion of a panel that is thicker than its edges, so that it projects above the surrounding frame or wall surfaces. 2. That portion of the upper part of a wall between the **cornice** and **dado** or between the **frieze** and dado**.**

fielded panel Same as **raised panel.**

fieldstone Loose stone, as found on the surface of the ground; commonly used for masonry fences constructed with or without mortar; also used in the construction of chimneys, fireplaces, and wall constructions.

figured glass A type of **glass** in which patterns have been etched, cut with a rotating grinding wheel, or produced by pressing against the molten glass with a machine roller having a decorative design on its surface.

fillet A molding consisting of a narrow flat band. This term is loosely applied to almost any rectangular molding set between other moldings.

filling Same as **infilling.**

finial An ornament that terminates the point of a pediment, pinnacle, spire, or the like.

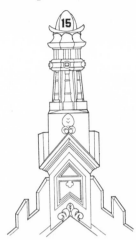

finial: a fireman's hat terminates the finial atop Engine 15 Firehouse (1885), San Francisco, Calif.

finish carpentry Same as **joinery.**

finish floor The walking surface in a room. In the earliest colonial American houses, the finish floor was often wide boards about one inch (2.5cm) thick, commonly of heavy oak or ash in the earliest houses and of hard pine or a variety of other types of wood later.

finish string Same as **face string.**

fireback An ornamental plate of cast iron, at the rear vertical surface of a fireplace, whose function is to reflect heat into the room and to protect the rear surface of the fireplace. As early as the mid-17th century, ornamented cast-iron firebacks could be obtained from the Hammersmith Ironworks in Lynn, Massachusetts. Also called a chimney back.

fireback: cast iron, from George Washington's study in his headquarters at Rocky Hill, N.J.

firebrick A very durable brick made of a ceramic material that can resist high temperatures; sometimes used to line fireplaces and chimneys.

fired brick A brick that is burnt in a kiln at a high temperature, in contrast to air-dried **adobe** brick.

firemark A plaque, usually cast in lead and affixed to the façade of a colonial American house, indicating that the owner of the house had contributed money to the local volunteer fire department.

firemark: cast in lead

fireplace An opening at the base of a **chimney** in which a fire may be built. In America prior to the manufacture of cast-iron stoves, fireplaces were the principal means of heating a house, usually being the central focus of the main room in colonial homes of the 17th century and an important architectural feature. They were usually constructed of fieldstone or roughly dressed stone, and later of brick. By necessity the fireplace had to be large enough to heat much of the house, hold a sizable log, and provide adequate space for cooking, commonly accommodating a roasting spit between 7 and 12 feet (2.1–3.6m) long. Because of this

fireplace: cottage of John and Abigail Adams, Quincy, Mass.

length, the horizontal structural member that supported the wall above the fireplace opening had to be massive; thus, a wood beam that served this function could be as large as 12 by 18 inches (30 x 46cm) in cross section and was typically set 4 to 5 feet (1.2–1.5m) above the **hearth**. Some fireplaces contained an auxiliary chamber in which meat could be hung and exposed to the smoke for curing. Later, when fireplaces were no long used for cooking, the openings were greatly reduced in size to improve their efficiency in heating the house. They also became more ornate, often being faced with marble or decorative tiles. *See also* **Rumford fireplace** and **Franklin stove.**

fireplace cheek One of the two splayed sides of a fireplace opening.

fireplace crane A wrought-iron horizontal bar, usually attached to the rear wall of a colonial fireplace and pivoted so that it could be swung out at any desired angle over the fire; often served as a support on which to hang pots and kettles. *See also* **randle bar** and **trammel.**

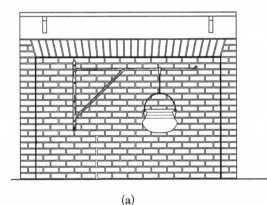

(a)

(b)

fireplace cranes

fireplace damper A device for controlling the draft (i.e., the flow of air and gaseous products) through a fireplace and up the chimney; a pivoted metal plate set just above the **chimney throat** permits the chimney to be closed off when the fireplace is not in use.

fireplace lintel A horizontal structural member that supports the weight of the wall above a fireplace opening; same as **manteltree**. If fabricated of metal, it is usually called a chimney bar; if wood, it is often plastered to increase its fire resistance.

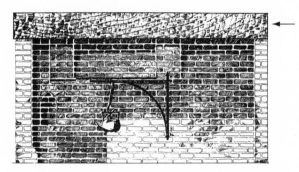

fireplace lintel: 11 feet (3.4m) long and
13 inches (33cm) high, Gibbon Homestead (1730),
Greenwich, N.J.

fireplace mantel *See* **mantel.**

fireplace surround A decorative element or structure around a fireplace, ranging from simple brick to more elaborate tile, marble, or decorative woodwork.

fireplace throat Same as **chimney throat.**

fireplace tile Tile used as a decorative facing around a fireplace opening; Delft tiles from Holland were popular in America during colonial times.

fire protection *See* **heavy-timber construction, lightning rod, textile mill.**

fire-resistance rating The time in hours that a material or construction can withstand fire exposure, as determined in conformity with generally accepted standards or from information derived from standard tests.

fireroom A term occasionally used in colonial times for any room having a fireplace.

fireside The **hearth** or area around a fireplace.

firestone Any stone, such as sandstone, that is heat resistant and therefore especially suitable for use in fireplaces.

firing port Same as **rifle hole.**

First Period Colonial architecture A term occasionally used for architecture of the American colonies from the time of their initial settlement until the emergence of the Georgian style at the start of the 18th century. Also called First Period English style. *See* **American Colonial architecture.**

fishscale pattern Same as **imbrication.**

five-part mansion A pretentious colonial home connected to two **dependencies** (one on each side of the house) by links called *hyphens*; all five units usually formed a straight line or a curve.

fixed light, fixed sash A window that does not open; the glazing is set in a fixed frame. A large fraction of the glazed openings in early colonial homes were of this type.

flagstone A flat stone, usually one to four inches (2.5–10cm) thick, often used as a stepping stone or as outdoor paving; usually either naturally thin or split from rock that cleaves readily, although sometimes produced by sawing. Flagstone imported from England was widely used in colonial America.

flanker A **dependency** or a service wing on a side of a building.

flank window Same as **sidelight.**

flared eaves That part of a roof that has a gradually diminishing slope and that projects beyond the face of an exterior wall, flaring upward near its lower end. Flemish in origin, such **eaves** were especially common in **Dutch Colonial architecture, French Colonial architecture, French Eclectic architecture, French Vernacular architecture.**

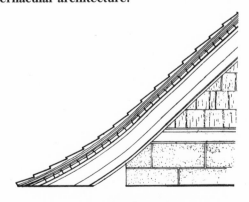

flared eave
Christie-Parsils House, Tenafly, N.J.

flared post A heavy **post,** often located at the corners of a **timber-framed house,** that has a flare at its upper end to provide a larger area for supporting the load imposed on it from above; occasionally located at the middle of a wall to provide additional support for a massive **summerbeam.**

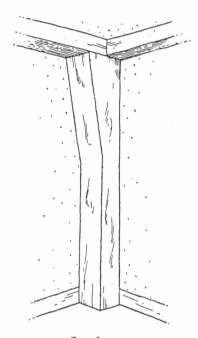

flared post
Lyon House, Greenwich, Conn.

flat arch A arch whose **soffit** (i.e., lower face) is horizontal. Also called a Dutch arch, French arch, jack arch, or straight arch.

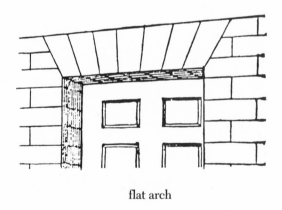

flat arch

flat-head dormer Same as **shed dormer.**

flat joint Same as **flush joint.**

flat keystone arch A **flat arch** with a **keystone** at its center.

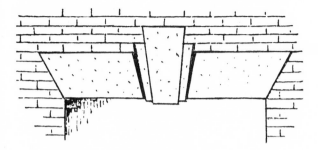

flat keystone arch

flat roof A horizontal roof having either no slope or a slope sufficient only to effect drainage, its pitch being usually less than 10 degrees; it may be surrounded by a parapet or it may extend beyond the exterior walls. Flat roofs that are usually *symmetrical* are found in the **Beaux-Arts style, Federal style,** and **Italian Renaissance Revival**; flat roofs that are usually *asymmetrical* are found in the **International style, Pueblo Revival, Spanish Colonial architecture,** and **Spanish Eclectic architecture.**

Flemish bond A brick pattern in which each course consists of **headers** and **stretchers** that are laid alternately; each header is centered with respect to the stretchers above and below it; perhaps the most popular brick pattern in the American colonies. Same as **Dutch bond.**

Flemish bond

Flemish Colonial architecture *See* **Dutch Colonial architecture.**

Flemish eaves Same as **flared eaves.**

Flemish gable A **gable** having a pediment whose outline contains two or more curves on each side of its highest point.

Flemish gables

Flemish gambrel roof Same as **Dutch gambrel roof.**

flier Any of the steps in a straight flight of stairs, each tread of which is of uniform width, as distinguished from the treads in a winding stair (called *winders*), which are wedge-shaped.

flight A continuous series of steps with no intermediate landings.

float glass *See* **plate glass.**

floor 1. In a room, the surface on which one walks; the **finish floor.** 2. A division between one story and another. *See also* **counterfloor, earth floor, finish floor, subfloor.**

flooring Any material used for the surface of a floor, such as boards, bricks, planks, or tile. In colonial America, the flooring was commonly heavy oak, ash, or pine planks 1 inch (2.5cm) thick and as much as 20 inches (50.8cm) wide. A double thickness was sometimes used to provide greater thermal insulation, particularly if the flooring were laid directly over the ground rather than over a cellar. In many very early houses, the flooring was plain, composed of bleached unfinished pine planks; later such planks became the base for a more decorative **finish floor.** In **Georgian style** houses, polished finish floors of narrow tongue-and-groove boards (**matchboards**) were popular.

flooring brick A dense, hard brick that is especially resistant to heavy surface wear.

floor plan A drawing showing, diagrammatically, the enclosing walls of a building, its doors and windows, and the arrangement of its interior spaces. *See* **plan.**

Florentine mode *See* **Italian Renaissance Revival.**

floriated, floreated Decorated with floral patterns.

flounder house A two- or three-story house that is only one room deep but several rooms wide; its roof is in the shape of an inclined plane that runs the full length of the house, giving the appearance of half a gable roof.

flounder house
Alexandria, Va.

flounder roof Same as **shed roof.**

flue *See* **chimney flue.**

flush chimney An **interior chimney** whose outer surface is flush with an exterior wall.

flush door A door having smooth, plain faces that conceal the elements of its internal structure, such as the **door rails** and **door stiles.**

flush joint, flush-cut joint In brickwork, a **masonry joint** in which an excess of mortar is applied; then a trowel is held flat against the brick surface and moved along the surface, so as to cut away the excess mortar. The resulting joint is flush with the wall but is often not watertight because the cutting action can produce hairline cracks in the mortar.

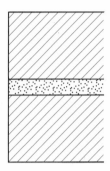

flush joint

flush siding A wood exterior covering on the walls of a colonial New England house of **wood-frame construction;** particularly used in parts of Connecticut and Rhode Island; commonly made of pine boards that have been sawn and planed smooth. These boards, applied horizontally, are usually wider than ordinary **clapboards** and are nailed flat against the studs; the upper edge may be beveled and overlapped by the board above.

flute A lengthwise groove or channel, especially one of many such parallel grooves; used decoratively, as along the shaft of a column.

fluting A series of **flutes,** as on a column. Also called channeling.

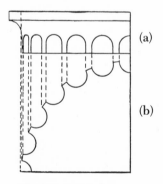

fluting: on a column
(a) elevation; (b) partial cross section

flyer *See* **flier.**

flying façade Same as **false front.**

fly rafter In a gable roof, a **rafter** whose lower end projects beyond the face of the wall.

fodder house A small shedlike structure for storing coarse food for livestock.

fogón In early **Spanish Colonial architecture** and in some **American Indian dwellings** of the Southwest, a cooking stove or fireplace with a chimney; usually constructed of adobe brick and finished with adobe plaster. It was commonly bell-shaped or quarter-round and located in one corner of a room.

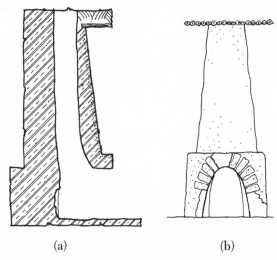

(a)   (b)

fogón: Laguna, N.M. (1706): (a) section showing the flue; (b) elevation showing face of fireplace

foil In **tracery**, any of several rounded lobes that meet each other in points called **cusps**; widely used in American **Gothic Revival** and **Collegiate Gothic** architecture. *See* **trefoil** (three lobes), **quatrefoil** (four lobes), **cinquefoil** (five lobes), and **multifoil** (usually greater than five lobes).

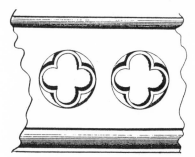

foil: a quatrefoil with four lobes

folding door One of a pair of doors that are hinged together so they can be folded into a confined space.

folding door
Camp Mansion, Sackets Harbor, N.Y.

folding partition A movable door or partition comprising a number of individual sections that are hinged and folded against each other; they can be lowered to form a continuous vertical surface that divides a large space into two smaller ones; used in America as early as the 17th century. Compare with **falling wainscot.** *See also* **sliding door.**

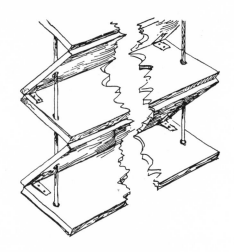

folding partition

folding shutter Same as **boxing shutter.**

foliated A term descriptive of a surface decorated with conventional leafage, as on a Corinthian capital or on some friezes.

folk architecture An imprecise term descriptive of relatively simple structures usually intended to provide only basic shelter suitable for the surrounding terrain, with no pretense of following current styles of architecture. Such houses were built of local materials using available tools, often by the people who planned to live in them. Folk architecture was usually based on traditional building techniques brought to America by immigrants, sometimes in combination with building techniques used by the indigenous inhabitants. Folk architecture has been strongly affected by the availability of local construction materials and therefore has varied significantly from region to region. Examples include: **Cajun cottages** built by the Acadians who fled from Canada to Louisiana between 1760 and 1790; **Plains cottages, sod houses, dugouts, half-dugouts,** or **straw bale houses** of the Great Plains (i.e., the region between the Mississippi River and the Rocky Mountains, from Canada to Texas) in the late 1800s, since such dwellings required a minimum of wood construction in areas where lumber was scarce and fuel was not readily available for firing bricks; **adobe** houses of the American Southwest that combined adobe building techniques imported by the Spanish Conquistadors with those of the local Indian tribes; **log cabins, log houses, shotgun houses,** which were located primarily in the rural regions of the United States, especially from the early 1800s to the early 1900s; **board houses, palma huts,** and **tabla houses** of Spanish Colonial Florida; and houses of **wood-frame construction** such as **Cape Cod houses** of Massachusetts, which used hand-split wood shingles to cover the roof and walls. In addition, some architectural historians include all types of **American Indian dwellings** in this classification. Folk houses became less common after railroad transportation made available inexpensive sawn lumber and a much wider range of building materials; by the beginning of the 20th century, building components, or even complete houses, could be ordered by catalog and shipped to most construction sites in the United States. *See also* **Gingerbread Folk architecture.**

Folk Victorian architecture Same as **Gingerbread folk architecture.**

folly A structure that is functionally useless, designed primarily for effect, such as a fake ruin in a landscaped park or an elaborate gazebo that is built to highlight a view. Also called an **eye-catcher.**

folly: Hexagon House, Mineral Wells, Texas

footing That portion of a building's **foundation** that transmits imposed loads directly to the earth or rock below.

footing stone A broad, flat stone used as a **footing.**

foot scraper Same as **boot scraper.**

footway A raised walkway, usually of brick, flagstone, tile, or the like.

forebay That part of a structure's upper story that significantly overhangs the story below; usually an integral part of the structure.

forebay barn A **barn** on a hillside having a **forebay,** usually on its downhill side, that is often supported by a series of heavy posts or pillars; particularly found in Pennsylvania.

forebay barn

forecourt A courtyard forming an entrance plaza for a single building or several buildings in a group.

formal garden A garden whose fountains, plantings, pools, walks, and the like follow a definite, recognizable plan that emphasizes geometrical forms.

fort A fortified place, exclusively military in nature, that is strengthened for protection against enemy attack and commonly incorporates a series of bastions (i.e., projections from the outer wall of the fort) to defend the adjacent perimeter; usually occupied by troops. A number of early forts and the surrounding houses later became cities; for example, in 1664, when the English took control of Fort Orange, established by the Dutch in 1624 in what is now New York State, they renamed it Albany. *See* **bastion, battlement, breastwork,4, casemate, embrasure, loophole, rampart.**

foundation A substructure that transmits the structural load of a building to the earth or rock below it. In colonial America the foundation was usually constructed of **coursed rubble** or **uncoursed rubble**, timber posts, and stone or brick **footings**; the very earliest foundations often were laid without mortar. In modern construction reinforced concrete is widely used for foundations. *See also* **chimney foundation.**

foundation stone Same as **cornerstone.**

four-crib barn *See* **crib barn.**

four-over-four (4/4) A term descriptive of a double-hung window having four panes in the upper sash over four panes in the lower sash. *See* **pane.**

four-square house Same as **American four-square house.**

four-square plan A **floor plan** for a house consisting of four rooms that form a square or rectangle.

frame The timberwork or steelwork that encloses and supports structural components of a building. *See* **bent frame, door frame, space frame, window frame, framing.**

frame construction Any building primarily supported by wood or steel structural members or some combination thereof. *See* **steel-frame construction** and **wood-frame construction.**

formal garden
at entrance to Valley View, Cass County, Ga.

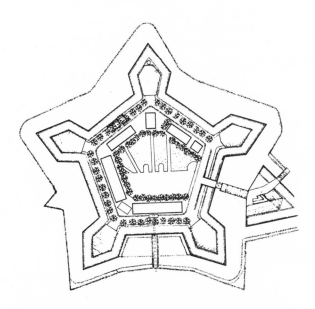

fort: 'twas o'er these ramparts at Fort McHenry in Baltimore, Md., that Francis Scott Key watched the British attack during the War of 1812 and was inspired to write "The Star-Spangled Banner"

framed building A type of building construction in which the loads are carried to the ground through a structural framework, rather than through **load-bearing walls.**

framed house A house of **wood-frame construction.** *See also* **timber-framed house.**

framed overhang The projection of an upper story of a house beyond the story immediately below it. Compare with **false overhang** and **hewn overhang**.

framing 1. The rough timber structure of a building, including flooring, partitions, and roofing. 2. Any framed work, as around an opening in an exterior wall. 3. A system of structural woodwork or structural steelwork. *See also* **balloon framing, braced framing, platform framing, post-and-girt framing, post-and-lintel construction.**

framing timber One of the structural members of a timber-framed house; in colonial America, often a massive timber of hand-hewn oak.

Franco-Italianate style Same as **Second Empire style.**

Franklin An obsolete term for a **lightning rod.**

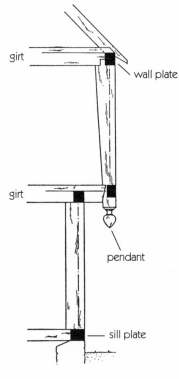

framed overhang

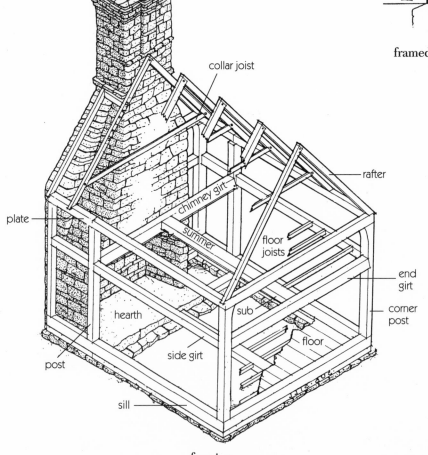

framing

Franklin stove A freestanding, enclosed, cast-iron stove that is set on short legs with provision for air circulation around, over, and under its surfaces; serves the function of a fireplace incorporating a grate; fuel-efficient and far superior to a fireplace as a means of heating a house because the source of heat is brought out into the room itself. The amount of heat the stove radiates can be controlled by means of a front door that has an adjustable opening for controlling the draft through the stove. This stove is usually attributed to Benjamin Franklin (1706–1790), who first investigated heating efficiency in one of his publications in 1744. In a later communication to the American Philosophical Society in Philadelphia in 1785, Franklin described another stove having an operable cast-iron door in front, fueled by coal rather than wood, but did not build an actual working model of it. Later, several manufacturers in Pennsylvania produced commercial models of cast-iron stoves somewhat similar to the one described by Franklin, which they called Franklin stoves, but there is no firm evidence to link him to these products.

Franklin did not apply for a patent for his cast-iron stove, saying: "That as we may enjoy great advantages from the invention of others, we should be glad of an opportunity to serve others by inventions of ours, and we should do so freely and generously." *See also* **Rumford fireplace.**

Franklin stove

freestanding A term descriptive of a structural element that is fixed at its lower end but not constrained throughout its vertical height.

freestone A fine-grained sandstone or granular limestone that is easily quarried; it has no tendency to split in any preferential direction, so is especially suitable for carving and elaborate milling.

French arch Same as **flat arch.**

French-Canadian traditional architecture *See* **Cajun cottage, galerie house.**

French casement window Same as **French window.**

French Colonial architecture A term descriptive of architecture developed by French colonists in America, particularly in New Orleans from about 1699 onward. The earliest colonists from France, often well-to-do and well educated, settled in New Orleans; it is primarily their architecture that is described by this term, and it varied not only with the financial status of the individuals but also with the particular time period. Although the Louisiana Territory was sold to the United States in 1803, the French influence persisted at least until 1830, not only in Louisiana but also in neighboring areas, especially along the Mississippi River Valley, all of which were once French territorial possessions. *See* **French Vernacular architecture** for a more appropriate term describing domestic architecture that exhibits the strong ethnic influences of the immigrant populations of the Acadians and the Creoles, including **Cajun cottage, Creole house, plantation house, raised house.**

French Colonial architecture usually includes many of the following characteristics:

Façade and exterior wall treatments: A high masonry foundation, resulting in a **raised basement,** often with plaster or stucco exterior walls, which was generally used for utility or commercial purposes and storage; commonly, a symmetric façade with a centrally located front door; a porch, called a **galerie,** reached by steps and often covered by a projecting roof extending across the entire front of the house and sometimes along the sides or completely surrounding it; in New Orleans, wrought-iron balconies extending over the sidewalk and surrounding the upper stories of many houses; later many of these balconies were replaced by more elaborate cast-iron balconies.

Roof treatments: Typically, a high, steeply pitched **hipped roof,** a **pavilion roof** (occasionally with flared eaves), or a dual-pitched **bonnet roof** that projects considerably beyond the walls, often decorated with

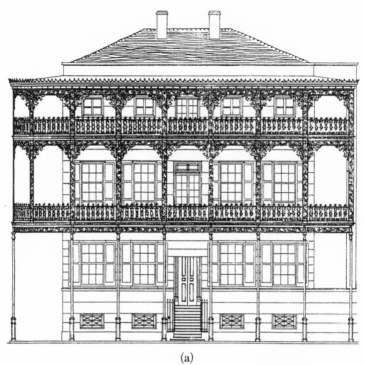

(a)

(b)

French Colonial architecture
(a) Le Prêtre Mansion, New Orleans, La.;
(b) view of corner in old New Orleans

ornamental finials at each end of the roof ridge; above the porch, a roof structure supported by wood posts and/or brick columns; hand-split cypress shingles covering the roof; a brick chimney. The urban house was often side-gabled, with flared eaves projecting over the front façade.

Window treatments: **French windows,** usually with battened or paneled shutters.

Doorway treatments: **French doors,** typically battened or paneled; often, transom lights or fanlights above the doors of the more elegant homes.

French door One of a pair of doors having **stiles,** a **bottom rail,** and a top rail, with glass panes covering nearly its entire vertical length. Also called a casement door.

French door: Fannie Riché Plantation, Louisiana

French Eclectic architecture Domestic architecture in America, primarily from about 1920 to 1950 and beyond, that suggests or emulates many of its French antecedents, such as **Beaux-Arts style, Châteauesque style,** or **Second Empire style;** sometimes it loosely imitates aspects of different styles in the same structure. Compare with **Neo-French architecture.**

Typical characteristics of French Eclectic architecture include many of the following:

Façade and exterior wall treatments: A wall cladding of brick, stone, or stucco; quoins at the wall intersections; occasionally, decorative half-timbering; a circular stair tower having a steep, conical roof; a small porch having a balustrade over the door; a **porte cochère.**

Roof treatments: A tall, steeply pitched, hipped roof with one or more gables, often tiled or shingled; flared eaves; one or more massive chimneys; arched dormers, gabled dormers, or hipped **wall dormers** that break the line of the cornice; occasionally, dentils along the cornice.

Window treatments: French windows or double-hung windows; upper-story windows that break the roof line; occasionally, **window surrounds.**

Doorway treatments: An entry door having a stone or terra-cotta **door surround** or having pilasters on each side; French doors.

French Revival *See* **French Eclectic architecture.**

French roof A term sometimes used for **mansard roof.**

French Second Empire style *See* **Second Empire style.**

French Vernacular architecture Architecture, found primarily in Louisiana and in settlements along the Mississippi River, that exhibits the ethnic influences of two major immigrant populations. The first group, the Acadians, were French-speaking refugees who came from Acadia, a region in what is now a part of Canada's Maritime Provinces, in the last half of the 18th century; their descendants are commonly called *Cajuns.* Their modest houses, which made maximum use of regional materials such as cypress, are described under **Cajun cottage.** The second major ethnic group was the *Creoles:* persons of European ancestry born in the Mississippi Valley, on the Gulf Coast, or in the West Indies, who usually spoke French patois and whose dwellings are described under **Creole house.** For other descriptions and illustrations related to French Vernacular architecture, *see* **abat-vent, banquette cottage, barreaux, bluffland house, bonnet roof, bousillage, briquette-entre-poteaux, cabanne, columbage, faux bois, faux marbre, gaulette, maison pièce sur pièce, pièce sur pièce construction, pierrotage, pilier, plaunch debout en terre, poteaux-en-terre house, poteaux-sur-solle house, raised house.**

French window A pair of **casement sashes** that extend down to the floor; the sashes swing open as they rotate on hinges fixed to the upright sides of the opening and may serve as an entrance or exit to the room.

fret 1. Same as **Greek key**. 2. Similar to a **Greek key** but having fillets that intersect at oblique angles rather than at right angles.

fretwork Ornamental openwork or interlaced work in relief, often elaborate and minute in its parts and of patterns of contrasting light and dark.

frieze 1. In Classical architecture and derivatives, the middle horizontal member of three main divisions of an **entablature**; it is above the **architrave** and below the **cornice**. 2. A decorative band at or near the top of an interior wall below the cornice. 3. In house construction, a horizontal member connecting the top row of the siding with the underside of the cornice. *See also* **cushion frieze.**

frieze-band window One of a series of small windows that form a horizontal band directly below the cornice, usually across the main façade of a building; found often in **Greek Revival style** architecture.

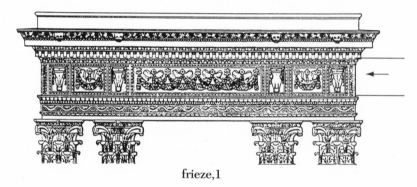

frieze,1

frieze-band window
LeMoyne House (1812), Washington, Pa.

frieze panel The topmost panel(s) in a paneled door.

front elevation The **façade** or principal elevation of a building.

front-gabled, front-facing gable A term descriptive of a house having a **gable** on its façade. Also called gable-fronted.

front girt A horizontal member (**girt**) or beam along the front face in the framing of an early American house. *See* illustration under **timber-framed house.**

frontispiece 1. The principal façade of a building, the main pediment, or the most important bay of a building. 2. An ornamental doorway or porch.

frosted work Any type of ornamental rusticated work having the appearance of frost on plants.

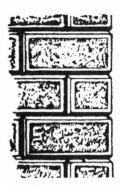

frosted work

full Cape house A one-and-a-half-story **Cape Cod house** of wood-frame construction whose façade has two double-hung windows on each side of the front door; its roof and exterior walls are covered with wood shingles, typically unpainted and gray in color when weathered; a partial basement; usually several windows in the end gable to provide light and ventilation in the attic. This version of the Cape Cod house was occasionally created by building an addition onto a **half Cape house.** On Cape Cod, also called a double house. (*See illustration* under **Cape Cod house.**)

full-façade portico A **portico** that extends the full height of the house, usually two stories high, and the full width of a house.

frontispiece,2
with Ionic columns

full-façade portico
Mount Vernon (1743–1787), Fairfax County, Va.,
inherited by George Washington in 1761;
alterations completed after the Revolution

full-height porch A roofed porch, usually occupying part of the façade of a house, that extends the full height of the house but not the full width; often pedimented; found, for example, in the **Classical Revival style, Greek Revival style, Gingerbread folk architectecture, and Neoclassical style.**

full-width porch A porch that extends the full width of a house, usually at the ground-floor level; most common in regions where the summers are hot.

Functionalism A philosophy of architectural design asserting that the form of a building should follow its function, reveal its structure, express the nature of its materials, construction, and purpose; purely decorative effects are excluded or minimized. Although this philosophy is frequently thought to be an expression of the early 20th century, its essence was stated by Ralph Waldo Emerson (1803–1882), who wrote in his essay "Thoughts on Art" in 1841: "Whatever is beautiful rests on the foundation of the necessary." For Louis H. Sullivan's 1896 statement on this subject, "… form ever follows function," *see* **Sullivanesque.**

furring Wood strips or metal channels that are fastened to the walls, ceiling, joists, or studs to provide a means of attachment for the finish surface; may also provide an air space to act as thermal insulation.

furring strip A flat strip of wood attached to a wall as a base for lath or the like.

G

gable A vertical surface on a building usually adjoining a pitched roof, commonly at its end and triangular-shaped, although the specific shape of the vertical surface depends on the type of roof and parapet; often extends from the level of the cornice up to the ridge of the roof; may also be on the façade of the building. If the gable is at the façade, it is said to be front-gabled or gable-fronted. For definitions and illustrations of particular types of gables, *see* **bell gable, clipped gable, corbiestep gable, cross gable, crowfooted gable, crowstep gable, curvilinear gable, docked gable, Dutch gable, end gable, façade gable, Flemish gable, hanging gable, intersecting gable, multicurved gable, parapeted gable, side gable, stepped gable, straight-line gable, wall gable.**

gableboard Same as **bargeboard.**

gable dormer, gabled dormer Same as **triangular dormer.**

gabled roof *See* gable roof.

gable end, gable-end wall An end wall of a building having a **gable** at one or both of its ends.

gable: House of Seven Gables (1669), Salem, Mass.

gable end (17th cent.): Massachusetts

gable-front-and-wing plan The **plan** of a house having a gable facing the street and an added side-gable wing, at right angles to the front gable, at the rear of the house. A porch is often situated within the **L** formed by the intersection of the front of the gable with the wing. Sometimes found, for example, in the **Greek Revival style.**

gable-fronted Same as **front-gabled.**

gable-on-hip roof A roof, symmetric about the roof ridge, that comprises flat surfaces that slope upward from each side of the roof as in a **hipped roof** but do not continue all the way to the ridge; instead each of these end surfaces turns vertically so as to form a small gable at each end.

gable-on-hip roof

gable ornamentation Any type of decorative element, such as **spindlework**, at the apex of a **gable.**

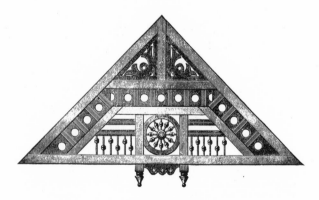

gable ornamentation

gable post A post directly under the ridge of one end of a **gable roof**; supports the intersection of the **bargeboard** at the roof ridge.

gable roof A roof having a single slope on each side of a central ridge; usually with a **gable** at one or at both ends of the roof.

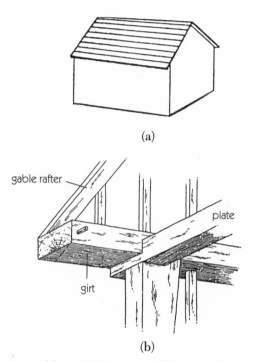

(a)

(b)

gable roof: (a) exterior; (b) interior framing

gablet A small ornamental **gable.**

gable wall Same as **gable end.**

gable window 1. A window in the face of a **gable.** 2. A window shaped like a gable.

gable window

galerie, gallery In **French Vernacular architecture** of Louisiana, a roofed porch, usually open-sided, about 6 to 12 feet (1.8–3.7m) wide; it often extends across the entire front, across the front and one or both sides, or completely around the building and provides useful living space in the open air, of particular value in a hot, humid climate. It is occasionally enclosed or partially enclosed. On a **raised house,** the *galerie* is usually on the first floor, i.e., the upper level; in a **Creole house,** there is sometimes a *galerie* across the front of the house and a loggia at the rear.

galerie house, gallery house In **French Vernacular architecture** of Louisiana, a one- or two-story farmhouse or plantation house, at the top of which is an attic or garret; developed by French-speaking settlers in the Louisiana Territory; has a roofed **galerie** either along the façade or along the façade and one or both sides of the house. This type of house displays characteristics also occasionally found elsewhere in the South and Southwest, such as gabled dormers to provide light within the loft and promote air circulation, an asset in very warm, humid climates; if the *galerie* is along the upper story, there is a balustrade between relatively simple wood posts that support the roof and, in turn, are usually supported by substantial columns at ground level. *See also* **Cajun cottage** and **Creole house.**

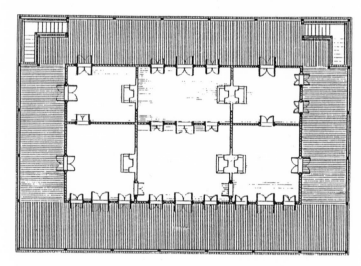

galerie: floor plan showing *galerie* surrounding house
at Destrehan Plantation (1787), Destrehan, La.

galerie house
Riverlake Plantation (1830), Point Coupee Parish, La.

gallery 1. A long, covered area acting as a corridor, either inside or on the exterior of a building, or between buildings. 2. An elevated area, interior or exterior, such as a **veranda**. 3. Same as **galerie.**

galleting Stone chips that are inserted into the joints of a rough masonry wall to reduce the amount of mortar required to seal the joints, to wedge larger stones in position, or to add detail to the appearance.

gambrel end An end wall of a structure having a **gambrel roof.**

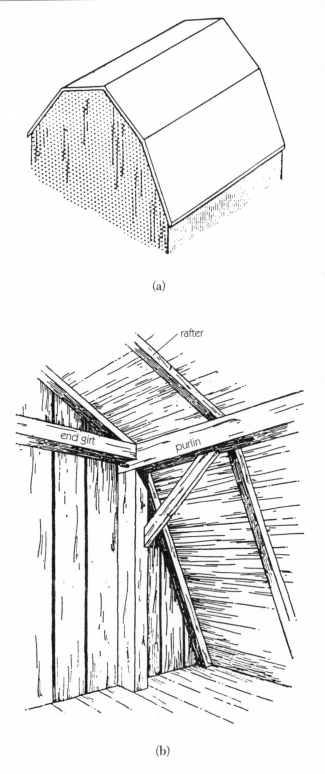

(a)

rafter

end girt

purlin

(b)

gambrel roof
(a) exterior view;
(b) interior view showing structural members

gambrel end

gambrel roof A roof having two flat surfaces on each side of a central ridge; each surface is at a different pitch; the shorter upper surface has a low pitch, and the longer, lower surface has a steep pitch. A gambrel roof is more complicated to build than a gable roof, but it provides greater headroom under the roof than does a **pitched roof** covering the same floor area, hence its wide use in barn construction. The earliest gambrel roof in America is said to be the second Harvard Hall (1677) at Harvard College in Cambridge, Massachusetts. Common in the Georgian period, gambrel roofs continue to be used today, as, for example, in **Colonial Revival** architecture. Occasionally called an English gambrel roof. *See also* **Dutch gambrel roof, New England gambrel roof, Swedish gambrel roof.**

garçonnière In **French Vernacular architecture** of Louisiana and the Gulf Coast, a bachelor's residence that is separate from the main house.

garçonnière
Houmas-Burnside Plantation (1840), Louisiana

garden apartment 1. A ground-floor apartment with access to a garden or other adjacent outdoor space. 2. One of several two- or three-story apartment buildings with communal gardens, often located in the suburbs.

garden arch An archway in a garden, often of lattice construction, that serves as a decorative structure on which to grow vines, roses, or other climbing plants.

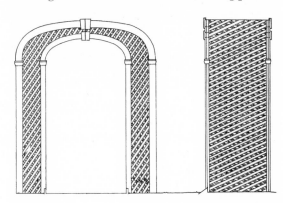

garden arch (c. 1830–1835): Newburyport, Mass.

garden city A residential development specifically planned to provide considerable open space that is well planted with trees and shrubs.

garden house A small structure for shelter in a garden; same as **gazebo.**

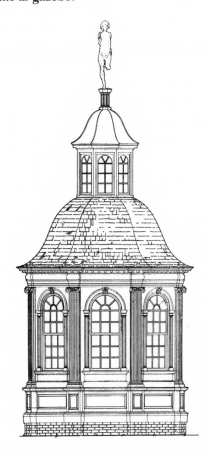

garden house: on grounds of Col. Isaac Royall House (1737), Medford, Mass.

gargoyle A grotesque carved figure projecting from the face of a building; may be merely decorative but may also function as a **waterspout,** projecting from a roof gutter to discharge rainwater.

gargoyle
Cleveland Arcade (1890), Cleveland, Ohio

garland Same as **festoon.**

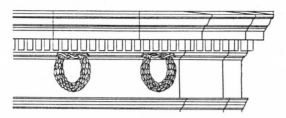

garland
frieze, Boston Symphony Hall, Boston, Mass.

garner Same as **granary.**

garret Same as **attic** or **loft.**

garreting Same as **galleting.**

garrison house 1. A fortified early American house generally constructed of stone or hewn logs, commonly with a second-story overhang, as deep as 24 inches

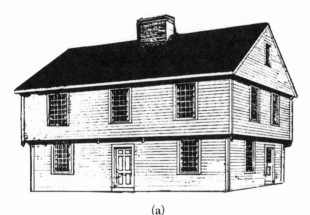

(a)

(b)

garrison house
(a) Does House, Newmarket, N.H.;
(b) modern garrison house

(61cm), along the front of the house, but occasionally on all four sides; commonly fitted with **loopholes,** slots through which defenders could fire in the event of an enemy attack. Used as a one-family dwelling in times of peace, a garrison house provided a family with a safe haven in times of emergency. They were built along the Atlantic coast as early as 1660; later, during the opening of the Far West, similar buildings served as defensive structures; compare with **blockhouse.** 2. A modern term sometimes applied to any **Colonial Revival** house having an overhanging second story.

gate A passageway through a fence, wall, or other barrier, that slides, lowers, or swings open or shut.

gate: entrance to Westover (1734),
Charles City County, Va.

gatehouse A small building adjacent to or built over a gate; may provide living quarters for the gatekeeper.

gatepost A **post**, usually one of a pair between which a gate swings or slides.

gauged arch An **arch** built of wedge-shaped **gauged bricks,1.**

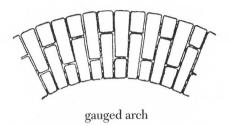

gauged arch

gauged brick 1. Any brick that tapers in the direction of its length; used in a curved arch or circular construction. 2. Brick that has been manufactured to close tolerances or that has been roughly sawn or cut and then ground to accurate dimensions.

gaulette In **French Vernacular architecture** of Louisiana, a wood bar; a variant of **barreaux.**

gazebo A small ornamental structure, such as a pavilion, often providing a fine view; usually built in a garden, park, or the like. Also called a garden house or summerhouse.

General Grant style A seldom-used term for the **Second Empire style.**

geodesic dome A relatively lightweight **dome** having a framework consisting of an assemblage of many identical, straight-line, rigid members that provide considerable structural strength for its weight; conceived and developed by R. Buckminster Fuller (1895–1983) in 1954.

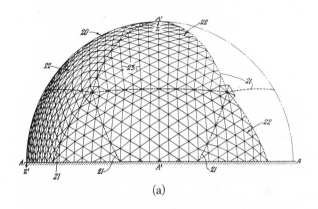

(a)

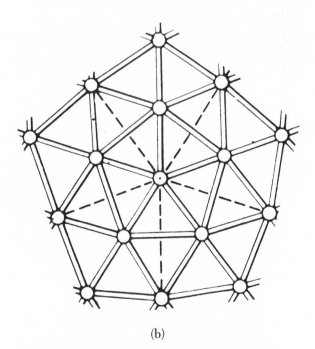

(b)

geodesic dome: from R. Buckminster Fuller's
U.S. Patent 2,682,235 (1954)
(a) dome showing numbers referring to
items covered in the patent application;
(b) detail showing connection of the rigid
members assembled to form a dome

gazebo
Askhurst Estate, Mt. Holly, N.J.

geometrical stair A stair constructed around a stairwell without the use of a central post around which the steps wind; the steps are continuous from top to bottom.

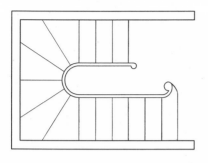

geometrical stair

Georgian Colonial architecture *See* **Georgian style.**

Georgian plan A **floor plan** of a Georgian-style house; often two rooms deep on each side of a central hall, with a kitchen added at the rear; the chimneys of the house are usually located on the end walls on each side of the house.

Georgian Revival *See* **Colonial Revival** and **Georgian style.**

Georgian style A style of architecture that emerged about 1700 and flourished until about 1780 in the American colonies along the Atlantic coast. The Georgian style varied with geographical region. For example, in New England, where there was an ample supply of wood, two-story timber-framed houses with

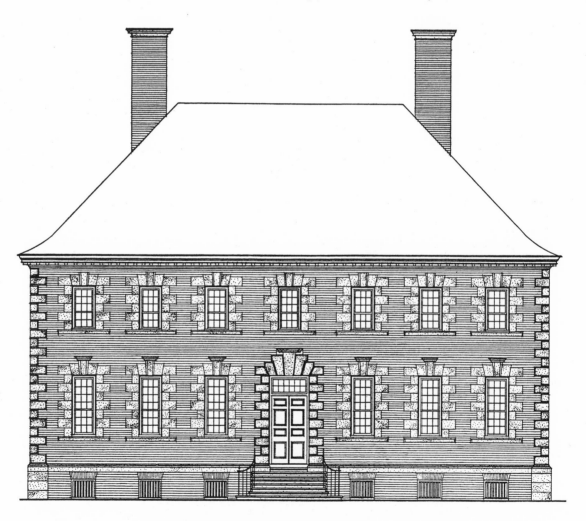

Georgian style: (a) Cleve (1754), King George County, Va.

central chimneys predominated because a central chimney helped to warm the entire house during the cold winter months. In the southern colonies, where good clay for bricks and lime for mortar was plentiful, brick houses were widely used; fireplace chimneys were usually placed at the ends of the house to minimize the heat generated during the hot summer months when the fireplace was used for cooking. Along the mid-Atlantic coast, stone and brick were both widely used for the exterior walls. Over time the Georgian style became more elaborate, and the houses themselves grew larger, wider, and often as high as two-and-a-half stories. Because of such changes in style with time, a distinction is sometimes made between *Early Georgian* and *Late Georgian*, with the year 1750 as the approximate time of transition. This

date is arbitrary, however, because many changes occurred gradually and at different times in different colonies; moreover, some attributes labeled Early Georgian can be found in Late Georgian style and vice versa. Outstanding examples of the Georgian style include Westover (1734) in Charles City County, Virginia; Mount Pleasant (1761) in Philadelphia; and Cliveden (1764) in Germantown, Pennsylvania.

Georgian-style houses, commonly rectangular in plan, often with symmetrical wings flanking each side, usually include many of the following characteristics:

Façade and exterior wall treatments: In Early Georgian, a relatively plain, unbroken, symmetrical façade with geometric proportions; frequently, a pedimented gable. In Late Georgian, the façade was more highly ornamented, often with a projecting central

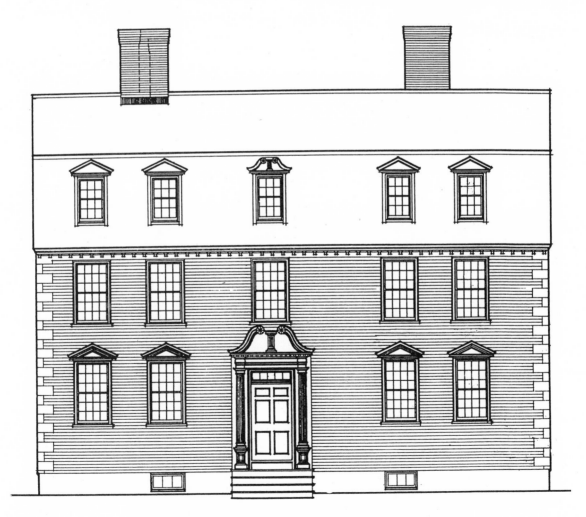

Georgian style: (b) Cutts Mansion (1782), Saco, Maine

pavilion or a portico with two-story columns. In the second half of the 18th century, monumental pilasters extended the full height of the façade, usually at or near the corners of the house and also on the pavilion or portico; often the rear entrance to the house was similar to the front entrance (*see* illustration of Thomas Jefferson's retreat under **octagon house**.). Brick walls were common, often laid in a **Flemish bond** pattern, but clapboard, shingle, stone, or wood decorated to look like stonework were also widely used, typically with quoins at the corners. The façades commonly were brick or stone, especially along the mid-Atlantic coast, often with a **belt course** of stone or projecting

bricks, and occasionally a **water table.** In Pennsylvania a **pent roof** between the first and second stories was common; in large houses in the South, a **raised basement,** with its ceiling extending well above ground level (sometimes by as much as a full story) was typical.

Roof treatments: A hipped roof, gable roof, or gambrel roof, commonly with slate shingles; a truncated hipped roof (particularly popular after 1750), providing a flat surface that could be enclosed with a balustrade, as in a **captain's house**. Typically, a roof pitch of about 30 degrees, i.e., somewhat lower than many earlier colonial roofs; often gabled dormers, boxed eaves with little overhang; often a classical cor-

Georgian style: (c) Late Georgian door, Wentworth-Gardner House (1760), Portsmouth, N.H.

Georgian style
(d) Georgian door with window above

nice decorated with dentils, modillions, or moldings. Commonly, a brick or stone chimney, sometimes plastered; occasionally **double chimneys** at one or both ends of the house.

Window treatments: Typically, larger, more numerous, and more highly decorated windows than in earlier American colonial architecture; usually, rectangular double-hung sashes having heavy frames, with thick **muntins** that became thinner over time; often nine panes in the upper sash and nine panes in the lower sash, i.e., (9/9), although other popular configurations included (6/6), (9/6), and (12/12). Many elegant houses were *five-ranked*, i.e., had five windows across on the second story and four windows plus a door on the ground floor, the door being tallied as one of the windows. In the Late Georgian style, a flat lintel having a prominent keystone above the rectangular windows; front windows on the ground floor, often pedimented. In homes along the mid-Atlantic coast, occasionally a **Palladian window,** primarily after about 1750.

Doorway treatments: A somewhat elaborate front entrance, usually having either a six-paneled single door or a double door with multiple panels in each leaf; often decoratively crowned, commonly with an **entablature** above; often, a triangular, segmental, or scroll pediment over the door; frequently, a projecting hood above the door; prominent decorative elements around the main doorway, for example, a transom light or a row of small panes of glass above the door and **sidelights** on each side of the door; occasionally a horizontal row of small panes of glass in the door itself. In the Late Georgian style, a semicircular or elliptical fanlight over the door, as in the Federal style; decorative pilasters or engaged columns (plain or fluted, full height or raised on pedestals) flanking the door. In elegant homes the front door opened into a spacious **entrance hall** that often featured an elaborate staircase ascending to the floor above.

Georgian style: (e) Georgian dormer window, Hope Lodge (1773), Philadelphia, Pa.

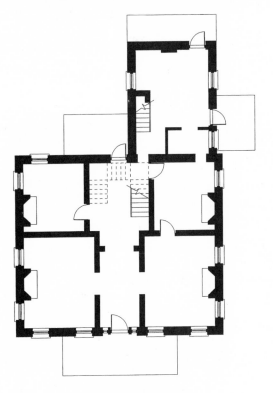

Georgian style
(f) common Georgian floor plan

German barn, Swiss barn Any one of a variety of barns, often serving as a combination barn and place to live, built during the 18th and 19th centuries by German-speaking immigrants to America; especially characterized by a gambrel roof or a gable roof with hand-split shingles; a second floor overhanging one side of the barn, well beyond the foundation; usually an inclined driveway (i.e., a *bank*) providing direct entry to the *threshing floor* where wheat was threshed, hay was stored, and where the family lived. The floor below, called the *basement*, was used as a stable for horses, cattle, and sheep. This type of barn was often constructed of masonry up to the threshing floor; above this, wood construction was typical. Many stone barns of this type had long, vertical slots in the walls, called **slit ventilators**, for supplying the barn with fresh air. German barns are most often found in the area around Lancaster, Pennsylvania, and in northern Delaware. Also called a **bank barn, forebay barn, grundscheier, Pennsylvania Dutch barn, Sweitzer barn.**

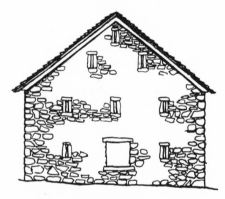

German barn
Glen Fern Farm, near Philadelphia, Pa.

German Colonial architecture Architecture attributed to German-speaking immigrants to America primarily in the years from about 1680 to 1780, especially in Pennsylvania and environs, but extending as far west as Wisconsin and as far south as North Carolina. Many of these early colonists first built a **log house** of hewn square timbers as a temporary home until they could construct more substantial, permanent housing. Common characteristics of the permanent houses included a symmetrical façade, thick stone walls, a steeply pitched end-gabled roof usually covered with hand-split wood shingles or red clay tiles; an attic story with windows at the gable ends and **shed dormers** on the roof; a porch at the gable end of the

house or at the front of the house; small casement windows with battened shutters, later replaced by double-hung windows with paneled or decorative shutters. Such dwellings were often called *bank houses* because they were built on the bank of a hill and had a room, dug into the hillside, that remained relatively cool throughout the year. If the room were located over a spring providing cool water, some of this water was piped to another room used for storing perishable foods. *See also* **fachwerk, grundscheier, Pennsylvania Dutch, rauchkammer, springhouse.**

German siding A type of **drop siding** (i.e., an exterior wall cladding of horizontal wood boards) in which each board has a concave upper edge that fits into a corresponding groove in the lower edge of the board above.

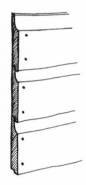

German siding

giant order In Classical architecture, an **order** in which the columns rise more than one story, most commonly two or three stories. Also called a colossal order.

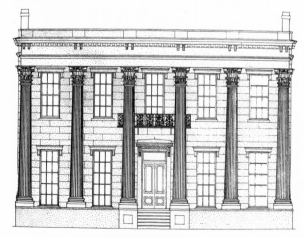

giant order
Corinthian, Pollard Mansion, Montgomery, Ala.

Gibbs surround In masonry, a decorative frame around the exterior side of a door or window; composed of alternating larger and smaller blocks of stone, usually with a triple **keystone** at the head of the door or window. Named after the English architect James Gibbs (1682–1754).

Gibbs surround
First Presbyterian Church, Newark, N.J.

gingerbread Highly decorative woodwork, usually turned on a lathe and/or fashioned on a jigsaw; characteristically elaborately embellished.

gingerbread

Gingerbread folk architecture A type of **folk architecture** widely applied to one-, one-and-a-half-, and two-story homes in America from about 1870 to 1910; particularly popular during the 1880s and 1890s. It was especially characterized by the heavy use of **gingerbread**, including the use of elaborate **Neo-Victorian** details such as **spindlework**, as well as some details borrowed from the **Italianate style**. Often these highly ornate decorative elements were simply added to the exterior of an older house in an attempt to give it a more current appearance or were added to a new house in traditional folk-house style. Both the ornamentation and the houses themselves could be purchased by mail-order from a catalogue and shipped to the building site by railroad. Heavily ornamented porches were common; in larger houses they were often two stories high and had decorative balustrades with spindlework balusters and lacelike **spandrels**. Ornate **bargeboards** hung from the projecting edge of a sloping gable roof. Although ornamentation of this type is found in the **Queen Anne style**, here it was applied with a semblance of order and symmetry, in contrast to the arbitrary character of Queen Anne adornments. Also called Folk Victorian architecture and Gingerbread style. *See also* **Carpenter Gothic** and **Steamboat Gothic**.

girder 1. A large horizontal beam used to support concentrated loads at points along its length. 2. Same as **girt**.

girt A horizontal member in the **framing,3** of an early American **timber-framed house**, typically supporting the ends of the ceiling joists and acting as the main horizontal support for the floor above. Girts, usually of hewn oak or another very hard wood such as walnut, were often located about halfway between the **groundsill,2** and the horizontal timber at the top of the wall (the **top plate**). The term *girt* often is preceded by an adjective indicating its position; for example, **front girt** denotes a girt that runs horizontally along the front of the house. *See also* **chimney girt** and **end girt**. *See* illustration under **timber-framed house**.

girt: mortise-and-tenoned to a summerbeam

glass A hard, brittle inorganic substance, ordinarily transparent or translucent, produced by melting a mixture of silicates (such as sand) with a flux (such as lime and soda). While molten, glass may be blown, cast, drawn, rolled, or pressed into a variety of shapes. In colonial times glass was imported from England and was generally of poor quality, often green or violet in hue, streaked with air bubbles, and only about 1/16 inch (1.6mm) thick. Because glass panes were expensive, window sizes were small except in the more affluent homes. In some areas small size was considered an asset since it was said to provide increased security against enemy attack. Glass manufacturing in America was attempted as early as 1609, but this attempt met with failure, as did many subsequent ventures. It was not until 1792 that the manufacture of window glass became commercially viable in America. The price of glass then dropped significantly, the use of window glass became much more widespread, and the sizes of panes increased. One of the most successful of the early manufacturers was the New England Glass Company of Cambridge, Massachusetts, founded in 1818. The **Crystal Palace,** built in New York City for the 1853 Exhibition, provided a dramatic early example of the use of glass in building construction. *See also* **art glass, broad glass, crown glass, cylinder glass, figured glass, float glass, opalescent glass, painted glass, plate glass, sheet glass, stained glass, Tiffany glass.**

glass brick, glass block A hollow block of glass, usually translucent, often with textured faces; used for decorative purposes in non-load-bearing walls; provides relatively poor thermal insulation and low fire resistance. Occasionally found in modern architecture, particularly in **Art Moderne** and **Streamline Moderne.**

glass house A residence having exterior walls that are almost completely glass. A notable example is the Philip Johnson house (1949) in New Canaan, Connecticut.

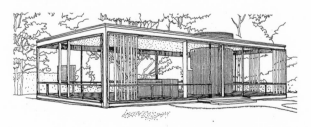

glass house

glazed 1. A term descriptive of an opening that is filled with sheets of glass, as in a window. 2. A term descriptive of a finish that is composed of ceramic materials fused into its surface, usually making it essentially impervious to moisture.

glazed brick A **brick** that has been fired (i.e., burnt) in a kiln at a temperature sufficiently high to fuse the clay and sand on its surface, usually forming a bluish black glassy coating. In some areas of colonial America, it was common practice to lay such bricks in a decorative pattern or in a pattern called **diaperwork.** The pattern frequently indicated the house owner's initials and/or the date of construction.

glazing The sheets or panes of glass that are set in windows and doors or other openings.

glazing bar One of the vertical or horizontal wood dividers within a window frame that hold the panes of glass; also called a **muntin.** With the introduction of the **Federal style** in about 1780, these dividers became thinner and more elegant.

glyph A **V**-shaped groove used as a wall ornament in the **Classical Revival style** and its derivatives; usually found on a Doric frieze. *See* **triglyph.**

good-morning stair In a **Cape Cod house,** a stair having a single flight from the front entry hall up to an intermediate landing, from which a pair of single flights lead to each of two bedrooms in the garret above. According to legend, the name is derived from persons greeting each other with "Good morning" on leaving their respective bedrooms at the start of the day.

gorge Same as **cavetto.**

Gothic arch A loose term denoting any **arch** with a point at its apex, such as a **lancet arch;** found in many **Gothic Revival** buildings in America.

Gothic architecture The architecture of the style prevalent during the High Middle Ages in Western Europe; emerging from Romanesque and Byzantine forms in France during the mid-12th century and lasting until the 16th century. Its great works were cathedrals, usually characterized by flying buttresses, pointed arches, rib vaults, and a system of richly decorated **fenestration.** Gothic architecture lasted until the 16th century, when it was succeeded by the classical forms of the Renaissance. Served as a prototype for Gothic Revival architecture in America.

Gothic Revival A style of architecture in America aimed at reviving the spirit and forms of Gothic architecture; applied to country cottages, churches, some public buildings, and a few castlelike structures, primarily from about 1830 to 1880. The earlier phase of this architecture is sometimes called *Early Gothic Revival*; the later phase, *Late Gothic Revival*, *High Victorian Gothic*, or *Victorian Gothic*. An outstanding example of Early Gothic Revival is Trinity Church (1839–1846) in New York City, designed by Richard Upjohn (1802–1878), who is often regarded as the father of Gothic Revival in America. A well-known example of Late Gothic Revival is Saint Patrick's Cathedral (1858–1879) in New York City, by James Renwick (1818–1895). The application of Gothic Revival was stimulated by widely available **pattern books**, particularly the publications of Andrew Jackson Downing (1815–1852) and Alexander Jackson Davis

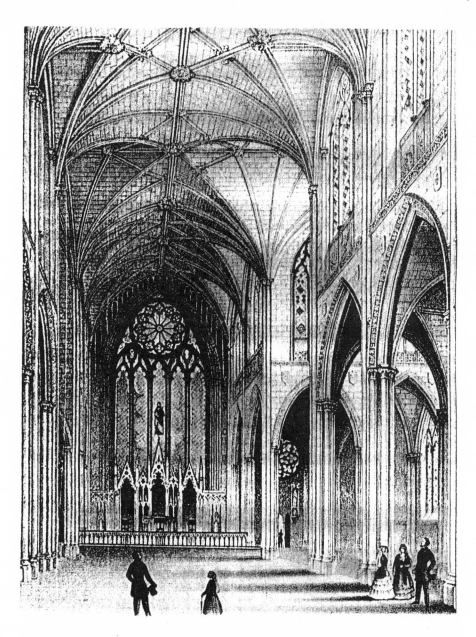

Gothic Revival: (a) Grace Church (1848), New York City; James Renwick, Architect

Gothic Revival: (b) Greystone, Pevely, Mo.;
(c) Wadsworth Athenaeum (1842–1844), Hartford, Conn.; Alexander Jackson Davis, Architect

(1803–1892). Gothic Revival buildings constructed of wood, and often designed by carpenters and builders, are described and illustrated under **Carpenter Gothic.** *See also* **Collegiate Gothic** and **High Victorian Gothic.**

Gothic Revival buildings usually exhibit many of the following characteristics:

Façade and exterior wall treatments: Walls of a variety of building materials and finishes (commonly, **ashlar masonry**, **polychromed** brickwork, and wood), often extending into the gables without interruption to promote a vertical emphasis; Gothic motifs such as battlements, decorative brackets, finials, foliated ornaments, hood moldings, label moldings, pinnacles with crockets, pointed arches, quatrefoils, towers, trefoils, turrets, and wall dormers. Often, a full-width or partial-width one-story porch with flattened Gothic or Tudor arches; occasionally a recessed entry. Small houses in this style commonly have a symmetrical façade.

Roof treatments: A steeply pitched gable roof, usually with the gable at the center of the façade or with cross gables; intersecting gables; gables that are decorated with highly ornate, lacy, gingerbread **bargeboards** suggestive of Gothic architecture; projecting eaves; decorative slate or shingle patterns on the roof; occasionally, a flat roof with crenellated and castellated parapets; high, ornamental chimney stacks with clus-

ters of chimney pots; a cast-iron decorative strip at the ridge of the roof.

Window treatments: Windows that extend into the gables; bay windows; lancet windows, ogee arch windows, oriel windows, triangular arch windows, often with mullions and relatively thin tracery, including **foils**; casement windows with diamond-shaped panes or small rectangular panes set diagonally, sometimes of stained glass; **label moldings** over some windows, particularly on the ground floor.

Doorway treatments: Often, an elaborately paneled front door set into a **lancet arch**, partially glazed, either with Gothic motifs or in a simple rectangular or diamond-shaped pattern; infrequently, a battened door suggestive of a similar door from the medieval period; the entry door sometimes within a recessed porch or under a doorhood, occasionally bordered with sidelights; above the doorway, often a label molding terminated with label stops.

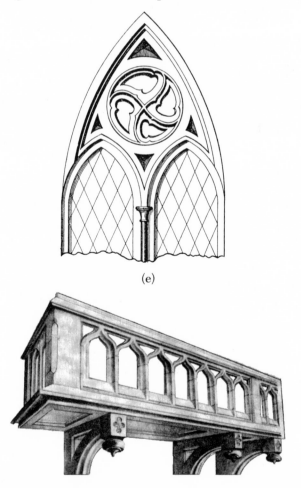

(e)

(f)

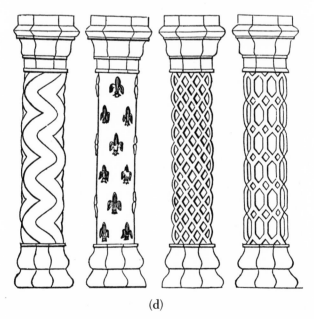

(d)

Gothic Revival: (d) Gothic Revival chimney tops; (e) window detail; (f) balcony with a series of ogee arches

Gothic sash A term occasionally applied to a **lancet window.**

Gothic survival The survival of Gothic forms and construction techniques in America long after the demise of Gothic architecture, usually in a provincial context, as distinct from **Gothic Revival.** On rare occasions this term is applied to early colonial American churches with medieval motifs; an outstanding example is the Old Brick Church, in Newport Parish, Virginia (1680).

gougework An ornamental wood surface having decorative surface marks made with a chisel whose blade is curved.

grade The ground elevation or level at the outside walls of a building, or at a specified point on the building site.

graining *See* **false woodgraining.**

granary A storehouse for grain, usually after it has been threshed, or for the storage of corn after it has been husked; typically rectangular in shape. In the 19th century, such structures were supported by smooth stone shafts about three feet (1m) in height, capped with flat stones about two feet (0.6m) in diameter. The smooth surfaces of the stone provided some protection against vermin that would otherwise crawl up the supports.

granary

granite 1. An igneous rock having crystals or grains of visible size, consisting mainly of quartz, feldspar, and mica. 2. A crystalline silicate rock having visible grains; this term includes gneiss and igneous rocks that strictly speaking are not granite.

grapevine ornament A **running ornament** usually consisting of a grapevine with bunches of grapes and grape leaves; used as a decorative element, particularly below a ceiling.

grapevine ornament: ceiling, Edward Carrington House (1810), Providence, R.I.

grass house 1. A round primitive dwelling primarily constructed by American Indians of the Great Plains (i.e., the region between the Mississippi River and the Rocky Mountains, from Canada to Texas), for example, the Wichitas; had a framework that consisted of vertical poles, bent over and lashed together across the top, with other branches tied around the framework horizontally, thereby creating a domed structure that supported heavy layers of prairie-grass thatching in overlapping courses, usually with a smoke hole at the top; similar to **bent-frame construction.** 2. Any similar primitive house having a round or rectangular shape; for example, *see* **palma hut** and Hawaiian **hale.**

grass house,1: constructing a framework for a typical house of the Wichitas: poles are tied together in a ring at the top; light poles are tied completely around the structure to form a base for the heavy grass thatching

great house The main or central residence of an large estate, farm, or plantation; usually the home of the owner. In the South from 1830 to 1860, a number of magnificent great houses erected on plantations along the Mississippi River were fine examples of **French Vernacular architecture**; many others were built in the **Greek Revival style** or in the **Italianate style.**

great room The main room of a house of some pretension, usually the room largest in size.

Greek key, Greek fret An ornament that is incised or raised and formed of fillets, bands, or moldings variously combined, but usually consisting of continuous lines arranged in rectangular forms. Frequently used in the **Greek Revival style.** Also called a key pattern, labyrinth fret, or meander.

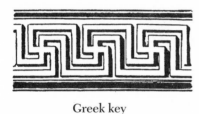

Greek key

Greek Revival style A style of architecture, widely used in America from about 1820 to the 1860s (most popular from 1820 to 1850) for public buildings, detached houses, and town houses, based on the reuse of ancient Greek forms in architecture, i.e., the Greek **orders** (Doric, Ionic, and Corinthian). Ornaments were used more often than before the American Revolution; for example, cast-iron capitals or elaborate plaster decorations cast from stock patterns. Homes in the Greek Revival style were commonly two rooms deep with four rooms on the first floor. Public buildings in this style were usually symmetrical in plan and rectangular in shape, or a combination of such rectangles. Outstanding contributors to this style included the architects William Strickland (1788–1854), Robert Mills (1781–1855), and Thomas Ustick Walter (1804–1887). *See* **Classical Revival style** and **Neoclassical style.** Also called National Style during the height of its popularity.

Buildings in the Greek Revival style, greatly fostered by the spread of **pattern books** in which many of the classical elements were reproduced with exactitude, commonly exhibit many of the following characteristics:

Greek Revival style: (a) the Gordon House (1843), near Waynesburg, Greene County, Pa.

(b)

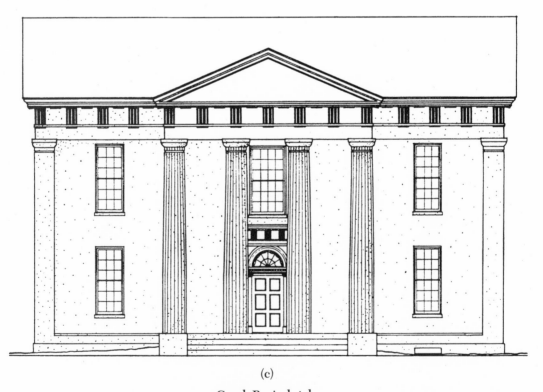

(c)

Greek Revival style
(b) Doric, Second Bank of United States (1824), Philadelphia, Pa.; William Strickland, Architect;
(c) Doric, Lyceum (1840), Alexandria, Va.

Façade and exterior wall treatments: In public buildings and detached houses, a symmetric front-gabled façade with a one-story or full-height classical pedimented portico extending the full width or partial width of the building; a façade of brick, wood clapboard, or stone construction (or wood stuccoed to imitate stone); a partial-height porch, sometimes with a porch roof having a raked cornice supported on round or square columns of the Doric or Ionic orders, or occasionally the Corinthian order; pilasters, especially at the corners; regular-spaced openings in the façade, including the use of blank windows and blank doors in order to achieve symmetry of design; often, a plain wide band of trim below a heavy cornice just below the roof line; walls that tend to imitate flat stonework, often painted white; typically, sparse ornamentation that occasionally included decorative motifs such as the Greek key, the anthemion, dentils, and egg-and-dart moldings.

Roof treatments: Typically, a low- to moderate-pitched gabled or hipped roof that may be partially hidden by prominent cornices or parapets; in town houses in this style, flat roofs, frequently with decorative parapets.

Window treatments: Commonly, widely spaced double-hung windows with six panes in the upper sash over six panes in the lower sash (6/6); occasionally, nine panes in the upper sash and six in the lower (9/6); usually, tall double-hung windows on the ground floor; broad architrave trim around the windows; decorative window crowns; often, louvered shutters. Occasionally, **frieze-band windows** directly below the cornice.

Doorway treatments: Usually, a wide, imposing, intricate entryway, often recessed, framed by pilasters or engaged columns; an **entablature** that may or may not be pedimented; the entry door, either a single or double door, usually having one, two, four, six, or eight raised panels; typically, a horizontal transom above the door in the form of a line of small **lights**, and a vertical line of small lights on each side of the door.

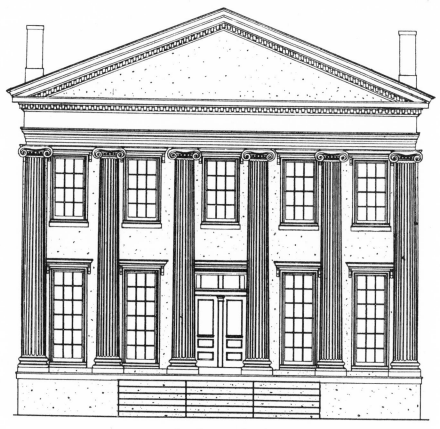

Greek Revival style
(d) Ionic, Redstrake House, Salem, N.J.

green *See* **village green.**

greenbelt A wide area of parks, farmland, or undeveloped land surrounding a community.

greenhouse A glass-enclosed structure, often heated, for growing flowers, plants, and out-of-season fruits and vegetables under controlled, protected conditions. More or less temporary structures for the same purpose may be covered by plastic sheeting over a framework, rather than glass. *See also* **conservatory, hothouse, orangery.**

grille A grating or openwork barrier, often fabricated of metal but also of wood or other material, used to cover, conceal, decorate, or protect an opening.

gristmill A mill for grinding grain, especially grain brought to the mill by customers. In colonial America such mills were usually powered by the wind, a stream or river, or by tidal water.

groin The ridge, edge, or curved line formed by the intersection of two curved surfaces.

groined vault A compound vault in which **barrel vaults** intersect, forming **groins.**

grotto A structure constructed and decorated to resemble a picturesque cave or cavern.

ground A nailing strip fixed to brickwork or to a concrete wall as a base for attaching wood trim or the like.

ground beam Same as **groundsill,2.**

ground plan The **plan** of a building taken at ground level.

groundsill, groundplate 1. In timber-framed construction, a horizontal timber, usually laid on a foundation, into which the posts or other wall members are framed; may also receive ground-story floor members; infrequently, laid directly on the ground or on stones set into the ground; also called a sill plate. 2. The structural timber that is nearest the ground or on the ground itself; used to distribute concentrated loads; also called a ground beam.

ground table Same as **earth table**

group house Same as **row house.**

grout Mortar containing sufficient water so that the resulting mixture has the consistency of a viscous liquid, thereby permitting it to be troweled, poured, or pumped into joints, confined spaces, and/or cracks.

grille
wrought iron, The Arsenal, New Orleans, La.

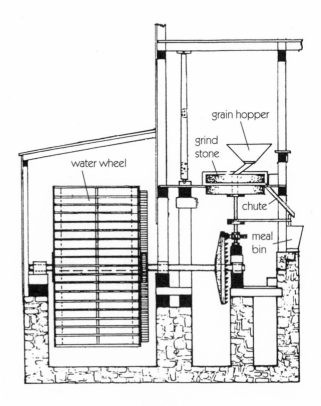

gristmill
Bollinger's Mill (water-driven), near Alpine, N.J.

grundscheier A barn constructed by early German-speaking immigrants to America; of varied construction, depending on the terrain and available materials. Usually built on slightly sloping ground. *See* **German barn.**

guard bar A vertical bar, of wrought iron or wood, that was fastened to the frame of a **casement window** in a colonial American home to stiffen the frame.

gudgeon A metal pin used to hold two blocks or slabs of stone together.

guildhall In colonial America, the place of assembly for a society of craftsmen or merchants for their mutual assistance; an outgrowth of similar medieval organizations or guilds.

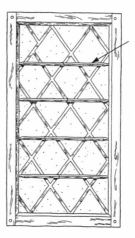

guard bar

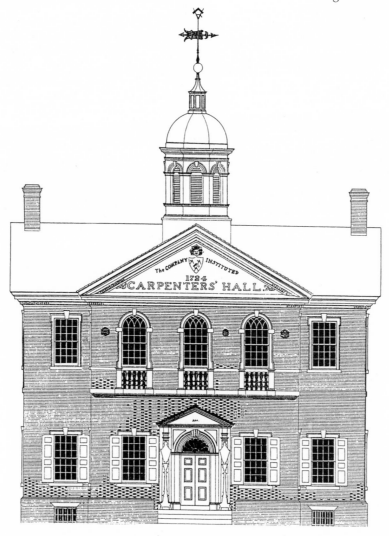

guildhall: Carpenters' Hall (1770–1774), Philadelphia, Pa.; First Continental Congress met here in 1774

guilloche An ornament formed by two or more curved bands twisted over each other in a continuous series, leaving circular openings that are often decorated.

gun hole, gun port, gun slot An **embrasure.**

gunshot house Same as **shotgun house.**

gun-stock post Same as **musket-stock post.**

gutta (*pl.* **guttae**) In Classical architecture, one of a series of pendant ornaments, generally in the form of an inverted frustum of a cone, i.e., a cone in which the upper tip has been lopped off; usually found on the underside of the **mutules** of a Doric entablature; occasionally used in America in the **Greek Revival style.**

gutter A shallow horizontal channel of metal or wood usually set immediately below and along the eaves of a building to catch and carry off rainwater from the roof. Gutters became popular after the introduction of the **Georgian style,** i.e., after 1700. Prior to that, they were used only on some of the better homes and public buildings; on most buildings, rainwater fell from the roof directly to the ground below. *See* **box gutter, standing gutter, sunk gutter.** Also called an eaves trough.

guttered A term descriptive of a structural framing member, such as a corner post, that is encased or cut away (for example, a corner cut off) to hide its appearance, a practice that began in some areas of the South toward the end of the 17th century.

gypsum A soft mineral consisting of hydrated calcium sulfate from which gypsum plaster is made; colorless when pure.

gypsum mortar A plastic mixture of gypsum, water, and often sand; can be troweled in the plastic state; hardens in place when the water it contains evaporates.

guilloche

guttae: end view

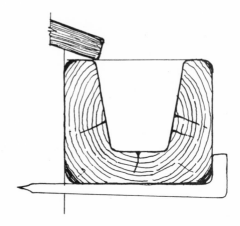

gutter: hand-hewn from a solid piece of wood

H

HABS Abbreviation for **Historic American Buildings Survey.**

hacienda In the American Southwest, the main house of a Spanish Colonial estate or ranch; usually, the house is part of a complex having adobe walls that enclose a corral and a courtyard or patio; rooms in the house usually open onto a patio. *See also* **placita** and **zaguán.**

ha-ha A barrier once used to prevent livestock from crossing a boundary without interrupting the view with a fence; usually consists of a trench or ditch that may or may not have a fence along its bottom. A good early example of a ha-ha is at Bremo (1815), in Fluvanna County, Virginia. Also called a sunk fence.

hale A primitive Hawaiian house consisting of a wood framework covered by a thatched roof, commonly of grass.

half baluster A **baluster** that is **engaged** and that projects from the surface to which it is attached by about one-half of its diameter.

hale
pili grass thatching tied to a pole framework

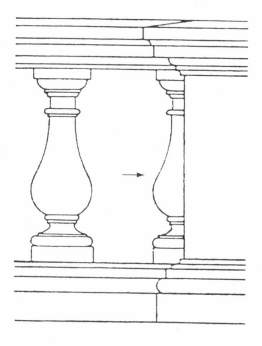

half baluster

half Cape house Typically, a one-and-a-half-story rectangular house of wood-frame construction developed in the 1700s on Cape Cod, Massachusetts; has two double-hung windows in the façade on one side of the front door but, unlike a **full Cape house**, no rooms or windows on the other side of the door; usually, a window in one or both end gables to provide light and ventilation in the attic; a massive central chimney that serves all fireplaces; a roof covering and wall covering of hand-split unpainted shingles that become gray when weathered.

half Cape house

half column An **column** that is **engaged,** attached, or apparently attached, to a wall and projects from it by about one-half its diameter.

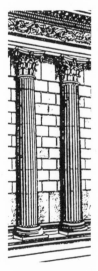

half columns

half-cut notch A simple joint between the timbers at a corner of a **log house**; formed by cutting away the lower half of the end of one timber and placing it over and at right angles to another timber in which the upper half of the end has been cut away. A spike or **treenail** is usually driven through the two ends to secure the joint.

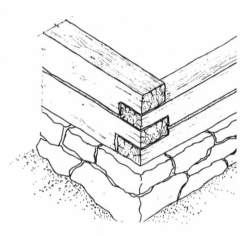

half-cut notch

half dovetail A wood joint similar to a **dovetail** but having only one side flared; the other side is straight.

half-dovetail notch At a corner of a **log house**, a notch in the shape of a **half dovetail** at the end of a rectangular exterior timber; forms an interlocking joint when mated with an appropriately notched timber at right angles to it; widely used because it is relatively easy to make, yet provides a rigid joint with a good slope for water runoff. Compare with **dovetail notch.**

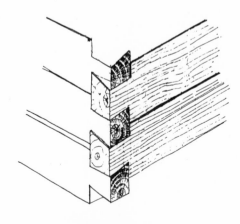

half-dovetail notch

half-dugout A primitive shelter, partially dug below ground level, but having a significant portion of its structure above ground level. The depth of ground excavated depended on soil conditions, but a depth of about four feet was typical. Often, the excavation was in a bank of sloping terrain; commonly had sod walls and a **sod roof**. Used by some early colonists in America until they built more permanent houses, and later by homesteaders on the Great Plains (the region between the Mississippi River and the Rocky Mountains, from Canada to Texas). *See* **sod house.**

half-gabled Descriptive of a **shed roof**, i.e., a roof having the shape of a flat inclined plane.

half house 1. Same as **half Cape house.** 2. Same as **flounder house.**

half-house plan *See* **one-room plan.**

half landing Same as **halfpace landing.**

half-lap joint A joint at the intersection of two wood members of equal thickness in which half the thickness of each is removed so that they fit together to form a flush continuous surface.

halfpace landing, halfpace A **landing** between two adjacent flights of stairs where the two flights turn in opposite directions.

halfpace stair A stair making a 180-degree turn, usually has a **halfpace landing.** Compare with **quarterpace stair.**

half-round molding A convex **molding** of semicircular profile.

half story A partial story under a sloping roof that forms an attic, garret, or loft space; often has dormers projecting above the roof and/or windows in a gable-end wall to provide daylight and ventilation in this space. A half story has less usable area than the floors below it.

half-timbered construction A term descriptive of a type of timber-framed construction in which all supporting and bracing members consist of heavy timbers. In colonial America the space between the structural framing of the walls had an **infilling** of brick, mud plaster, **nogging**, or **wattle-and-daub** to provide additional rigidity and improved thermal insulation; usually the structural timbers of the exterior walls were exposed. Found, for example, in **Queen Anne style, Tudor Revival, French Vernacular architecture** of Louisiana. *See also* **columbage, fachwerk, false half-timbering, pierrotage.**

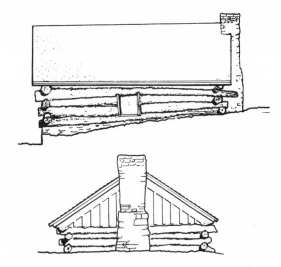

half-dugout: Dickens County, Tex.

half-lap joint: roof ridge of Lydia Lester House, near Gettysburg, Pa.

half-timbered construction
Hermann-Ahem House, Kimmswick, Mo.

hall 1. In an early American colonial house, the low-ceilinged main room that served as the center of family life, usually combining the functions of a kitchen, dining room, living room, and workroom for activities such as spinning, sewing, and candle making; in colonial days, often called a keeping room; *see also* **hall-and-parlor plan.** 2. An imposing entrance hall; also called a living hall. 3. A large room for assembly, entertainment, and the like. 4. A small, relatively primitive dwelling having a **one-room plan**, built by some early settlers in America. 5. A manor house. 6. A **corridor.**

which contained the best furniture, as well as a bed for the parents. These rooms were separated by a wall containing a massive chimney that served both rooms. Access to the loft space above was usually provided by a stairway in the hall, near the chimney. As the family prospered, windows were added in the loft space, either in dormers or in the gable-end walls, thereby providing light and ventilation, and making this space much more livable. In colonies in the South, the hall-and-parlor plan commonly included a central corridor running from front to back between the two rooms; **exterior chimneys** were located in the end walls.

hall,2

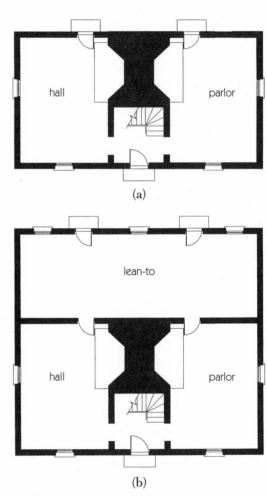

(a)

(b)

hall-and-parlor plan
(a) plan; (b) plan with added lean-to

hall-and-parlor plan A relatively common **floor plan** of many early colonial American houses, especially during the latter half of the 17th century and the early part of the 18th century; essentially a **two-room plan.** In New England the front door opened into a small vestibule, called a **porch,** which contained two interior doors leading to the two rooms of the house. One room was the **hall,1** which served as the center of activity for the entire family; the other was the **parlor,**

hall chamber In an early colonial American home having a **hall-and-parlor plan,** a bedroom directly above the **hall.**

halved-and-lapped notch Same as **half-cut notch.**

hammer beam A short, massive horizontal wood beam that projects from a wall at the foot of a **principal rafter** which it supports; extends from the wall to the end of a **wall bracket.**

hand-wrought nail *See* **wrought nail.**

hanging gable At the **gable end** of a barn or house, a small extension of the roof structure beyond the end wall, usually located at the ridge; encloses a heavy beam that supports the rigging used to hoist materials to the storage area directly under the roof.

hanging pew In Anglican churches in Virginia during the first half of the 18th century, a pew raised on posts and usually set apart from the less prestigious seating, with access by a private stair. Worshipers paid for this privilege.

hanging stile Same as **hinge stile.**

hard-burnt brick, hard-fired brick A brick or clay unit that has been molded to the desired shape and then baked in a kiln at an elevated temperature, thereby considerably increasing its mechanical strength and resistance to moisture and greatly improving its weather resistance. *See* **brick.**

hatch In a floor or roof of a building, an opening that is equipped with an operable cover; used for ventilation or to allow the passage of people or goods from one level in the building to another level. Also called a bulkhead.

haunch That part of an arch between the **crown** of the arch and the masonry units that receive and distribute the stress at the ends of the arch.

hay barrack An open-sided structure in which hay is stored; usually had a four- or five-cornered roof that moved up and down on poles to provide direct cover for the hay stored under the roof; usually used to store the overflow of hay from the main barn, offering a modest amount of protection against the weather. Once found on Dutch colonial farms and in the western United States following the great migration to the West. Also called a Dutch barn.

hay hood Same as **hanging gable.**

hayloft The upper part of a barn in which hay is stored.

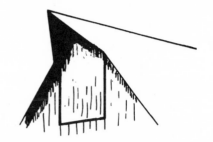

hanging gable

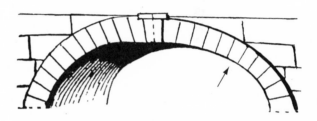

haunch

hay barrack

head The top or upper member of any architectural element; for example, the horizontal cross member, atop the frame of a door or window, between the **jambs**.

head: door to Declaration Chamber, Independence Hall (1731–1736 and later), Philadelphia, Pa.

header 1. A brick or stone, laid horizontally, with its length perpendicular to the face of the wall and its end exposed so that its smallest dimension is vertical; *see* **brick.** 2. A framing member that crosses and supports the ends of joists, rafters, or the like.

header bond A pattern of brickwork consisting entirely of **headers,1;** usually, each **course** of headers is displaced by half the width of one header with respect to the headers in the course above and the course below; found, for example, in early eastern Maryland brickwork.

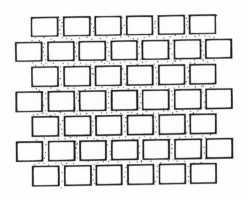

header bond

head molding Same as **hood molding.**

hearth The floor of a fireplace, usually composed of brick, tile, or stone; may extend into the room. *See also* **back hearth.**

hearth (1680): Connecticut

hearthstone A single large stone forming the **hearth** of a fireplace. This term is also used as a synonym for the hearth itself.

heavy-timber construction Wood construction in which fire resistance is increased by (a) using structural timbers of specified minimum dimensions; (b) using wood floors and roofs of specified minimum thickness and composition; (c) using bearing walls and nonbearing exterior walls of noncombustible construction; (d) using approved fastenings, construction details, and adhesives for structural members; and (e) avoiding concealed spaces under floors and roofs. Such construction, devised in the early 19th century in response to numerous fires in New England textile mills, represented a major step forward in the fire protection of timber-framed buildings in America.

hedgerow Trees and shrubs planted in a row, forming a fence that encloses or separates fields.

helical stair Same as **spiral stair.**

helm roof A sloping roof having four flat faces, each of which is steeply pitched and rises to a point, forming a spire; each of these flat faces has a gable at its base.

helm roof

henhouse *See* **poultry house.**

heptastyle A term descriptive of a **portico** having seven columns in front.

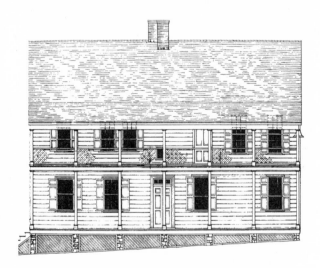

heptastyle
portico, Washington's Headquarters, Rocky Hill, N.J.

hermitage A private retreat or secluded hideaway in a garden, usually on an estate.

herringbone, herringbone pattern A directional zigzag pattern formed by assembling adjacent rows of rectangular bricks, strips of wood, or other finishing materials.

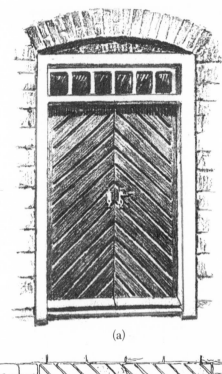

(a)

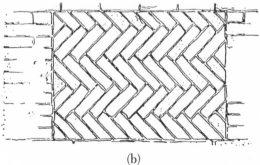

(b)

herringbone pattern
(a) entry door of a Moravian house (c. 1773),
Bethlehem, Pa.; (b) brick bond pattern on a wall

herringbone matching An arrangement of wood-veneered surfaces in which the veneer has been taken from the same log, thereby permitting successive side-by-side sheets of veneer to be alternately placed faceup and facedown. This alternation produces a symmetrical mirror image of the joints between pairs of adjacent sheets.

hewn-and-pegged joint   A **mortise-and-tenon joint** formed by cutting a tenon to fit a corresponding mortise, joining these two members, and then securing them with a wood pin. Such joints are used, for example, in **post-and-girt framing.**

hewn overhang   In an early colonial **timber-framed house**, the modest projection of an upper story beyond the story immediately below it, usually no more than a few inches. A heavy timber post extended from the foundation of the house to the top of the upper story; this post was hewn away from just below the upper story down to the **groundsill**, creating the appearance of an upper story slightly overhanging the lower one. Also called false overhang. Compare with **framed overhang.**

hexastyle   A term descriptive of a **portico** having six columns in front.

hex barn   A barn decorated with painted hex symbols called *hexenfoos*, i.e., colorful geometric patterns set within circles, particularly found on barns in areas settled by the Pennsylvania Dutch. The symbols, derived from similar ones in Switzerland, probably were originally intended to protect the animals from harm cast by the "evil eye."

hick joint   In masonry work, same as **flush joint.**

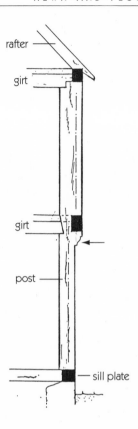

hewn overhang

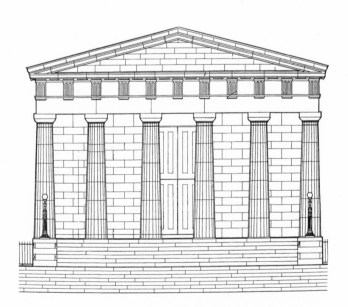

hexastyle: Old Customs House (1839), Erie, Pa.

hex barn decorations

H-hinge A type of **strap hinge** forming the letter **H** when the hinge is open; usually fabricated of wrought iron in colonial America; now made of steel or brass.

high relief Sculptured, carved, or embossed work in which the figures project considerably beyond the plane of the background. Also called alto-relievo.

high-rise building A building having many stories; sufficiently tall so that an elevator is essential. *See also* **skyscraper.**

High-Tech architecture A loose term applied to architecture, from about 1950 onward, that has as its goal the conspicuous use of factory-made or prefabricated building components. Mechanical and electrical building services and pipes often are not only revealed but emphasized, thereby accentuating the machinelike aspects of the building; for example, ducts and pipes may be painted in different bright colors to indicate their respective functions. The Eames House (1949), in Palisades, California, designed in collaboration with Eero Saarinen, represents an early outstanding example of the use of factory-made and prefabricated components in domestic architecture.

High Victorian architecture *See* **Victorian architecture.**

High Victorian Gothic A very elaborate, highly detailed interpretation of the **Gothic Revival** in its last phase in America, from about 1860 to 1890; may have bands of **polychromed** masonry, and brickwork or roofing tiles of different colors; is heavy in appearance, as exemplified by its massive gables and porches, and can be difficult to categorize because many examples of the earlier Gothic Revival are also very elaborate. This adaptation is sometimes referred to as Late Gothic Revival or as Ruskinian Gothic, after the influential English writer and art critic John Ruskin (1819–1900). As described under **Victorian architecture**, some architectural historians shun the use of any stylistic term making use of the adjective *Victorian*, contending that the term is merely descriptive of an age that encompassed a number of specific exuberant, ornate, and highly decorative architectural styles.

High Victorian Italianate A term sometimes applied to the latter phase of **Italianate style**, from the 1860s to 1880. In general, it is more elaborate than the earlier Italianate style, but this difference can be difficult to discern since earlier work also may be fairly ornate.

H-hinge
Old Wails House, Hopewell Township, N.J.

High Victorian Gothic
St. Clemens Church (1859), John Notman, Architect, Philadelphia, Pa.

hinge A movable joint used to attach, support, and turn the frame of a door or window sash about a pivot; consists of two plates, joined together by a pin, that support the door and connect it to its frame, enabling the door to swing open or closed. *See also* **butterfly hinge, butt hinge, dovetail hinge, H-hinge, HL-hinge, side hinge, strap hinge.**

hinge: carved from wood, used only in colonial areas where metal was scarce

hinge stile The vertical structural member of a door frame on which the hinges are fixed and about which the door pivots. Also called a hanging stile.

hip The inclined external angle formed at the junction of two adjacent sloping sides of a roof or the sloping side and sloping end of a roof.

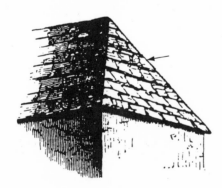

hip

hip knob A vertically projecting ornament placed atop an end of the ridge of a **hipped roof,** at a point where the hip rafters meet.

hip-on-gable roof Same as **jerkinhead roof.**

hipped dormer A **dormer** whose roof has flat surfaces that slope upward at the front of the dormer as well as on both sides; may be truncated to form a horizontal surface on top; especially found, for example, in **French Eclectic architecture, Prairie style, Shingle style.**

hipped dormer

hipped-gable roof A seldom-used term for a **jerkinhead roof.**

hipped roof, hip roof A roof comprising adjacent flat surfaces that slope upward from all sides of the perimeter of the building, requiring a **hip rafter** along each intersection of the inclined surfaces. *See also* **pyramidal roof.**

hipped roof

hip rafter A rafter located along the intersection where two sloping roof surfaces meet in a **hipped roof.** Also called an angle rafter.

Hispanic Colonial architecture *See* **Spanish Colonial architecture.**

Historic American Buildings Survey (HABS)
A collection of **measured drawings**, photographs, and
records of American buildings, constructions, or sites
that (a) are of particular historical interest, significance, or are representative of a particular architectural style; (b) represent important methods of construction; (c) were designed by a major American
architect; and/or (d) are typical of work by an ethnic
group within the United States. Housed in the Library
of Congress, HABS represents an important, useful,
and significant resource for anyone having a serious
interest in American architecture. Address: National
Park Service, Department of the Interior, P.O. Box
37127, Washington, DC 20013-7127.

historic preservation *See* **building preservation.**

HL-hinge A type of **H-hinge** that has a horizontal
extension added to one foot of the hinge; in colonial
days, usually fabricated of wrought iron; now, usually
made of steel or brass.

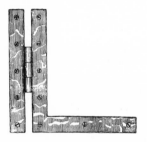

HL-hinge

hob At the back or side of a fireplace, a built-in ledge
or shelf on which a pot or kettle can be placed for
warming.

hob

hogan The traditional single-family dwelling of the
Navajo of the American Southwest, primarily in Arizona and western New Mexico; usually has a framework constructed of logs, poles, branches, and sticks
that is covered with a layer of bark and then a thick
layer of mud or sod; the entryway usually faces east.
The floor is often partially below ground level and can
be as large as 30 feet (9m) in diameter. A smoke hole
centered at the top of the structure provides light and

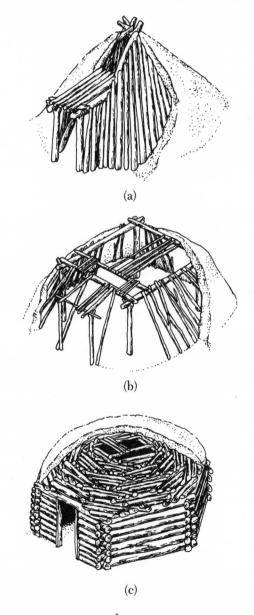

(a)

(b)

(c)

hogan
(a) a conical forked-pole hogan; (b) four-sided leaning-
log hogan; (c) six-sided stacked-log hogan

carries off fumes and smoke from an open firepit located directly below; there are no windows in a hogan. The design of such dwellings has varied with time and with the construction materials available. Although there are variations, most hogans fall into one of the following categories:

Conical forked-pole hogan: The earliest type of hogan, this dwelling had a framework of three heavy poles with forks at their upper ends. These forks were lashed together at their tops; additional lighter poles leaned against this conical forked-pole framework. The spaces between the poles were filled with chinking and sealed, forming a somewhat conical dwelling.

Four-sided leaning-log hogan: A dwelling having a framework consisting of four vertical logs with forks at their upper ends, which are set into the ground in a rectangular array. The poles are then interconnected at their upper ends by horizontal beams. Light poles are then leaned against this four-sided structure, forming a rigid framework that is somewhat domelike in character.

Stacked-log (hexagonal) hogan: A six-sided dwelling, constructed of horizontally stacked logs, arrayed in the shape of a hexagon at the base of the structure; this shape is carried up to a level just above the wood entry door; above this height, the shape is maintained but each hexagon decreases in size with increasing height, so that the roof is domelike.

hollow molding A concave, often circular molding. Also called a cavetto or scotia.

hollow-newel stair Same as **open-newel stair.**

hollow wall Same as **cavity wall**.

homestead A tract of land, 160 acres in area, that settlers acquired under the Homestead Act of 1862, passed by Congress to promote westward expansion; also, the house built on such a tract. This amount of acreage was deemed adequate for the support of one family under the provisions of this act. Any citizen who was head of a family and over 21 years of age could purchase surveyed public land from the government. The land would be acquired after 5 years of continuous occupancy and the payment of a fee ranging from $26 to $34. The Homestead Act had the general effect of fostering the Jeffersonian ideal of the nation having self-sufficient farmers who owned and tilled their own land.

honeysuckle ornament Same as **anthemion.**

hood 1. A covering or housing above a door or window to provide shelter and/or a decorative element. 2. A covering or housing over a fireplace to direct the smoke, odors, or noxious vapors into the chimney flue.

hood,1: supported by brackets, above a doorway (1814), Charlestown, Mass.

hooded crown The upper termination of a window that is covered by a **hood,1.**

hood molding The projecting **molding** of the arch over a door or window, usually intended to discharge rainwater from the face of the wall; usually called a label molding if it extends horizontally across the opening. Found, for example, in the **Châteauesque style** and the **Italianate style.**

hopper head Same as **leader head.**

hopper window A window having a **sash** that is hinged along the lower edge of its frame; the sash is usually much wider than it is high and tilts inward when the window is opened.

horse block In America before the advent of paved streets, a block or platform, with steps, used for mounting or dismounting from a horse; often set near the front door of a building. Also called an upping block.

horse shed A rough structure having one or more open sides, once used to shelter horses temporarily.

horseshoe arch A rounded arch whose curve is a little greater than a semicircle so that the opening at the bottom is narrower than the widest span of the arch; occasionally found in **Moorish Revival** buildings in America. Also called a Moorish arch.

horseshoe arch

hot closet In colonial days and beyond, a closet adjacent to a fireplace or oven; used for drying damp clothes.

hothouse A **greenhouse** that is artificially heated. *See also* **conservatory** and **orangery**.

house-and-a-half Same as a **three-quarter Cape house**.

house raising The erection of structural framing for a **timber-framed house** with the assistance of neighbors who gather at the site of the house for this purpose. *See* **barn raising**.

H-plan The basic **plan** of a building having the shape of a capital letter **H**, with an open courtyard at both the front and the back.

hull An obsolete term for the framework of a building.

hydraulic cement *See* **cement.**

hyperbolic paraboloid roof A roof in the shape of a geometric figure called a *hyperbolic paraboloid*. The entire roof structure rests on only two supports, giving it an appearance somewhat resembling a bird in flight. An outstanding example is the Catalano house (1955) in Raleigh, North Carolina, by Eduardo Catalano (1917–   ).

hyphen A connecting link (for example, a covered walkway) between a large, centrally located house and its dependencies or wings. The house and its hyphens may be in a straight line or form a curve. *See also* **five-part mansion.**

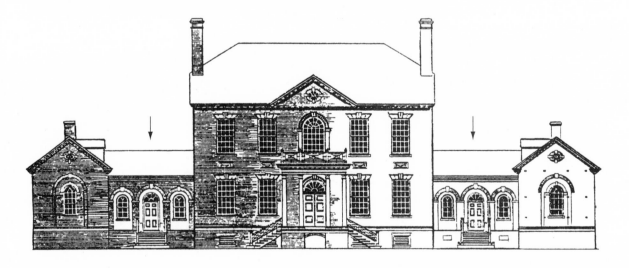

hyphen

I

icehouse From colonial America until well into the 19th century, a building for storing ice, usually cut from lakes or ponds, for use in the spring and fall. It was often located in a shady area and usually had overhanging eaves and thick exterior walls, packed with straw or sawdust to minimize thermal loss; commonly painted white to lessen the absorption of radiation from the sun. The ice was usually contained in a space at least partially below ground level. The melted ice water was drained through a pipe to a lower elevation; sometimes it was fed through in a room below, where it served to cool a room used as a storage area for dairy products. In some areas of the South, ice was shipped in from as far away as New England. Thomas Jefferson (1743–1826) designed two icehouses for his home Monticello, one of which had a depth of 16 feet (4.9m) and could hold as much as 60 wagonloads of ice.

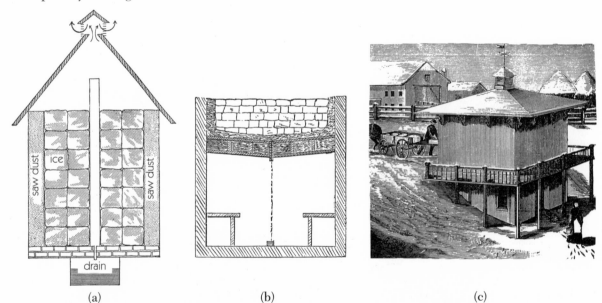

(a)   (b)   (c)

icehouse: (a) basic components, including thermally insulated walls and a drain; (b) melted ice water drains to a reservoir in the room directly below, used for storing dairy products; (c) an exterior view of an icehouse

iglu, igloo A hemispherical shell, built of blocks of ice or packed snow by Eskimos in Alaska, which served as a temporary dwelling for a single family. It was usually about 10 to 15 feet (3–4.5m) in diameter at its base, with the floor often partially below the surrounding terrain. Daylight within was provided by one or more blocks of relatively transparent freshwater ice or by an opening covered with a piece of translucent seal intestine. Entry was usually through a domed passageway that prevented snow or wind from being blown directly into the interior. For other types of Eskimo dwellings, *see* **barabara, pole house, sod house, winter house.**

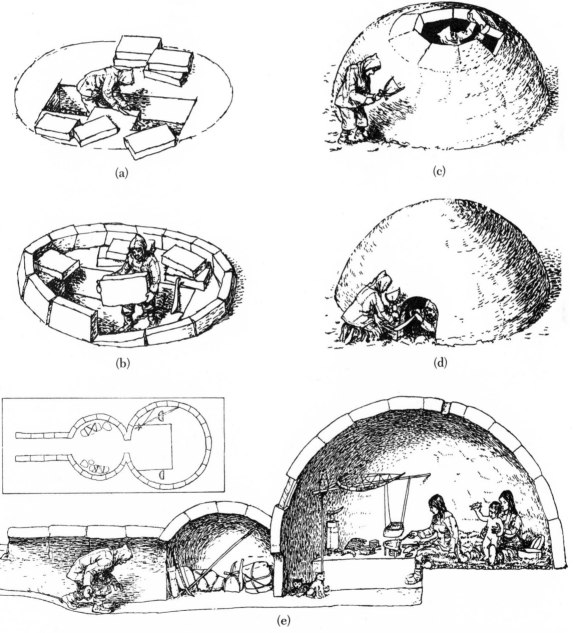

(a)

(b)

(c)

(d)

(e)

iglu: construction technique: (a) cutting the blocks of ice or packed snow; (b) placing the blocks in spiral-shaped rows to create a dome-shaped structure; (c) completing the dome and plastering the exterior of the blocks with snow to provide a tight seal; (d) cutting a hole in the wall to provide an entrance; (e) the completed dwelling with the addition of a domed passageway to the entrance

I-house A side-gabled house, usually one-and-a-half or two stories high, one room deep, and two rooms wide; the two rooms usually have an entrance hall between them containing a central stairway. Such houses were popular in the Tidewater region of the colonial south before about 1750, were very popular as folk houses from about 1850 to 1890, and were again used widely throughout the country as one type of Gingerbread folk architecture between about 1870 and 1910.

imbrication Overlapping rows of shaped tiles or shingles that resemble overlapping fish scales; often used, for example, in the **Queen Anne style.** Also called fishscale pattern.

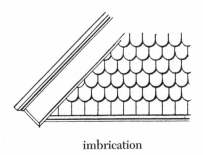

imbrication

impost A masonry unit, or course of units, often distinctively profiled and decorative, that receives and distributes the thrust at one end of an arch. *See also* **abutment** and **springer,1.**

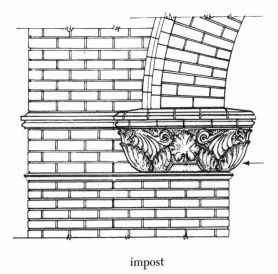

impost

in antis *See* **anta, distyle in antis.**

Indian dwellings *See* **American Indian dwellings.**

infilling In **timber-framed houses** in early colonial New England, a mixture of clay and chopped straw, mud, plaster, **wattle-and-daub,** or brick, set between the heavy structural timbers of a wall to improve its structural rigidity, thermal insulation, and fire resistance. This construction technique, used well into the 1700s, followed its prototypes in England, where the use of infilling was an established tradition. The infilling in exterior walls was often given a covering such as stucco, plaster, or clapboards to protect the surface from rain and snow. *See also* **bousillage, fachwerk,** and **pierrotage.**

infilling: in a timber-framed house

inflatable structure *See* **pneumatic structure.**

inglenook A corner adjacent to the hearth of a fireplace, often provided with seating.

inglenook

inlay A shaped piece of one material embedded in another material as a form of surface ornamentation. *See also* **intarsia** and **marquetry.**

inner hearth That part of a **hearth** contained within a fireplace.

inset dormer A **dormer** that is partially set *below* a sloping roof, unlike the usual dormer that projects entirely *above* the sloping roof.

inset porch Same as **integral porch.**

inside chimney Same as **interior chimney.**

intarsia Mosaic inlay, especially a form of wood inlay, sometimes used in **Italian Renaissance Revival** buildings in America from about 1890 to 1930.

integral garage A garage that is part of the structure of a building. Garages of this type were not built in America until around 1920.

integral lean-to A colonial New England timber-framed house with a **lean-to** that was part of the original construction, not a later addition or separate structure. This permitted the use of continuous rafters between the roof ridge and the eaves, thus providing a long, sloping roof of uniform pitch. This construction gave the house a profile resembling a box for holding salt then much used in the British colonies in America, from which the term **saltbox house** is derived. Also called original lean-to. *See also* **lean-to** and **added lean-to.**

inlay

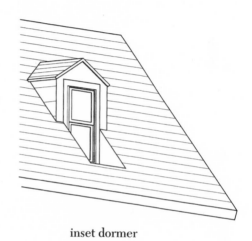

inset dormer

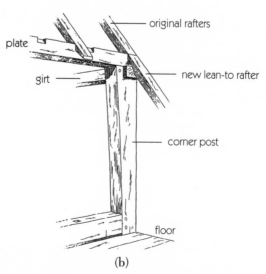

(a)   (b)

integral lean-to: (a) section through a two-story colonial New England house shown on the right, with lean-to addition, on the left; (b) detail showing a lean-to rafter joined to an original rafter to support a saltbox roof

integral porch A porch whose floor is set within the main structure of a house, rather than being attached to the house, as in a **projecting porch.** Also called an inset porch.

integral porch

intercolumniation The clear space between two adjacent columns in a series of columns, usually measured at the lower parts of the shafts of the columns; if the spacing is equal to 1½ diameters of the columns, it is called *pycnostyle*; if the spacing is 2 diameters, it is called *systyle*; if the spacing is 2¼ diameters, it is called *eustyle;* if the spacing is 3 diameters, it is called *diastyle*; if the spacing is 4 diameters, it is called *areostyle*.

interfilling Same as **infilling.**

interior chimney A chimney that is built within the walls of a building; often categorized according to its location, e.g., **centrally located chimney, end chimney,** or **inside chimney.** Compare with **exterior chimney**.

International Revival A term occasionally used to describe a 1970s adaptation of the **International style** that emphasizes the use of pure geometric forms.

International style A style of architecture applied to residences and public buildings that is minimalist in concept, is devoid of regional characteristics, stresses functionalism, and rejects all nonessential decorative elements; typically this style emphasizes the horizontal aspects of a building. It developed during the 1920s and 1930s, in western Europe principally in the **Bauhaus** school under Walter Gropius (1883–1969), and in America particularly as a result of a highly successful exhibit at the Museum of Modern Art in New York City entitled *International Style: Architecture in 1932* and a book entitled *The International Style— Architecture since 1922* by Henry-Russell Hitchcock (1903–1987) and Philip Johnson (1906–   ). Outstanding early examples in America of the International style include the buildings on the campus of the Illinois Institute of Technology (1939–1956) in Chicago, designed by Ludwig Mies van der Rohe (1886–1969). *See also* **Bauhaus** and **Miesian.**

Buildings in the International style usually exhibit many of the following characteristics:

Façade and exterior wall treatments: Simple geometric forms, often rectilinear, making use of reinforced-concrete and steel construction with a nonstructural skin; occasionally, cylindrical surfaces; unadorned, smooth wall surfaces, typically of glass, steel, or stucco painted white; a complete absence of ornamentation and decoration; often, an entire blank wall; often, a cantilevered upper floor or balcony. Houses in this style are characterized by open interior spaces and are commonly asymmetrical. In contrast, commercial buildings in this style are not only symmetrical but appear as a series of repetitive elements.

Roof treatments: A flat roof, without a ledge, eaves, or coping, that terminates at the plane of the wall.

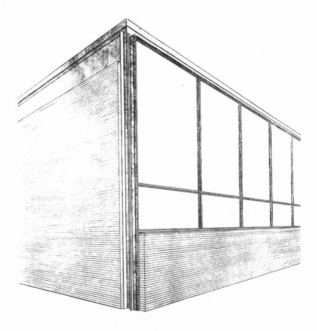

International style: Library and Administration Building, Illinois Institute of Technology (1944), Chicago, Ill.; Ludwig Mies van der Rohe, Architect

Window treatments: Large areas of floor-to-ceiling glass or curtain walls of glass; metal window frames set flush with the exterior walls, often in horizontal bands; casement windows; sliding windows; glass-to-glass joints at the corners, without framing.

Doorway treatments: Conspicuously plain, lacking decorative detailing.

intersecting gable *See* **cross gable.**

intertie A horizontal structural member that interconnects upright **posts**. Also called a nogging piece.

intrados The inner face or interior surface of an arch or vault, forming the underside.

Ionic capital The topmost member of a column of the **Ionic order**; the twin **volutes** in the Greek Ionic order are larger and more conspicuous than the corresponding volutes in the Roman Ionic order.

Ionic order One of the five **orders** in Classical architecture, originated by the Ionian Greeks; the shafts of the columns usually have twenty-four **flutes** and are separated by narrow fillets rather than meeting in sharp arrises; has capitals with large **volutes**, a fasciated entablature, a **frieze** having no triglyphs (sometimes adorned with a continuous band of figures), and dentils in the cornice; elegant detailing; is less heavy in appearance than the Doric and less elaborate than the Corinthian; the pilasters are often fluted shafts with a capital consisting of a band of anthemions, with egg-and-dart molding above. *See also* illustrations under **base** and **entablature.**

iron A ductile metallic element from which pig iron and steel are made; used in its relatively crude form for making tools, castings, and the like. *See* **bar iron, cast iron, malleable iron, pig iron, wrought iron.**

iron back A cast-iron **fireback.**

iron framing A system of structural ironwork for buildings; often considered to have been first developed at the end of the 18th century. The **Crystal Palace,** constructed in New York City in 1853, provided a dramatic example of its application in America. *See* **cast iron** and **cast-iron architecture.**

ironwork Objects or parts of objects made of **cast iron** or **wrought iron;** frequently utilitarian in colonial America, but thereafter often elaborate and ornamental. *See also* **cast-iron lacework.**

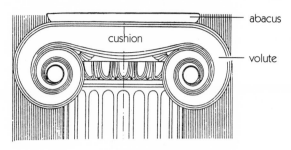

Ionic capital

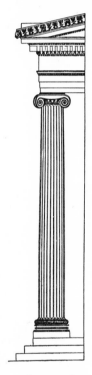

Ionic order

ironwork: Le Prêtre Mansion, New Orleans, La.

Italianate style A broad term generally representing an eclectic style of Italian-influenced residential and commercial architecture that was fashionable in America from the 1840s to around 1890 and beyond, with its peak popularity in the 1850s. Italianate-style residential buildings may be divided into the following categories:

Villas: Domestic architecture intended to resemble prosperous farmhouses or country manor houses of northern Italy; commonly two stories in height, with an **attic story.** Because a very large number of such houses were built, some writers use the term **Italian Villa style** as a synonym for the Italianate style.

Town houses: Urban row houses from about 1860 to 1880, commonly three or four stories in height; a loose interpretation of more formal **Renaissance architecture.**

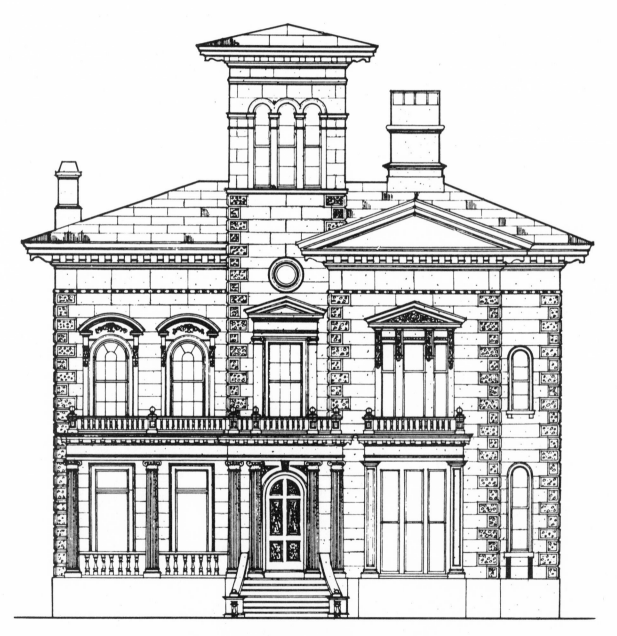

Italianate style: Libby House (1859), Portland, Maine

Palazzi: See **Italian Renaissance Revival.**

Commercial Italianate style: A style having features somewhat similar to the Italianate style, but with buildings usually having a raised pediment above the roof line at the center of the façade, often with the name of the building and/or the date of its completion, and a cast-iron façade. *See also* **Tuscan Villa style.**

A division is sometimes made between early and late Italianate-style architecture. The latter phase, sometimes referred to as **High Victorian Italianate**, is usually more highly decorated than its earlier counterpart. However, this division is often arbitrary, because some earlier Italianate can be equally ornate.

Residential buildings in the Italianate style commonly exhibit many of the following characteristics:

Façade and exterior wall treatments: Either a symmetrical or an asymmetrical façade; houses are usually two-storied with wall surfaces of smooth ashlar masonry, rough-cast brick, or (less often) stucco or wood clapboard siding; classical columns, sometimes of cast iron, and pilasters; balustraded balconies; often, a **belt course** encircling the building; wide, projecting cornices with decorative brackets for support; corner quoins; a square tower; a porch, often arcaded, on one or more sides.

Roof treatments: Usually, a low- to moderate-pitched gabled roof and/or **hipped roof**, sometimes front-gabled; often, a cupola; typically, widely overhanging eaves supported by elaborate wood or pressed-metal brackets (often in pairs) evenly spaced along the eaves; chimney shafts with ornate caps. The town house usually has a flat or very low-pitched roof.

Window treatments: Typically, tall, relatively narrow double-hung window sashes, particularly on the ground floor; windows frequently in pairs or triple units treated as a single architectural element; occasionally, bay windows; commonly, windows with arched rather than rectangular sashes; windows typically topped with a segmental arch, with a hooded crown, or with a crown supported by decorative brackets. Occasionally, rectangular windows set between the brackets supporting the eaves. Frequently, a cupola or belvedere on the roof, often with two or three arched windows set in each face; operable windows in this location could aid air circulation throughout the house. In row houses, in both the upper and lower sashes, mullions divide the sash vertically into two panes.

Doorway treatments: Commonly, a pair of decoratively paneled double doors at the main entrance, the upper parts of which are glazed; often, a round-topped door or a door set in a round arch.

Commercial Italianate style: bank in the Midwest

Italian molding A wide, heavy **bolection molding**, often used to surround a fireplace.

Italian order Same as **Composite order.**

Italian Renaissance Revival A style of architecture emulating the Renaissance palazzi of northern Italy; most popular in America from about 1890 to 1930. Buildings are usually rectangular or square in plan. Houses are usually ornate and two or three stories high; public buildings are usually imposing and also three or four stories high. An outstanding example of this style, long before it became popular, is the Athenaeum (1847) in Philadelphia, designed by John Notman (1810–1865). Sometimes called Italian Renaissance style or Second Renaissance Revival. This style is occasionally subdivided into the *North Italian* or *Venetian mode* and the *Romano-Tuscan* or *Florentine mode.* These are somewhat similar, although the North Italian has arched windows that are usually larger than those in the Romano-Tuscan; the North Italian façades tend to be more ornamented and elaborate than those of the austere Romano-Tuscan mode.

Italian Renaissance Revival buildings usually exhibit many of the following characteristics:

Façade and exterior wall treatments: The façades of homes are commonly symmetrical and flat, with masonry or stucco walls; often, with a different architectural treatment on different stories, for example, rusticated masonry at the ground-floor level but stucco on the floors above; frequently, an elaborate **belt course** between stories; a massive cornice that rests directly on the architrave, the frieze being omitted; often, rusticated quoins, pilasters, dentils, and decorative detailing; a recessed entry porch flanked with classical columns or pilasters; often, a **raised basement**, resulting in a short flight of stairs from street level up to a **piano nobile**; occasionally, a balustraded balcony;

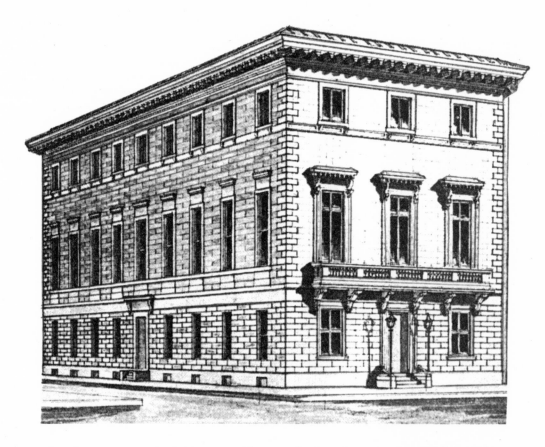

Italian Renaissance Revival: (a) a very early example, the Athenaeum (1847), Philadelphia, Pa.

round arches and arcading on porches. Public buildings, usually of stone masonry, may have prominent arcading on the ground floor and a recessed arcaded gallery on the floors above.

Roof treatments: Commonly, a low- to moderate-pitched, ceramic-tiled **hipped roof**; widely overhanging eaves with decorative supporting brackets. If the roof is flat, there is frequently a balustrade or roof-line parapet above an elaborate cornice that may be ornamented with dentils and modillions.

Window treatments: Full-length ground-floor windows, often with arches above; commonly, a different type of window on each story, the windows on the uppermost story usually being the smallest and simplest, square in shape; three adjacent windows often treated as a single architectural unit. In elaborate

examples of this style, on the second story, **window heads,** often pedimented (triangular arches, flattened arches, or segmental arches) and supported by **ancons**; on the ground floor, elaborate, tall, narrow windows placed in a regular pattern, set symmetrically on both sides of the main entrance; window sashes with multiple lights within the sashes, framed with moldings and an **architrave** above.

Doorway treatments: Frequently, arches above the exterior doors; a hooded entryway; often, an **entablature,** supported by pilasters, over the entrance.

Italian Renaissance style Same as **Italian Renaissance Revival.**

Italian roof *See* **hipped roof.**

Italian Villa style *See* **Italianate style.**

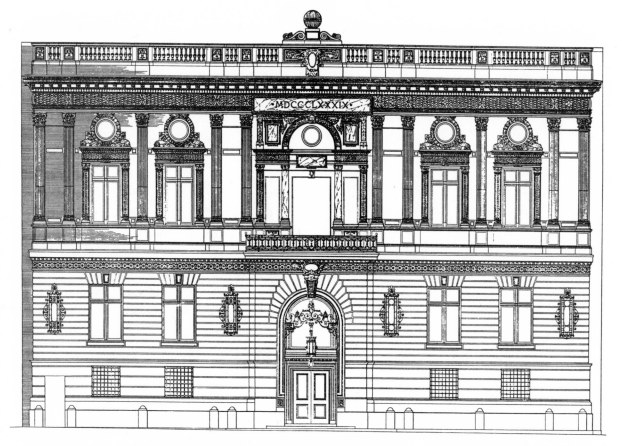

Italian Renaissance Revival: (b) Century Association (1889), New York City; McKim, Mead & White, Architects

J

jacal 1. A rectangular structure, either partially enclosed or open on all four sides, used as a temporary storage place, such as for grain; the roof is usually flat, and is supported by two to four posts on each side of the structure (depending on its size) and often covered with a layer of adobe mud or straw. 2. In the American Southwest, a crude house having walls built of closely spaced upright sticks or poles driven into the ground, with small branches interwoven between them; then covered with mud or an adobe clay; usually plastered to provide additional weather protection; a flat roof is supported by horizontal logs (**vigas**) and then covered with thatching, often with a layer of adobe mud atop the thatching. 3. Same as **wigwam.**

jack arch Same as **flat arch.**

jack rafter Any **rafter** that is shorter than the usual length of the rafters used in the same roof.

jack rib Any rib in a framed arch or dome that is shorter than the other ribs.

jack timber Any timber in a framework which, being intercepted by some other piece, is shorter than the rest.

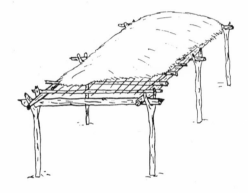

jacal,1

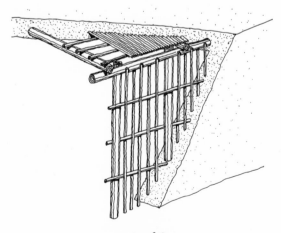

jacal,2

Jacobean architecture An imprecise term applied to early-17th-century English architecture in the Tudor Gothic, Elizabethan, or Early Stuart styles, or applied to buildings erected during the reign of James I (1603–1625) but continuing beyond his death, rarely used in America. Houses were usually two to three stories high and might have elaborate multicurved Flemish gables, Tudor arches, and high, decorative chimneys; outwardly swinging, hinged casement windows were separated by stone or cement mullions that had small diamond-shaped panes of glass held in place by grooved strips of lead (i.e., by lead **cames**). Jacobean architecture was seldom used in America because its high cost restricted its use to the very affluent, but a few outstanding examples survive in Maryland and Virginia. One of the best-known is Bacon's Castle (1655) in Surry County, Virginia, which has a plan similar to that of a **cross house.**

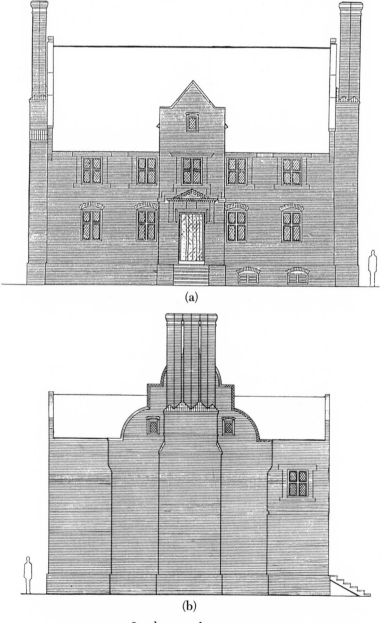

(a)

(b)

Jacobean architecture
Bacon's Castle (c. 1655), Surry County, Va.: (a) façade, restored; (b) west elevation

Jacobethan style, Jacobethan Revival A type of **Tudor Revival** architecture, of limited popularity in America from about 1895 to 1920 and beyond. This term, popularized by Henry-Russell Hitchcock (1903–1987), is a compound of the words *Jacobean* and *Elizabethan*.

Buildings in this style usually exhibit a number of the following characteristics:

Façade and exterior wall treatments: Often, front-facing gables that rise above the roof line; frequently, elaborate brickwork or stonework; quoins at the corners of the building; occasionally, turrets or towers.

Roof treatments: Stone **straight-line gables**, or **multicurved gables**, as in Flemish gables; tall, decorative chimneys.

Window treatments: Rectangular window frames, usually containing small, leaded panes of glass set in hinged casement sashes.

jail A place where individuals are confined, either while awaiting trial or serving time for minor offenses. In the early days of the American colonies and later, on the western frontier, jails often were built of masonry or thick hardwood planks, with window bars and hardware fabricated of wrought iron.

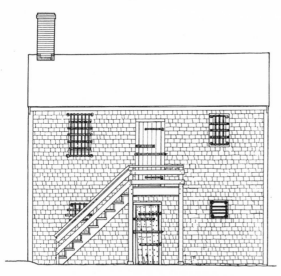

jail (1711): Nantucket, Mass.

jalousie A shutter or blind with fixed or adjustable slats, often of wood or glass; used to exclude rain and provide ventilation, shade, and visual privacy, found particularly in southern regions of the United States from the beginning of the 19th century onward.

jamb One of the vertical members at each side of an opening, such as a door frame, window frame, or fireplace.

jamb post An upright member (for example, a timber) at the side of a door opening.

Jeffersonian Classicism, Jeffersonian style A term occasionally applied to houses in the colonial South having a two-story pavilion and a full-width one- or two-story portico. *See* **Classical Revival style.**

jerkinhead roof A combination of a **gable roof** and a **hipped roof**. The gable rises vertically about halfway up to the ridge, then the roof is tilted back at a steep incline. Also called a clipped gable, docked gable, hipped gable, or hip-on-gable roof.

jerkinhead roof

jettied house A house having an overhanging second story. *See also* **garrison house.**

jettied house: birthplace in 1706 of Benjamin Franklin in Boston, Mass.; destroyed by fire in 1810

jetty *See* **overhang.**

jib cupboard A built-in cupboard that is covered by doors that are flush with, and treated in the same manner as, the surrounding wall so that it is concealed.

jib door A door that is flush with, and treated in the same manner as, the surrounding wall so that it is concealed; its hardware is not visible on the room side.

jigsaw work Wood boards cut with a jigsaw, ordinarily in elaborate patterns. *See also* **gingerbread** and **scrollwork.**

joinery The craft of woodworking by joining pieces of wood, especially the finish and trim on the interior of a structure, such as doors, paneling, sashes, or the like, as distinguished from carpentry, which suggests wood framing and rough woodwork.

joint The junction between adjacent surfaces (for example, between two wood members, masonry units, sheets, tiles, or timbers), or the place where two members or components are firmly held together by nails, cement, fasteners, mortar, or the like. For examples of specific types of joints, *see* **masonry joint** and **wood joint.**

joist One of a series of parallel horizontal beams of timber, reinforced concrete, or steel used to support floor and ceiling loads; the widest dimension of the beam is vertically oriented. In early colonial American timber-framed houses, the lower edges of exposed joists were often **chamfered** in an uncharacteristic display of ornamentation. They usually supported the flooring in two spans, for example, from **front girt** to the **summerbeam** and from **summerbeam** to the **rear girt**. *See also* **binding joist, boarding joist, ceiling joist, common joist, principal joist, sleeper joist.**

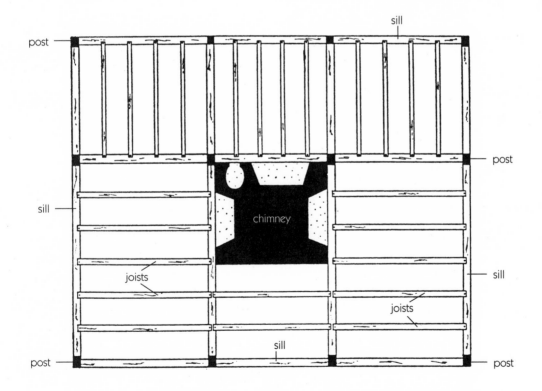

joists
shown on typical first floor framing plan of an early American Colonial home

K

keeping room In a colonial New England house, the principal room that served as a combination dining room, kitchen, living room, and workroom. A stairway or ladder usually led from the keeping room to a bedroom in the loft space above. Same as **hall,1.**

kettle crane Same as **fireplace crane.**

key pattern Same as **Greek key.**

keystone, key block The central wedged-shaped masonry block of an arch; often embellished. Until this block is in place, the arch cannot support any superimposed weight.

keystone arch An **arch** having a keystone at its center.

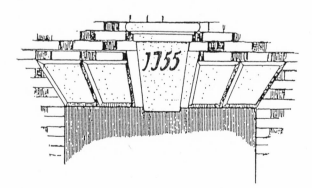

keystone: in splayed lintel, Pennsylvania Hospital (1755), Philadelphia, Pa.

keystone arch
New York City Public Library (1906)

ki One of a number of small dwellings used during the winter months by the Papago and Pima Indians of southern Arizona. In the 19th century, both these tribes lived in domed, circular structures having a post-and-beam framework at its center; saplings were bent over and tied together at their tops to form a domelike configuration that was covered with bark, a layer of grass, or the like that was then covered with an **adobe** plaster. The floor was partially excavated, and earth was banked around the perimeter at the base of the thatched walls. Later the Papago developed a rectangular flat-roofed structure of somewhat similar construction. During the very hot summers, the tribes lived chiefly in open-air shaded structures called **ramadas,2.**

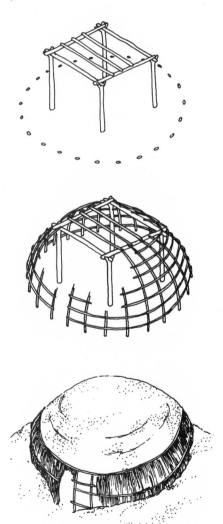

ki: construction sequence, Pima tribe

kick roof A roof having **flared eaves.**

kiln-fired brick *See* **burnt brick.**

king-post truss A structural support for a roof formed by two inclined rafters joined at the apex of their intersection; a horizontal **tie beam** connects the rafters near their lower ends, and a vertical central member (called the *king post*) connects the apex with the midpoint of the tie beam. Found, for example, in **French Vernacular architecture** of Louisiana.

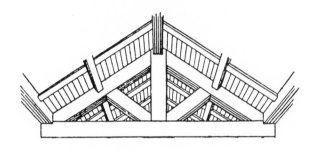

king-post truss

kitchen A room intended for the preparation and cooking of food; often, also where meals are eaten. In early colonial American houses, food was usually prepared in a multipurpose room called the **hall.** If one room were set aside to be used only as a kitchen, it was often located in a **lean-to** at the rear of the house. In more elegant homes, meals were usually prepared in a separate nearby building called an **outkitchen;** *see also* **cocina, cuzine, summer kitchen.**

kitchen: in a typical Shaker dwelling (c. 1820), Mt. Lebanon, N.Y.

kiva An assembly room, often partly or wholly underground, found in villages of certain tribes of Hopi and Pueblo Indians of the American Southwest; used for religious observances, ceremonial rituals, as a forum for clan discussion, for weaving, as a men's dormitory, and as a lounging area. The earthen floor is packed smooth by tamping and often surfaced with flat stones; there is a firepit in the center. The roof is supported by light hewn logs covered by small branches, matting, and a layer of earth commonly about six inches (15cm) thick. The structure is usually entered through a roof hatchway by means of a ladder whose poles extend well above the flat rooftop; this hatchway also serves as a smoke outlet for the firepit below. The earliest kivas, centuries ago, were circular in plan; after the arrival of Europeans, a rectangular plan evolved, usually having a north–south orientation along the long axis. *See also* **earthlodge.**

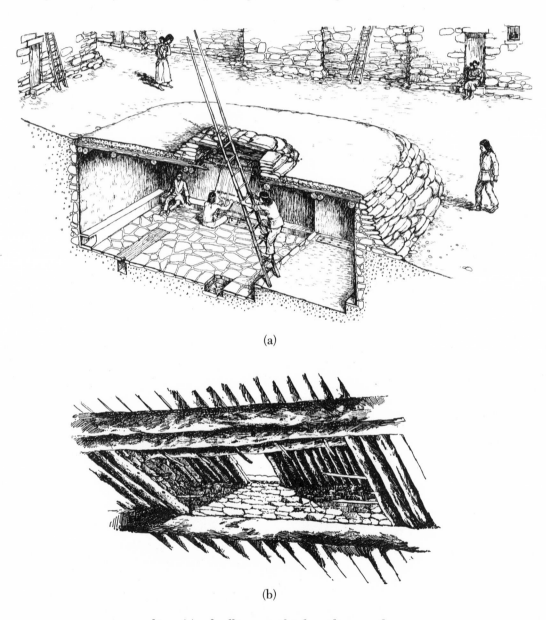

(a)

(b)

kiva: (a) a dwelling completely underground;
(b) detail showing a hatchway to a kiva, viewed from below

knee A piece of wood having a bend, either natural or artificially set.

knee brace A diagonal support placed across the angle between two members that are joined; serves to stiffen and strengthen the members.

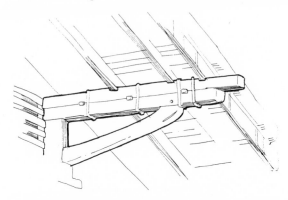

knee brace: Pitcairn House (1906), Pasadena, Calif.; Greene and Greene, Architects

knee rafter 1. A brace between a **principal rafter** and a **tie beam.** 2. In colonial America, a **principal rafter** having a bend in it.

knee roof A roof that slopes away from the ridge of the roof in two successive planes; symmetrical about its ridge, as a **mansard roof.**

knocker A hinged knob, bar, or ring of metal attached to the outer surface of an exterior door, which enables a person to announce his or her presence by striking it against a metal plate fastened to the door, or against the door itself.

knocker
Elizabeth Haddon House (1713), Haddonfield, N.J.

L

label molding A projecting molding on a building's exterior surface, usually over a door or window, which extends horizontally across the top of the opening and then vertically downward; used to discharge rainwater from the face of a wall. Especially found in **Carpenter Gothic, Châteauesque style, Collegiate Gothic, French Eclectic architecture, Gothic Revival, Tudor Revival.**

label stop The termination of a **label molding** in which the lower ends of the vertical portions of the label molding turn in a horizontal direction, away from the opening which it frames.

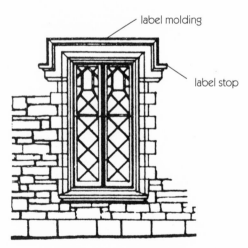

label molding and label stop

labyrinth fret Same as **Greek key.**

lacework *See* **cast-iron lacework** and **jigsaw work.**

ladrillo In **Spanish Colonial architecture** and derivatives, an adobe brick that has been kiln-dried rather than merely sun-dried, thereby providing increased durability, increased mechanical strength, and much greater protection against rain; usually about three inches (8cm) thick.

laid-on molding A **molding** that is nailed or otherwise fastened to a surface, rather than cut into the surface itself.

lamb's-tongue The end of a handrail that turns outward and downward from the rail; shaped somewhat like a tongue.

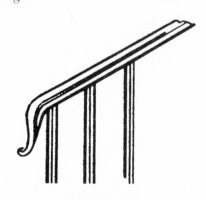

lamb's-tongue

lancet arch A sharply pointed two-centered arch whose centers of curvature are farther apart than the width of the arch; in America, especially found in **Carpenter Gothic, Châteauesque style, Collegiate Gothic, French Eclectic architecture, Gothic Revival, Tudor Revival.** Also called an acute arch.

lancet arch

lancet window A narrow window having the shape of a **lancet arch.**

lancet window

landing The horizontal platform at the end of a flight of stairs or between two flights of stairs.

landing newel A post that supports one end of a stair handrail; located on a stair landing or at a point where stairs change direction.

landmark 1. Any building, structure, or place that has a special character, special historic interest, and/or special aesthetic interest or value, as part of the devel-opment, heritage, or cultural characteristics of a town, city, state, or nation. 2. A formal designation of such status for a building by a national or local authority; *see also* **National Register of Historic Places.** 3. A monument, fixed object, or marker on the ground that designates the location of a land boundary.

landscape architect A person whose profession is the design and development of landscapes and gardens, whether as self-contained areas or to harmonize with existing or new buildings; often accomplished by modifying natural scenery, draining or adding small lakes or ponds, placing new trees, shrubs, and plants, and designing small buildings such as pavilions, pergolas, and recreational facilities. Andrew Jackson Downing (1815–1852), author of the popular book *A Treatise on the Theory and Practice of Landscape Gardening* in 1841, was greatly influential in establishing landscape architecture as a profession. Another early major figure in this field was Frederick Law Olmsted (1822–1903). He and Calvert Vaux (1824–1895), his partner in many projects, were the designers of Central Park (1857–1859) in New York City.

landscape window A **double-hung window** whose upper sash is highly decorated with small panes of colored glass; the lower sash of clear glass is a single pane and is larger than the upper sash.

lantern, lantern light A superstructure crowning a roof or dome, often glazed; provides light and/or ventilation to the space below. *See also* **belvedere** and **cupola.**

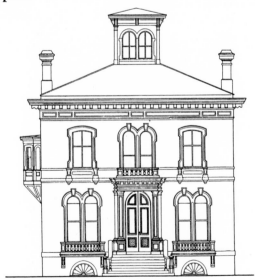

lantern
Albert Scott House (1861), Petersburg, Va.

lap notch Same as **half-cut notch.**

lap siding, lapped siding Same as **clapboards.**

lap splice The connecting, joining, or uniting of two similar members or pieces by overlapping their ends and fastening them, for example, by nails, screws, or rivets.

larder A place where food is stored; a **pantry.**

latch A simple fastening device for holding a door or gate in the closed position, for example, by means of a thin flat bar that falls or slides into a notch; such a latch is operated from the interior side of the door by lifting the lever. In colonial America latches could be operated from the exterior by pulling on a string that was passed through a hole in the door and tied to the lever, thus giving rise to the phrase "the latch string is out" as an indication of hospitality. *See also* **door latch, lift latch, Norfolk latch, Suffolk latch, thumb latch.**

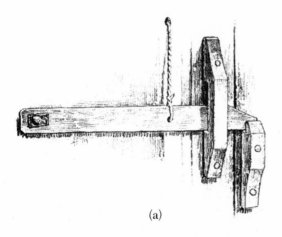

(a)

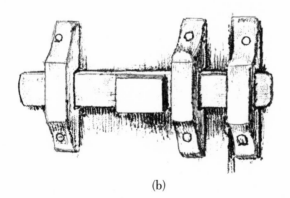

(b)

latch: constructed of wood,
(a) latch operated by a "latch string";
(b) a sliding latch

latch plate An **escutcheon** that protects the area of a door around a **latch.**

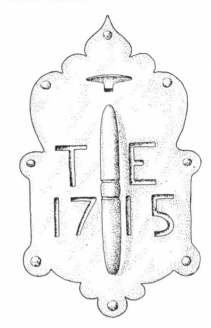

latch plate

Late Georgian style *See* **Georgian style.**

Late Gothic Revival The last phase of the **Gothic Revival** (*see* **High Victorian Gothic**); descriptive of the **Collegiate Gothic** style in America in the early part of the 20th century, in which an attempt was made to emulate its **Gothic architecture** prototype with some degree of accuracy.

Late Victorian architecture A term occasionally applied to architecture in the **Queen Anne style.**

lath A building material used as a base for the application of plaster. *See* **wood lath, expanded-metal lath,** and **metal lath.**

latia In **Spanish Colonial architecture** of the American Southwest and its derivatives, one of a number of light, relatively straight saplings, usually about three feet (0.9m) long, that have been stripped of their bark and laid across log beams (**vigas**) of a structure, either diagonally, so as to create a herringbone ceiling pattern, or at right angles to the vigas. A matting of reeds or the like, placed over the latias, is then covered with a layer of tamped earth, dried mud, or adobe mixed with grass to serve as the roof of the structure.

latia labrada A **latia** that has been split along its length; usually laid across **vigas** with its flat side down.

lattice A structure formed by the crossing of laths, rods, bars, or thin strips of wood or metal, usually arranged in a diagonal pattern or a square pattern; often used as a screen, as ornamental grillwork, or as a barrier to prevent entry into an area intended to be private.

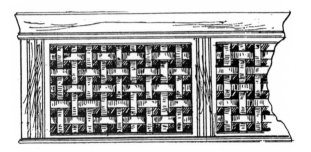

lattice
fabricated of wrought iron, The Arsenal,
New Orleans, La.

lattice porch A **porch** enclosed by a **lattice**; provides limited privacy, yet permits breezes to flow through the porch.

lattice window A term occasionally applied to a **casement window**, fixed or hinged, in which the glazing bars are set diagonally.

leaded light, leaded window A window having small diamond-shaped or rectangular panes of glass set in grooved lead strips called **cames.**

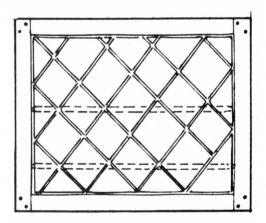

leaded light
Fairbanks House (1636), Dedham, Mass.

leader A vertical metal or wood pipe used to conduct rainwater from a gutter to the ground or to a cistern. Also called a conductor or downspout.

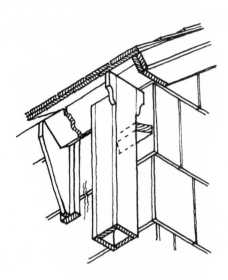

leader: constructed of wood

leader head An enlargement at the top of a **leader** to receive the rainwater from a gutter; usually fabricated of metal, although some of the very earliest in America were made of wood. Also called a conductor head.

leader head: fabricated of lead

leaf 1. One of the hinged or sliding components of a **folding door**. 2. One of the two major components of a **cavity wall.**

lean-to A building extension, one side of which is usually supported on one side by a wall of the building; commonly has a roof of single pitch. In colonial America such an extension was often added to a **timber-framed house** to increase its floor area; it was typically located at the rear of the house for use as a large kitchen, one or two small bedrooms, or storerooms. *See also* **integral lean-to.**

lean-to house A term sometimes used for a **saltbox house.**

lean-to roof A roof having a single pitch, carried by a wall that is higher than the roof.

ledged-and-braced door A **batten door** with the addition of diagonal bracing. Same as **Z-braced battened door.**

ledged door Same as **battened door.**

ledgement table A **belt course**, usually molded, especially one that is carried along the lower portion of a building.

library A place for maintaining a permanent collection of books for public or private use. In a home, it usually consists of a single room; in a public or private facility, it may occupy an entire building. Among the first library buildings was the Redwood Library in Newport, Rhode Island, completed in 1750, for which Peter Harrison (1716–1775) was the architect. This building, his first, is significant because it introduced the classical temple form to America long before the Greek Revival period. The design of this wood building, stuccoed to simulate rusticated stone construction, owes much to the work of the Italian Renaissance architect Andrea Palladio (1508–1580); it has the portico of a Roman Doric temple with small side wings that might be characterized as half-porticos.

lift latch A **latch** that fastens a door by means of a pivoted bar that engages a hook on the doorjamb; a lever lifts the pivoted bar to unfasten the door. It is usually operable from both sides of the door and contains no provisions for locking with a key. *See also* **Norfolk latch, Suffolk latch, thumb latch.**

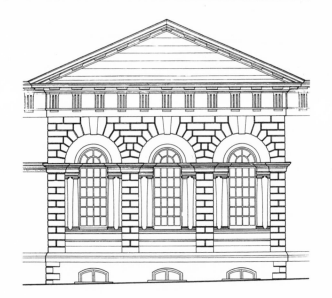

library
side elevation of wing of Redwood Library (1750),
Newport, R.I.

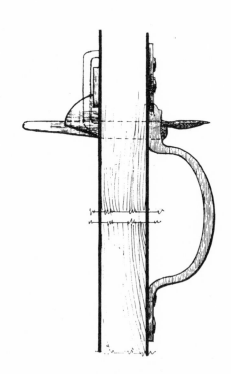

lift latch
van Schaick Mansion (1718), Cohoes, N.Y.

light 1. A pane of glass in a window or a subdivision of a window; usually one of a number of such panes combined in groups to provide a window of much larger area; *see* **pane.** 2. An aperture through which daylight is admitted to the interior of a building. *See* **deadlight, divided light, dome light, elliptical fanlight, fanlight, lantern, leaded light, pavement light, quarter-round light, semicircular fanlight, semielliptical fanlight, sidelight, skylight, sunburst light, transom light.**

lighthouse A tall structure, such as a tower, with a powerful source of light on top; located on a seacoast and designed to provide guidance for mariners at sea. Lighthouses were important facilities in establishing seafaring commerce along the Atlantic coast of the American colonies and continued to be influential until the latter half of the 20th century, when they were gradually largely replaced by electronic guidance and warning signal systems.

lightning rod A rodlike electrical conductor attached to the highest exterior point of a building; provides a direct electrical path to the ground if lightning strikes the building. In his famous kite experiment in 1752, Benjamin Franklin (1706–1790) established that lightning is an electrical phenomenon. Shortly thereafter, he invented the lightning rod, which, when correctly installed on a building, protects it from lightning-induced damage.

lime A white or grayish white caustic substance, calcium oxide, usually obtained by heating **limestone** or marble at a high temperature; used chiefly in plasters, mortars, and cements. In many areas in the English colonies along the Atlantic seacoast where limestone was scarce, seashells were heated to obtain lime; similarly in California the early Spanish missionaries heated seashells to obtain much-needed lime for plaster used as a protective coating for their adobe constructions. *See also* **lime mortar** and **shell lime.**

lime mortar A mixture of lime, fine aggregate (such as sand), and water; used in good-quality plasters and in cements until about 1880, when it was largely replaced by **gypsum mortar,** which has superior hardness and strength when dry. *See also* **mortar.**

lime plaster *See* **plaster.**

limestone Rock of sedimentary origin; a mineral form of calcium carbonate; particularly used as building stone or as the basic material that is heated at a high temperature to produce **lime.**

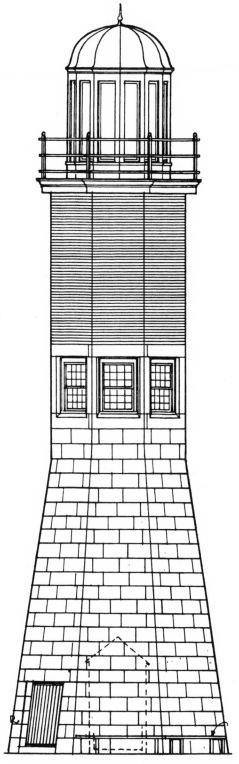

lighthouse (1810)
Scituate Harbor, Mass.

limewash Same as **whitewash.**

linear plan A house **plan** that is either one room wide and two or more rooms deep or one room deep and two or more rooms wide.

lining Material that covers any interior surface, such as the framework around a door, panel, or window, or **wainscoting** that covers an interior surface.

lintel A horizontal structural member (for example, a beam of iron, stone, wood, or steel) that spans the top of an opening such as a window; supports the weight of the wall directly above it. *See also* **eyebrow lintel, fireplace lintel, splayed lintel, through lintel.**

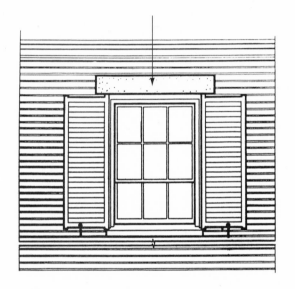

(a)

(b)

lintel
(a) unadorned rectangular block of stone;
(b) door lintel at a Harmony Society building (1811), Butler County, Pa.

lintel course A **course** of masonry units, set at the level of a **lintel**, commonly differentiated from the wall by its greater projection, its finish, or its thickness.

little house An 18th-century euphemism for an outdoor toilet.

living hall, living stair hall A large room at the entry of a house, especially in an elegant **Georgian style** or **Queen Anne style** home; frequently contains an imposing staircase, fireplace, and seating area; commonly called the **hall.** *See also* **entrance hall.**

load-bearing wall A wall capable of supporting an imposed load in addition to its own weight. Compare with **non-load-bearing wall.**

loam In building construction, a mixture composed chiefly of moistened sand, silt, and clay. In colonial America it was often used as a mortar when mixed with lime or used as a plaster with the addition of chopped straw.

lock A mechanical device that secures a door, gate, cabinet, or the like. Door locks were not in general use in America until after the Revolution. In colonial times the common method of securing a door from the inside was by means of a **door bar** or a door bolt. The earliest door locks had a hardwood casing with working parts fabricated of metal; later, these were replaced by all-metal locks. A further significant advance in lock design was made by Linus Yale (1821–1868), who patented the pin-tumbler **cylinder lock,** operated by a small flat key, in 1848. *See* **box lock, case lock, door lock, rim lock, stock lock.**

lock stile The vertical structural member of a door that is located on the side of the door farthest from the hinges; closes against the **jamb** of the surrounding **door frame.**

lodging house A building containing two or more rooms used or rented for sleeping purposes by paying guests or unmarried workers in a local mill; the minimum number and maximum numbers of rooms may be specified by the applicable local **code;** especially found in the past in early mill towns of New England. *See also* **boardinghouse.**

loft The space above the uppermost floor in a house, usually beneath a sloping roof; often used for storage or sleeping quarters. In colonial America windows were often added on the gable-end wall, or dormers were installed to provide light and air in the loft. Also called an attic or garret.

loft building A building containing open, unpartitioned floor space, usually with high ceilings; usually used for commercial or industrial purposes.

log cabin A general term often applied to two quite different types of dwellings, both of which are constructed of logs. The first is called a *log cabin*; the second is called a *log house*. In a log cabin, the logs are simply stripped of their bark and assembled to form a structure. In a log house, described in a subsequent entry, the logs are *hewn* to form square timbers before they are assembled as a structure. The construction of these two types of dwellings differs with regard to the tools, skill, and time required for their construction.

A log cabin is constructed of straight, relatively smooth, round logs usually laid horizontally, one above the other, and notched or otherwise fastened at their ends to prevent the joints from spreading at the corners and to provide rigidity and strength; the logs protrude at the corners beyond the joints; typically, there is a **pitched roof**. Log cabin construction requires only an ax, a minimum of skill, and a minimum of construction time. The walls are usually waterproofed by filling the cracks between adjacent logs with mud or clay mixed with wood chips or straw, or with some other type of filling, occasionally in combination with scraps of wood or small stones wedged in the cracks.

The earliest log cabins were usually built of round logs with **saddle notches** at their corners, and consisted of a single room (often referred to as a **single-pen cabin**); they had a battened door and a **clay-and-sticks chimney** built of twigs or branches mixed with mud and stones, which was largely replaced by chimneys of masonry construction at a later date. The introduction of these cabins on the American continent is often attributed to the Swedes in the Delaware Valley. Log cabins were also favored by the Scotch-English and Scotch-Irish, as well as by some American Indian tribes in the Southeast; they were used by early pioneer colonists not only for housing but also for barns, churches, storage, and other facilities, especially in the frontier regions. *See also* **log house, dogtrot cabin, double-pen cabin, notch, planking,2, saddlebag cabin, vertical log cabin.**

log-cabin siding A finish covering of an exterior wall that gives it the appearance of having been constructed of unhewn logs.

(a)   (b)

log cabin
(a) exterior view; (b) detail of wall construction at eaves

loggia An arcaded or colonnaded porch or gallery attached to or contained within a larger structure; usually located in a prominent part of the building; open on at least one side to provide a protected outdoor sitting area, sometimes contains an upper story.

log house A house constructed of square timbers that have been hewn from round logs, thus requiring an adze and other tools to shape them. The timbers are laid horizontally and notched or otherwise fastened to prevent their spreading at the corners and to provide rigidity and strength; the timbers do not protrude at the corners as in a **log cabin**. Commonly the roof is shingled; there is often a chimney on a gable-end wall. A log house requires considerably more skill and time to construct than a log cabin, although the square-timbered walls require less filling between the cracks to be made weather-tight than do the round logs of a log cabin. This type of construction was favored by many early German-speaking settlers in colonial America.

log notch *See* **notch.**

Lombard style 1. A synonym occasionally used for the **Italianate style**. 2. A term once applied to **Romanesque Revival**, now usually called **Richardsonian Romanesque style.**

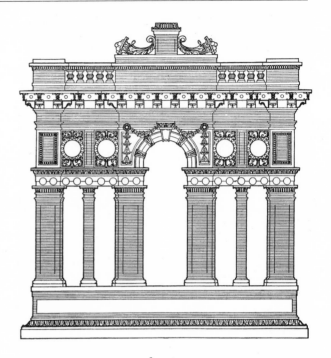

loggia
in tower of Madison Square Garden (1891),
New York City; McKim, Mead & White, Architects

log house: Cane Ridge Meeting House (1791), near Paris, Ky.

longhouse 1. A multifamily dwelling or a council house of American Indians in the Northeast, primarily the Iroquois of central New York and the Huron who settled near Lake Huron; it had a rectangular plan, vertical side walls, and a barrel-vaulted roof built on a framework of bent poles usually covered with elm bark, hides, mats, and/or thatch. Holes in the roof provided outlets for smoke and furnished some light; there was a hide-covered entrance to the longhouse at each end of the structure. Families lived in compartments, divided by thatched partitions, that ran along each side of a central longitudinal aisle. Two families, on opposite sides of the aisle, usually shared a firepit; thus, the length of the dwelling and the number of firepits was determined by the number of families. Some longhouses were several hundred feet long and between 15 and 25 feet (4.6–7.6m) in width. 2. A house similar to that of **longhouse,1** but having a removable roof covering. 3. A 20th-century term for a building that included both the domestic quarters for a family and housing for animals.

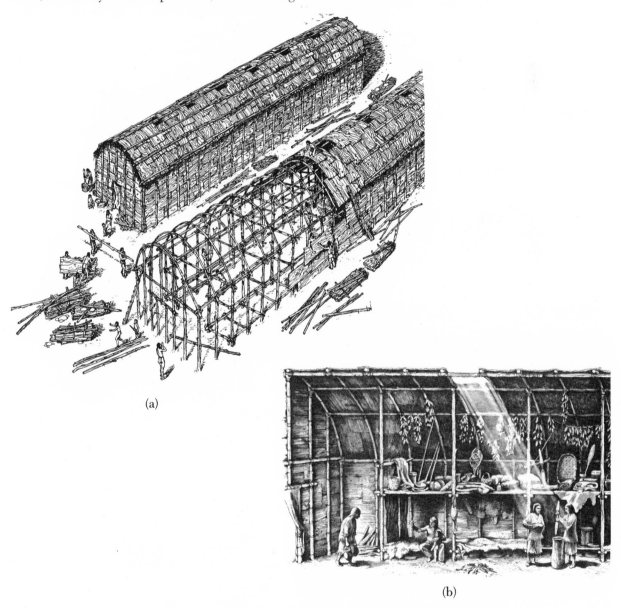

(a)

(b)

longhouse,1: (a) exterior; (b) interior

long room In colonial days, a room for social gatherings, usually attached to a tavern.

lookout 1. A rafter, bracket, or joist at the ridge of a roof that projects beyond an end wall of a building; may support the overhanging portion of the roof or cornice; also called a rafter lookout. 2. An elevated place or structure that provides a wide view for observation of the countryside; in particular, as a lookout for protection against marauders.

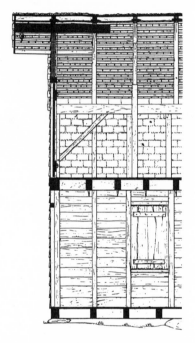

lookout,1

lookout,2

loom house Same as **spinning house.**

loophole In early American fortifications, one of a number of long, narrow slits in the walls, either or horizontal or vertical, usually widening inward to permit a musket to be fired over a wide angle in the event of an enemy attack.

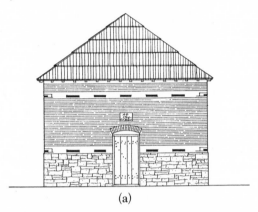

(a)

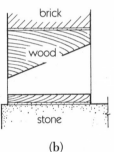

(b)

loopholes (horizontal): wood, (a) set in the brick walls of Block House (1764), Pittsburgh, Pa.; (b) detail of loophole

lotus capital, lotiform capital The topmost structural member of a column or pilaster that has the shape of a lotus bud or flower; found in some **Egyptian Revival** structures in America.

lotus capital
atop a column, Grove Street Cemetery,
New Haven, Conn.

Louisiana Vernacular architecture *See* **French Vernacular architecture, Cajun cottage, Creole house.**

louver An assembly of sloping, overlapping blades, slats, or narrow boards, often set in a door, window, or other opening; may be fixed or may be adjustable to admit air and/or light in varying degrees, and to exclude rain and snow.

louvered shutter *See* **shutter.**

low relief Same as **bas-relief.**

lozenge In a **double lancet window**, a small glazed opening that pierces the space between the heads of the two lancet windows; used, for example, in the **Gothic Revival** style.

L-plan A **plan** having the shape of a capital letter **L**.

lucome window In colonial New England, a wide dormer providing light for a room in a loft or attic.

luffer An obsolete term for **louver.**

Lutheran window Same as **dormer.**

lozenge

M

magazine In early America, a storage place for gun-powder, loaded cartridges, arms, and military supplies. *See also* **powder house.**

maison de maître *See* **Creole house.**

maison de poteaux-en-terre *See* **poteaux-en-terre house.**

maison pièce sur pièce In **French Vernacular architecture** of northern Louisiana, primarily in the early 1800s, a term usually used for a **dogtrot cabin** consisting of two single-room cabins separated from each other by an open passageway; both cabins shared this passageway and a common wood-shingled roof. Occasionally this term is also used to describe a one-room **log cabin**. *See also* **pièce sur pièce construction.**

mall 1. A public plaza, walk, or system of walks, often set with trees and designed for pedestrian use. 2. *See* **shopping mall.**

malleable iron A low-carbon cast iron that has been annealed and allowed to cool slowly; capable of being beaten into shape to form decorative ironwork.

manor house 1. An important house in a country-side, often the residence of a landowner with a farm of considerable acreage; generally a home of elegance, although some were relatively simple. 2. A term some-times used to describe a one-room house built by set-tlers in the early American colonies; usually had a **gable roof**, clapboard walls, a battened door, a window at the front of the house with solid shutters, and a chimney at one or at each gable end.

mansard roof A hipped roof usually having a dou-ble slope or compound curve on all four sides of the roof, the lower slope often being much steeper than the upper slope; alternatively, the sides may have a concave, convex, or **S** shape, as illustrated under **Second Empire style**. Named after the French architect François Mansart (1598–1666). Found, for example in the **Beaux-Arts style, Richardsonian Romanesque style,** and **Second Empire style.**

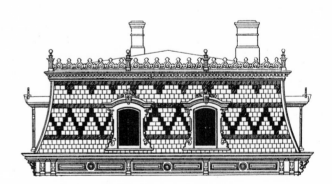

mansard roof: one example

Mansard style 1. A term sometimes used as a syn-onym for **Second Empire style**. 2. A loose term applied to architecture that makes use of, or suggests, a **mansard roof.**

mansion 1. A very large, imposing, stately residence. 2. In colonial times, the residence of a landholder.

mantel 1. A projection or facing around a fireplace opening, often decorative. 2. Same as **mantelpiece**. 3. The construction that serves as a support for the masonry above a fireplace.

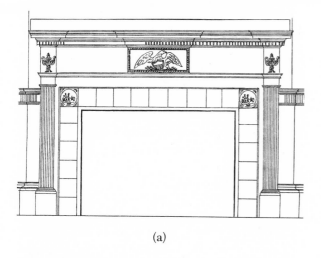

(a)

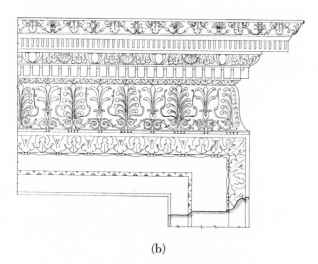

(b)

mantel,1
(a) Registry of Deeds Building (1800), Salem, Mass.;
(b) Whitehall, Anne Arundel County, Md.

mantelpiece 1. The fittings and decorative elements of a **mantel** above a fireplace; unusual in America before the year 1725. 2. A shelf above a mantel; often called a mantelshelf.

mantelshelf That part of a mantelpiece which constitutes a shelf.

manteltree A wood, stone, or iron structural member that spans the opening over a fireplace. In colonial American homes, an oak timber as large as 12 inches by 18 inches (30 x 46cm) in cross section often served to support the wall construction above; it was typically placed 4 to 5 feet (1.2–1.5m) above the hearth, high enough to prevent its burning, and was sometimes plastered to improve its fire resistance.

manufactured house Same as **prefabricated house.**

marble A metamorphic rock composed largely of calcite or dolomite; often highly polished to enhance its appearance. The differences in color among various types of marbles are a result of differences in their mineral content. Until the early 1800s, most marble was imported to American cities from abroad.

marbling Treating a wood surface to give it the appearance of marble by the special application of paint. *See also* **faux marbre.**

market house, market hall In towns in colonial America, usually a one- or two-story rectangular building where butchers, fishmongers, grocers, and peddlers sold their goods, usually under the supervision of the town's officials. The ground floor was often open to the outdoors; sometimes arches or heavy posts supported a second story that housed municipal offices.

marquee A permanent canopy, usually of metal and glass, that projects over an entrance to a building, especially that of a theater or hotel; may include lettering or signs indicating the current presentation.

marquetry Inlaid pieces of a material, such as wood or ivory, fitted together and applied to a surface for decorative purposes. *See also* **inlay, intarsia.**

marquetry

martin hole *See* **owl hole.**

masonry 1. The craft of shaping, arranging, and uniting brick, blocks of stone, and concrete blocks, usually by a mason. 2. The work constructed by a mason.

masonry bond *See* **bond.**

masonry course A layer of masonry units running horizontally, or more or less horizontally, in a wall.

masonry joint A **joint** between two masonry units held together by mortar. *See* **colonial joint, concave joint, excess joint, flat joint, flush joint, hick joint, raked joint, rodded joint, rough-cut joint, scribed joint, skintled joint, struck joint, tooled joint, troweled joint, V-joint, weather joint, weather-struck joint**. *See also* **pointing.**

masonry veneer A facing of **masonry** laid against a wall but not structurally bonded to it.

matchboards Boards that have a tongue along one side edge and a groove along the opposite edge; when installed, the tongue of one board fits into the corresponding groove of the adjacent board. *See* **tongue-and-groove joint.**

matched siding Same as **drop siding.**

matching A system of **matchboards** or of sheets of wood veneer arranged to emphasize grain pattern, as in **book matching** or **herringbone matching.**

mat house A multifamily dwelling of some American Indians of the Northwest, often as much as 60 feet (18m) long and 15 feet (4.6m) wide. The framework is composed of a series of **A**-frames lashed together by a ridgepole and by a series of horizontal poles that act as **purlins**, forming a gable roof; the two ends of the dwelling are rounded. The framework of the house is usually covered with a matting of grass, cattails, tule, or the like. The floor may be excavated slightly below the surrounding ground level.

meal house A structure used for storing grain that has been ground.

meander Same as **Greek key.**

measured drawing An architectural drawing of an existing building, object, site, structure, or detail thereof; accurately drawn to scale on the basis of field measurements; usually one of a set of such drawings.

meat house Same as **smokehouse.**

medallion 1. An ornamental plaque (often round, oval, or square, but may be any form) representing an object or design in relief, such as a figure, flower, or head; usually applied to a wall frieze near its center. 2. A ceiling ornament, often cast in plaster, at the center of which is often hung a chandelier or luminaire; also called a rose or rosette.

medallion,1

medallion,2
First Presbyterian Church, Newark, N.J.

Medieval architecture Architecture of the European Middle Ages, from about the 5th to the 15th centuries. Found, in particular, in the pre-Romanesque, Romanesque, and Gothic styles that served as prototypes for a number of styles of architecture in America, such as Richardsonian Romanesque and Gothic Revival. Traditional methods of timber construction employed in Medieval architecture were used in **American Colonial architecture of early New England**.

Mediterranean Revival An imprecise term (*not* a **Revival architecture** as the name implies) for a mixture of **Spanish Colonial Revival, Mission Revival,** and the **Italian Villa style**; popular in some regions of America in the latter part of the 20th century. Usually a one- or two-story house with a red tile roof and stuccoed walls, typically with rounded or arched windows; occasionally referred to as Mediterranean style.

meeting house In colonial New England and as far south as North Carolina, a house of worship. The earliest meeting houses not only served as places for organized worship, but also as centers of community activity; they were usually built and owned by the town and were the seat of local government, in which public notices were posted and where able-bodied men gathered in case of emergency, since many meeting houses were built so they could be defended. In some areas a sentinel in a lookout was stationed atop the roof during services or meetings. The earliest meeting houses were notably plain structures, often having a square **floor plan**, with fixed seating usually assigned according to the presumed "dignity," social rank, and wealth of each individual; men and women often sat apart, on opposite sides of the central aisle. A meeting house was not considered a sacred edifice or a consecrated place and was not a synonym for church; the term *church* usually referred to the congregation itself. Most often meeting houses were the places of worship of Protestant dissenters, such as the Quakers and the Congregationalists.

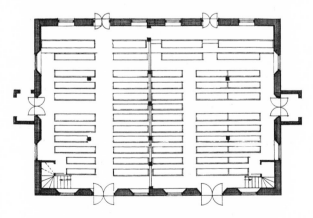

meeting house plan,
Society of Friends (1772), Salem, N.J.

megalopolis An urban area consisting of several large, densely populated cities that abut one another.

member A constituent component of a framework or of a structure.

memorial arch An arch commemorating a person or event.

memorial arch
The Washington Arch (1892), New York City;
McKim, Mead & White, Architects

memorial plaque, memorial tablet A flat stone, often inscribed, affixed to, or set into, a surface; used to commemorate some special event or to serve as a memorial.

1778
HANCOCK HOUSE
IN MEMORY OF THOSE PATRIOTS
WHO WERE MASSACRED BY THE
BRITISH IN THIS HOUSE
MARCH 21 1778

ERECTED BY OAK TREE CHAPTER
DAUGHTERS OF THE AMERICAN REVOLUTION
SALEM NEW JERSEY
1903

memorial plaque
erected in memory of martyred patriots
(1778), Hancock House, Hancock Bridge, N.J.

meridian stone A stone placed along a meridian (i.e., an accurately determined line running north and south) to delineate the eastern or western boundary of a town or village.

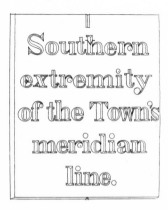

meridian stone (1840)
Nantucket, Mass.

merlon In a **battlement**, the solid part between two openings (called **crenels**); often found in **Gothic Revival** architecture in America.

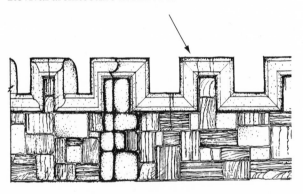

merlon

messuage A dwelling with all attached and adjoining buildings and **curtilage,** together with adjacent lands used by the household.

metal ceiling *See* **pressed-metal ceiling.**

metal lath A building material, fabricated of metal, used as a base for the application of **plaster;** *see* **expanded-metal lath.** Compare with **wood lath,** which was used as a base for plaster walls in early American homes.

metal roofing *See* **sheet-metal roofing.**

metope In Classical architecture and derivatives, the vertically oriented panel between the **triglyphs** in a frieze of the **Doric order**; often carved.

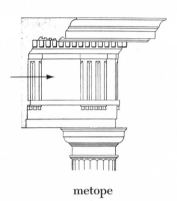

metope

mews An alley or court in which stables are, or once were, located; now mostly converted to housing. In New York City, a well-known example is the Washington Mews near Washington Square.

Mid-Colonial architecture A term occasionally used for **Georgian style** architecture.

Miesian A term descriptive of the style of Ludwig Mies van der Rohe (1886–1969), a German-American architect who was a principal exponent of the **International style.** An outstanding example of his work is the Seagram Building in New York City (1958), designed by Mies with Philip Johnson (1906–).

milestone, milepost A marker showing the distance in miles from a designated location. In colonial and post-Revolutionary America, such markers were especially helpful to those traveling between communities.

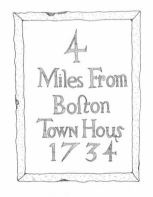

milestone (1734)
near Boston, Mass.

milk house In colonial America and beyond, a small subsidiary structure in which milk and other dairy products were stored at a cool temperature. The milk was usually kept in open pans until the cream rose to the surface and could be skimmed. It was necessary for the storage temperature to be low enough to prevent souring, so the typical milk house had overhanging eaves to shade it, double walls, and a ceiling filled with sawdust or the like for thermal insulation. Cooling was usually provided by slow-running cold spring water or the runoff from an **icehouse**. A milk house commonly had a concrete floor to promote cleanliness and louvers for ventilation and was separated from the barn for reasons of sanitation. Starting in the 1800s, the term *milk house* was gradually replaced by the word *dairy*. Health regulations have made such structures obsolete.

mill *See* **bark mill, bolting mill, gristmill, sawmill, textile mill, tide mill, water mill, windmill.**

millwork A variety of wood products that are manufactured by machines such as wood planers; includes cabinets, doors, door frames, moldings, panels, stair components, and window sashes (but does not include ceiling boards, flooring, or wood siding).

mirador In **Spanish Colonial architecture**, any architectural feature that provides a view of the landscape, for example, a roof pavilion.

mission In **Spanish Colonial architecture of the American Southwest**, a church and complex of buildings usually dependent for support on a monastic order.

(a) (b)

(c)

mission: (a) Royal Chapel of San Carlos, Monterey, Calif.;
(b) San Luis Rey, San Luis Rey, Calif.; (c) San Juan Capistrano, Calif.

Mission architecture Church and monastic architecture of Spanish religious orders in the American Southwest, primarily in the 18th century. It exhibits considerable regional variation; for example, Mission architecture in New Mexico is usually relatively unadorned, evidencing the influence of the local laborers; in contrast, Mission architecture in Arizona, California, and Texas is more elaborate, often with ornamentation imitative of the elaborate and lavish **Baroque** or the **Churrigueresque style**. The tamped earth floors of the missions were commonly covered with square tile. *See also* **Spanish Colonial architecture** and **Mission Revival.**

Mission architecture usually exhibits many of the following characteristics:

Façade and exterior wall treatments: Massive walls of adobe brick, often three to five feet (0.9–1.5m) thick, laid with lime mortar where available, commonly with wall buttresses to provide additional stability. Adobe walls were usually coated with lime-and-sand stucco to reduce the effects of erosion of the adobe, although a few California missions were constructed of kiln-burnt brick less subject to erosion. Arcaded walkways with arches were usually built around the patios; missions commonly had multicurved gables, a belfry (**campanario**), bell tower, or twin bell towers.

Roof treatments: A flat roof or a low-pitched roof with multicurved parapets. Support for the roof usually provided by round horizontal logs (vigas) resting on decorative brackets called bolsters. Many of the earliest mis-

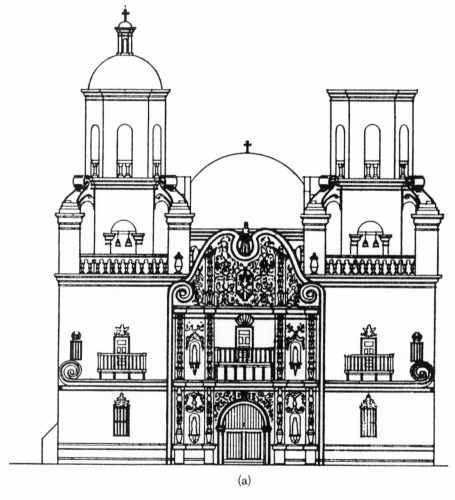

(a)

Mission architecture
(a) church façade, Mission San Xavier del Bac (1797), Tucson, Ariz.

sions had thatched roofs. One of the first tiled roofs was installed at Mission San Luis Obispo (1772) in California, spurred by the burning of the mission's original thatched roof by flaming arrows during an Indian attack.

Window treatments: Windows in mission churches were usually located high in the walls; occasionally clerestory windows. Windows facing the street were commonly protected by grilles (**rejas**), usually fabricated of wrought iron.

Doorway treatments: A massive wood door at the main entrance; on important buildings, heavily carved or paneled, often set in elaborately sculptured portals.

(b)

(d)

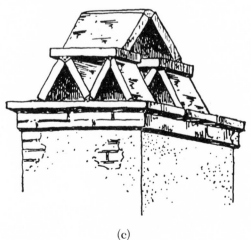

(c)

Mission architecture
(b) baptistry window, Mission San José de Aguayo
(1720–1731), San Antonio, Tex.; (c) chimney cap,
Mission San Juan Capistrano, California;
(d) belfry, Mission San Xavier del Bac

mission dormer In Mission Revival architecture, a **dormer** that projects above a tiled roof; the face of the dormer has a multicurved shape similar to that of a **mission parapet.**

mission parapet In Spanish missions of the American Southwest, a low **freestanding** wall at the edge of a roof; typically, the upper edge of the parapet is multicurved.

mission parapet

Mission Revival, Mission style A style of architecture popular in the southwestern United States and in Florida from about 1890 to 1930 and beyond; suggestive or imitative of the earlier **Mission architecture**, although usually much simpler because of the absence of sculptured ornamentation. Compare with **Pueblo Revival** and **Spanish Colonial Revival**.

Mission Revival architecture usually exhibits many of the following characteristics:

Façade and exterior wall treatments: Stucco-finished exterior walls, occasionally with terra-cotta ornamentation; often, balconies or balconets; semicircular arches; a porch roof supported by massive piers with broad arches between them, forming arcaded walkways; multicurved gables with parapets.

Roof treatments: A red mission-tile roof of low pitch; often a **hipped roof**; open eaves having a exposed rafters and a significant overhang; roof ridges topped with a red-tiled protective cap; roof or wall dormers; roof drainage provided by waterspouts (**canales**) that pierce the walls; often, tile-faced bell towers.

Window treatments: Typically, double-hung rectangular windows; occasionally **fixed lights** in a **quatrefoil** pattern.

Doorway treatments: A main entry door often located within a recessed porch.

Mission Revival

mission tile 1. A red-clay roofing tile, approximately semicylindrical in shape; laid in courses, with adjacent tiles having their convex side alternately up and down; especially found in **Mission architecture, Mission Revival, Spanish Eclectic architecture;** also called Spanish tile. 2. Same as **pantile,2.**

mission tile

miter arch Same as **triangular arch.**

miter joint A wood joint between two members at an angle to each other, often a right angle; each member is cut at an angle equal to half the angle of the junction.

miter joint

mode *See* **architectural mode.**

Modern architecture A loosely applied term, used since the late 19th century, for buildings, in any of number of styles, in which emphasis in design is placed on functionalism, rationalism, and up-to-date methods of construction; in contrast with architectural styles based on historical precedents and traditional ways of building. Often includes **Art Deco, Art Moderne, Bauhaus, Contemporary style, International style, Organic architecture,** and **Streamline Moderne.**

Moderne A loose term occasionally applied to **Art Deco, Art Moderne, PWA Moderne, Streamline Moderne.**

Modernistic style *See* **Art Deco** and **Art Moderne.**

Modern style A vague term that often includes **Contemporary style** and **Shed style.**

modillion A horizontal bracket that supports a cornice on its underside; often has the form of a scroll. If the support is a plain slab, it is called a *block modillion.*

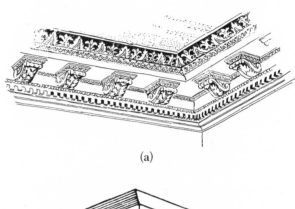

(a)

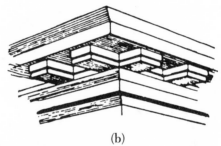

(b)

modillion: (a) Thomas Ives House (1806), Providence, R.I.; (b) block modillion

modillion cornice A **cornice** supported by a series of modillions; occasionally used in Classical Revival or derivatives.

modular construction Building construction based on the use of a number of relatively small units, often factory-built, that are assembled at the job site. Because these modules are transported to the job site by truck, they usually have a width of 12 feet (3.7m) or less, the legal limit for transporting wide loads in most jurisdictions in America.

molded brick A specially shaped brick, usually for decorative use.

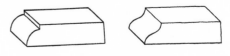

molded brick

molding A long, relatively narrow, decorative surface that may be flat, curved, or somewhat irregular, often with a more or less uniform cross section; especially used as a decorative element at the edges of or joints between surfaces on bases, capitals, cornices, doors, panels, and windows; usually formed by cutting or otherwise shaping the building material of which the molding is fabricated. Most moldings are derived at least in part from wood or stone prototypes of Classical architecture. Moldings may be generally divided into three categories: rectilinear, curved, and composite-curved. For definitions and illustrations, *see* **applied molding, bead-and-reel molding, bead molding, bolection molding, cyma, drip molding, egg-and-dart molding, half-round molding, head molding, hood molding, Italian molding, label molding, laid-on mold-**ing, ogee, ovolo molding, planted molding, quarter-round molding, rope molding, scotia, struck molding, sunk molding, tongue-and-dart molding, weather molding.**

monial Archaic term for **mullion**

monitor A superstructure that straddles the ridge of a roof or that crowns a roof or dome; may be glazed to provide light below or may be louvered to provide ventilation below.

monolith 1. An architectural member, such as the shaft of a column, that is formed from a single block of stone. 2. A term descriptive of concrete that is cast in one large piece.

monitor
General Salem Towne House (1796), Charlton, Mass.

Monterey style, Monterey Revival A style of architecture that originally came into existence in Monterey, California, between about 1835 and 1840; typically, a two-story house with a full-façade balcony supported by plain wood posts and enclosed by wood railings. From about 1920 to 1960, there was a reuse of a modified version of this style, which combined Spanish Colonial architecture with some elements of early New England colonial architecture and was especially popular in the 1930s. The balcony of the 20th-century house is typically cantilevered rather than supported by wood columns from ground level, as in the earlier version. Compare with **Mission Revival** and **Spanish Colonial Revival.**

Monterey-style houses usually exhibit a number of the following characteristics:

Façade and exterior wall treatments: Nineteenth-century houses in this style had whitewashed adobe walls up to two feet (0.6m) thick; in contrast, the 20th-century houses have much thinner walls with a finish material such as stucco, brick, and/or wood, which may differ on each of the two stories.

Roof treatments: A low-pitched **gable roof** or **hipped roof** with its ridge parallel to the façade; usually covered with hand-split wood shingles, but sometimes tiled; occasionally has a decorative chimney cap or chimney hood in the shape of a miniature house.

Window treatments: Double-hung wood-frame windows with mullions; often, window shutters; occasionally, full-length windows opening onto the balcony.

Doorway treatments: Nineteenth-century houses in this style usually had relatively simple paneled doors; many 20th-century houses in this style have doors imitative of those found in **Colonial Revival** architecture, including paneling, a fanlight over the door, and **sidelights** flanking the door. Very occasionally, there may be some elements of Greek Revival wood trim around the doors and windows.

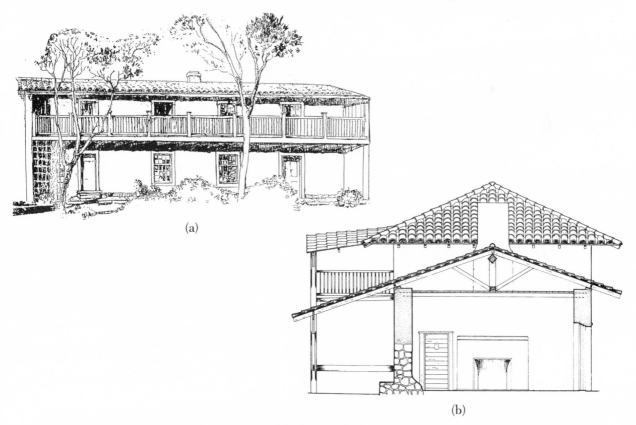

(a)

(b)

Monterey style
(a) typical home; (b) section through the Custom House, Monterey, Calif.; construction started in 1814 under the Spanish flag; continued from 1822 to 1846 under the Mexican flag; completed in 1848 under the American flag

monument A stone, pillar, structure, or building erected in memory of the dead, of an event, or of an action such as a battle.

Moorish arch Same as **horseshoe arch.**

Moorish Revival A rarely used type of **Exotic Revival** architecture in America from about 1845 to 1890; occasionally used in some American synagogues constructed during this period. Buildings in this style are usually characterized by **horseshoe arches, multifoil arches,** and **multifoil** window tracery.

mopboard Same as **baseboard.**

Mormon thatched-roof shed Same as **jacal,1.**

morning room In a house, a sitting room that is usually situated so as to be sunlit in the early part of the day.

mortar A plastic mixture of cementitious materials (such as lime or cement) with water and sand; can be troweled in its plastic state; hardens in place as it dries; used in building construction to bond brick, stone, and the like. It is often subdivided into categories, depending on its principal ingredient(s), such as clay mortar, lime mortar, and gypsum mortar. Lime mortar was used in America until about 1880; thereafter, gypsum mortar came into popular use because of its superior hardness and strength. *See also* **cement, clay-and-hair mortar, gypsum mortar, lime mortar.**

mortar brick A type of brick used in America primarily in the 18th and 19th centuries; usually consisted of a mixture of sand and 20 to 40 percent lime, to which water was added; then molded into bricks and allowed to harden in the open air. It was primarily used in early America in regions where clay for making a better grade of bricks was unavailable.

mortar joint *See* **masonry joint.**

mortise A cavity, hole, notch, recess, or slot cut into a piece of wood or other material, usually to receive a **tenon,** i.e., another piece of wood having a reduced cross section at one of its ends that fits into the mortise.

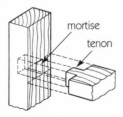

mortise and tenon

mortise-and-tenon joint, mortise joint A joint between two wood members that is formed by fitting a **tenon** at the end of the one member into a **mortise** in the other member. In colonial America the mortise and the tenon were usually cut or shaped with a mallet and chisel. After fitting the tenon into the mortise, a hole was drilled through them with an auger; then a wooden peg (a **treenail**) was driven in the hole to secure the joint. Also called a mortise-and-pegged joint.

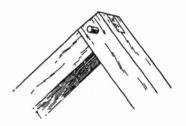

mortise-and-tenon joint

mosaic A pattern formed on a surface by applying small pieces of stone, tile, glass, or enamel to a matrix of cement, mortar, or plaster spread on the surface.

motif A principal repeated element in an ornamental design.

mouse-tooth pattern, mouse-tooth finish *See* **tumbling course** and **straight-line gable.**

M-roof A roof formed by joining two parallel gable roofs so as to make a valley between them; somewhat resembles the letter **M** in section.

M-roof

mud-and-sticks chimney Same as **clay-and-sticks chimney.**

mud brick A term occasionally used for **adobe** that has been shaped in a brick form and then sun-dried.

mud house 1. A dwelling of American Indians of the Southwest; usually has a shaded entrance and framework of branches covered with some combination of thatching, cactus stalks, grass, or brush that is then overlaid with mud plaster. 2. Any primitive dwelling having walls of unbaked earth, constructed either of **puddled adobe** or molded sun-dried blocks of mud usually mixed with straw, manure, or another material to increase the mechanical strength of the construction. *See also* **jacal,2** and **prairie cottage.**

mud plaster A plaster, usually a mixture of heavy clay and water, that often contains chopped straw, manure, or a like additive to improve its mechanical strength when dry.

mud room A small room adjacent to an exterior door, usually at the back or side of a house, used for temporary storage of dirty or wet boots or outer garments; found especially in northeastern regions of the United States where there is heavy snowfall.

mud sill In a **timber-framed house**, the lowest horizontal timber at the base of the wood structure, usually laid directly on the ground; used to distribute concentrated loads.

mud wall A wall usually constructed of a mixture of clay and a binder such as chopped straw; often gravel is added.

mullion A vertical member that separates lights in a window, leaves of a door, or panels in a wainscot that are set in series; for example, the vertical bar that separates the two leaves of casement windows in some colonial American houses.

multicurved gable A **gable** having an outline containing two or more curves on each side of a central ridge, as in a **Flemish gable** Also called a curvilinear gable.

multicurved gable

multicurved parapet At the edge of a roof, a **free-standing** wall whose outline contains a number of curves, as in a **mission parapet.**

multifoil In an opening, a pattern usually having more than five **foils**, lobes, or arcuated divisions separated by cusps; if there are five or fewer, the terms **trefoil, quatrefoil,** and **cinquefoil** are customarily used.

muntin 1. A secondary framing member to hold glass panes within a window frame, a window wall, or a glazed door; often decoratively molded; relatively thick muntins were used until about 1780, when thinner muntins became more fashionable; also called a glazing bar, muntin bar, sash bar, or window bar. 2. An intermediate vertical member that divides the panels of a door.

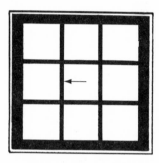

muntin,1: in a window

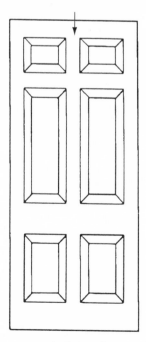

muntin,2: in a door

musket-stock post In an early colonial American **timber-framed house**, a principal vertical structural support, i.e., a **post**, that has a shape similar in appearance to an inverted musket stock; the additional thickness at the top of the post provides an added bearing surface to support the load imposed on it. Also called a gun-stock post or a shouldered post. Compare with **flared post.**

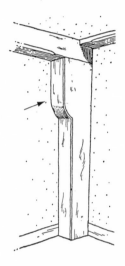

musket-stock post

mutule A flat block on the underside of a Doric cornice, usually decorated with inverted conelike ornaments called **guttae**; found, for example, in the **Greek Revival style** in America.

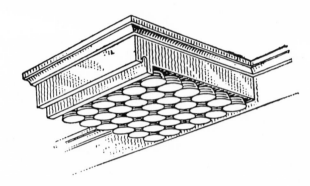

mutule
showing guttae, Redwood Library (1750),
Newport, R.I.

nail A straight, small, rigid, slender shaft of metal, one end of which is usually pointed; the other end has a head that may be driven with a hammer; used as a fastener to join separate pieces of wood, to attach tiles to a wood sheathing on a roof, etc. Before the American Revolution, hand-wrought nails were usually imported from England. Machine-made nails were manufactured in America for the first time in the 1780s, but their quality was poor, and production was relatively small. By the 1800s the quality of manufactured nails had greatly improved. This improvement, in combination with **balloon framing**, was among the principal factors that made it possible to construct relatively inexpensive homes in the years that followed. *See also* **cut nail, dog nail, hand-wrought nail, wire nail, wrought nail.**

National Historic Landmark *See* **landmark,2.**

National Register of Historic Places A government organization that maintains lists and files of documentation of buildings, structures, objects, districts, and sites that are of national, state, or local significance. Buildings on the register may be marked with plaques that provide historical information about them. Address: National Park Service, U.S. Department of the Interior, P.O. Box 37127, Washington, DC 20013-7127. Also called the National Register.

National style A term sometimes used as a synonym for **Greek Revival style** during the height of its popularity, from about 1830 to 1850.

National Trust for Historic Preservation A national, nonprofit private organization chartered by Congress to encourage public participation in the preservation of buildings, objects, and sites that have been significant in American history. Address: 1785 Massachusetts Avenue NW, Washington, DC 20036.

Native American dwellings *See* **American Indian dwellings** and **Eskimo dwellings.**

nave 1. The middle aisle of a church, extending from the church entrance to the **transept** or **chancel**. 2. By extension, the middle and side aisles of a church from the entrance to the chancel. 3. That part of the church intended primarily for the laity.

necking In **Classical architecture** and derivatives, the space between the top of the **shaft** of a column and the bottom of the **capital**; usually marked by a recess or a ring of moldings.

necking: in a Doric capital

needlework In early colonial American house construction, the filling in of a timber structural framework with masonry or the like. *See also* **half-timbered construction.**

Neo-Adamesque style *See* **Neo-Federal style.**

Neoclassical Revival Since about 1965, a rather free interpretation of the **Neoclassical style** with little attempt to emulate the original style accurately; usually has a pedimented portico with full-height columns.

Neoclassical style A style of architecture, most popular in America from about 1895 to 1950 and beyond, based primarily on the use of forms of classical antiquity; as a result of a renewed interest in classical forms, stimulated by the Columbian Exposition at the Chicago World's Fair in 1893, widely used for both public buildings and residences in America. Homes are usually two or two-and-a-half stories high; public buildings in this style are generally multistoried and may have a smooth ashlar façade, an **attic story**, an enriched entablature, and a parapet. Aspects of this style are imitative of the earlier **Classical Revival style** (often called Early Classical Revival) that was most popular from about 1770 to 1830; others are imitative of the **Greek Revival style** that was most popular from about 1830 to 1850. The terms **Classical Revival style, Neoclassical Revival**, and **Neoclassicism** are sometimes used as synonyms.

The Neoclassical style usually exhibits many of the following characteristics:

Façade and exterior wall treatments: A symmetrical façade, commonly having a visually important full-width portico with full-height wood or stone classical columns (often having Corinthian, Doric, or Ionic capitals) or with square columns (sometimes paired) and full-height pilasters; or a similar portico only one story high.

Roof treatments: An unadorned roof line; often a side-gabled roof, although hipped or gambrel roofs are not uncommon; a moderate overhang at the eaves or boxed eaves; balustrades frequently located just above the eaves; occasionally, modillions and dentils below the eaves; often ornamented with statuary; a wide **frieze,2** below the cornice.

Window treatments: Double-hung, symmetrically arranged windows with lintels above, sometimes occurring in pairs or in groups of three; in homes, an upper sash usually with either six or nine panes, and a lower sash with either the same number of panes or a single pane; occasionally, arched windows or bay windows (particularly those that are canted in plan).

Doorway treatments: A doorway at the center of the façade that may be capped with a decorative lintel or with a **broken pediment**; ornamental elements usually surround the door, as in earlier prototypes.

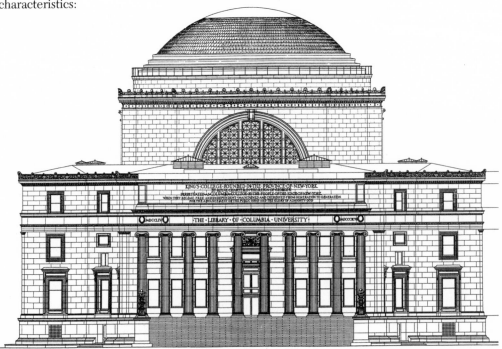

Neoclassical style
Low Library, Columbia University (1893), New York City; McKim, Mead & White, Architects

Neoclassicism In the late 18th and the early 19th century and beyond, a reinterpretation of the principles of Classical architecture. This term is sometimes used to include the **Classical Revival style, Federal style,** and **Greek Revival style.** Usually characterized by: monumentality, colossal porticos, and columns; strict use of the Greek and Roman **orders**; sparing application of ornamentation, an unadorned roof line, and an avoidance of moldings. The term **Neoclassical style** is occasionally used as a synonym.

Neo-Colonial architecture In the last half of the 20th century, a loose term applied to architecture imitative of 19th-century **Colonial Revival** architecture but usually a poor emulation of its prototype; has many variations; occasionally called Neo-Colonial Revival.

Neo-Eclectic architecture One of any number of domestic modes of architecture in America during the second half of the 20th century that freely borrows from, but does not copy, an earlier traditional style and detailing, making little effort to be precise in imitating its prototype. For examples, *see* **Neoclassical Revival, Neo-Colonial architecture, Neo-French architecture, Neo-Mansard, Neo-Tudor, Neo-Victorian,** and **Mediterranean Revival.** Some features of **Post-Modern architecture** can be called Neo-Eclectic.

Neo-Federal style An loose term applied to architecture imitative of the **Federal style** of architecture; moderately popular in the 1920s.

Neo-French architecture A free interpretation of **French Eclectic architecture** in America in the latter part of the 20th century, often vaguely recalling Normandy farmhouses. Usually characterized by steeply pitched hipped roofs, sometimes with **flared eaves**; a cylindrical tower with a conical roof; occasionally, **false half-timbering**; often, rounded or segmental arches over the windows that extend above the line of the eaves.

Neo-Georgian A loose term applied to architecture that emulates features and details of the **Georgian style,** including a symmetrical façade, but usually with a significant lack of historical accuracy; popular at various times, including the 1980s.

Neo-Gothic A term descriptive of the reuse of Gothic forms during the second half of the 19th century and the early part of the 20th century. *See also* **Collegiate Gothic, Gothic Revival,** and **Steamboat Gothic.**

Neo-Grec A mode of architecture, primarily in the 1870s, that sought to follow the **trabeated**, rectangular construction of the early Greeks; especially characterized by the combination of brickwork and cast iron.

Neo–Greek Revival An inexact term for architecture loosely based on the Greek Revival style with little regard for historical accuracy.

Neo-Greek Revival

Neo-Mansard A loose term applied to architecture since about 1960 that has some form of **mansard roof** but usually has little else in common with the **Mansard style**.

Neo-Mediterranean *See* **Mediterranean Revival**.

Neo-Romanesque A term sometimes used for **Richardsonian Romanesque style,** particularly in its early phases, or for **Romanesque Revival**.

Neo-Tudor Descriptive of a **Neo-Eclectic architecture** of limited popularity in America primarily after about 1955; vaguely imitative of its earlier **Tudor Revival** prototypes that were popular from about 1880 to 1940. Houses are usually one or two stories with front-facing gables and exhibit many of the following characteristics: false half-timbering employed as a decorative element; masonry or stucco walls on the ground floor, sometimes with a different wall treatment on the floor above; occasionally, an overhanging upper story; a steeply pitched roof, often covered with slate or wood shingles; prominent chimney stacks; groups of tall, narrow windows separated by mullions, often set with small panes of leaded glass that are either diamond-shaped or square-shaped set diagonally.

Neo-Tudor

Neo-Victorian A term descriptive of a Neo-Eclectic architecture somewhat imitative of features and details of the traditional 19th-century **Queen Anne style**; used in America during the second half of the 20th century, particularly after the 1970s; especially characterized by porches of wood construction having wood brackets and a profusion of **spindlework**.

New Brutalism *See* **Brutalism**.

newel 1. The central post or column around which the steps of a circular staircase wind, that provides a central support for the stair. 2. A post, often ornamental, that supports one end of a handrail at the bottom or top of a flight of stairs.

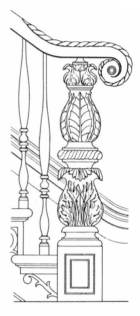

newel,2

newel cap The upper terminal feature of a **newel,2**; often turned on a lathe, molded, or carved in a decorative shape.

newel stair A stair whose tapered treads wind around and are supported by a solid central column.

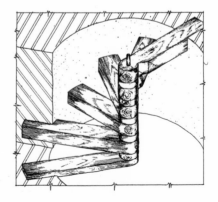

newel stair
San Esteban del Rey (c. 1642), Acoma, N.M.

New England Colonial architecture *See* American Colonial architecture of early New England, Cape house, captain's house, Corporate style, meeting house, New England gambrel roof, Sabbath house, saltbox house, stone-ender, whale house.

New England connected barn *See* continuous house.

New England Federal style *See* Federal style.

New England gambrel roof A gambrel roof in which the upper and lower slopes are of approximately equal length, but the lower slope is of steeper pitch, usually about 60 degrees. *See also* gambrel roof.

New Shingle style A term occasionally used to describe a late-20th-century modern shingled house having many of the basic characteristics of a **Shingle style** house built between 1880 and 1900.

niche A decorative recess in a wall, often containing a sculpture or an urn; often semicircular in plan, may be surmounted by a half-dome.

nidged ashlar, nigged ashlar Stone masonry that has been dressed on its exterior surface with a pick or sharply pointed hammer.

nine-over-nine (9/9) A term descriptive of a double-hung window having nine panes in the upper sash and nine panes in the lower sash. *See* pane.

nogging The **infilling**, such as bricks, between the logs in a log cabin or between the framing members of a **timber-framed house** of the colonial American period; used to increase the rigidity of the framing system, provide increased thermal insulation, and improve fire resistance.

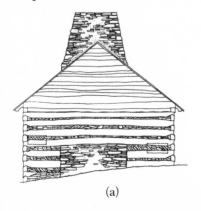 

(a)   (b)

nogging: (a) Robert Neal Cabin, Pittsburgh, Pa.;
(b) detail of wall construction

non-load-bearing wall A wall capable only of supporting its own weight and, if it is an exterior wall, capable of resisting the force of the wind blowing against it; it cannot support an imposed load. Compare with **load-bearing wall.**

Norfolk latch A type of **thumb latch** for a door, with a metal plate behind the latch to protect the door finish. Originally made of iron wrought by hand and imported from England, manufactured latches of this type came into use in America in the early 1800s. Compare with the **Suffolk latch.**

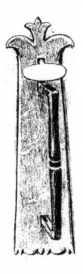

Norfolk latch

Normandy cottage *See* **French Eclectic style** and **Neo-French architecture.**

North Italian mode *See* **Italian Renaissance Revival.**

nosing, nose The prominent, usually rounded edge of a horizontal surface that extends beyond an upright face below; on a stair, for example, the projection of a tread beyond the riser that supports it at one end.

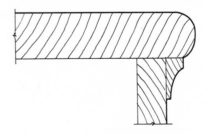

nosing

notch A cutout in a log or timber, at or near one of its ends, that is used to form a rigid joint when mated with another appropriately notched log or timber at right angles to it; for example, at the corners of a **log cabin** or **log house**. Considerations that enter into the choice of notch usually include the time required in its preparation, its rigidity, its effectiveness in draining moisture that may collect within it, whether the notch is cut in a round log or in a square timber, and its appearance. In the earliest log cabins and log houses in America, the **half-dovetail notch** was widely used because of its rigidity and its ability to drain rainwater. The **square notch** was also popular because of its simplicity, although it required a peg driven through the joint to make it rigid and secure the joint. The **saddle notch** was often used in frontier dwellings and outbuildings because it required a minimum of skill and preparation time. The **V-notch** was used to a lesser extent because it required more care in preparation. For definitions and illustrations of various types of notches, *see* **corner notch, diamond notch, double-saddle notch, dovetail notch, half-cut notch, half-dovetail notch, halved-and-lapped notch, lap notch, round notch, saddle notch, single notch, single-saddle notch, square notch, V-notch**.

notched-log ladder A primitive form of ladder, once used by some American Indian tribes, such as the Pueblos; consisted of a log, set at an angle with respect to the vertical, that was notched to provide a crude series of steps.

notched rafter A **rafter** having a notch on its underside near its lower end, enabling it to be fitted over and fastened to a **wall plate,** i.e., to a horizontal timber supporting the rafter.

novelty siding Same as **drop siding**.

nutmeg ornament An ornament resembling half a nutmeg; Connecticut is called the Nutmeg State in reference to wooden nutmegs reputedly made there.

notched-log ladder
in a Hopi Indian pueblo

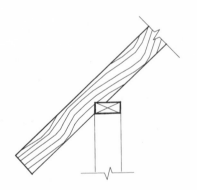

notched rafter

obelisk A monumental, tapering, four-sided stone shaft; may be topped by a decorative element, but usually has a pyramidal tip. A splendid example is the Washington Monument, 555 feet (169m) high, originally designed by Robert Mills (1781–1855), and completed in 1884.

observatory A room that provides a wide view; a term popularly used for the **cupola** of an **Italianate style** home.

octagon barn A barn having an eight-sided plan. Structures of this type were found in modest numbers in America prior to 1880, stimulated by interest in octagon houses. However, barns having this shape lost their popularity when the development of the circular **silo** demonstrated the practicality and superiority of a barn having a round plan; *see* **circular barn.**

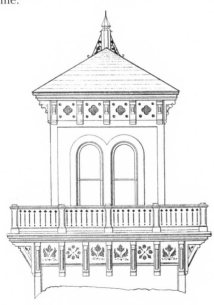

observatory

octagon barn (1885)

octagon house An eight-sided house, usually two to four stories high. Thomas Jefferson's retreat, Poplar Forest (c. 1811), near Lynchburg, Virginia, was a very early example of an eight-sided house; like many elegant southern homes, it had a portico at the rear as well as on the façade. According to a letter written by Jefferson from Poplar Forest in 1811, "I have fixed myself comfortably, keeping some books here, bringing others occasionally, am in the solitude of a hermit and quite at leisure." Nevertheless, he continued work on the interior of this house until 1823. Perhaps the individual who promoted the octagon house the most was Orson S. Fowler (1809–1887) author of *The Octagonal Mode*, published in 1848. Fowler was a persuasive lecturer (and phrenologist) who advocated innovations that emphasized functionality in housing, such as central heating, indoor plumbing, and simple conveniences such as **dumbwaiters** and **speaking tubes**. Octagon houses were numerous in the Hudson Valley of New York but were also built throughout the United States, mostly between 1850 and 1870, and were especially popular in the 1850s. The house was often encircled, or partially encircled, by a porch; it had a low-pitched roof, often topped with an eight-sided cupola, and occasionally a raised basement. In one arrangement all rooms opened into a large, full-height central space that served as a vertical shaft connected to the cupola, thereby promoting excellent air circulation. The exterior walls were usually of wood or concrete, though stone was sometimes used.

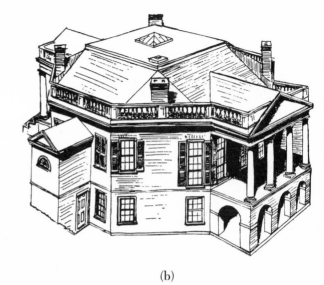

(b)

(a)

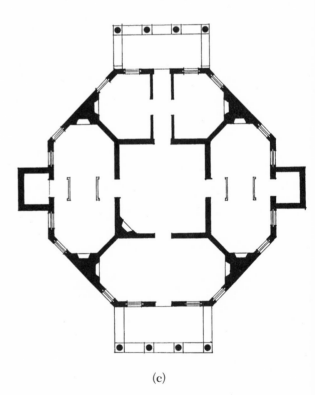

(c)

octagon house
(a) typical octagon house with encircling balcony;
(b) Thomas Jefferson's octagonal retreat, Poplar Forest, near Lynchburg, Va.;
(c) floor plan of Poplar Forest; even the nearby privies were octagonal and domed

octastyle A term descriptive of a **portico** having eight columns in the front.

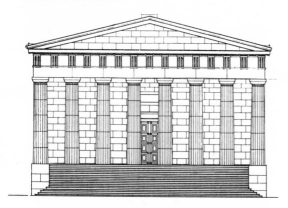

octastyle
Greek Revival style

oculus 1. A small circular window or panel, especially an opening at the crown of a dome. 2. Same as **bull's-eye window.**

oeil-de-boeuf A small round or oval window; same as **bull's-eye window.**

offset chimney Same as **stepped-back chimney.**

ogee 1. A double curve, formed by joining a convex line with a concave line, somewhat suggestive of the letter **S**. 2. A term descriptive of a pediment, molding, or roof having such a shape.

ogee,2: an ogee pediment

ogee arch A pointed arch, each side of which has the shape of an **ogee**, the lower curve being concave and the upper curve being convex.

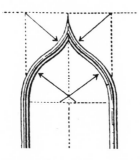

ogee arch

ogee pediment A pediment in the shape of an ogee.

ogee roof A roof whose **section** is an **ogee.**

ogee roof

one-and-one-half-bay cottage Same as a **three-quarter Cape house.**

one-and-one-half-story house A one-story house having a loft space between the ceiling of the first floor and the roof directly above; windows in the gable-end walls and/or dormers provide light and ventilation in this loft space, making it more livable and giving the house an additional half story.

one-and-one-half-story house

one-bay cottage Same as **half Cape house.**

one-centered arch Any arch struck from a single center of curvature, such as a **round arch** or **segmental arch.**

one-over-one 1. A two-story colonial cottage having two rooms, one directly over the other; usually the result of the expansion of a cottage having a **one-room plan** by the addition of a second floor above it; once especially found in Pennsylvania. 2. A term descriptive of a pattern in a double-hung window having one pane in the upper sash and one pane in the lower; *see* **pane.**

one-room cottage A cottage having a **one-room plan**, usually with loft space above.

one-room plan The earliest and simplest **floor plan** for a dwelling, especially used in 17th-century colonial New England, Pennsylvania and parts of the South; consisted of a single room, usually called a **hall** or **keeping room**, that served as a combination living room, dining room, kitchen, and workroom. Cooking was done in a large fireplace set into a massive chimney. In some regions the front door of the house opened into a small vestibule called a *porch*; in others it opened directly into the hall. Access to a loft above was provided either by a staircase in the vestibule or by a ladder in the hall. As the colonists prospered, many such houses were enlarged by adding a second room, called a *parlor*, giving rise to the **hall-and-parlor plan**. The parlor served as a combination living room and sleeping room for the parents. Also called a single-room plan. *See also* **one-over-one.**

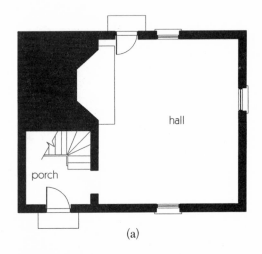

(a)

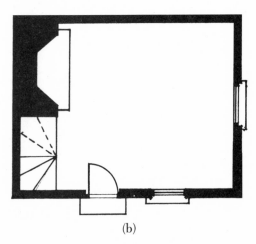

(b)

one-room plan
(a) with a porch; (b) without porch

one-room schoolhouse A school in which all elementary-grade students were taught in a single room. Such schools were common in sparsely populated areas in America before the 20th century; many had a bell at the ridge of the roof for summoning students at the start of the school day.

one-room schoolhouse
Old-stone Schoolhouse (1810), New Jersey

opalescent glass A type of iridescent **glass** of many colors; first used by the painters Louis Comfort Tiffany (1848–1933) and John La Farge (1835–1910) in the late 19th century; now often referred to as *Tiffany glass.*

open cornice A **cornice** in which the rafters supporting the roof are visible from below.

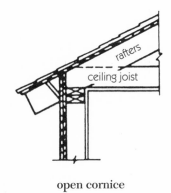

open cornice

open eaves Overhanging **eaves** in which the roof rafters are visible from below.

open-newel stair A spiral stair constructed around an open cylindrical space without a central post (i.e., **newel,1**), in contrast to a **solid-newel stair** built around a post. Also called a hollow-newel stair.

open pediment Same as **broken pediment.**

open plan A **floor plan** in which there are either no internal walls or a minimum number of internal walls that subdivide the space; often there are many partial-height partitions.

open roof A roof construction in which the rafters and roof sheathing are visible from below. There is no ceiling between the underside of the roof construction and the floor below.

open stair A **stair** whose treads are visible from one or from both sides of the stair. Also called an open staircase or an open-string stair.

open stair

open string An inclined board, parallel to the slope of a stair (i.e., a **string**), whose upper edge is cut to fit the profile of the **treads** and **risers** of the steps; the treads of the stairs project beyond the face of the string and are visible. Compare with **closed string.**

open-timbered roof Same as **open roof**.

openwork Any work, especially ornamental, that is characterized by perforations or openings, such as **scrollwork.**

operable transom Above a door, a solid or glazed panel that may be opened for ventilation.

operable window A window that may be opened for ventilation, as opposed to one that is fixed.

orangery A building, or sometimes a part of a building, once used in especially lavish homes for cultivating orange trees and other ornamental or exotic plantings in a climate where they would not grow outdoors; usually had large, tall windows along its southern exposure. A splendid early example of this type of building is The Orangery (1685) at the Palace of Versailles, said to be its finest piece of architecture. Some orangeries in America were provided with central heating systems as early as the middle of the 19th century. *See also* **conservatory, greenhouse, hothouse.**

orangery
at Wye House (1812), Talbot County, Md.

order In Classical architecture, a particular style of column having a prescribed **entablature** and standardized details, including its capital and base. The term is often limited to a single shaft of a column with its associated appurtenances; the distinction between one order and another is marked by the details of one such unit of a colonnade. The Greeks developed the **Doric order, Ionic order**, and **Corinthian order**; the Romans added the **Composite order** and **Tuscan order.** For each order the height and spacing of the columns were established in terms of a specified number of diameters of the lower part of the columns, and the design of the base was also prescribed; the height of the **entablatures** was determined by the height of the columns. Often used in **Classical Revival style, Greek Revival style,** and **Neoclassical style** buildings in America before the 20th century.

ordinary An obsolete term for a village tavern licensed to sell alcoholic beverages and to accommodate travelers.

Organic architecture A style of architecture of American origin that emerged in the early 20th century, based largely on the design philosophy of Frank Lloyd Wright (1867–1959). He asserted that the structure and appearance of a building should be based on forms that are in harmony with its natural environment and that the materials used on the exterior should be sympathetic to the building's locale, thereby relating the building to its setting. Thus, use should be made of low-pitched overhanging roofs to provide protection from the sun in the summer and to provide some weather protection in the winter; and maximum use should be made of natural daylighting.

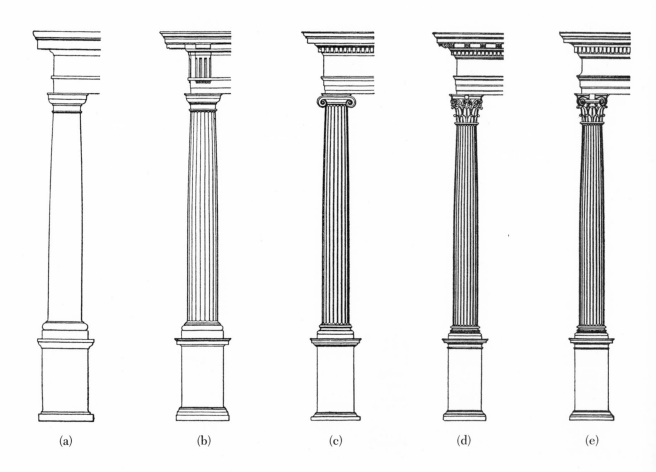

(a) (b) (c) (d) (e)

order
(a) Tuscan; (b) Doric; (c) Ionic; (d) Corinthian; (e) Composite

oriel A bay window that projects from the face of a wall; usually cantilevered out, corbeled out, or supported by brackets; found, for example, in the **Châteauesque style** and in **Tudor Revival** homes.

oriel: 18th cent.

Oriental Revival A loose term applied to **Exotic Revival** architecture that is suggestive of the architecture of the Middle East and the Far East. *See also* **Moorish Revival.**

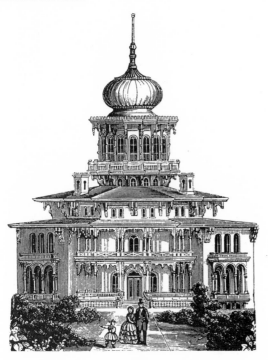

Oriental Revival: Longwood (1861; unfinished), an Eclectic style home in Natchez, Miss., designed by Samuel Sloan, exhibits Oriental Revival influences

original lean-to Same as **integral lean-to**.

ornament In architecture, a detail of shape, texture, and/or color (such as an embellishment or decoration) that is deliberately exploited to attract the attention of an observer.

ornamental cast iron *See* **cast-iron lacework**.

ornamental plaster A **plaster** detail that is decorative in nature, such as a ceiling medallion; usually cast in **plaster of paris**.

orthostyle A term descriptive of a colonnade arrayed in a straight line.

osier A flexible, slender twig or branch, especially used to tie down the thatching on a roof.

outbuilding A building subsidiary to, and separate from, the main house or building; a **dependency**.

outer string An inclined board, parallel to the slope of a stair, that is located at the end of the steps away from the wall and that supports these outer ends of the steps.

outhouse 1. A detached outdoor structure housing a primitive toilet; usually constructed of wood, not the proverbial brick. 2. A small accessory building generally located at the rear of a house and used for domestic animals, storage, etc.

outhouse,1 (1700)
Danvers, Mass.

outkitchen In early America and extending into the 19th century, a kitchen that is subsidiary to, but separate from, the main house. This separation avoided overheating the house during hot summer weather, eliminated cooking odors, reduced noise emanating from the kitchen, and minimized the possibility of accidentally setting the house on fire.

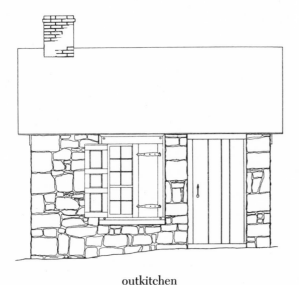

outkitchen

outlooker 1. Same as **outrigger**. 2. A covering over a doorway or opening in the face of a building to provide a small degree of shelter.

outrigger A beam at the ridge of a roof that extends beyond the end wall of the building to serve as a support for hoisting tackle or the like.

outrigger

outshot An addition to a building that adjoins but is structurally independent of it, often resulting in an **L-plan**.

outside chimney Same as **exterior chimney**.

oval window A window having the shape of an ellipse or a shape between an ellipse and a circle.

oval window

overdoor The wall area or decorative element directly above a doorway; often ornamented.

overhang, overshoot The projection of an upper story beyond the wall of the story below, commonly on the front of the house, but sometimes on the sides as well; frequently called a jetty. This term is also applied to the **forebay** of a Pennsylvania Dutch barn. *See also* **framed overhang** and **hewn overhang**.

overhang
front of Boardman House (1687), Saugus, Mass.

overmantel An ornamental panel or structure above a **mantelpiece.** In American homes during the Victorian era, a mirror was sometimes set in the overmantel to reflect light into the room from a candelabra placed on the mantelpiece.

oversailing A term descriptive of a surface that overhangs or projects beyond the surface immediately below. For example, an oversailing course of brickwork projects beyond the general face of a wall; an oversailing **gable end** is a gable end that overhangs the floor below.

overstory 1. An upper story. 2. Same as **clerestory.**

ovolo molding A convex molding, usually having a profile of approximately a quarter-circle or quarter-ellipse.

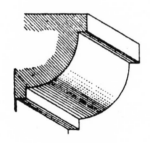

ovolo molding

owl hole An opening in an exterior wall of a barn that permits owls, martins, or other mice-eating birds to enter; often cut in a distinctive or decorative pattern near the top of a **gable end.**

ox-eye molding A concave molding having less of a hollow than a **scotia,** but a deeper hollow than a **cavetto.**

oxeye window, oxeye Same as **bull's-eye window.**

pace A seldom-used term for **stair landing.**

packaged house A **prefabricated house** composed of building components cut to size at the factory.

pad stone A block of stone, embedded in a wall, to support a beam or girder.

painted glass A type of **stained glass** formed by painting a plain or tinted glass with an enamel containing the desired pigment and then baking or firing the glass in a kiln at a high temperature.

paired brackets Two closely spaced brackets that form a pair. Also called coupled brackets.

paired gables A façade having two **gables**; found in America, for example, in the façades of **Gothic Revival** structures of wood construction.

palazzo In Italian cities, a large separate dwelling, usually sumptuous. One of the major categories into which the **Italianate style** is often divided. Palazzi of northern Italy were widely emulated in America in the Italian Renaissance Revival period from about 1890 to 1930. *See also* **Italianate style** and **Italian Renaissance Revival.**

pale, paling 1. A tall stake, usually of wood; one of a series set vertically into the ground to form a fence or protective barrier. 2. The protective barrier itself, i.e., a **palisade.** 3. The area enclosed by a **palisade.**

palazzo: American style
University Club (1900), New York City;
Charles Follen McKim, Architect;
bears a remarkable resemblance to
Palazzo Strozzi (c. 1480), Florence, Italy

palisade A series of stout poles, pointed on top, set vertically into the ground close to each other; used as a fence or fortification.

palisado house A primitive house or building, built in frontier areas, whose walls were constructed by setting two parallel rows of logs, pointed on top, upright into the ground; the space between the rows was usually filled with mud and twigs or with clay mixed with stones.

Palladian door A door topped with a rounded arch and flanked by vertical rectangular areas of fixed glass on each side that are narrower than and usually not as high as the door; suggestive of the conformation of a **Palladian window.**

Palladian dormer A **dormer** having a window, divided into three parts, that is suggestive of a small **Palladian window.**

Palladianism A style of building that follows the strict use of Roman forms, as set forth in the publications of the Italian Renaissance architect Andrea Palladio (1508–1580).

Palladian window A large window divided into three parts: a central **sash** that is arched at the top and two sashes on each side of it that are smaller than the central sash; the smaller sashes are rectangular, usually topped with flat lintels. Although a few Palladian windows appeared as early as 1750, they were not widely used in America until the **Federal style** became popular. Also used in the **Neoclassical style, Queen Anne style, Shingle style, Colonial Revival.** Compare with **three-part window.**

palma hut, palma cottage A primitive one-room dwelling having a relatively steeply pitched gable roof that was thatched with overlapping palmetto fronds attached to a wood framework, so as to provide a relatively watertight surface on the roof and side walls. Such temporary dwellings were constructed by early Spanish colonists in Saint Augustine, Florida, and environs in imitation of similar dwellings of the Seminole. The Seminole huts usually had a **smoke hole** in the ridge of the roof. *See also* **chickee.**

palm capital A type of **capital** resembling the spreading crown of a palm tree; sometimes used in America in **Egyptian Revival** structures.

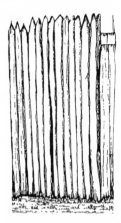

palisade

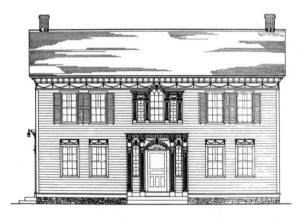

Palladian door with a Palladian window above
Harris House (1800), Castleton, Vt.

(a)   (b)

palma hut:
(a) method of construction; (b) detail showing method
of attachment of the palmetto fronds

pampre An ornament consisting of vine leaves and grapes used as a decoration.

pane 1. A flat sheet of glass, cut to fit a window or door or part of a window or door; often of small size, the larger ones usually being called *sheets*. Once installed in a window sash, a pane is often referred to as a *light*. A window sash may be subdivided into a number of smaller panes, often for decorative purposes. Thus, in specifying the configuration of a **double-hung window** having divided lights, the number of panes in the upper sash is specified first, followed by the word *over* and the number of panes in the lower sash. For example, a "six-over-three (6/3) pattern" indicates that the upper sash is divided into six panes and the lower sash is divided into three panes. Popular arrangements of panes in colonial America were six-over-six (6/6), nine-over-nine (9/9), and twelve-over-twelve (12/12). 2. A panel of a door, wainscot, or the like. 3. A rectangular division having a plane surface on the face or side of a building.

pane,1
a Georgian-style (9/9) window

panel A portion of a flat surface usually either sunk below or raised above the surrounding area; often set off by a molding, border, or some other decorative device, to distinguish it from the surface into which it is set.

paneled door A door having **stiles**, **rails**, and sometimes **muntins,2** which form one or more frames around thinner recessed panels; commonly referred to by the number of panels it contains, usually between one and eight; for example, a *two-paneled door*. Doors are also characterized by their panel arrangements; *see* **Christian door, cross-and-Bible door, witch door**.

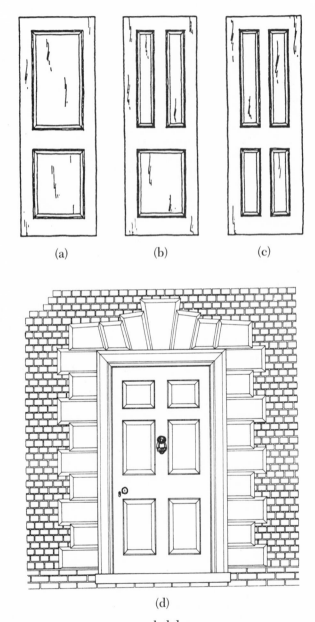

(a)   (b)   (c)

(d)

paneled door
(a) two panels; (b) three panels; (c) four panels;
(d) six-panel door, Hayes Manor House,
Chevy Chase, Md.

panework In **Tudor Revival,** the decorative panels formed by half-timbering.

pantile 1. An **S**-shaped rectangular roofing tile that is straight along its length but curved along its width; laid in courses so that each tile hooks over the adjacent tile. 2. A roofing tile whose cross section is semicircular and tapered; the large lower end fits over the tile directly below it.

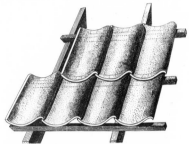

pantile,1

pantry 1. A room for the storage of food supplies; also called a larder. 2. A serving room between the kitchen and dining room. *See also* **butler's pantry** and **scullery.**

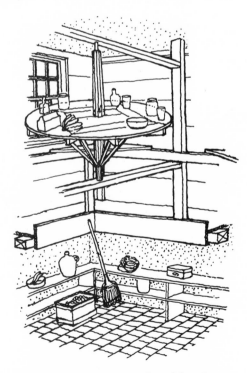

pantry,1: the Lovering colonial farmhouse, Kensington, N.H.; note an early version of a "lazy Susan," the revolving shelf

parapet 1. A low protective wall or similar barrier at the edge of a roof, balcony, terrace, or the like; often decorative, as in a **mission parapet, multicurved parapet,** or **stepped parapet.** 2. A wall of a fortification that rises above the main wall.

parapeted gable A **gable** having a face that rises above the roof line and carries a parapet. For example, *see* **Flemish gable, multicurved gable, stepped gable, straight-line gable.**

parge coat, pargeting 1. A plaster coat, especially one that is elaborate or ornamental. 2. The interior lining of a chimney flue, used to improve its fire resistance and to provide a smooth surface. 3. A coat of cement mortar on the face of rough masonry construction.

parlor In past eras in America, a room chiefly for the entertainment of visitors. In colonial America it was the room in the house where the most valuable furnishings were kept; usually somewhat smaller than the **hall,1.** This room was intended primarily for entertaining guests and important visitors as well as for special family gatherings. Because floor space was scarce in most colonial American houses, the parlor usually contained the best bed and so served as the parents' sleeping area. The bed vanished in subsequent periods, but the parlor remained a room more for special occasions than for family use.

parlor chamber A bedroom above the parlor in a two-story colonial American house having a **hall-and-parlor plan.**

parquetry A flat inlay pattern, usually geometric, consisting of closely fitted pieces of wood and employing two or more tones or colors; frequently used for ornamental flooring.

partition A divider, barrier, or internal wall that separates one space from another within a building; may either be **load-bearing** or **non-load-bearing.**

party wall A common wall shared by, and set between, two adjoining properties; used jointly by the owners of both properties under an easement agreement; usually half the thickness of the wall is on each property. The party wall must have a **fire-resistance rating** sufficiently high to prevent fire on one side of a wall from spreading to the other side. Also called a common wall.

party-wall house Same as **row house.**

passive solar-energy system In a **solar house**, a system by which energy is collected from the sun and stored, then distributed throughout the house predominantly by natural means, i.e., by convection, conduction, or radiation. Compare with **active solar-energy system.**

patera A small square, round or oval ornament, often decorated with leaves, petals, or the like; sometimes used as a decorative element, such as on a **corner block.**

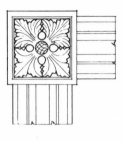

patera

paternoster A small molding in the form of a series of round beads; also called a bead molding.

patina A greenish coating that develops on a copper surface after it has been exposed to the atmosphere for a long period of time and has oxidized; seen, for example, on copper roofing.

patio 1. An outdoor area or courtyard, open to the sky but enclosed, or partially enclosed, by the walls of a building. While the term originally described such an area in a Spanish Colonial house, it is now used for any outdoor space next to a house that is used for relaxing, recreation, and family activities. *See also* **placita** and illustration under **U-plan.** 2. A large quandrangle of an early Spanish-American mission, usually surrounded on all four sides by a series of abutting structures for protection; these structures often included facilities for weaving, candle- and soap-making, carpenter and blacksmith shops, olive presses, winery, kitchen, and refectory.

patio: adjacent to an adobe house

patten A base or **groundsill** that supports a column, post, or pillar.

pattern book A useful book on architectural practice that served as a builders' manual, builders' guide, or handbook containing plans and/or patterns of houses and building details such as columns, cornices, doors, porches, and windows. Pattern books imported from England introduced the **Georgian style** of architecture to colonial America. One early influential example was *The Builder's Jewel* by Batty and Thomas Langley, published in London in 1741. Later, similar publications prepared by American architects were also important in spreading the latest architectural styles throughout the land. Among them was *The American Builders' Companion, or A New System of Architecture: Particularly Adapted to the Present Style of Building in the United States of America*, published in 1806 by Asher Benjamin; he also wrote other similar books, the last of them in 1833. Another significant publication was *The Young Carpenter's Assistant* by Owen Biddle, published in 1810. The *Young Builder's General Instructor* by Minard Lafever, published in 1829, presented the **orders** and elements of Greek architecture and was an important influence in spreading the **Greek Revival style** in America; Lafever also wrote a later book on **Gothic Revival** architecture.

patterned brickwork Masonry of bricks that are laid with more than one color, are laid in different directions, or have different textures, so as to form a decorative design.

patterned brickwork
Dickinson House (1754), Salem, N.J.

pavement light One of many heavy, translucent glass disks or prisms set into a section of pavement to convey light to a space beneath.

pavilion 1. A prominent structure projecting from a façade; usually located at the center of the façade or at each end. 2. A detached or semidetached structure used for entertainment or for specialized activities; for example, at a fair or park. 3. A temporary structure, usually ornamented, in a garden or at an exhibition.

pavilion roof A steeply pitched **hipped roof** whose upper termination is usually a ridge somewhat shorter than the length of the building. If the four sloping surfaces terminate in a peak, it is often called a **pyramidal roof** or a pyramidal-hipped roof.

pavilion roof: Avery Hall, Columbia University;
McKim, Mead & White, Architects

peak-head window 1. A window that has a triangular **head**; most often found in **Gothic Revival** church architecture 2. Same as **lancet window.**

peak-head window

pebble dash A stucco exterior finish in which large pebbles or shells are embedded in the stucco base by throwing them against a fresh base surface before it has hardened. Also called **rough-cast.**

pedestal A support for a classical column consisting of three parts: the uppermost, called the **cornice** or **cap**; the middle, called the **dado** or **die**; and the lowest, called the **base** or **plinth**. In contrast, in modern architecture a pedestal often consists of an unadorned block.

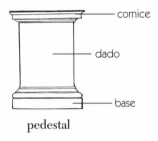

pedestal

pediment 1. In Classical architecture and its derivatives, a low triangular gable usually having a horizontal cornice enclosing a tympanum, with **raked** cornices on each side, surmounting or crowning a portico or another major division of a façade, end wall, or a colonnade. 2. A gable above or over a door, window, or hood; usually has a horizontal cornice, crowned with slanting sides forming a triangle, but may also be crowned other with configurations, such as curved or broken sides. For definitions and illustrations of specific types, *see* **angular pediment, broken pediment, broken-scroll pediment, center-gabled pediment, curved pediment, open pediment, pointed pediment, round pediment, scroll pediment, segmental pediment, split pediment, swan's-neck pediment, triangular pediment.**

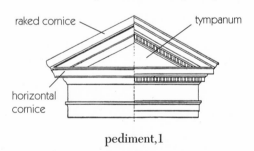

pediment, 1

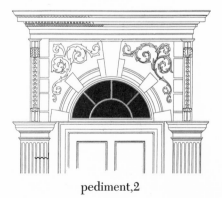

pediment, 2

pen 1. A term occasionally used as a synonym for *room* in a four-sided enclosure constructed of logs; for example, a one-room log cabin is sometimes referred to as a *single-pen cabin*, and a **dogtrot cabin** (consisting of two single-room cabins) is sometimes referred to as a *double-pen cabin*. 2. An enclosure for animals, such as a pigpen.

penciled A term descriptive of a mortar joint in a brick wall used in the early 19th century. The wall, with mortar joints flush with the brick surface, was first painted the color of the brick over its entire surface. Then a narrow white line was painted along the center of the mortar joints to create the illusion of an extremely thin mortar joint.

pendant, pendent, pendent drop 1. In the late 17th century, the 18th century, and beyond, a hanging carved-wood ornament used as an exterior decorative feature on New England colonial houses having an overhanging second story; commonly suspended from the overhang at the corners of the façade and called a **corner drop,** and also often suspended on each side of the front door; usually the only decorations on the façade; also called a drop. 2. A suspended feature or hanging ornament sometimes used in vault and timber roofs of **Gothic Revival** architecture.

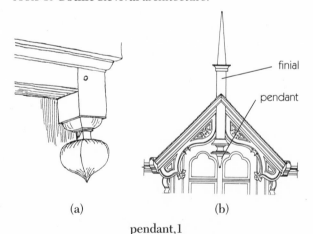

(a)   (b)

pendant, 1
(a) suspended from overhang at front corner of a colonial house; (b) on each side of the entry door

pendant, 2: Shrine House, Mobile, Ala.

pendentive 1. One of a set of curved wall surfaces that form a transition between a dome (or its **drum,1**) and its supporting masonry. 2. One of a set of surfaces vaulted outward from a pier, corbel, or the like.

pendentive,2

pendill Same as **pendant.**

Penn plan Similar to the **Quaker plan**, but having an **interior chimney** rather than an **exterior chimney.**

Pennsylvania Dutch The name given to German-speaking immigrants who settled in Pennsylvania and its environs primarily during the 18th century. For examples of their architecture, *see* **bank barn, forebay barn, German Barn, hex barn, Pennsylvania Dutch barn, pfeiler, rauchkammer, springhouse.**

Pennsylvania Dutch barn, Pennsylvania barn A **bank barn** having a **forebay.**

pent 1. Same as **chimney pent.** 2. A small room, **lean-to,** or **shed**, often with one or more open sides. 3. Same as **pent roof,1.**

pentastyle A term descriptive of a **portico** having five columns in front.

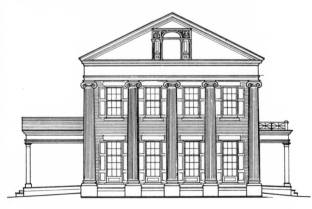

pentastyle: Harold Brooks House, Marshall, Mich.

pentice A small **pent roof,1** on a side of a building, often restricted to the area over a door.

pent roof 1. A small false roof having a single slope, placed between the first and second floors of a house; may provide very limited shelter for a window or door directly below but is usually merely decorative; frequently called a visor roof; *see also* **skirt roof** and **visor roof.** 2. Same as **shed roof.**

pent roof,1: on a barn

pergola A garden structure of open timber-frame construction, often latticed and supported by regularly spaced posts or columns and usually covered by climbing plants such as vines or roses.

pergola

Period Revival A general term, rather than a specific architectural style, that usually denotes some type of historical Revival architecture; for example, **Colonial Revival, Georgian Revival, Mission Revival, Pueblo Revival, Spanish Colonial Revival, Tudor Revival.**

peripteral A term descriptive of a classical building that is surrounded by a single row of columns.

peristyle A walkway, with a roof supported by columns, surrounding the exterior of a building or an open space. Such a colonnade is especially found on plantation houses in the vicinity of New Orleans and along the Mississippi River.

perpend, perpend stone A rectangular stone set with its longest dimensions perpendicular to the face of a masonry wall; extends through the entire thickness of the wall so that it is exposed on both faces of the wall.

perron 1. A formal terrace or platform, especially one centered on a gate or doorway. 2. An outdoor flight of steps, usually symmetrical, leading to a terrace, platform, or doorway of a large building.

pew In a house of worship, one of a number of fixed benches with backs.

pfeiler A pillar or pier that supports the **forebay** in a Pennsylvania Dutch barn.

piano nobile The principal story of a large house, usually one flight above street level; often contains formal reception rooms and dining rooms; especially found in **Italian Renaissance Revival** buildings.

piazza A term occasionally used for a raised porch or veranda in American Colonial architecture and derivatives, especially in the South; often supported by columns or posts.

piazza house A term occasionally used for a **Charleston house.**

picket fence A fence formed of a series of vertical pales, posts, stakes, or rods that are usually driven into the ground, joined together by horizontal rails, and sometimes brought to a point at the upper ends.

Picturesque Gothic A term sometimes applied to **High Victorian Gothic** architecture.

Picturesque movement The development of the concept, by a group of architects from about 1840 to 1900, that architectural ideals should look away from formal Classical architecture and instead should embrace the romanticized past. The modifier *Picturesque* is not indicative of a particular style but is suggestive of a number of styles or modes of architecture that were related to this movement, including: **Exotic Revival, Gothic Revival, Italianate style, Queen Anne style, Richardsonian Romanesque style, Second Empire style, Stick style, Swiss Cottage architecture**.

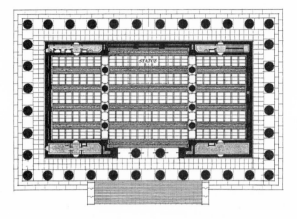

peripteral: plan of building (with superimposed reflected ceiling plan), Lincoln Memorial (1923), Washington, D.C.; Henry Bacon, Architect

piano nobile: W. M. Sledge House, Chappell Hill, Tex.

piazza

pièce sur pièce construction In French Vernacular architecture, a method of construction brought to Louisiana by the Acadians from Canada between about 1760 and 1790; used in building small houses of well-finished, heavy, rectangular hewn timbers (*pièces*), usually 4 to 6 inches (10–15cm) thick by 8 to 16 inches (20–40.6cm) wide. Each timber, laid horizontally, had a dovetail notch at each end, forming a strong, interlocking rigid joint with another appropriately notched timber at right angles to it. The timbers were fitted closely together so that little **chinking** was required.

pier A column, masonry support, or other structural member used to sustain a concentrated load, generally as a thickened section forming an integral part of a wall; usually set at intervals along the wall, which is thicker at such placements.

pierced work Ornamentation that is characterized by patterns formed by perforations. *See also* **gingerbread, openwork.**

pierrotage In **French Vernacular architecture** of Louisiana and the Mississippi Valley, lime mortar or clay mixed with small stones; used as **infilling** between half-timbering with diagonal braces (**columbage**). *See also* **bousillage.**

pigeonnier In **French Vernacular architecture** of Louisiana, same as **dovecote.**

pig iron Crude high-carbon iron ore that has been smelted and cast into ingots; may be remelted and used as a source of material for architectural cast-iron products or further refined for use in producing steel. In the 1800s the pig-iron industry in America was largely concentrated in the Ohio River Valley and in Pennsylvania.

pilaster A pier or pillar attached to a wall, often with a capital and base, that projects slightly from the wall, sometimes to provide added strength and sometimes merely for ornamentation. Full-height pilasters at the corners of building façades, often called *corner pilasters*, first made their appearance in America around 1750.

(a)

pigeonnier
Uncle Sam Plantation, St. James Parish, La.

pigeon roof Same as **pyramidal roof.**

(b)

pilasters: (a) on façade of Foster-Hutchinson House, sacked by a mob protesting the Stamp Act in 1765, Boston, Mass.; (b) corner pilaster, Corinthian order, Goodring House (c. 1806), Bristol, R.I.

pilastered chimney A **chimney shaft** having pilasters on two or more sides to provide a decorative effect and to enhance its structural strength.

pile 1. A wood, concrete, or steel column that is driven into the ground, usually to support a vertical load imposed from above. 2. A term used to indicate the number of rooms in a house from front to rear; for example, a double-pile house has two rooms between the façade and the rear wall of the house.

pilier In **French Vernacular architecture** of Louisiana, a stack of rectangular blocks of cypress wood used to support a **Creole house,** transferring the load of the structure to the earth below. The use of cypress is advantageous in that this wood resists rot resulting from an unusually high moisture content in the ground.

pillar Any isolated vertical structural member that is capable of providing major vertical support, such as a column, pier, pilaster, or post.

piloti (*pl.* **pilotis**) One of a number of isolated columns, posts, or piles that support a building, raising it above ground level; the ground floor is open to the exterior.

pin A dowel, peg, or **treenail** used to secure a joint between two members.

pineapple ornament A decoration, usually cast in plaster or carved in wood, that resembles the cone of a pine tree or a true pineapple; said to be a symbol of hospitality. Often found in American Colonial architecture, for example, as a **pendant** or a **finial.**

pine shingle A shingle of pine wood, usually hand-split along the grain; much used in America in the colonial past and still used today, for example, on **Cape Cod houses.**

pinnacle A small, largely ornamental upright structure, usually more or less tapered, rising above the roof of a building, commonly capping a tower, crowning a buttress, or the like.

pisé 1. Same as **rammed earth.** 2. A mixture of clay and chopped straw, sometimes with the addition of gravel; particularly used in wall construction.

pitched-face masonry In masonry, having all arrises cut true and in the same plane, but with the face beyond the arris edges left comparatively rough, being simply dressed with a pitching chisel.

pilastered chimney
home (c. 1715), East Greenwich, Conn.

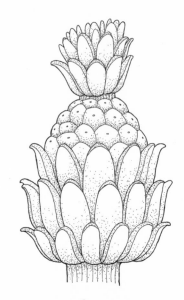

pineapple ornament
Wanton-Hunter House (c. 1746), Newport, R.I.

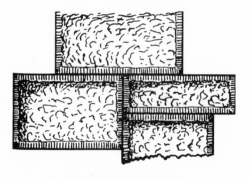

pitched-faced masonry

pitched roof 1. A gable roof having the same pitch, usually steep, on each side of a central ridge. On early colonial New England houses, the pitch was most often 45 degrees but in unusual cases could be as much as 60 degrees. 2. Occasionally, a synonym for a **gable roof.**

pitched-roof dormer A **dormer** having a triangular-shaped gable.

pit house 1. Same as **dugout**. 2. A multifamily dwelling once used by American Indians of the West Coast, approximately circular in shape. Set partially below ground level, it had a framework constructed of heavy logs that supported layers of tightly spaced poles on which were placed a heavy layer of earth and grass or the like; an opening at the top provided some light and permitted smoke to escape from a firepit on the dirt floor below.

pit house,2

pivot window A window that turns about hinges, usually aligned along a vertical axis.

placita A central enclosed courtyard in Spanish Colonial ranches of the American Southwest; usually entered through a massive gate (**zaguán**) set in a high wall built of adobe bricks.

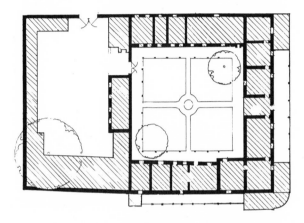

Plains cottage, Plains house A relatively simple single-family, single-story house, constructed primarily of sod, with two to five rooms and a depth usually somewhat greater than its width; primarily built in the 19th century in those parts of the Great Plains (i.e., the region between the Mississippi River and the Rocky Mountains, from Canada to Texas) where homes were usually constructed of sod, the only material conveniently obtainable. *See also* **sod house** and **straw bale house.**

placita
plan of La Casa del Rancho, near San Diego, Calif.

plan 1. A two-dimensional graphic representation of the design, location, and dimensions of a building, or the components thereof, seen in a horizontal plane viewed from above. *See* **center-hall plan, cruciform plan, community planning, floor plan, four-square plan, gable-front-and-wing plan, Georgian plan, ground plan, half-house plan, hall-and-parlor plan, H-plan, linear plan, L-plan, one-room plan, open plan, Penn plan, Quaker plan, reflected ceiling plan, side-hall plan, single-room plan, three-room plan, T-plan, two-room plan, U-plan.** 2. When used in the plural, a set of drawings, including elevations and sections, that collectively define a building. 3. *See* **city plan** and **town plan.**

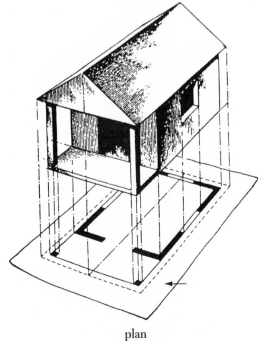

plan

plancier, plancer The soffit (underside) of any projecting member, such as a **cornice.**

plank A long, wide, square-sawn piece of timber. The contemporary specifications for planks vary, but the minimum width is usually about six to eight inches (15–20cm), and the minimum thickness is usually about two inches (5cm) for softwood and one inch (2.5cm) for hardwood.

plank fence Same as **board fence.**

plank-frame house A type of house in 17th-century colonial America constructed of heavy wood **planks**, usually erected vertically by setting them into grooves in a **sill plate,1** for support; they were then drilled and pegged or otherwise held firmly in place.

(a)

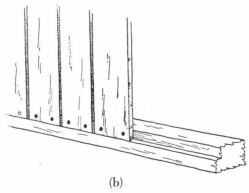

(b)

plank-frame house: (a) Glebe House, Woodbury, Conn., with 2-inch-thick planks; (b) detail showing the fastening of planks to the sill plate

plank house An Eskimo dwelling primarily along the Alaskan coastline; often a shedlike structure built either entirely above ground or partially below ground level; usually rectangular in plan and of **post-and-lintel construction.** The heavy plank walls and the roof were largely independent of each other; they were supported by columns consisting of logs stripped of their bark or of very heavy planks cut from logs. The typical Tlingit house was built without nails but was tenoned. Upon completion the entire structure was covered with a thick layer of sod. The doorway always faced the water.

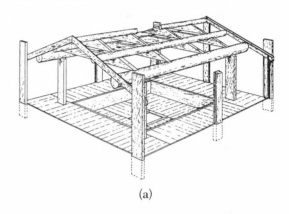

(a)

(b)

plank house: (a) framing for a typical Tlingit dwelling; (b) in Alaska

planking 1. A covering or flooring made of planks. 2. In log cabin construction, a term occasionally applied to a log that has been hewn only on two sides; the flat surfaces of these logs form the inner and outer walls, leaving bark between the horizontal joints; the cracks between these joints are usually filled with a mixture of clay and chopped straw or the like.

plank-in-the-ground construction *See* **plaunch debout en terre.**

planning *See* **community planning.**

plantation house The principal house of a Southern plantation, usually of very large acreage, on which cash crops such as cotton, sugar, rice, or tobacco were cultivated. In regions influenced by **French Vernacular architecture**, particularly in Louisiana and in other areas having a high humidity, houses were usually designed to take maximum advantage of natural ventilation, with very tall windows, two stories, and a veranda (commonly called a **galerie**) on the second story that extended cross the entire façade and sometimes along the sides and back as well; large plantation houses often had a galerie on all four sides of the house. The walls at ground level were thick, of brick construction, usually stuccoed; the flooring was brick; on the upper floor, the walls were often of cypress construction. Many of the most fertile plantations were along rivers that flooded periodically, resulting in soil so rich that fertilizers were not required. Because of the high water table, the plantation houses usually had no basements. Instead, the ground floor, called a **raised basement**, was often the location for service facilities, pantries, wine cellar, servants' rooms, and sometimes for a dining room. Thus, the principal floor of the plantation house was the floor above, which provided much better air circulation than if it were at ground level; French windows were numerous to promote cross-ventilation. The *galerie* was supported by stucco-covered brick columns having a classic appearance. In many plantation houses, above each of these columns, on the second floor there were lighter wood columns supporting the roof. An exterior staircase often provided access to the principal floor from ground level. Cooking was done in the **outkitchen** near the house. Many of the more pretentious houses in other areas of the South were in the **Greek Revival style**, the **Italianate style**, or a mixture of several styles or influences. *See also* **American Colonial architecture of the early South**.

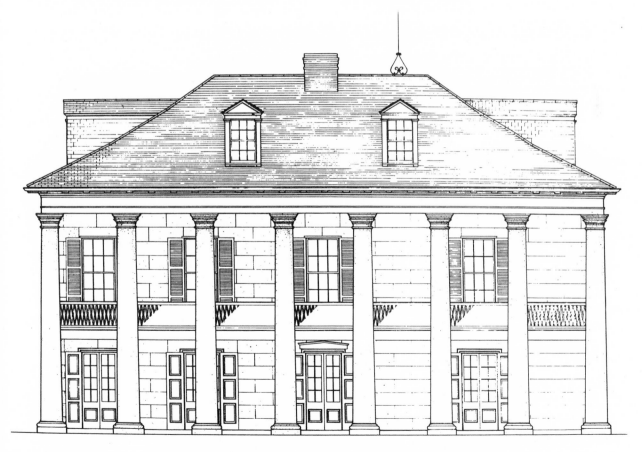

plantation house: René Beauregard House (1830), Chalmette, La.

planted molding A molding that is nailed on, laid on, or otherwise fastened to a surface, rather than cut into the surface itself.

plaque A tablet, often inscribed, that is affixed to the surface of a wall or set into a wall; usually commemorates some special event or serves as a memorial.

plaque
showing date of construction of the Old Mill,
Cumberland County, N.J.

plaster A mixture of lime or gypsum with sand and water, producing a pastelike material that is applied in the plastic state, usually over **lath** fastened to a surface such as a wall or ceiling or sometimes directly onto brick; it forms a hard surface when the water it contains evaporates. In very early settlements in America, when lime or gypsum was not available, a so-called plaster of fine white clay mixed with chopped straw was sometimes troweled onto a surface to produce a smooth finish on a wall or ceiling. By the middle of the 17th century, **lime** was available in some of the colonies, particularly along the seacoast where it could be obtained by heating seashells. Cow hair and/or cow dung often was added to the plaster mixture to increase its mechanical strength when dry. In the late 19th century, gypsum supplanted lime as the plaster of choice because of its superior properties. In **Spanish Colonial architecture of the American Southwest,** a mixture of clay, chopped straw, and water (called *mud plaster*) was widely used as a plaster finish on adobe walls. *See also* **stucco.**

plaster of paris A calcined gypsum containing no additives to control the rate of evaporation of the water it contains, so that it dries very quickly; especially suitable for use in fine ornamental plasterwork because it fills all the crannies of a mold.

plat An archaic term for a map, plan, or chart of a city, town, section, or subdivision, indicating the location and boundaries of individual properties.

platband 1. Any flat, rectangular, horizontal molding of slight projection in comparison with its width. 2. A decorative **lintel** over a doorway. 3. The **fillets** between the **flutes** of a column.

plate A structural timber, laid horizontally on its widest surface; provides bearing and anchorage for other timbers, joists, trusses, or rafters. If located at the top of a wall, it is called a **wall plate** or **raising plate**; if laid on the ground, it is called a **ground plate** or **groundsill**. *See also* **crown plate, curtail plate, false plate, ground plate, roof plate, sill, sill plate, soleplate, top plate.**

plate glass A high-quality glass sheet having both its sides plane and parallel so that it is free of distortions and flaws; has much greater mechanical strength than ordinary window glass, so it can be used to glaze large, undivided areas. It is usually formed by a *rolling process,* then ground and polished, but can also be formed by the *float-glass process,* in which molten glass floats on a layer of molten metal to smooth out surface irregularities. This produces a flat sheet of glass when the temperature of the molten metal is gradually reduced. *See also* **glass.**

Plateresque architecture A richly decorative style of Spanish Renaissance architecture of the 16th century; its decorative elements are considered to resemble the intricate work of silversmiths in delicacy, hence its name. Occasionally emulated in **Spanish Colonial Revival** architecture in America.

platform framing A system of framing for a building of wood construction several stories high, in which the studs are only one story high. The floor joists for each story rest on the **top plates** of the story below; the bearing walls and partitions rest on the subfloor of each story, i.e., on the rough floor that serves as the base for the finish floor. Compare with **balloon framing.** Also called western framing.

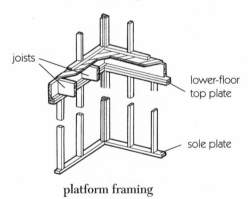

joists
lower-floor top plate
sole plate

platform framing

plaunch debout en terre In **French Vernacular architecture** of Louisiana and the lower Mississippi Valley in the early 1700s, a system of construction in which closely spaced planks were driven several feet into the ground; **bousillage** was applied between the vertical boards above ground level and then covered with horizontal clapboards. It was relatively easy to build and therefore was widely used in southern Louisiana, but it had the disadvantage of impermanence, because the wood below ground tended to rot over a period of time.

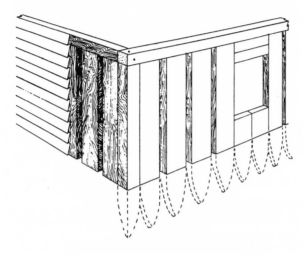

plaunch debout en terre

plaza A public square that is usually centrally located, found especially in towns of the American Southwest of Spanish heritage.

plinth 1. A square or rectangular base for a column, pedestal, pier, or pilaster. 2. A solid monumental base, often ornamented with moldings, bas-reliefs, or inscriptions; sometimes used to support a statue or memorial.

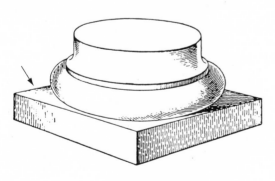

plinth,1

pneumatic structure A very lightweight temporary exterior structure, usually fabricated of a membrane of an impervious material and supported not by a structural framework but by the difference in air pressure between the exterior and the interior. The interior pressure must be maintained slightly in excess of normal atmospheric pressure by fans; otherwise the structure will slowly deflate and collapse. Used primarily as a temporary enclosure or for housing sports facilities such as tennis courts and swimming pools during inclement weather. Also called an air-supported structure.

pocket door 1. A single door leaf that slides into a vertical rectangular slot on one side of the doorway. 2. A pair of door leaves, each of which slides into a vertical slot in a side of the doorway. Because such doors do not require room to swing open, they are especially useful where space is limited.

pocket-head window A window in which a part of the **sash** slides upward through an opening in the head of the window frame.

pointed arch Any **arch** with a point at its apex, for example, a **lancet arch** or **triangular arch**.

pointed architecture Architecture characterized by **Gothic arches;** *see* **Gothic Revival.**

pointed dormer Any **dormer** having a point at its apex, for example, a **gabled dormer.**

pointed pediment A **pediment** having a triangular shape. Also called a triangular pediment.

Pointed style A term once used for **Gothic Revival,** but such use is now rare.

pointed work In masonry, the rough finish that is produced on a stone by repeated impacts of a pointed tool on its face.

pointing 1. The removal of old mortar from between existing bricks and its replacement with new mortar; also called repointing. 2. In brickwork, the final treatment of **raked** joints by troweling mortar into the joints. *See also* **recessed pointing** and **tuck pointing.**

pole-frame construction Same as **bent-frame construction.**

pole house A boxlike, rectangular, timber-framed house constructed by Alaskan Eskimos on King Island in the Bering Sea.

polychromed 1. A term descriptive of a building façade exhibiting a distinctive masonry pattern of contrasting colors, usually in the form of horizontal bands across the façade and/or bands around arches, doorways, or windows; a feature of the latter phase of **High Victorian Gothic**. 2. A term descriptive of a surface that is painted in a variety of colors to emphasize the differences among various elements.

poorhouse In colonial America, a building, often supported by a religious organization, that provided housing and minimal services for the indigent. *See also* **almshouse** and **bettering house**.

porch 1. A small vestibule inside the front door of a 17th-century colonial American house, usually containing a steep stair leading to the loft space above. 2. An exterior structure that shelters a building entrance. 3. An exterior structure that extends along the outside of a building; usually roofed and generally open-sided, but may also be screened, semienclosed, or glass-enclosed; it may be an addition to the main structure or may be set within the house structure, in which case it is called an **integral porch**. 4. A **veranda**, **galerie**, or **piazza**. *See also* **carriage porch, double-decker porch, double-tiered porch, engaged porch, full-height porch, full-width porch, inset porch, integral porch, lattice porch, projecting porch, raised porch, sleeping porch, storm porch, two-tiered porch, wraparound porch, portale**.

porch chamber A bedroom above an unheated entrance porch or veranda of a house.

portal An impressive entrance, gate, or ostentatious door to a building or courtyard.

portale In **Spanish Colonial architecture**, a covered porch, usually long and narrow, on the front of a house or on the side; provides direct access to individual room entrances. Its roof is supported by wood posts capped with **bolsters,1**.

polychromed,1: arch

porch,1
in a 17th-cent. colonial home, a vestibule showing stair to the attic

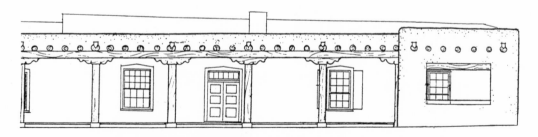

portale: El Palacio Real de Santa Fe (1614), Santa Fe, N.M.

porte cochère 1. A covered carriage or automobile entryway to provide shelter from inclement weather for persons arriving or leaving a building by a vehicle. 2. A covered carriage or automobile entryway leading to a courtyard.

porte cochère

portico A covered entrance having a roof supported by a series of columns or piers, commonly at the front entrance to a building. Porticos appeared in America after about 1750. In the North they were usually small. In the South they were usually larger, commonly being two stories high in elegant homes and sometimes placed on both the front and rear of the house, as at Thomas Jefferson's house Poplar Forest, illustrated under **octagon house.**

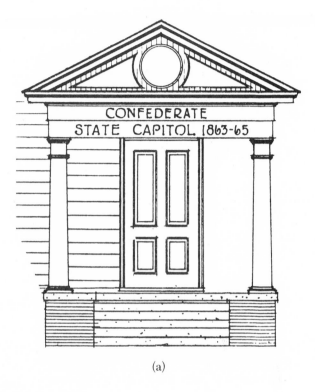

(a)

(b)

portico: (a) State Capitol (from 1863–1865), Washington, Ark.; (b) a two-storied portico

portico-in-antis A **portico** that is recessed within a structure instead of projecting from the façade. *See also* **antae** and **in antis**.

portland cement A generic term for a cementitious binder used in most modern structural concrete; manufactured by grinding and burning a mixture of limestone with clay or shale with a small amount of gypsum. This product is then mixed with water and an aggregate (such as sand and gravel) to form a monolithic product when dry. Although **cement** was developed by the ancient Romans, the first *portland cement* was developed in England by a bricklayer, John Aspdin, in 1824. Modern portland cement has greatly increased in tensile strength. *See also* **cement.**

posada In **Spanish Colonial architecture**, an inn.

possum-trot cabin Same as **dogtrot cabin.**

post A strong, stiff, vertical structural member or column, usually of wood, stone, or metal, capable of supporting a **framing** member of the structure above it and/or providing a firm point of lateral attachment; posts may divide the structural framework of a building into **bays**. In early colonial days, posts provided the main vertical supports in timber-framed houses. In such houses the term *post* was often preceded by an adjective that indicated the its location, as a **corner post**, or by an adjective that indicated its shape, as a **musket-stock post**. For definitions and illustrations of specific types of posts, *see* **chimney post, corner post, crown post, door post, flared post, gable post, gatepost, gun-stock post, jamb post, musket-stock post, prick post, principal post, shouldered post, sure post, teagle post, wall post.**

post-and-beam framing Same as **post-and-lintel construction.**

post-and-girt framing In an early colonial American **timber-framed house**, a medieval system of structural wood-frame construction characterized by the use of heavy corner **posts,** horizontal **girts** to carry the superimposed loads, and summerbeams to carry the floor joists. Structural members were interconnected by **mortise-and-tenon joints** that were held fast by wood pins or dowels. Post-and-girt framing was replaced by **balloon framing** in the early 19th century, a construction technique that spread after the invention of machines for manufacturing good-quality nails and as the availability of commercial lumber in standard sizes increased.

post-and-lintel construction A system of construction characterized by the use of vertical columns (**posts**) and heavy horizontal beams (**lintels**) to carry a load over an opening, in contrast to systems employing arches or vaults. Also called post-and-beam framing.

post-and-pane, post-and-petrail A system of timber construction consisting of a framework of structural timber posts with an **infilling** (such as brickwork) between the posts.

post-and-rail fence A fence having a series of posts set into the ground, usually interconnected by three or four horizontal rails between consecutive posts.

Post-Colonial period The years from about 1780 to 1830, during which time buildings were commonly built in the **Classical Revival style, Greek Revival style,** or **Federal style.**

postiche Decorations added after a work is finished, especially when superfluous, inappropriate, or in questionable taste.

postigo In **Spanish Colonial architecture** of the American Southwest, a small door set in a door of much larger size, such as a **zaguán.**

post-in-the-ground house A relatively simple type of wood building construction in which the **posts** were set directly into the ground, as for example in a **poteaux-en-terre house.** The life span of such buildings was usually limited because of the wood rot that eventually developed at the base of the posts. This type of construction was therefore usually limited to temporary or subsidiary buildings near or adjoining a principal structure.

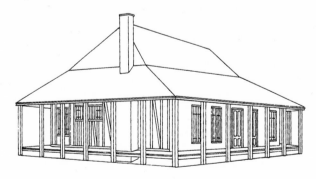

post-in-ground house

Post-Medieval architecture *See* **American Colonial architecture.**

Post-Modern architecture Since the late 1960s, a term describing architecture that connotes a break with the canons of **International style** modernism. Functionalism and emphasis on the expression of structure are rejected in favor of a greater freedom of design, including classical historical imagery. This leads to a new interplay of contemporary forms and materials with frequent historical allusions, often ironic, as, for example, in the use of nonsupporting classical columns and medieval arches. Post-Modern architecture also accepts the manifestations of commercial mass culture, such as bright colors, neon lights, and advertising signs. Especially influential in the formulation of post-modernism were the works of Robert Venturi (1925–) and Denise Scott Brown (1931–), Peter Eisenman (1932–), Michael Graves (1934–), Robert A. M. Stern (1939–), Charles Moore (1925–1993), and Philip Johnson(1906–); an example is Johnson's AT&T Building, 1984, in New York City. *See also* **Neo-Eclectic architecture.**

post-on-sill house Same as **poteaux-sur-solle house.**

potato barn A **barn** for the long-term storage of potatoes, sunk below ground level to provide a cool temperature that remains above freezing in the wintertime; often has a gambrel roof.

potato barn

poteaux-en-terre house In **French Vernacular architecture**, a dwelling of the earliest French settlers, primarily in Louisiana but also farther to the north in the Mississippi Valley, before the introduction of building techniques adapted to the prevailing climatic conditions. Posts (*poteaux*), usually of cypress, acted as the vertical structural elements, supporting the walls; the posts were close together and driven several feet into the ground (*terre*). The space between them was usually filled with a mixture of clay and Spanish moss (**bousillage**), clay and small stones (**pierrotage**), or **briquette-entre-poteaux.** Although this construction was simple and easy to erect, it had a limited life because that part of the posts below ground level tended to rot. Compare with **poteaux-sur-solle house.**

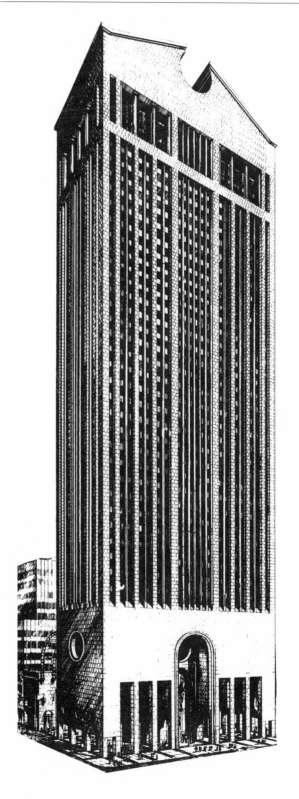

Post-Modern architecture: AT&T Building (1984), New York City; Philip Johnson, Architect

poteaux-sur-solle house In early **French Vernacular architecture** of Louisiana, a dwelling similar to a **poteaux-en-terre house** but supported by a hewn-log structural framework that usually rested on a **sill,1** (*solle*), i.e., a heavy horizontal timber that was supported by cypress blocks. This construction obviated the problem of wood rot that occurred with *poteaux-en-terre* construction; the cypress blocks could be replaced when necessary. The space between the hewn logs was filled with **pierrotage** or **briquette-entre-poteaux**, then plastered and whitewashed in a manner similar to that of medieval half-timbering. The houses commonly had a **bonnet roof** covered with hand-split cypress shingles, although some houses of this type had a hipped roof. Access to individual rooms was from the **galerie** that ran across the face of the house, through battened doors, or through French doors. The spelling *solle* is Cajun; the standard French spelling is *sole*, which is also sometimes used in Louisiana.

poultry house A place for housing fowl, particularly hens; a dependency considered essential for most rural houses, farms, plantations, and estates before refrigerators, since it provided a source of freshly killed meat as well as a daily supply of fresh eggs. *See also* **dovecote.**

poured concrete *See* **concrete.**

powder house An isolated storage place for gunpowder; especially found in areas of colonial America that were subject to Indian attack. Also called a powder magazine.

prairie box A **Prairie style** house having a square floor plan, usually having a symmetrical façade and four rooms on the ground floor, a **hipped roof**, occasionally **hipped dormers**; somewhat popular from 1900 to 1920. Also called an American four-square house.

prairie cottage A cottage constructed of large adobe bricks, built during the late 1800s by settlers on the prairies in the western states where stone was scarce but clay suitable for brick-making was usually available within 15 inches (38cm) of the surface of the ground. Often sand, ashes, and linseed oil were added to the clay. After the bricks air-dried for 10 to 12 days, they were laid with mortar in a construction that required minimal technical skill. The exterior walls were commonly 12 inches (30cm) thick, and interior walls were 6 inches (15cm) thick. **Battened doors** were common. The roof, usually shingled or thatched, had a minimum overhang of 2 feet (0.2m) to give the adobe walls some protection against rain. Contrast with **Prairie style** house.

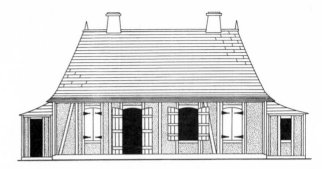

poteaux-sur-solle house (1730): New Orleans, La.

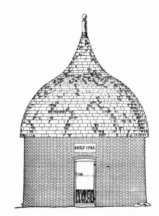

powder house: Marblehead, Mass.

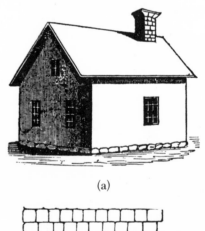

(a)

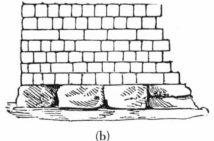

(b)

prairie cottage:
(a) typical example; (b) detail of a foundation

Prairie School A highly original group of influential architects in Chicago, closely associated with the early work of Frank Lloyd Wright (1867–1959). Many of his early works are in the **Prairie Style** created by this school. Wright is considered the acknowledged master of this group, and to a much lesser extent Louis H. Sullivan (1856–1924). Their followers, from about 1900 to 1930, included Walter B. Griffin (1876–1937), George G. Elmslie (1871–1952), and William G. Purcell (1880–1965). This school was also strongly influenced by the **Arts and Crafts movement** in England. *See* **Prairie style.**

Prairie style An American style of architecture that originated with the **Prairie School,** primarily domestic architecture although also applied to commercial buildings; especially popular in the Midwest from about 1900 to 1930; typically, a two-story house having one-story wings and/or porches, integrated with its site to provide a low-to-the-ground horizontal appearance.

Prairie-style houses commonly exhibit many of the following characteristics:

Façade and exterior wall treatments: Exterior walls commonly of light-colored stucco, light-colored brick, or concrete block; the central portion of the house usually higher than the adjacent flanking wings; contrasting wood trim between stories; a **porte cochère** and/or a porch having a roof typically supported by heavy columns that are either square in cross section or have slanted sides; a terrace and/or balcony; often, **Sullivanesque** ornamentation such as friezes and/or door surrounds.

Roof treatments: A broad, low-pitched roof, either hipped or gabled; eaves with a considerable overhang; hipped or gabled dormers; a prominent, large, relatively low plain rectangular chimney.

Window treatments: Often, a series of ribbon windows below the roof overhang, tending to emphasize the predominantly horizontal, low-to-the-ground appearance of the house; commonly, windows having small diamond-shaped or rectangular panes of glass set in grooved lead strips called **cames**; often set in geometric patterns; commonly one-over-one (1/1) double-hung sashes or tall casement windows; windows often grouped in pairs or sets of three; occasionally, stained-glass clerestory windows.

Doorway treatments: Doors hving windows often glazed with highly decorative geometric patterns associated with the work of Frank Lloyd Wright.

prefabricated house A house assembled from components cut to size at a factory or from entire building modules shipped for subsequent assembly at the construction site. As early as 1908, precut and pre-marked building components or entire houses could be ordered by catalogue from firms such as Sears, Roebuck and Company.

Pre-Revolutionary architecture *See* **American Colonial architecture.**

preservation *See* **building preservation.**

presidio In **Spanish Colonial architecture**, a frontier outpost or fort.

pressed-metal ceiling A thin sheet-metal ceiling embossed in a decorative pattern; usually coated with a layer of tin and lead or a coat of paint primer as a protection against oxidation. Much used on the ceilings of stores in America after about 1875, especially during the early part of the 20th century.

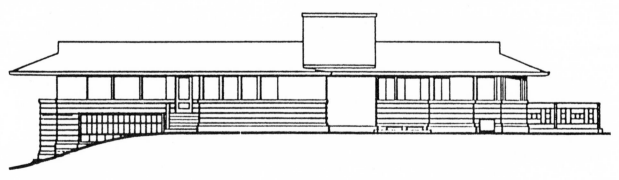

Prairie style
Glasner House (1905), Glencoe, Ill. (south elevation); Frank Lloyd Wright, Architect

pretil In **Spanish Colonial architecture** of the mid-19th century, a **parapet**, a breast-high wall, or a brick **coping** atop an adobe wall.

prick post In a wood-framed structure, any secondary post or side post.

principal elevation The façade or front **elevation** of a building.

principal joist In a **timber-framed house**, a large **joist** that carries much of the floor load.

principal post A **corner post** in a timber-framed house.

principal purlin In timber-framed construction, a **purlin** that is somewhat more massive than a **common purlin**; runs parallel to the ridge of the roof about halfway between the ridge and the top plate. The only purlin on each side of the roof ridge, it is framed into and joins the **principal rafters**, thus providing lateral stability for the entire roof framing system and supporting a number of common rafters.

principal rafter In a timber-framed house, one of several such **rafters** that extend from the ridge of the roof down to the **wall plate**; somewhat more massive than a **common rafter**; typically located at a corner post, story post, or chimney post and framed into a **tie beam**. Together with the **principal purlins**, the principal rafters form a roof-framing system with considerable stability. Also called a blade.

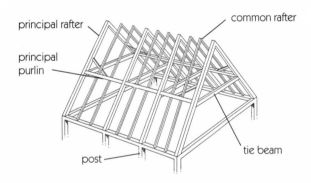

principal rafters and principal purlins

principal roof, principal rafter roof A **roof** supported by **principal rafters**.

prize house In tobacco-growing states of the South, a structure that once housed a press (called a *prize*) for compacting cured tobacco leaves.

projecting porch A **porch** that extends beyond the face of a house, in contrast to an **integral porch**, which is set within the main structure of the house.

promenade A suitable place for walking for pleasure, as along a lake, river, terrace, or public setting.

proscenium The frame or arch that separates the stage and seating areas of an auditorium.

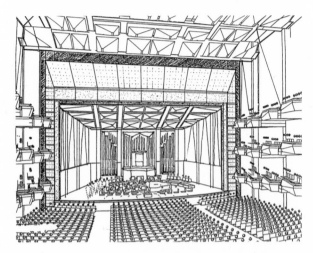

proscenium: Benaroya Hall (1998), Seattle, Wash.; LMN Architects

prostyle A term descriptive of a **portico** having columns across the entire front of a building but not at its sides or rear.

public house Same as **tavern**.

pudding stone A composite rock containing rounded pebbles or gravel embedded in a siliceous matrix.

puddled adobe construction In the Southwest, a type of wall construction used by American Indians long before the appearance of the first Spaniards; built up of successive layers of an adobe mixture containing enough water so that it could be poured. The first layer was poured directly on the ground. This layer, about two feet (0.6m) high, was allowed to dry before the next one was poured on top of it; in this way, successive layers were build up until the wall reached its full height. The practice of placing the lowest layer of the wall directly on the ground contributed to erosion of the wall because of puddles of water that collected on the ground after a rain. The Spaniards introduced the American Indians to an improved technique of wall construction in which adobe, in the form of brick, was laid on a foundation to reduce erosion of the wall at ground level.

pueblo architecture Multistoried communal housing, as much as five stories high with stepped-back roof lines, containing a large number of individual family units; built by the "Pueblo Indians," linguistically unrelated tribes who live in villages in New Mexico and Arizona. Among the most widely known pueblos in the Southwest are those of the Acoma, Hopi, Zuni, and Taos peoples. Their homes are constructed of **adobe** or a combination of adobe and stone; the actual combination depended on the accessibility of water at any given location. The exterior walls are thick (at the Acoma pueblo, for example, the average thickness is two feet[0.6m]) and are usually coated with adobe plaster to help protect them against erosion caused by rain. The stepped-back flat roofs are drained by waterspouts (**canales**). They are supported by roof beams (**vigas**) on which poles (**latias**) or smaller branches or saplings (**savinos**) have been laid and then are blanketed by a matting of reeds covered by a thick layer of adobe that acts as the roof. Typically the interior walls are finished with adobe plaster and then whitewashed; some rooms are heated by a fireplace (**fogón**) in one corner. The rooms are entered through a hatchway in the roof reached by a ladder whose poles typically extend far above roof level. The windows are small to keep the interior relatively cool during hot weather and to minimize heat loss during the winter.

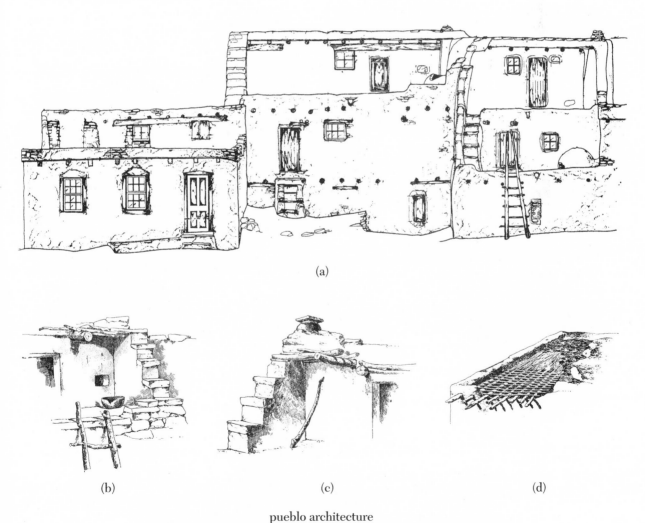

(a)

(b)　　　　(c)　　　　(d)

pueblo architecture
(a) Acoma, N.M.; (b) ladder to a higher story at the Old Acoma Pueblo;
(c) stone steps with platform at chimney; (d) detail of roof construction

Pueblo Revival, Pueblo style In the American Southwest, primarily from about 1910 to 1940, a style intended to suggest **pueblo architecture**; usually includes a mixture of **Spanish Colonial Revival** and **Mission Revival**.

Pueblo Revival buildings usually exhibit a number of the following characteristics:

Façade and exterior wall treatments: Typically, earth-colored stucco walls that provide a low-profile, adobelike appearance; rounded corners and wall intersections; sometimes, battered walls; often, brick flooring on the porches and terraces.

Roof treatments: Stepped-back roof lines in imitation of pueblo architecture; parapeted, flat, adobe-covered roofs drained by waterspouts (**canales**); rows of wood beams (**vigas**), resting on unpainted wood posts and protruding through the exterior walls, provide structural support for the roof.

Window treatments: Commonly, **casement windows**, usually recessed, with roughly hewn lintels.

Doorway treatments: Often, **battened doors.**

pugging A heavy loose-fill material, such as ashes or sand, placed between the joists in floor-ceiling assemblies to improve the sound insulation between the spaces above and below. Such construction was used in multiple-dwelling housing units in New York City in the middle of the 19th century, emulating an earlier construction practice in England.

pug-mill brick Same as **adobe quemado.**

pulpit An elevated stand or structure in a house of religious worship from which a cleric conducts services or delivers a sermon. In many colonial American churches, a **sounding board** was placed above the pulpit to help reflect the cleric's voice toward the congregation. *See* illustration at **sounding board.**

pulvinated A term descriptive of a surface that is cushion-shaped, bulging outward as in a **cushion capital** or **cushion frieze.**

pulvinus The **baluster,2** on each side of an Ionic capital.

pump *See* **water pump.**

puncheon A short, rough timber usually having only one relatively smooth face; easily and economically produced and therefore especially used as flooring in buildings of a temporary nature.

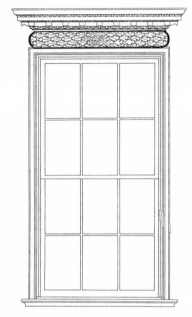

pulvinated frieze

pulpit
in a colonial New England church

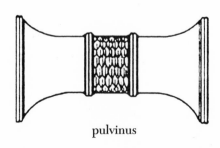

pulvinus

purlin A timber laid horizontally, below and parallel to the ridge of a roof, on the principal rafters, on which the roofing is laid. *See also* **common purlin** and **principal purlin;** compare with **subpurlin.**

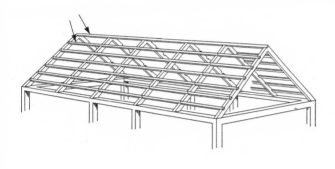

purlins

purlin roof A roof construction in which purlins are laid between the principal rafters; they support the boards that run in a vertical direction between the ridge and eaves of the roof and serve as **sheathing**.

putty A heavy paste used to fill holes and cracks prior to painting, and to secure glass panes. Once composed of a mixture of a pigment (such as whiting) and linseed oil. Other compounds, sometimes in powdered form to be mixed with water, are now widely used.

PWA Moderne Architecture that combined elements of **Art Deco** and **Streamline Moderne** with elements of the **Beaux-Arts style**; employed in the design of many large public buildings, civic centers, theaters, and other buildings constructed between 1933 and 1944 by the Public Works Administration (PWA), an agency of the federal government set up to provide jobs during the Great Depression.

pycnostyle *See* **intercolumniation.**

pyramidal house A one- or two-story house having a **pyramidal roof**. In various regions of America, the one-story house was the more common, particularly in the first half of the 20th century. Many houses of this type were decorated to suggest a particular type of architecture; others were unadorned.

pyramidal roof A **hipped roof** that has four slopes terminating either in a peak or very short ridge; found, for example, in the **Châteauesque style** and in **Gingerbread folk architecture.**

pyramidal roof
the first meeting house in Connecticut

Q

quadrel A square brick, tile, or stone.

Quaker plan In the late 17th and early 18th centuries, the **plan** of a three-room stone or brick house found primarily in Pennsylvania but as far south as North Carolina; typically had one large room with a fireplace in one corner and an exterior chimney, alongside of which were two small rooms, one serving as a vestibule and the other as a bedroom. There were many variations in this plan, some with additional rooms or a second story. *See also* **Penn plan.**

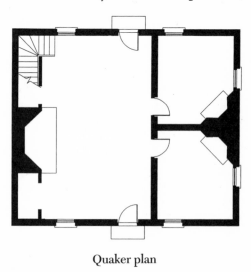

Quaker plan

quarrel A small pane of glass, usually diamond-shaped or square and set diagonally; framed and held in place by slender grooved strips of lead (**cames**). Quarrels were used extensively in windows until 1792, when the manufacture of window glass in the United States became commercially feasible, making larger-sized glass panes available at less cost than previously. *See also* **glass.**

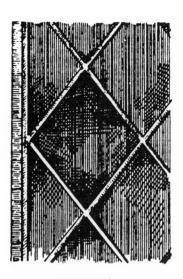

quarrel

quarry-faced masonry A term descriptive of masonry construction in which rectangular stone blocks are roughly dressed on the side of the block that is to form the exterior surface of the building; usually found in buildings whose design is intended to express massiveness, as in the **Richardsonian Romanesque style.**

quarry-faced masonry

quartering house In early America, a subsidiary building that provided housing for servants; usually near or adjoining the principal structure.

quarterpace stair A stair incorporating a **stair landing** between two flights that are at right angles to each other. Also called a quarter-turn stair. Compare with **halfpace stair.**

quarter-round light A window, usually one of a pair, that has the shape of one-quarter of a complete circle.

quarter-round molding A convex molding whose cross section is a quarter of a circle.

quarter-turn stair Same as **quarterpace stair.**

quatrefoil A four-lobed pattern in an opening that is subdivided by **cusps**; particularly found in **Gothic Revival** architecture. *See* **foil.**

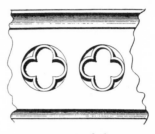

quatrefoils

Queen Anne arch An **arch** having three openings: a large central opening that is rounded at its top, and two narrower rectangular openings, one on each side.

quarterpace stair
in a Craftsman-style home

Queen Anne style An eclectic, picturesque style of domestic architecture in America from the 1870s to 1910 and beyond; based on country-house and cottage Elizabethan architecture and a blend of Tudor, Gothic, English Renaissance, and American Colonial architecture. It is to the reign of Queen Elizabeth I that this term should really refer, rather than to the reign of Queen Anne (1702–1714). Occasionally called *Victorian Queen Anne style* to avoid confusion with the 18th-century Queen Anne style in England, from which it differs considerably. It may safely be said that the Queen Anne style abhors any unadorned large flat surface.

Queen Anne–style houses, often timber-framed and irregular in plan and elevation, usually exhibit many of the following characteristics:

Façade and exterior wall treatments: An asymmetrical façade with emphasis on verticality; often, a front-facing gable; decorative trusses, bracketed posts, **gingerbread** in the form of spindlework, finials, and cast-iron cresting; occasionally, a cornice enriched with dentils. Textured shingles and masonry that provide variations in wall surface treatment and color; carved ornamentation, and patterned horizontal siding; contrasting wall materials, such as brick, decoratively patterned clapboards, half-timbering, stone, and stucco, used in combination; the stories often decorated differently, for example, by cladding

(a)

Queen Anne style

the first story with one type of material and the second story with another; typically, a one-story, asymmetrical porch covering much of the lower façade, or covering all of the lower façade and also wrapping around one or both side walls; asymmetrical porches often set within the main structure of the house, usually on the upper stories.

Roof treatments: Typically, a roof irregular in shape or parapeted; sometimes hipped; high, steeply pitched, ornamented gables and cross gables, ornamental ridges, overhanging eaves, bargeboards, second-story projections, various-shaped ornamental dormers, cresting, finials, pendants, and/or pinnacles; shingles laid in decorative patterns; tall chimneys of molded, ribbed, or patterned brickwork; corbeled chimney caps; frequently, a cylindrical tower with a conically pointed or bulbous roof, or a square or polygonal tower.

Window treatments: Large window sashes, usually with the upper sash multipaned or set with many small, square stained-glass lights and with a single pane in the lower sash; casement windows, often in groups; three-part windows; bay windows; oriel windows.

Doorway treatments: A paneled main entry door typically located off the central axis of the façade; the upper part of the door set with a single pane or many small panes; occasionally, a stained-glass **transom light** above the door or **sidelights** flanking the door.

(b)

Queen Anne style

queen-post truss A roof truss having two vertical posts (called *queen posts*) that rest on the **tie beam** between the rafters; the upper ends of these vertical posts are connected to a horizontal member (called a *straining piece*) above the tie beam.

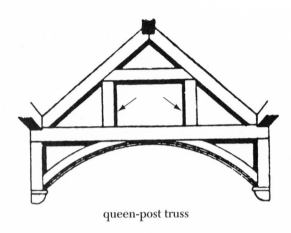

queen-post truss

quicklime *See* **lime.**

quirk An indentation or groove separating one element from another, as between moldings.

quoin One of the flat stones at an external corner of a building, usually distinguished decoratively from adjacent masonry by color, size, texture, or the masonry joints; occasionally imitated, for decorative purposes, by wood that has been finished to look like masonry. Found, for example, in the **Beaux-Arts style, Federal style, French Eclectic architecture,** and **Georgian style.**

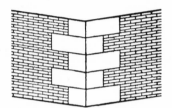

quoins: set in brickwork

Quonset hut A prefabricated structure, developed during World War II, that has a semicylindrical shape; commonly constructed of corrugated steel fastened to arched steel ribs that are attached to a concrete slab floor; used for a wide variety of temporary structures, such as barracks, storage sheds, and transient housing. First erected at Fort Davis in Quonset, Rhode Island.

R

rabbet A long groove or channel that is cut into the edge or face of a board to receive another board that is fitted into the groove at a right angle to it.

rabbeted siding Same as **drop siding.**

rad and dab Same as **wattle and daub.**

radius brick Same as **arch brick.**

rafter One of a series of inclined structural members from the ridge of the roof down to the **eaves,** providing support for the covering of a roof. Rafters are of two general types: **common rafter** and **principal rafter.** For special types, *see* **fly rafter, hip rafter, jack rafter, knee rafter, notched rafter.**

rafter house In colonial America, especially in the Chesapeake Bay area, a house of a relatively temporary nature, in which the lower ends of the roof rafters rested directly on the ground; a forerunner of the modern **A-frame house.**

rafter lookout Same as **lookout,1.**

rafter tail That part of a rafter that overhangs the wall at the eaves.

rag rubble Thin, small stones of irregular shape and size; used in **uncoursed** masonry work in the construction of foundations, paving, and walls.

ragwork Crude masonry, most commonly of undressed flat stone, laid horizontally in a random pattern in a wall.

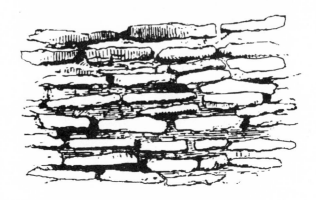

ragwork

rail A bar of wood or other material connecting one post, pale, or baluster to another.

rail fence Same as **zigzag fence.**

railroad flat A single apartment containing a series of rooms in a straight line, through which one passes in going from the front to the rear of the apartment; there is no internal corridor. In substandard buildings, often called a **dumbbell tenement**.

rainbow roof 1. Same as **compass roof**. 2. Same as **ship's-bottom roof**.

rainbow roof: Meeting House, Church Family of Shakers, Mount Lebanon, N.Y.

rainwater conductor Same as **leader**.

rainwater conductor head, rainwater hopper head Same as **leader head**.

raised barn A term sometimes used as a synonym for a **bank barn**.

raised basement A **basement** whose floor level is much higher than usual, so that its ceiling extends well above ground level. In early American architecture of the South, it was common for the basement floor to be at ground level and the basement ceiling to be a full story above it. *See also* **plantation house.**

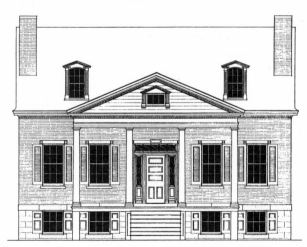

raised basement: Greek Revival home

raised house, raised cottage A house or cottage having a raised basement with its cellar floor at ground level or raised on piers as a precaution against floods; in the South its exterior walls typically are white-washed brick, stone, plaster, or stucco; the cellar sometimes functions as a service area, shop, office, or stable. The main floor, one story above the cellar, contains the family living quarters; a porch (**galerie**) extends across the entire façade and sometimes along both sides as well; French doors usually open onto the porch so as to promote the flow of air during very hot weather. It is especially found in **French Vernacular architecture** of Louisiana and in other areas having a similar climate.

raised cottage
St. Martinsville, La.

raised house
Maison Chenal (c. 1790), Pointe Coupee Parish, La.

raised joint Same as **excess joint.**

raised panel A panel whose center portion is thicker than its edges, so that it projects above the surrounding frame or wall surfaces. Also called a fielded panel.

raised porch In **French Vernacular architecture** of Louisiana, the **galerie** on a raised house.

raising bee *See* **barn raising.**

raising piece A piece of timber laid atop a brick wall or along the top of the **posts** of a timber-framed house that supports one or more wood beams.

raising plate Same as **wall plate.**

rajones The term for **shingles** in **Spanish Colonial architecture of the American Southwest.**

rake On roofs of early colonial American houses, a flat board covering the lower ends of the rafters.

raked A term descriptive of any surface that is inclined with respect to the horizontal, such as a *raked molding* or the inclined surface of a *raked cornice* in a triangular pediment.

raked: molding

raked joint In brickwork, a masonry joint formed by using a square-edged tool to remove some of the mortar in the joint while it is still soft; produces dark shadows and tends to darken the overall appearance of the brick wall.

raked joint

ramada 1. In **Spanish Colonial architecture,** an arbor. 2. An open-air structure with a pitched, thatched roof that is usually supported by heavy logs at the four corners; provides a shaded outdoor area; especially used during the hot summer months by American Indians of the Southwest, such as the Papagos and the Pimas of Arizona and New Mexico.

ramada,2

rambler A one-story dwelling having a large floor area; a **ranch house.**

rammed earth A material, usually consisting of clay and sand or clay and some other aggregate such as pebbles or seashells, that is made by adding water to this mixture, compressing it in a form while it is still slightly damp, and then allowing it to dry. In some regions of the Southwest, walls are still constructed using this technique, especially in buildings that are derivatives of **Spanish Colonial architecture.** Also called pisé.

rampant arch An arch in which the impost (i.e., the unit which on one side of the arch that receives and distributes the thrust of the arch) is higher than the similar unit on the other side.

rampart An earthen wall for purposes of defense, located on the inner side of a ditch surrounding a bastioned **fort**; usually directly atop and behind a wall of masonry. Such forts were designed primarily for defense, rather than for attack against an enemy.

ranch house A rambling one-story house, found from the 1930s on, but especially popular during the 1950s and 1960s, particularly in the West; usually designed to emphasize the width of the façade. Typically characterized by: an asymmetrical plan; a low-pitched roof with eaves having a moderate-to-wide overhang, a hipped, cross-gabled, or side-gabled roof; exposed rafters; exterior wall cladding of stucco, brick, wood, or some combination thereof; ribbon windows, windows decorated with shutters; frequently, glass sliding doors at the side or rear of the house that open onto a porch or patio; usually has an attached garage.

randle bar A horizontal iron bar, built into a **jamb** of a colonial fireplace, that projected over the fire so that pots could be suspended from it for cooking. *See also* **chimney crook, fireplace crane, trammel.**

random ashlar Masonry in which rectangular stones are set without continuous joints and appear to be laid without a fixed pattern, although there may actually be a repeated pattern. Also called random bond or random work.

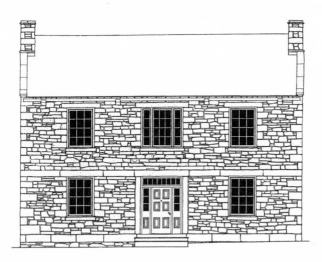

random ashlar
Stewart House (1844), Schenley, Pa.

random course One of a number of horizontal stone masonry **courses** that are of unequal height.

rangework Masonry in which the stones are of equal height within each **course**; all courses need not be of the same height.

ranked A term preceded by a digit (usually from two to nine) that indicates the number of windows across the façade of a house. For example, a four-ranked house has four windows across the upper floors; on the ground floor, the entry door is tallied as one of the windows, so it has three windows plus the door.

ranked
a four-ranked Georgian house in Pennsylvania

rauchkammer A garret in a **Pennsylvania Dutch** colonial house that was set aside for the curing of meat; an opening in the chimney stack that passed through this space allowed smoke to enter the garret. The meats to be cured were hung from hooks attached to the underside of the roof framing.

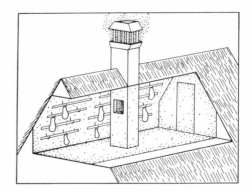

rauchkammer
in garret of a colonial Pennsylvania Dutch home

ready-cut house Same as **prefabricated house.**

rear girt A **girt** that runs horizontally along the rear wall of an American colonial house. *See* illustration under **timber-framed house.**

rebar A steel bar having ribs or slightly projecting patterns on its surface to provide a greater bond with concrete when used in **reinforced concrete**, increasing its mechanical strength.

rebate Same as **rabbet.**

recessed dormer A **dormer**, all or part of which is set below the main roof surface.

recessed pointing A treatment of masonry joints in a brick wall in which the mortar is pressed back from the face of the wall into the joint by about a quarter-inch (0.6cm) to protect the face of the mortar.

reed house Same as **brush house.**

reeding An ornament of adjacent, parallel, protruding half-round moldings; the reverse of **fluting.**

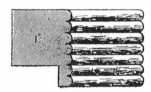

reeding

reflected ceiling plan The **plan** of a ceiling as if it were projected downward onto a flat surface directly below.

Regency Revival A mode of **Revival architecture** found to a very limited extent in America in the 1930s that borrowed features of its **Georgian style** and **Regency style** prototypes. A house in this style was usually two stories high with a hipped roof; brick walls with **quoins** at the corners and sometimes at the main entrance; often, painted white walls; double-hung windows with shutters; an entrance porch; typically, a small octagonal window above the door. Examples of this style are found in particular in the works of the architectural firm of William A. Delano (1874–1960) and Chester A. Aldrich (1871–1940).

Regency style A colorful style prevalent in England between 1811 and 1830 during the regency and reign of George IV; later, very occasionally emulated in America in Regency Revival; often combined with Oriental motifs.

reglet A **fillet** or small flat-faced projection; used, for example, to cover a joint between two boards.

reinforced concrete Concrete in which steel **rebars** are embedded to provide additional mechanical strength so that the combination acts effectively in resisting imposed forces; used as a structural material in the United States since the beginning of the 20th century.

reinforcing bar *See* **rebar.**

reja In **Spanish Colonial architecture,** a grille or grating over windows facing the street, often projecting from the face of a house into the street.

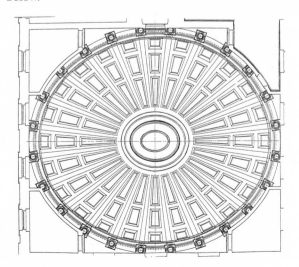

reflected ceiling plan
dome of Old St. Louis Courthouse, St. Louis, Mo.

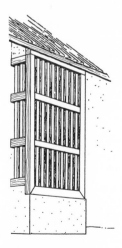

reja
Spanish Colonial house (late 18th cent.),
St. Augustine, Fla.

relief Sculptured work, carving, casting, or emboss-ing that is raised above the plane of its background. *See also* **bas-relief, high relief,** and **sunk relief.** Also called relievo.

relieving arch Same as **discharging arch.**

Renaissance architecture, Renaissance Classical architecture The architectural style devel-oped in early-15th-century Italy during the rebirth (*rinascimento*) of classical art and learning. After the mid-16th century, it succeeded Gothic architecture as the dominant style throughout Europe and evolved into Baroque and, in the early 17th century, into architecture based on the correct use of Roman and Greek **orders**; also characterized by round arches and symmetrical composition. Elements of Renais-sance architecture are found in the **Italianate style** in America.

Renaissance Revival A term occasionally used as a synonym for **Italian Renaissance Revival.**

repointing Same as **pointing,1.**

restoration *See* **building restoration.**

retaining wall A heavy wall, usually constructed of stone or concrete, that bears laterally against a mass of earth, thereby preventing the mass from sliding to a lower elevation; often **battered.**

reticulated Having a distinct pattern of two sets of parallel lines that crisscross.

return The continuation of a cornice, molding, pro-jection, or the like in a different direction from its main direction. For example, *see* **cornice return** and **label stop.**

reveal The side of an opening for a door or window between its frame and the outer surface of the wall.

reveal lining Any finish, such as moldings, applied over a **reveal.**

reverse-flight stair *See* **dogleg stair.**

revetment Any facing of metal, stone, or wood over a less attractive or less durable substance or construc-tion, for example, a facing on a retaining wall to pre-vent it from eroding.

retaining wall

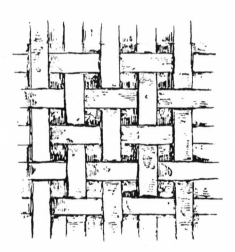

reticulated

return

Revival architecture Architecture that makes use of elements of an earlier style that it seeks to emulate, borrowing many of the features of its prototype. *See* **Adam Revival, American Colonial Revival, American Renaissance Revival, California Mission Revival, Carpenter Gothic Revival, Châteauesque Revival, Classical Revival style, Classic Revival, Colonial Revival, Dutch Colonial Revival, Early Classical Revival, Early Gothic Revival, Egyptian Revival, Exotic Revival, Federal Revival, French Revival, Georgian Revival, Gothic Revival, Greek Revival style, International Revival, Italian Renaissance Revival, Jacobethan Revival, Late Gothic Revival, Mediterranean Revival, Mission Revival, Monterey Revival, Moorish Revival, Oriental Revival, Period Revival, Pueblo Revival, Regency Revival, Renaissance Revival, Romanesque Revival, Second Renaissance Revival, Spanish Colonial Revival, Spanish Pueblo Revival, Tudor Revival, Tuscan Revival**.

revolving door An entrance door usually consisting of four rigid leaves, set in the form of a cross, that rotate about a central vertical pivot; invented in the United States in 1900.

rib 1. A structural member supporting any curved panel or curved shape. 2. In vaulted roofs, a molding that projects from the curved surface and separates it into ceiling panels.

ribband Same as **ribbon strip**.

ribbon development Urban extension essentially in the form of a single depth of buildings along roads radiating from a city, along a highway between two cities, along the bank of a river, or the like.

ribbon strip A wood strip or board let into the studs to provide support for the ends of **joists**. Also called a girt strip or ledger board.

ribbon window, ribbon lights A horizontal band of at least three windows, separated only by **mullions**, on the façade of a building. Occasionally called a window band or band window.

ribbon windows
in a Greek Revival–style home (1812), Washington, Pa.

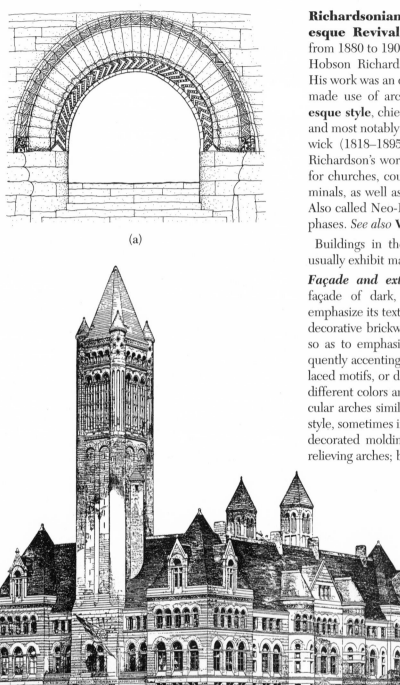

(a)

(b)

Richardsonian Romanesque style, Romanesque Revival The massive style of architecture, from 1880 to 1900 and beyond, as practiced by Henry Hobson Richardson (1838–1886) and his followers. His work was an outgrowth of earlier architecture that made use of architectural elements of the **Romanesque style**, chiefly in public buildings and churches, and most notably in buildings designed by James Renwick (1818–1895) and others, from 1840 to 1880. Richardson's work was especially popular in America for churches, courthouses, libraries, and railroad terminals, as well as some universities and large homes. Also called Neo-Romanesque, particularly in its early phases. *See also* **Victorian Romanesque.**

Buildings in the Richardsonian Romanesque style usually exhibit many of the following characteristics:

Façade and exterior wall treatments: Usually, a façade of dark, rock-faced masonry, rough-cut to emphasize its texture, occasionally in combination with decorative brickwork; often dramatically asymmetrical so as to emphasize a sense of massiveness, and frequently accenting structural features; flat lintels, interlaced motifs, or dentils that combine several types and different colors and textures of stone; massive semicircular arches similar to those used in the Romanesque style, sometimes in combination with flat arches; highly decorated moldings on the face of the arches; large relieving arches; blind arcades or corbel tables beneath

Richardsonian Romanesque style: H. H. Richardson, Architect (a) doorway, Ames Free (Memorial) Library (1879), North Easton, Mass.; (b) Allegheny County Courthouse and Jail (1888), Pittsburgh, Pa.

the eaves; clustered arches or piers, commonly with masonry mullions and masonry transom bars; frequently, a decorative tympanum; often, parapeted gable ends; one or more belt courses; short, thick columns, occasionally with cushion capitals; bands of engaged colonettes; decorative plaques; round, hexagonal, square, or polygonal towers topped with pinnacles.

Roof treatments: A steeply pitched hipped roof, occasionally flared at the eaves and supported by brackets; a roof covering of slate or tile; usually one or more **cross gables**; dormers set into the pitched roof; often, steep-gabled **wall dormers,** either parapeted or hipped; decorative cresting or decorative tile at the ridge of the roof, often with finials; little roof overhang at the eaves; cylindrical towers with steep conical roofs or peaked hexagonal roofs topped with a finial; a decorative chimney.

Window treatments: Usually, double-hung windows with a single pane in each sash, often arched or rectangular; deeply recessed window openings with deep window reveals to reinforce a sense of massiveness, often between colonettes; sometimes a number of windows treated as a single unit, particularly below the eaves; window openings framed by round arches having hooded moldings, often with **label stops** and with **spandrels** above; often, a circular or semicircular window in a wall gable.

Doorway treatments: Usually, deeply set within massive semicircular or segmental masonry arches, recessed within a porch or set between engaged columns; often, an entryway ornamented with Romanesque decorations. Above the entry door, occasionally a semicircular window.

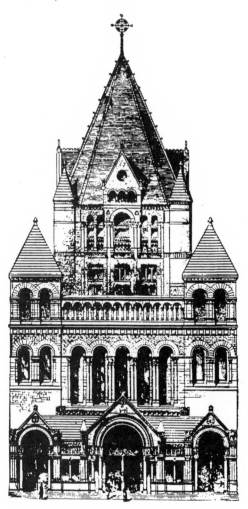

(c)

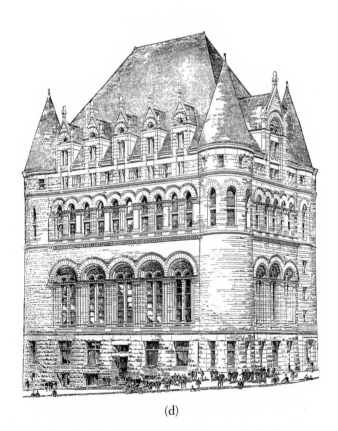

(d)

Richardsonian Romanesque style
(c) Trinity Church (1877), Boston, Mass.; (d) Chamber of Commerce Building, Cincinnati, Ohio

ridge The line at the intersection of the upper edges of two sloping roof surfaces.

ridgeboard, ridgepole The uppermost longitudinal structural member of a roof, located along the line of the **ridge**; supports the upper ends of the rafters. In some early colonial houses, the ridgeboard was omitted; instead, each pair of roof rafters met at the ridge in a **lapped joint**. Also called a ridge beam, ridgepiece, ridgeplate, or ridgetree.

ridge cresting *See* **cresting.**

ridge roll A rounded strip of wood, tile, metal, or composition material that is used to cover and finish a **ridge** of a roof. Also called a ridgecap.

ridge tile A tile that is curved or angled in section, often decorative, used to cover the **ridge** of a roof.

ridge tile

ridge ventilator A common type of **ventilator** that straddles a ridge of the roof of a barn; usually square in plan and constructed of wood and/or metal.

ridge ventilators

rifle hole A slot in an exterior wall of a structure used for defensive purposes. The sides of the slot are splayed so the opening is wider at the inner face of the wall than at its exterior face, thereby permitting a rifleman on the interior to fire over a wide angle; often the slots are vertical, but occasionally they are horizontal; particularly found in **blockhouses, forts, garrison houses.** Also called a firing port.

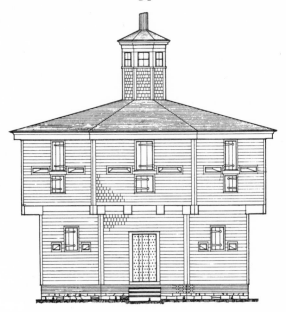

rifle holes
Ft. Edgecomb, Maine

rim lock In colonial America, a door lock in a metal casing that is surface-mounted at the edge of the door opposite the hinges. *See also* **lock** and **box lock.**

rinceau In Classical architecture and derivatives, an ornamental band of undulating plant motifs.

rinceau

riprap Random-sized pieces of quarry rock, ranging in size from small to very large. Sometimes used in foundations where the pieces are thrown together without any attempt to lay them in a regular structural arrangement.

riser The upright surface between two stair treads.

riven, rived A term descriptive of a piece of wood that has been shaped by splitting it along the grain instead by sawing it.

rivet A short pin of malleable metal, such as iron, with a head at one end; used to join two metal plates by passing it through a hole in both plates and then hammering the end down so as to form a second head.

rocaille Any ornament, usually asymmetrical, consisting of rock, plant, and shell forms in combination with artificial forms; widely used in America during the 18th century when **Rococo** was popular.

rock dash An exterior **stucco** finish containing crushed rock, large pebbles, or shells that are embedded in a stucco base. Also called slap dash.

rock-faced A term descriptive of the rough face of stone as it is split at the quarry and squared off only along the edges.

Rococo A style of architecture and decoration, primarily French in origin, that represents the final phase of the **Baroque style** around the middle of the 18th century. Characterized by profuse, often semiabstract ornamentation and lightness of color and weight. Rococo-style decorative elements were used in American Colonial architecture, for example, as decorative brackets.

rodded joint A masonry term occasionally used for a **concave joint**.

rollock arch Same as **rowlock arch**.

roll-up door A door fabricated of interlocking horizontal metal slats that are guided in a track; the configuration coils around an overhead drum that is housed at the head of the opening; may be manually operated or motor-driven.

Roman cement A quick-setting **cement** that can harden under water and is relatively impervious to water; made of a finely pulverized calcined argillaceous limestone that has been burnt at a temperature no higher than is necessary to drive off carbon dioxide.

Roman Classicism *See* **Classical Revival style**.

Romanesque Revival 1. Same as **Richardsonian Romanesque style**. 2. A term sometimes applied to the early works of James Renwick (1818–1895) and Richard Upjohn (1802–1878) using elements of the **Romanesque style**.

Romanesque style An architectural style emerging in Western Europe in the early 10th century and lasting until the advent of Gothic architecture in the middle of the 12th century; based on Roman and Byzantine elements; usually characterized by round arches and by massive articulated walls, **barrel vaults**, and **groined vaults**; served as the basis for the Richardsonian Romanesque style. Occasionally this term is used as a synonym for the **Richardsonian Romanesque style**.

Roman order *See* **Tuscan order**.

Romano-Tuscan mode *See* **Italian Renaissance Revival**.

Romantic style A loose term embracing a variety of styles of architecture, often including **Exotic Revival, Gothic Revival, Greek Revival style, Italianate style**.

rondel *See* **roundel**.

rood screen A screen, open or partly open, that separates the nave of a church from the chancel; intended to carry a large crucifix (rood).

roof The top covering of a building, including all materials and constructions necessary to support it on the walls of the building or on uprights; provides protection against rain, snow, sunlight, extremes of temperature, and wind. For definitions and illustrations of the different types, *see* **barrel roof, bell roof, bonnet roof, bowed roof, broken-pitch roof, bunker fill roof, butterfly roof, candle-snuffer roof, canopy roof, collar-beam roof, compass roof, conical roof, curb roof, deck roof, double-gable roof, double-hipped roof, double-pitched roof, dropped roof, dual-pitched roof, Dutch gambrel roof, Dutch roof, earth roof, English gambrel roof, flat roof, Flemish gambrel roof, flounder roof, French roof, gable-on-hip roof, gable roof, gambrel roof, helm roof, hip-on-gable roof, hipped-gable roof, hipped roof, hyperbolic paraboloid roof, Italian roof, jerkinhead roof, kick roof, knee roof, mansard roof, M-roof, New England gambrel roof, ogee roof, open roof, pavilion roof, pent roof, pigeon roof, pitched roof, principal roof, purlin roof, pyramidal roof, rainbow roof, round roof, saltbox roof, segmental roof, shed roof, ship's-bottom roof, single-pitched roof, skirt roof, sod roof, span roof, square roof, Swedish gambrel roof, terrace roof, truncated roof, umbrella roof, visor roof, wagon roof, whaleback roof**.

roof balustrade A railing with supporting **balusters** on a roof, often near the eaves or surrounding a **widow's walk**.

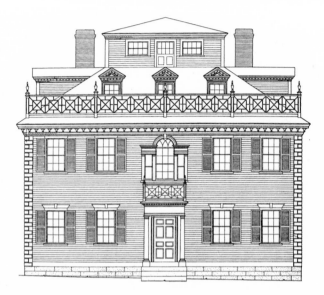

roof balustrade
Lt. Gov. Martin House, Seekonk, Mass.

roof board One of a number of boards that are placed over rafters to serve as a base for the application of a roof covering, such as shingles.

roof cresting *See* **cresting**.

roof deck The flat portion of a roof, used as a terrace for leisure activities; very widely used in large Georgian homes after 1750, and found in a wide variety of houses and high-rise buildings today. Compare with **deck roof**.

roof dormer *See* **dormer**.

roofer In early descriptions of American Colonial architecture, a term sometimes used for a **roof board**.

roof framing The assemblage of structural members that provides support for the exterior covering of a roof.

roofing Any material used as a roof covering, such as corrugated metal, sheet metal, shingles, slate, thatch, or tile; provides waterproofing, windproofing, and thermal insulation.

roofing tile A **tile** for roofing, often fabricated of burnt clay or slate but available in many types of materials and configurations. *See* **clay tile, mission tile, pantile, ridge tile, Spanish tile**.

roofing tile

roof plate A horizontal structural member that receives and supports the lower ends of the rafters of a roof. Same as **top plate,1** or **wall plate**.

rooftree The horizontal, longitudinal member at the ridge of a roof that supports the upper ends of the rafters. Also called a ridgeboard.

roof valley A trough or gutter formed by the intersection of two inclined planes of a roof.

roof ventilator An opening in the roof of a building to provide fresh air and/or to expel stale air; for example, *see* **ridge ventilator**.

root cellar A structure, either partially or wholly below ground level, that is used to store root crops such as potatoes and beets at a cool temperature. *See also* **potato barn**.

root cellar

rope molding A molding carved in imitation of a rope. Also called cable molding.

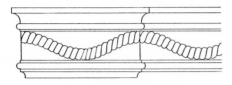

rope molding

rosette A round pattern with a carved, cast, or painted conventionalized floral motif. *See* **medallion,2.**

rosette

rotunda A circular hall in a large building, especially one covered by a dome.

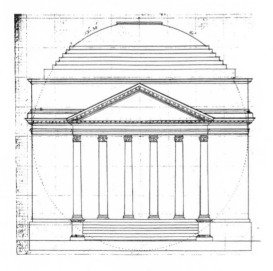

rotunda
University of Virginia (1821), as drawn by the architect, Thomas Jefferson

rough-axed brick Brick that has been shaped with an ax; requires thicker mortar joints than brick manufactured to close tolerances.

rough-cast A term descriptive of a stucco or plaster containing a crushed aggregate of pebbles that gives the surface a rough texture.

rough-cut joint In masonry, same as **flush joint.**

round arch An arch whose **soffit** (underside) is a full semicircle.

Round Arch style An American eclectic style that combines elements of the **Romanesque style** and **classicism;** especially characterized by arcaded round arches. Used primarily for public buildings in America in the mid-19th century, this style shows the strong influence of **Rundbogenstil** on the exterior of such buildings. A frequently cited example is the Union Depot (1848) in Providence, Rhode Island, by Thomas Tefft (1826–1859). Also called American Rundbogenstil from its German origins.

Round Arch style
Chapel at Bowdoin College (1853), Brunswick, Maine;
Richard Upjohn, Architect

round barn A **barn** having a circular plan. *See* **circular barn.**

round dormer A **dormer** having a circular window; a characteristic of the **Beaux-Arts style** and **French Eclectic architecture.**

rounded tile Same as **mission tile.**

roundel 1. A small circular panel or window; an **oculus**. 2. A small **bead** or **astragal**. 3. A circular plaster decorative element.

roundhouse 1. A large, round assembly hall having plank walls and a roof covered by hand-split wood shingles, usually with a gabled entrance; used in the 1800s by American Indian tribes of central California (for example, the Pomos) for ceremonial occasions and native dances. 2. A house that is round in **plan**, with no exterior corners; compare with **octagon house**.

round notch Same as **saddle notch**.

round pediment A **pediment,2** whose head is a semicircular arc.

round roof Same as **compass roof**.

round-topped A term descriptive of a window, door, or arch having a semicircular head.

row house One of a number of adjoining houses having a similar or identical appearance, similar plans, and constructed in an unbroken row; each house shares a common wall with the house on each side of it; most commonly they are two or three stories high. In the 1800s row houses frequently had a corresponding row of stables behind them. They remain distinctive examples of urban architecture in such cities as Baltimore and Philadelphia.

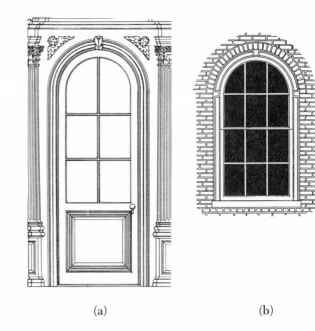

(a)   (b)

round-topped
(a) door, Wanton-Hunter House (c. 1746),
Newport, R.I.;
(b) round-topped window

row houses

rowlock 1. In brickwork, a **brick** laid on edge so that one end (i.e., its smallest surface) is visible. 2. One ring in a **rowlock arch**.

rowlock arch An arch composed entirely of wedge-shaped **rowlocks** or **voussoirs**; laid in separate concentric rings.

rubbed brick Brick having a smooth finish obtained by rubbing one of its surfaces (i.e., the exposed surface) with an abrasive or with another brick to remove surface irregularities and to promote a uniform color.

rubblework, rubble masonry Masonry built of rough stones of irregular shapes and sizes that are not laid in regular **courses**; used in the construction of walls, foundations, and paving.

Rumford fireplace An efficient fireplace invented by Benjamin Thompson (1753–1814), a Massachusetts-born loyalist who fled to England at the start of the American Revolution. For his services to the emperor of the Holy Roman Empire, he was later given the title of Count von Rumford. His innovative fireplace design increased the radiated heat and lessened the emitted smoke. These benefits were achieved by significantly reducing the size of the massive colonial fireplace opening (which typically had been about ten feet [3m] long and four to five feet [1.2–1.5m] high) and by introducing a constriction in the chimney directly above the hearth so as to increase the draft through the chimney. *See also* **Franklin stove**.

Rundbogenstil A German architectural style of the mid-19th century; especially characterized by round arches, often with Romanesque or Italianate features. It was the prototype of the **Round Arch style** in America.

running bond A pattern in which bricks or stones are laid lengthwise in a wall; all courses are laid as **stretchers,** with the vertical joints of one course falling midway between those of the courses directly above and below it. Also called stretcher bond.

running dog Same as **Vitruvian scroll**.

running ornament Any ornament in which the design is repetitive and continuous, often with flowing lines or with intertwining or interlocking lines, such as the **Greek key** design.

Ruskinian Gothic *See* **High Victorian Gothic**.

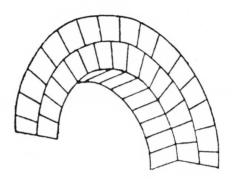

rowlock arch

rubblework

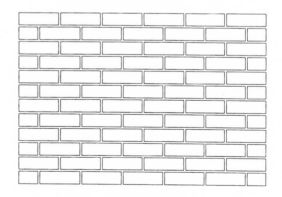

running bond

running ornament

rusticated stone Any stone masonry having strongly emphasized recessed joints; the exposed face of the masonry may be smooth or roughly textured. The border of each masonry block may be beveled (on all four sides, only at the top and bottom, or on adjacent sides) in an attempt to create an appearance of impregnability. Particularly found in banks and courthouses in the **Beaux-Arts style** and in **Italian Renaissance Revival.**

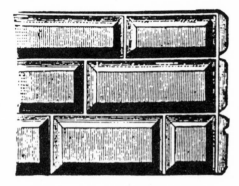

rusticated stone

Rustic order Same as **Tuscan order.**

rustic siding Same as **drop siding.**

Rustic style A vague term, used most often from about 1900 to 1930, denoting a style in the broadest sense of the word; usually applied to hunting lodges, ranger stations, or log cabins in mountainous or forested areas, and found especially in the northeastern United States. Buildings in this category, commonly front-gabled, often exhibit a number of the following characteristics: log-cabin siding, peeled logs, saddle-notch corner joints, and rough-cut lumber; a fieldstone chimney; a moderately to steeply pitched roof covered by hand-split wood shingles, a roof overhang with exposed rafters; one or more balconies or porches with flat balusters having decorative cutouts or decorative stickwork. Occasionally called Teddy Roosevelt Rustic or Adirondack Rustic style.

rustic work 1. Decorative or structural work constructed of logs from which the bark has not been removed. 2. Stonework, the face of which is roughly hacked or picked; the separate blocks are marked by deep **chamfers.**

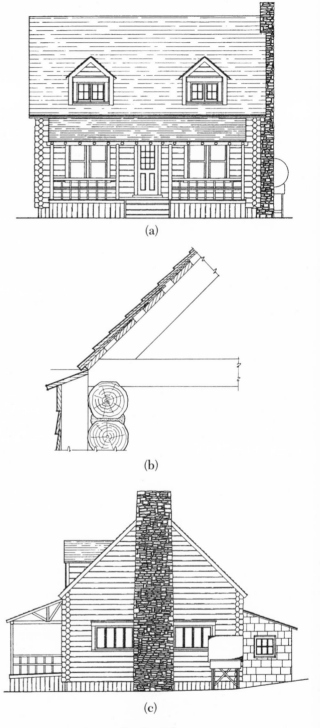

(a)

(b)

(c)

Rustic style
Storm King Ranger Station (1909), Olympic National
Park, Washington; (a) façade;
(b) detail of intersection of roof and walls;
(c) side elevation

S

Sabbath house, Sabbath-day house In colonial New England, a small house usually having a single room with a fireplace at one end, located near a house of worship; used on Sundays by a family as a place in which to warm and feed themselves during breaks in the all-day religious services, since such services typically were conducted in unheated **meeting houses.** Occasionally several families shared a two-room house with a centrally located fireplace; others had a small two-story house for this purpose, with the first story used as a stable. *See also* **Sunday house.**

saddle 1. Same as the **threshold** of a door. 2. Any structure suggesting the general appearance of a saddle.

saddlebag cabin A dwelling consisting of two one-room log cabins that are joined and share a roof having a single pitch on each side of a central ridge; the roof is usually shingled. The two cabins have separate entrances, and often there are no interior doors between them; there is often a full-width porch across the entire façade. In the North a central chimney is common, so the cabins are usually joined back-to-back, sharing the same chimney stack; in the South there is a chimney at the end of each cabin, a variation of the **dogtrot cabin.** Compare with **central-hall cabin.**

saddle bar A horizontal metal bar across a casement window frame that serves to stiffen the frame.

saddle notch At a corner in log-cabin construction, a rounded **notch** cut near one end in the lower surface of a horizontal log; forms an interlocking joint when mated with a similarly cut log set at right angles to it. (Such notches may instead be cut in the upper surfaces of the horizontal logs). Occasionally, this term is also used for a **double-saddle notch**, which is cut in *both* sides of a round log; in such instances, the logs at right angles are unnotched.

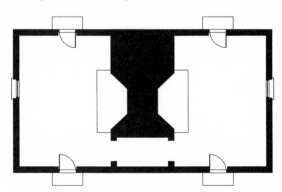

saddlebag cabin: plan

saddle notch

saddle roof A roof having a concave-shaped ridge with gables at each end of the roof, the configuration being suggestive of a saddle.

saddle stone The uppermost stone in a **gable** or **pediment**; often triangular or keystone-shaped and highly decorated. Also called an apex stone.

sailor A brick that is laid on end, i.e., positioned vertically, with its wider face showing on the wall surface. Compare with **soldier.**

sail-over Any outward projection beyond a general wall surface.

Saint Augustine house In Saint Augustine, Florida (first settled in 1565 by the Spanish), a two-story house having the following characteristics: walls constructed of blocks of **tabby** or **coquina,** as much as one foot (30.4cm) thick, to provide good thermal insulation against both the winter cold and the summer heat; a **hipped roof,** usually covered with hand-split cypress shingles; one room on the ground floor with windows facing the street through wood gratings, closed by solid-wood interior shutters. On the upper floor, two rooms, accessible by way of an exterior stairway; usually one or two balconies. *See also* **palma hut** and **tabla house.**

sala In **Spanish Colonial architecture of the American Southwest,** a reception room, main hall, or living room in a house; usually has windows facing the street that are protected by grilles or wood gratings (**rejas**) and also by heavy interior shutters.

salmon brick A brick of poor quality that lacks weather resistance; usually pink in color; commonly used to fill spaces between interior structural timbers in a **timber-framed house** in order to provide increased structural rigidity and improved thermal insulation.

salon A formal reception room for the entertainment of guests, usually in a central location in an elegant home; a **drawing room.**

saloon 1. A place where intoxicating liquors are sold and consumed; often the social center in the wide-open towns of the "Wild West." 2. A variant form of **salon.**

saltbox house A **timber-framed house,** commonly two-and-a-half stories high, having a **hall-and-parlor plan;** has gables at each end and a sloping roof in which the slope on the rear side of the ridge is much longer than the one in front. When such houses were originally built in colonial New England, this roof contour gave them a profile resembling the boxes that held salt then in use in the British colonies in America, giving rise to this term. Modern houses of this type are still popular, not only in New England, but elsewhere in the country. *See* **American Colonial architecture of early New England.** *See also* illustrations under **integral lean-to.**

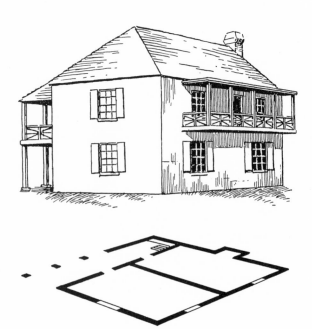

Saint Augustine house and plan

saltbox house: Baldwin House
(constructed before 1650), Branford, Conn.

saltbox roof Any roof having a configuration similar to that of a **saltbox house.** In the South, often called *catslides.*

sanctuary In a church, the immediate area around the principal altar.

sandstone Sedimentary rock composed of sand-sized grains naturally cemented by mineral materials; often used for decorative elements in buildings because it is easy to carve.

Santa Fe style A style in the broadest sense of the word, often suggestive of some combination of **Pueblo Revival** and **Spanish Colonial Revival** architecture.

sapling-frame construction Same as **bent-frame construction.**

sash The framework of a glazed window, either movable or fixed; may slide in a vertical plane (as in a **double-hung window**), may move in a horizontal plane (as in a **sliding sash**), may pivot about a vertical axis (as in a **casement window**), or may pivot about a horizontal axis (as in an **awning window**).

sash bar A secondary framing member to hold panes within a window, a window wall, or a glazed door; same as **muntin.**

saucer dome A **dome** that is very shallow, having a very large radius of curvature.

savino 1. In **Spanish Colonial architecture**, particularly in New Mexico, one of many saplings used in roof construction in **pueblo architecture**; such saplings are laid across the roof beams (**vigas**) to provide support for a blanket of fiber matting, which is then covered by a thick layer of tamped earth or dried mud to serve as a roof. 2. Red cedar posts once used in the wall constructions of Spanish Colonial homes in Saint Augustine, Florida, when it was a Spanish colony.

sawed-log house Same as **board house,1.**

sawmill A facility where timber is sawn by mechanical equipment into boards and planks. Important to the growth of the American colonies, many sawmills were operated by power generated by a stream, river, or tidal changes. As early as 1633, Dutch settlers in America had three sawmills operated by windmills. The efficiency of sawmills was greatly enhanced by the invention of the *gang saw,* which contained several parallel saw blades in a single frame; this was followed by the invention of the circular saw. On timbers in many extant early colonial buildings, the cut marks of circular saws are still visible.

saltbox roof

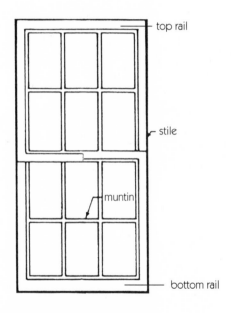

sashes: top and bottom sashes

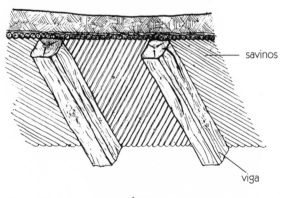

savinos

sawpit In colonial times, a pit dug in the ground and usually lined with boards, over which a timber to be sawn was laid during a hand-sawing operation. For ease of access, the sawpit was often was located on the side of a hill. One man (the *top sawyer,* placed above the pit) worked the upper handle of a two-handled saw; a second man (the *pitman,* below) worked the lower handle, providing motive power on the down-stroke. The sawn boards or planks were commonly 1, 1¼, or 2 inches (2.5, 3, or 5cm) thick.

sawpit

sawtooth pattern On a roof, a pattern of shingles or tiles resembling the teeth of a saw.

scagliola Plaster work having the appearance of decorative stone such as marble; formed by mixing marble dust and sizing with various pigments; often found in some elegant early American homes. *See also* **faux marbre.**

scallop One of a continuous series of curves resembling segments of a circle, used as a decorative element on the outer edge of a strip of wood, a molding, roofing tiles, or the like.

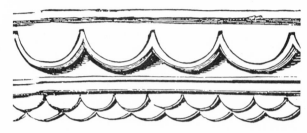

scallops

scamillus 1. In Classical and Neoclassical style, a plain block placed under the **plinth,1** of a column, thus forming a double plinth. 2. A slight bevel at the outer edge of a block of stone, as occurs between the **necking** of a Doric capital and the upper drum of the shaft.

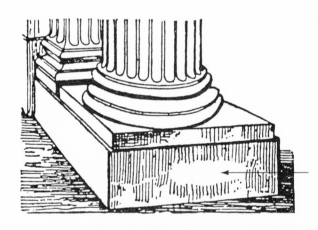

scamillus,1

scantling Any square-edged piece of lumber having a relatively small cross section.

scarf joint A joint between two pieces of timber or other structural members laid end to end and joined together; the timbers are usually notched and lapped, or otherwise fitted, to form a continuous piece that is able to resist compression or tension applied along its length.

schoolhouse A building in which classes are conducted at different educational levels to students under college age; instruction may be under private or public auspices. In colonial America some schoolhouses were located on the grounds of religious communities, plantations, or in meeting houses. *See also* **one-room schoolhouse.**

scored A term descriptive of a surface that has been grooved or channeled.

scotia A deep concave **molding**, especially one at the base of a column in Classical architecture and derivatives.

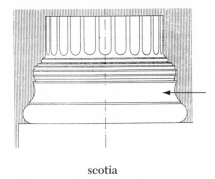

scotia

scribed joint A masonry joint in which a thin line has been cut in the face of the mortar between bricks after it has been smoothed with a metal tool.

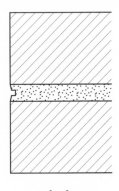

scribed joint

scroll An ornament consisting of a spiral form, either as a **running ornament** or as a terminal ornament such as the **volutes** of the Ionic capital or the ornaments on consoles and modillions.

scroll pediment A little-used synonym for **swan's-neck pediment.**

scroll step Same as **curtail step.**

scrollwork 1. Ornamental work that has been cut in wood by a scroll saw, a saw specifically designed for cutting decorative curved patterns such as those in the **bargeboards** on **Carpenter Gothic** homes; often suggestive of a series of waves or unrolled scrolls of paper. 2. Wrought-iron ornamental work in which scroll-like characters are an important element.

(a)

(b)

scrollwork,2
(a) on a 19th-century exterior door
(b) gate in colonial Charleston, S.C.

scullery A room, generally a kitchen annex, used to prepare food for cooking and/or as a pantry.

scuttle A hatchway or covered opening through a roof deck or ceiling; provides access through the opening.

seat cut A horizontal cut at the lower extremity of a rafter so that it fits against, and rests on, a **top plate,1** to which it is joined.

Second Classical Revival style A term sometimes used as a synonym for **Italian Renaissance Revival.**

Second Empire style A grand, eclectic style of architecture in America from about 1855 to 1890 and beyond, used in many public buildings and elegant homes; named after the French Second Empire of Napoléon III (1852–1870). Many important public buildings, commercial buildings, and some opulent homes in this style were designed by Richard Morris Hunt (1827–1895), the first American to study at the Ecole des Beaux Arts in Paris. It is frequently called *Mansard style* because it is characterized by a **mansard roof** often having the profile of a compound curve, with dormers. Occasionally called *General Grant style* because many public buildings were erected in this style during his presidency. Also called Second Empire Baroque.

Buildings in the Second Empire style usually exhibit many of the following characteristics:

Façade and exterior wall treatments: A central one-story pavilion projecting outward from a symmetrical façade; occasionally, corner or end pavilions; walls of brick, stone, or wood decorated to imitate stone; classical pediments and elaborate and heavy detailing and trim; often, a porch, with balustrades, supported by paired columns, usually with eaves having an overhang less than that in the **Italianate style**; a heavy cornice, typically supported by decorative brackets, often in pairs; a belt course; quoins; commonly, a square tower located at the center of the façade; occasionally a paneled **frieze**.

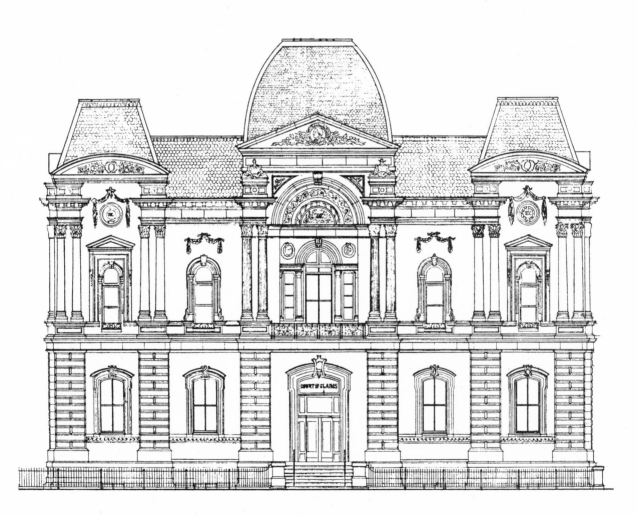

Second Empire style
(a) U.S. Court of Claims, Washington, D.C.

Roof treatments: A high **mansard roof** having a concave, convex, or compound-curve shape; the surface of the roof is usually broken by pedimented dormers; **terneplate** or multicolored slates forming decorative patterns covering the roof; often, a curb or railing around the roof, commonly enclosed with decorative metalwork cresting; occasionally, prominent chimneys, usually with decorative caps.

Window treatments: Often, an upper sash divided in two by a vertical secondary framing member, over a similar lower sash, in a **two-over-two** (2/2) arrangement of panes; pedimented, bracketed, or hooded windows, usually having a square or an arched head; windows sometimes flanked by pilasters or columns; tall, almost floor-to-ceiling, first-floor windows, occasionally with louvered shutters; frequently, windows in pairs or groups of three; dormer windows usually round or oval; one- or two-story **cant windows.**

Doorway treatments: At the main entry, a pair of paneled doors having glass in the upper panels; frequently, arched doorways; usually, steps leading from the street up to the level of the front porch, or if there is no porch, then to the doorway.

Second Empire style
(b) mansard roof with compound-curve profile

Second Period Colonial architecture A term occasionally applied to American Colonial architecture during the period from about 1700 (when **Georgian style** architecture emerged) to 1776.

Second Renaissance Revival   Same as **Italian Renaissance Revival.**

section A representation of a building, or portion thereof, drawn as if it were cut vertically to show its interior or internal structure.

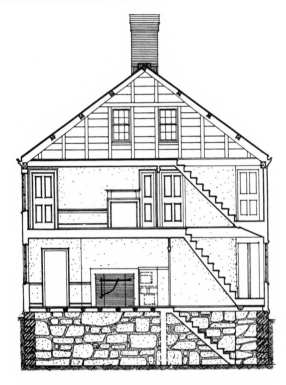

section: through a 2½-story house

segmental arch An arch whose **head** has the shape of an arc of a circle, usually an arc having a large radius of curvature; especially found in the architecture of the **Federal style, Georgian style,** and **Italianate style.**

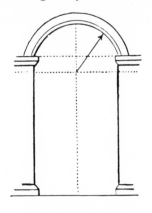

segmental arch

segmental dormer A **dormer** whose roof is an arc of a circle having a large radius of curvature.

segmental dormer

segmental pediment Atop a window or door, a decorative element in the shape of an arc of a circle. Also called a curved pediment. *See* **pediment,2.**

segmental pediment: above doorway

segmental roof Same as **compass roof.**

semicircular arch A round arch, the **head** of which is a full semicircle.

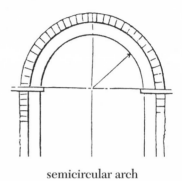

semicircular arch

semicircular fanlight A **fanlight** having a semicircular shape, usually located directly above the main entry of a house, often found in the **Federal style.**

semicircular fanlight

semicircular window 1. A window having a semicircle at its head. 2. A window having the shape of a semicircle, often placed above a door or in a **tympanum**; also called a **D**-window.

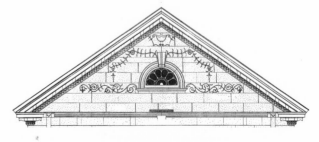

semicircular window
Meason House (1802), Fayette County, Pa.

semidetached house One of a pair of houses joined by a **party wall.**

semidetached house: a two-family dwelling

semielliptical arch An **arch** having the shape of half an ellipse. In construction, such a shape is often approximated by three adjoining circular arcs. Also called a basket-handle arch.

semielliptical fanlight A window, over the opening of a door, that has the shape of half an ellipse; often simply called an elliptical fanlight; commonly used, for example, in the **Georgian style** and the **Federal style,** among others.

semielliptical fanlight: doorway of (Federal-style) van Houten House (1831), Westside Park, N.J.

serpentine wall A wall that is not straight in plan but follows a winding course.

serpentine wall
University of Virginia, Charlottesville, Va.;
designed by Thomas Jefferson

servants' room In a large home of the past (or in a **dependency** of such a home), a common room in which the servants gathered, ate, and waited to be summoned.

setback The minimum distance between the front property line and the building line. This required distance is usually established by the applicable building code or ordinance.

Settlement phase The time period directly following the landing of the English settlers on the American continent, during which the colonists were providing themselves with basic shelter and were planting crops to ensure future supplies of food. *See* **American Colonial architecture.**

sexfoil A **foil** having six points called **cusps.**

sexfoil

shaft That portion of a column, colonette, or pilaster between the **base,2** and the **capital.**

shake A thick wood **shingle,** usually formed by hand-splitting a short log into tapered radial sections or by sawing; usually attached on sheathing in overlapping rows as a covering for a roof or wall.

Shaker architecture Architecture of the Shakers, a religious sect that founded its first community in America at Watervliet, New York, in 1776. Subsequent communities, usually consisting of 30 to 90 individuals, spread westward and southward; by 1826 there were Shakers as far west as Indiana. The sect reached a peak membership of 6,000 in the 1840s. For the most part, they were self-sufficient; they raised their own food, built their own housing, made their own furniture, wove their own cloth, and made their own clothing. Their structures were built of wood, stone, or bricks they made themselves. Their distinctive architecture is an attractive combination of unadorned simplicity, frugality, and functionality. Men and women lived in the same building in separate but equal facilities. The building was symmetrical in plan, with a wall dividing the men's and women's areas. In some communities even the hallways and stairways were separate. The staircases were unusual in that the stairs were built without continuous **carriages** for support; instead, the steps were bolted together so that each step provided support for the one above and the one below. The large meeting rooms for religious services, usually in a separate building, had no internal partitions or posts so as not to interfere with the fervent dancing that formed part of the religious rituals and from which the sect derived the name "Shaking Quakers" or "Shakers." Its original name was the United Society of Believers in Christ's Second Appearing. Since the Shakers were celibate and the sect was closed to new members in 1964, it is now extinct.

shaped parapet Any parapet whose edge does not follow a straight line; for example, a **multicurved parapet** as in a Flemish gable, or a **mission parapet.**

shay house Same as **coach house.**

sheathing 1. The covering placed directly over the rafters or the exterior studs of a building, for example, a covering composed of a layer of closely spaced boards; serves as a base on which to nail **cladding,** such as shingles, on the exterior walls or roof; introduced in the American colonies around the year 1700, sheathing layers greatly improved the thermal insulation of the exterior walls. 2. In colonial America, boards on the interior of a house that provided an interior surface finish.

sheathing,2
horizontal sheathing on the exterior wall of the bedroom; vertical sheathing on the fireplace wall,
Gilbert Stuart House (c. 1755), N. Kingston, R.I.

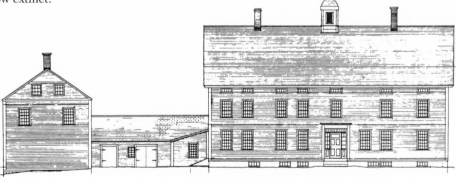

Shaker architecture: dwelling and washhouse (c. 1820), Harvard, Mass.

shed dormer, shed roof dormer A dormer whose eave line is parallel to the eave line of the main roof; its roof is a flat, inclined plane, sloping downward in a direction away from the ridge of the main roof; may provide a little more attic space than a gabled dormer.

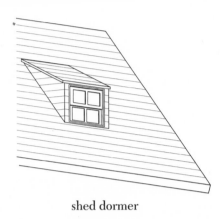

shed dormer

shed roof A roof having the shape of a single flat inclined plane.

Shed style In domestic architecture of the latter half of the 20th century, a mode of architecture characterized by its roof; houses commonly have two or more **shed roofs** that are generally steeply sloped in different directions. The roof surfaces usually have no significant overhang; the direction of the wall cladding can be vertical, horizontal, or sloped at an angle parallel to one of the major roof surfaces. The chief characteristic of the main doorway is its lack of prominence.

sheet glass Any type of glass in sheet form, for example, **plate glass.**

sheet-metal roofing A thin, rolled metal product, such as tin, used as **roofing**; usually flat or corrugated. *See* **corrugated metal** and **zinc.**

shell 1. A curved slab, curved plate, or the like, whose thickness is small as compared with its other dimensions. 2. Any framework or exterior structure that is regarded as incomplete. 3. An ornament similar in design to a seashell.

shell-headed A term descriptive of a decoration, generally concave in shape, that is similar in appearance to the shell of a sea scallop; often found at the **head** of a building component in **Spanish Colonial architecture.**

shell-headed cupboard A built-in cupboard, usually in one corner of a room, topped with a rounded arch containing a decorative element in the shape of a large seashell. Such cupboards were popular in colonial New England in the early 1700s.

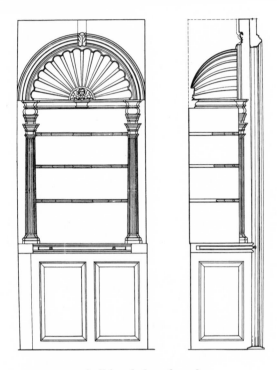

shell-headed cupboard
Wanton-Hunter House (c. 1746), Newport, R.I.

shell lime In early colonial America, a type of **lime** obtained by burning the shells of oysters, clams, or mussels; used in making lime mortar, particularly where limestone was not available for this purpose; the mortar often contained bits of shell as a result of incomplete calcination. Broken bit of shells could also appear in mortar because shell fragments were used as an **aggregate** with which the shell lime was mixed.

shingle A thin piece of slate, tile, or wood used as an exterior covering on sloping roofs and/or walls. Wood shingles are either hand-split or sawn along the grain from unseasoned wood and then kiln-dried; they are widely available in stock lengths, widths, and thicknesses. Shingles are applied in overlapping rows, usually in one of the following designs: **chisel pattern, coursed pattern, diamond pattern, fishscale pattern, sawtooth pattern**. *See also* **pine shingle, weather,** and **wood shingle.**

Shingle style An American eclectic style of domestic architecture used from about 1880 to 1900 and beyond. Houses in this style were usually two or three stories high, of wood construction, rambling and often asymmetrical in plan, with the walls and roof uniformly covered with wood shingles. The shingles, together with the overall lack of ornamentation, provided a uniform, continuous, fluid appearance, emphasizing the shingled surface and the horizontal aspects of the house. Outstanding examples, primarily located along New England's Atlantic coast, include some of the works of Henry Hobson Richardson (1838–1886), such as the Stoughton House (1883) in Cambridge, Massachusetts, and the Low House (1887) in Bristol, Rhode Island, by McKim, Mead & White. This style was given its name by the architectural historian Vincent J. Scully. More recently, Robert Venturi (1925–),

Charles Moore (1925–1993), and others have applied a modified Shingle style to shed-roof structures and other domestic forms of **vernacular architecture.**

Shingle-style houses usually exhibit many of the following characteristics:

Façade and exterior wall treatments: Extensive use of unpainted wood shingles, set in horizontal rows, as siding; the ground-story wall occasionally clad in some type of rough-surfaced masonry with shingles covering the stories above; large one- or two-story gabled porches incorporating circular or cylindrical shapes, set within the main structure or forming part of it; commonly, shingled arches and occasionally shingled porch posts.

Roof treatments: Commonly, a wood-shingled gable roof; typically, multiple gables that intersect; broad

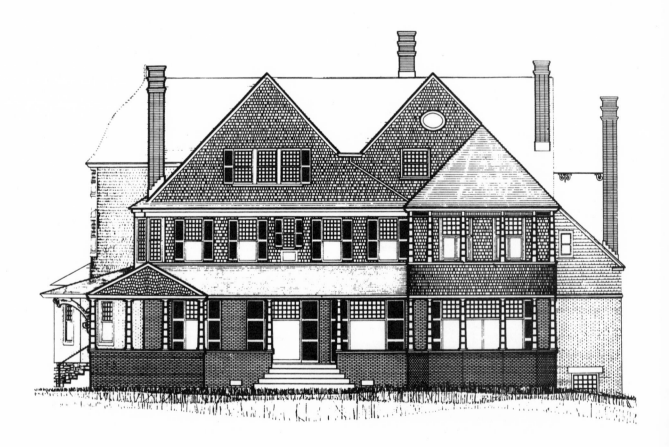

Shingle style: (a) Isaac Bell House (1883), Newport, R.I.; McKim, Mead & White, Architects

gable ends; less frequently, a gambrel roof; occasionally, a pent roof at a gable end; most commonly, pedimented dormers, although most other types of dormers are also used; often, multilevel eaves with little overhang; occasionally, a cylindrical or hexagonal tower having a conical or bell-shaped roof, usually topped with a finial, all unified in the overall design by the use of shingles; occasionally an **eyebrow dormer** with the roofing carried over the dormer in a wavy line to enhance the fluid appearance of the surface.

Window treatments: Usually, **double-hung windows** or **casement windows** with each sash having many panes; three or four windows often treated as a single unit; one- or two-story bay windows; occasional use of a Palladian window.

Doorway treatments: Prominent arches at entryways.

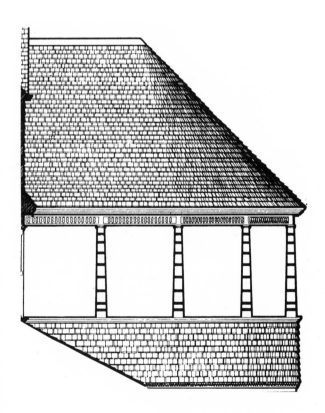

Shingle style: (b) Isaac Bell House, detail of porch

ship's-bottom roof A pitched gable roof whose slope on each side of a peaked ridge is slightly bowed, rather than constant. Also called a bowed roof, rainbow roof, whaleback roof.

ship's-bottom roof (c. 1800)

shopping center A group of retail stores and service establishments, especially in a suburban area, usually with associated parking facilities.

shopping mall A **shopping center** enclosed within a large structure; sometimes two or three stories high, placed around a central atrium; may have numerous stores, entertainment facilities such as movie theaters, fast-food outlets, restaurants, and public areas.

shotgun house Built primarily in the rural southern regions of the United States from the early 1800s to the early 1900s, a one- or one-and-a-half-story house, one room wide and several rooms deep, with the rooms placed in a straight line. According to folklore, one could fire a shotgun through the front door, hit the rear door, and leave the interior between undamaged; hence the name. The roof ridge was usually perpendicular to the street; there was a narrow gable front with a porch and often a similar porch at the rear. The house was commonly built on short piers. In the late 1880s and early 1900s, **prefabricated houses** of this design could be purchased in partial or complete form, occasionally with **gingerbread** ornamentation on the porch.

shot tower A very high structure, usually cylindrical and constructed of brick, that was once used in making lead shot for muskets. At the top of the tower, a molten alloy of lead was poured through a metal screen, forming small lead spheres that solidified as they dropped, falling into a container of water at the bottom of the tower. The first shot tower in America, 142 feet (43m) high, was constructed in Philadelphia in 1808; it is still in reasonably good condition.

shouldered arch A square-headed **trefoil arch.**

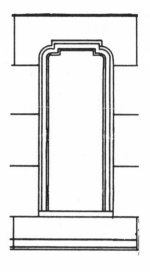

shouldered arch

shouldered post Same as **musket-stock post.**

shutter A movable panel, usually one of a pair used to cover an opening, especially a window opening; provides privacy and thermal insulation when closed. Solid-wood shutters were widely used until about 1760, when adjustable slat shutters were introduced and became popular. *See also* **battened shutter, boxing shutter,** and **folding shutter.**

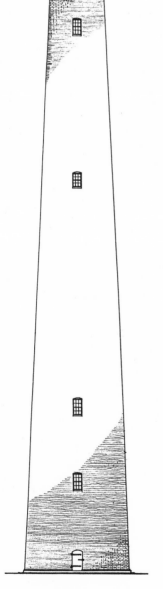

shot tower
Philadelphia, Pa.

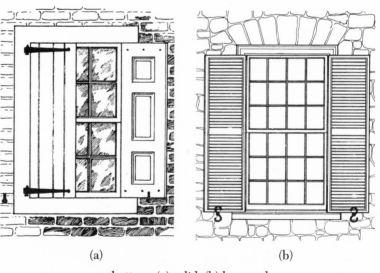

(a)   (b)

shutters: (a) solid; (b) louvered

shutter bar A hinged bar that can be fastened across the interior side of a pair of **shutters**. When the shutters are in the closed position, completely covering the window, the shutter bar prevents their being opened, adding a measure of security.

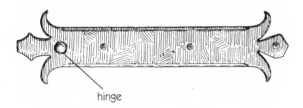

shutter bar

shutter box A pocket or recess located along the interior side of a window to receive **shutters** when folded.

shutter fastener A pivoted device, usually one of a pair, often made of decorative wrought iron, used to hold a **shutter** in the open position on the exterior side of a window. Also called a shutter catch, shutter dog, or a shutter holdback.

shutter fasteners

side bearer A structural member that runs horizontally along a side wall of a house and supports a load.

side gable A **gable** whose face is on one side (or part of one side) of a house, perpendicular to the façade.

side girt A **girt** between **corner posts** on the long side of a timber-framed house. *See* illustration under **timber-framed house.**

side-hall plan A **floor plan** of a house having a corridor that runs from the front to the back of the house along one exterior wall; all rooms are located on the same side of the corridor. Also called a side-passage plan.

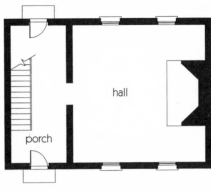

side-hall plan

side-hill barn A term occasionally used for a **bank barn.**

side hinge Same as **H-hinge.**

sidelight A framed area of fixed glass, usually comprising a number of small panes; commonly one of a pair of such **lights,** set vertically on each side of a door. Especially popular following the American Revolution and into the early 1800s. Compare with **fanlight.**

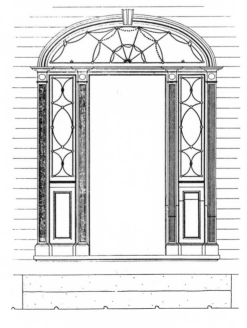

sidelight

siding A finish covering on the exterior walls of a wood-frame building; the covering may be a cladding material such as wood, aluminum, or asbestos-cement (but not masonry); long strips of the covering material are usually applied horizontally so as to provide water resistance at their joints. In colonial Connecticut, Rhode Island, the middle colonies, and the southern colonies, oak was the preferred material for siding, but in Massachusetts cedar and pine were more popular. Today aluminum and vinyl siding are widely used. *See* **bevel siding, bungalow siding, clapboards, colonial siding, drop siding, flush siding, German siding, lap siding, log-cabin siding, matched siding, novelty siding, rabbeted siding, rustic siding, shingle, vertical siding, weather slating.**

signature stone A stone, found on many 18th- and 19th-century dwellings, carved with the date of completion and the name or initials of the owner, and sometimes those of his wife; usually embedded in the wall over the entry door or in a gable.

sill 1. One of the structural members of an early colonial timber-framed house; same as **sill plate.** 2. A **doorsill** or **window sill.** 3. Same as **bed sill.**

sill course A band of stone masonry that extends horizontally across the façade of a building at window sill level; commonly differentiated from the wall by its greater projection, its finish, or its thickness.

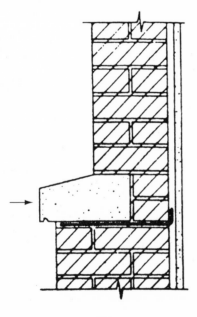

sill course

sill plate 1. A heavy horizontal timber at the bottom of the frame of a wood structure; the timber rests directly on a foundation. *See* illustration under **timber-framed house.** 2. Same as **groundsill.**

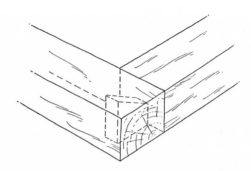

sill plate

silo A tall, enclosed structure used primarily to store grain, fodder, or chopped green plants (*silage*) and the like; commonly constructed of wood, masonry, or concrete. In 1882, Professor F. H. King of the University of Wisconsin developed the cylindrical silo, after having shown this shape to be most suitable for achieving the tightest packing of silage and therefore to result in minimum spoilage. As a result cylindrical silos proliferated across American farmlands. A silo is usually loaded from the top so that the weight of the silage forces air out as it settles; it may be unloaded either from the top or from the bottom.

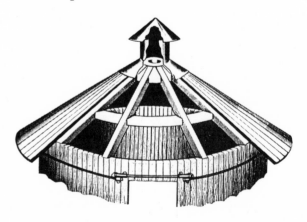

silo
detail showing vent at top

single-acting door A door provided with hinges or pivots that permit it to swing 90 degrees in one direction only.

single house A house having a long, narrow **plan**, only one room wide, with the narrow end of the house facing the street; popular in 18th-century Georgia and the Carolinas. The entrance from the street was up a short flight of stairs to a long, narrow, open porch, called a **piazza**, that extended along one side of the house and provided entry into the individual rooms. *See*, for example, **Charleston house.**

single-hung window A window having two sashes, only one of which (usually the lower one) is movable.

single notch Same as **half-cut notch.**

single-pen cabin A relatively crude one-story cabin, cottage, hut, or house having only one room.

single-pile house A house that is only one room deep. *See* **pile,2.**

single-pitched roof A roof having only a single slope on each side of a central ridge, for example, a **gable roof.** Compare with **shed roof,** which has a single slope but no central ridge.

single-room plan Same as **one-room plan.**

single-saddle notch Usually, a synonym for **saddle notch.**

sitting room A small living room or parlor in a house.

six-over-six (6/6) A term descriptive of a double-hung window having six panes in the upper sash and six panes in the lower sash. *See* **pane.**

six-over-six (6/6) window: Federal style

sizing A thick liquid applied over wood, plaster, or other porous surfaces to fill their pores; after the treated surface dries, it is more resistant to the further absorption of other liquids.

skeleton-frame construction A type of steel construction, usually for buildings of great height, in which the loads and stresses are transmitted to the foundations by a framework of steel columns and beams; the walls are supported by the framework. This technique avoids the problem faced in constructing very high buildings of masonry, which would require impractically thick walls at the lower stories in order to support the load imposed by the masonry above. *See also* **steel-frame construction** and **skyscraper.**

skew corbel A stone built into the bottom of a gable to form an abutment for a wall cornice or eaves gutter.

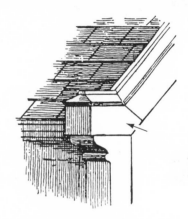

skew corbel

skid row, skid road An area of a town or city characterized by cheap barrooms, saloons, and run-down hotels; usually a gathering place for derelicts, vagrants, and alcoholics. This term originated in the early part of the 20th century in an area in Seattle, Washington, known as *skid road*, located near the foot of a skidway used for conveying cut logs from a higher location down to the waterfront. The logs were slid down a "road" consisting of greased logs laid perpendicular to the direction of travel.

skin A non-load-bearing exterior wall. In modern building construction, the skin is often composed of prefabricated panels. *See also* **curtain wall.**

skintled joint Same as **excess joint.**

skirt board Same as **baseboard.**

skirt roof A small **false roof** between the first and second stories of a house; provides some shelter for the windows and doors directly below it, but is primarily decorative in function; often completely encircles the perimeter of the house. If it extends only along the façade, usually called a visor roof or **pent roof**.

skirt roof

skylight In a roof, an opening that is glazed with a transparent or translucent material; used to provide light to the space below it. Compare with **dome light**.

skyscraper A very tall building, many stories high, with **skeleton-frame construction** supporting **curtain walls**. The development of the skeleton frame made the construction of modern skyscrapers practical. The invention of the high-speed electric elevator was also an important factor. Although there is some question as to which building should be designated as the world's first skyscraper—albeit a fairly primitive one— the one most cited for this distinction is the ten-story Home Insurance Building (1885) in Chicago, designed by William Le Baron Jenney (1832–1907). Prior to this date, buildings were of solid masonry construction; in high buildings of this type, very thick masonry walls were required in the lower stories to support the significant load of the masonry walls above. The use of skeleton-frame construction and a curtain wall avoided this problem by supporting the exterior walls independently at each floor. Jenney used a skeleton of cast-iron columns that were sheathed in masonry for his framing and wrought-iron beams to support the masonry walls. Three years after the erection of the Home Insurance Building, L. S. Buffington was granted a patent for a system of self-supporting wrought-iron framing for tall buildings (which he termed *cloudscrapers*) that did not depend on masonry for stiffening. Although he erected no building based on his patent, his system received considerable attention and stimulated contributions from others. *See also* **steel-frame construction**.

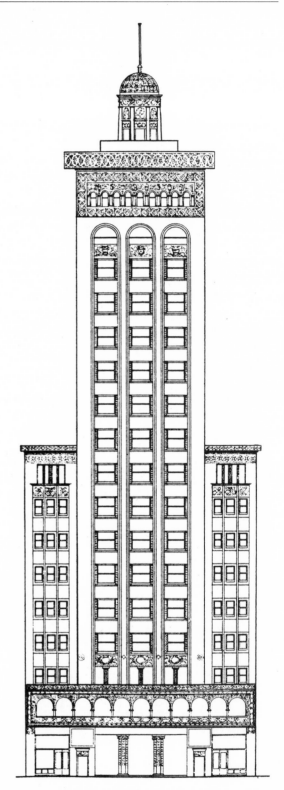

skyscraper: Schiller Building (1892), Chicago, Ill.; Adler and Sullivan, Architects

skyway An enclosed walkway, elevated above street level, that provides a passageway from one building to another.

slab board A board cut from the side of a log without removing the bark and sapwood.

slab house A house built of rough-hewn planks.

slaked lime A mixture of **lime** and water, used as mortar. *See also* **lime mortar.**

slap dash Same as **rock dash.**

slate A hard, brittle metamorphic rock consisting mainly of claylike minerals, characterized by good cleavage along parallel planes and available in a number of different colors; used extensively in thin sheets as shingles for roofing and as slabs for flooring. In Boston, after a serious fire in 1679, an edict mandated the use of slate or tile roofs on all buildings throughout the city, but the edict was not enforced because of the shortage and relatively high cost of slate. By 1830, half of the roofs in New York City were said to have had slate roofing.

slate: tiles at a roof valley

slate hanging Slate that is hung vertically, or nearly so, on the face of an exterior wall to prevent the penetration of moisture.

sleeper One of a number of long horizontal timbers that are laid on a concrete slab, or directly on the ground, to which the flooring is nailed.

sleeper joist Any **joist** resting directly on sleepers.

sleeping porch A **porch**, or a room lined with windows, used for sleeping; often located in an extension to a house, above another porch, or above a **porte cochère.**

sliding door A door, mounted on a track, that slides in a horizontal direction; used in America since the early 1800s to subdivide a large room; now often used as a segment of a glass wall, opening onto a patio.

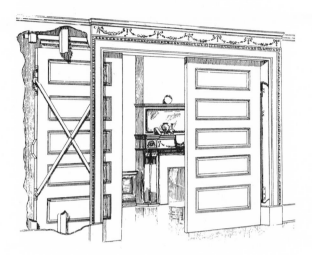

sliding door
invented c. 1892; requires no floor tracks or rollers

sliding sash, sliding window A window **sash** that is mounted on tracks or grooves in either the horizontal or vertical direction. Windows sashes of this type were installed in Williamsburg, Virginia, in the 1690s at the College of William and Mary, as well as in the capitol building in Williamsburg.

sliphead window A window in which part of the sash slides upward through the head of the window frame.

slit ventilator One of a number of long vertical slots in the masonry walls of a **German barn** to supply fresh air to the barn. Occasionally called a slit window.

slit ventilator

sloped offset chimney Same as **stepped-back chimney**.

smoke chamber Same as **rauchkammer**.

smoke hole In many types of primitive dwellings in America, a hole in the roof that permitted smoke and fumes to escape from an open firepit below; it also provided a source of light and ventilation.

smokehouse An enclosed **outbuilding** in which meat or fish is cured with smoke to preserve it; usually has a vent, no windows, and a single door. In colonial America the walls were usually constructed of boards, brick, logs, or stone with a gabled or pyramidal roof; the meat or fish, often partially preserved with salt before being placed in the smokehouse, was usually hung from wood beams or placed in boxes. Smokehouses about 10 to 12 feet (3–3.6m) square were common, although on plantations or in religious communities, where there were many mouths to feed, they were much larger in area and as high as 35 feet (10.6m). The type of fuel used to produce the smoke, such as wood from a fruit tree, hickory tree, or corncobs, affected the flavor of the cured meat or fish. Smokehouses have been common in America since the early 1700s.

snake fence Same as **zigzag fence**.

snecked rubble masonry Masonry that has been laid with rough irregular stones set so as to produce a strong bond.

snow guard Any device intended to prevent snow from sliding off a sloping roof.

snow house *See* **iglu**.

soapstone A massive variety of soft rock that contains a high proportion of talc. Because it is easy to carve, it was often used for ornamentation on early American fireplace mantels and the like.

Society of Architectural Historians A society dedicated to the encouragement of scholarly research in the field of architectural history; founded in 1940 as the American Society of Architectural Historians, and called the Society of Architectural Historians since 1947. Address: 1365 North Astor Street, Chicago, IL 60610.

sod The upper layer of soil covered by grass and containing grass roots.

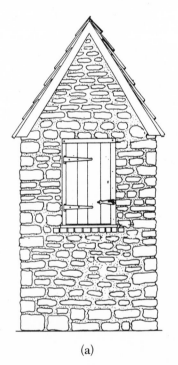

(a)   (b)

smokehouse
(a) Tallman Mansion (1757), Burlington County, N.J.;
(b) typical interior, with smoke rising through grille to smoke room above

sod dwelling   A partially underground dwelling used in some parts of Alaska by Eskimos; consisted of one large room, having a framework of driftwood and/or whalebone that was covered by a heavy layer of **sod**, which served as the center of all family activities. It was connected to the outdoors by an elongated passageway used as a storage area and to provide thermal insulation between the room and the exterior. Light entered the room through a hole, cut in one of the walls, that was covered with a slab of clear ice or a sheet of translucent sea mammal intestine. These dwellings were considered to be much more comfortable than an **iglu**. *See also* **sod house.**

sod house, soddie   A house of very economical construction, having walls about one (30cm) foot thick, built of large blocks of **sod** cut from an upper layer of grassland by means of a "grasshopper plow," which cut the sod into very long unbroken strips about three to four inches (7.6–10cm) thick; these strips were then cut with a spade into blocks about three feet (1m) long and one to one-and-a-half feet (0.46m) wide. Because the sod blocks were most easily handled when slightly damp, the sod was cut in the morning and laid in place the same day. An acre of land provided enough sod blocks to build a rectangular house about 14 feet by 16 feet (4.3 x 4.9m). Houses of this type were constructed quickly by early settlers in the Great Plains, from Oklahoma to North Dakota, where there were few stones, timber was scarce, and little fuel was available for making brick. Good-quality sod, usually permeated with buffalo-grass roots, was readily available; in Nebraska, for example, where essentially free land was available under the Homestead Act, such houses were popular from the late 1800s to 1910. Often they were built partially underground or into the side of a hill as protection against the wind. Floors were made of packed earth. Sod walls and **sod roofs** provided good thermal insulation, and plastering of the exterior and interior walls with clay or cement promoted cleanliness and reduced or prevented insect infestation. During a heavy rain, the roof usually leaked, as did the clay-and-sticks chimney, often making it difficult to start a fire. This type of building construction was also used by settlers for barns and other dependencies. *See also* **Plains cottage.**

sod roof   A roof composed of a thick layer of grassland containing roots; frequently pitched or barrel-shaped and supported by logs; usually prone to water leakage. In upscale modern sod houses, an impermeable plastic sheet is set beneath the sod roofing to reduce or eliminate water leakage.

sod dwelling

(a)

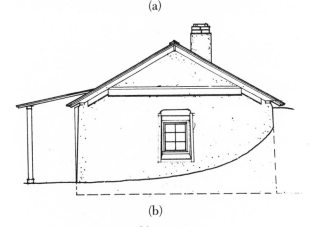

(b)

sod house,1
(a) under construction; (b) a completed house

sod roof: Pipe Spring Fort, Arizona

soffit The exposed undersurface of any overhead component of a building, such as an arch, balcony, beam, cornice, or lintel.

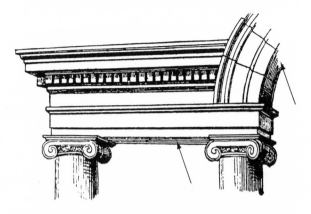

soffits

solar house A dwelling designed to utilize the sun's rays to maximum advantage for heating the house and providing hot water; an auxiliary heat source is usually provided. *See* **active solar-energy system** and **passive solar-energy system.**

solarium A glass-enclosed room, especially one with considerable exposure to sunlight.

soldier A brick that is laid on end, i.e., positioned vertically with its narrower face showing on the wall surface. Compare with **sailor.**

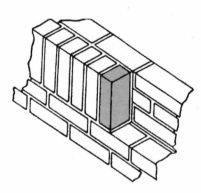

soldier

soleplate A horizontal timber used to distribute the thrust of one or more **posts** or **struts** that rest on it. Also called a solepiece, sole, or sill.

solid-newel stair A type of **spiral stair** whose wedge-shaped treads (**fliers**) wind around, and are supported by, a central post called a **newel.** Also called a newel stair.

sounding board In many early American churches, a solid surface above a pulpit that acts as a sound reflector; directs a small fraction of the sound of a speaker's voice toward the congregation.

sounding board: above a church pulpit

Southern Colonial architecture *See* **American Colonial architecture of the early South.**

Southern Colonial house 1. Any pre-Revolutionary house in the tradition of **American Colonial architecture of the early South.** 2. A term sometimes used to describe a full-colonnaded **Greek Revival style** mansion constructed *after* the colonial period. *See also* **plantation house.**

space frame A three-dimensional structure usually formed by an assemblage of many similar straight-line, rigid members such as beams, rods, or tubes, for example, the rigid **frame** of a multistory building or a **geodesic dome.**

span The distance between any two consecutive supports in a building, such as the distance between two supports of an arch.

spandrel   1. In a multistory building, a wall panel filling the space between the top of the window in one story and the sill of the window in the story above. 2. An area, roughly triangular in shape and often ornamented, included between the exterior surfaces of two adjoining arches and a line approximately connecting their **crowns;** or in the case of a single arch, a space approximately equal to half this area.

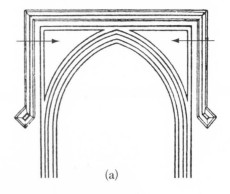

(a)

(b)

(a) spandrel,1; (b) spandrel,2, executed in cast iron; a box in the
Auditorium Building (1890), Chicago, Il.; Adler and Sullivan, Architects

Spanish Colonial architecture Because Spanish influence on architecture in America has been so widespread and has been so greatly affected by local culture, customs, traditions, and availability of materials, it is convenient to consider Spanish Colonial architecture in terms of distinct geographical areas, as in the two entries that follow.

Spanish Colonial architecture of the American Southwest Architecture of the Spanish settlers and missionaries in areas that later became Arizona, California, New Mexico, and Texas, from the middle of the 1500s onward. Many of the Spanish architectural contributions in this region are also described under **Mission architecture**. *See also* **Churrigueresque style**. Occasionally called Spanish Colonial style.

Spanish Colonial architecture of the American Southwest usually includes a number of the following characteristics:

Façade and exterior wall treatments: Thick, solid walls, usually constructed of **adobe** brick, often covered with a protective layer of stucco or plaster; typically a one-story building around an enclosed courtyard; a long, narrow covered porch (**portale**) either facing the street or facing a patio; if two stories, then a balcony, commonly supported by columns at ground-floor level, each column usually topped with a **bolster,** often decorated, to provide greater bearing area for sustaining the load imposed on the column.

Roof treatments: Commonly, a flat roof consisting of a very heavy layer of mortar or earth supported by round logs (**vigas**); because of the limited length of available logs, the rooms usually had a maximum width of about 15 feet (4.6m); the slope of the flat roof was only sufficient to effect rainwater drainage via waterspouts (**canales**) that penetrated the parapet surrounding the roof. In some regions of the Southwest, such as California, the roof often had a low or medium pitch and was covered with red clay tiles; it often had a substantial overhang.

Window treatments: In the earliest buildings, small windows because of the scarcity of glass; windows facing the street usually protected on the exterior side by ornamental grillwork (**rejas**) of wrought iron if available, otherwise of wood.

Doorway treatments: Doors to the various rooms opened directly onto a covered porch (**portale**) or onto the patio. *See also* **zaguán** and **zambullo door.**

Spanish Colonial architecture of Florida Architecture of the Spanish settlement in Saint Augustine, Florida, founded in 1565, described under **Saint Augustine house, azotea, board house, common house, coquina, palma hut, tabby, tabla house, thatch.**

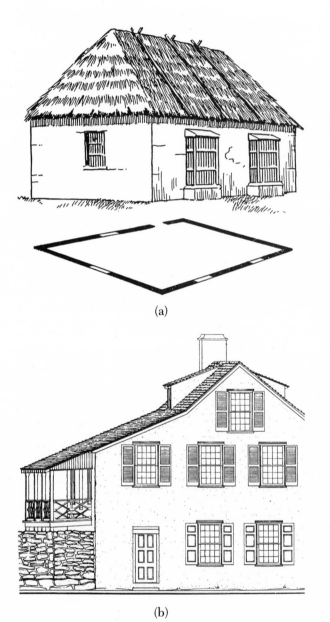

(a)

(b)

Spanish Colonial architecture of Florida
(a) one-room house and plan (18th cent.),
St. Augustine, Fla.; (b) two-story house
(c. 1804–1820), St. Augustine, Fla.

Spanish Colonial Revival An eclectic style loosely based on one or more phases of Spanish Colonial architecture, primarily found in residences but also in some public buildings and churches; most common in the southwestern part of the United States and in Florida from about 1915 to the present; particularly popular in the 1920s and 1930s. Occasionally called Spanish Eclectic style. *See also* **Mission Revival, Monterey style,** and **Plateresque architecture.**

Spanish Colonial Revival buildings usually exhibit many of the following characteristics:

Façade and exterior wall treatments: Commonly, a symmetrical façade with stucco or plastered walls, although occasionally, light-colored brick walls, usually unadorned, but some elaborately and lavishly decorated in the **Churrigueresque style,** displaying decorative elements of **Plateresque architecture** of the Spanish Renaissance of the 16th century; glazed and/or unglazed wall tiles; ornate low-relief carvings on window trim, around doors, or on columns and pilasters; highly decorated compound arches; molded, decorative cornices and enriched corbels; a long covered porch (**portale**) or arcade; occasionally, a **loggia**; commonly, a patio; wrought-iron balconies or balconets in front of one or more of the upper-floor windows; occasionally, a round, rectangular, or square tower intended to suggest a bell tower (**campanario**), emulating earlier Spanish Colonial architecture; occasionally, one or more decorative vents in walls.

Roof treatments: Typically, a low- to moderate-pitched, red mission-tiled, hipped and/or gable roof, although occasionally a flat roof; sometimes, multi-curved **mission parapets** with decorative tilework along the outer face of the parapet; usually little roof overhang at the eaves, in contrast to most earlier prototypes; often, a decorative **chimney hood.**

Window treatments: Round arches over the most prominent windows; often rectangular windows with **lintels**, sometimes crowned with an enriched cornice; cast-iron or wrought-iron window grilles; ornate, low-relief **window surrounds.**

Doorway treatments: Heavy wood doors, often elaborately paneled or carved, creating the appearance of massiveness; frequently, rounded arches over the exterior doors; occasionally, an elaborate portal; French doors at the rear of the house, providing easy access to a patio or outdoor terrace.

Spanish Colonial style *See* **Spanish Colonial architecture of the American Southwest.**

Spanish Eclectic architecture Same as, or an early phase of, **Spanish Colonial Revival.**

Spanish Colonial Revival

Spanish Mission Revival, Spanish Mission style *See* **Mission Revival.**

Spanish Pueblo Revival Same as **Pueblo Revival.** *See also* **Spanish Colonial Revival.**

Spanish Territorial style *See* **Territorial style.**

Spanish tile 1. A red roofing tile whose horizontal cross section has the shape of the letter **S** laid on its side. 2. Same as **mission tile.**

span roof A roof having the same slope on both sides of a ridge; the house has a gable at each end.

spar 1. A **common rafter**. 2. A bar for fastening a gate or door. 3. A heavy, round timber.

sparpiece A horizontal structural member that ties together, and stiffens, two common rafters on opposite sides of a roof ridge, as in a **collar-beam roof**; usually tied at a point about halfway up the rafters.

speaking tube A metal tube, usually of copper or tin, once used to transmit a speaker's voice from one part or one floor of a building to another; the mouthpieces were usually made of porcelain, ivory, or silver-plated metal.

sperm candle façade In **cast-iron architecture**, primarily in the 1860s, a commercial building in which the façade has a colonnaded base capped by an entablature and two upper tiers of stories; supported by relatively thin cast-iron **engaged** columns said to resemble the shape of candles made from sperm-whale oil. A number of such cast-iron façades still remain in New York City.

spindlework Wood details having circular cross sections, for example, **balusters**; usually turned on a lathe, although some shapes were once carved by hand; often used, for example, on porches of **Queen Anne style** and in some **Neo-Victorian** homes.

spinning house In colonial America and for a period thereafter, a subsidiary building devoted exclusively to spinning or weaving. Also called a loom house or a weaving house.

spiral stair A flight of stairs, circular in plan, having approximately wedge-shaped **treads** that wind around a solid, central column or around an open shaft. Also called a caracole, circular stair, helical stair, or solid stair.

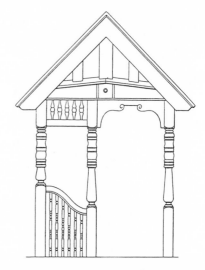

spindlework
ornamentation on a Queen Anne–style porch

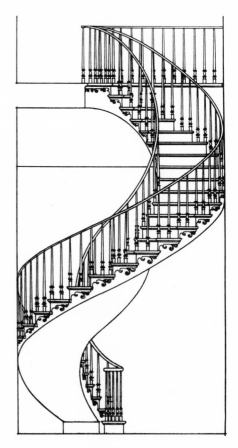

spiral stair: around a central shaft; Mission San Esteban del Rey (c. 1642), Acoma, N.M.

spire Any tall, sharply pointed rooflike construction atop a building, steeple, tower, or the like.

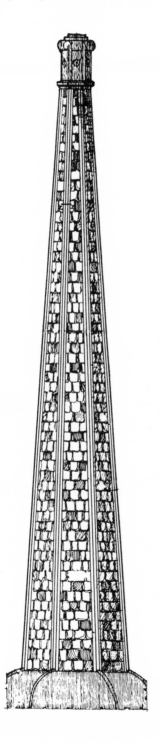

spire

splayed lintel A **lintel,** i.e., a horizontal structural member above a window, each end of which slants downward toward the centerline of the window; often has a keystone at its center.

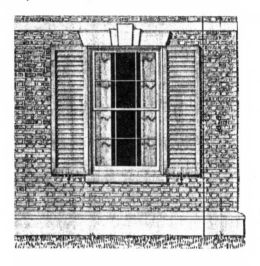

splayed lintel: above window (1819)

split-level house A house having its living room area on the main floor, with stairs leading upward to the bedrooms approximately a half-story higher; other stairs may lead downward from the main floor to the kitchen and/or dining areas and to a laundry or utility room; usually has no cellar, attic, or porch for reasons of economy; popular in America after about 1955.

split pediment Same as **broken pediment.**

split-rail fence *See* **zigzag fence.**

spoolwork Same as **spindlework.**

spraddle Same as **bonnet roof.**

springer 1. The **impost** or place where the vertical support for an arch terminates and the curve of the arch begins. 2. The lowest **voussoir,** or bottom stone of an arch, that lies immediately on an impost.

springhouse A small structure, typically of masonry construction, built into the slope of a hillside and enclosing a natural spring; the water flows into a small pool within the springhouse, keeping it cool at all times and providing an excellent place for storing dairy products, meats, fruit, and other perishable foods. Especially found in areas settled by the **Pennsylvania Dutch.**

springing wall Same as **buttress**.

square-headed window A window having a straight horizontal **lintel** above it.

square notch At the corner of a **log house**, a joint formed by cutting away part of the upper half of one end of a timber and placing this timber at right angles to the end of another timber whose lower half has also been partially removed; a spike (or other fastener) through the overlapping timbers is required to secure the joint.

square notch
with chinking between the notched timbers

square roof A **roof** in which the rafters on opposite sides of the ridge meet at an angle of 90 degrees; each side of the ridge has a pitch of 45 degrees with respect to the vertical.

stack *See* **chimney stack**.

stack bond A brick pattern in which the facing bricks are laid so that all vertical and horizontal joints are continuously aligned.

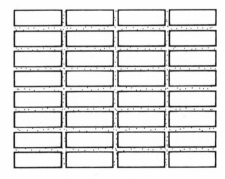

stack bond

stained glass A decorative glass that is given a desired color not by staining the glass, as the name implies, but by any one of the following techniques. One method, used in decorative windows or transparent mosaics, involves the application of an enamel paint onto a plain or tinted glass surface and firing it in a kiln. Another, widely used in Gothic architecture, fuses various metal oxides with glass while it is in its molten state; the resulting color, which has a jewellike quality, depends on the metal oxide used. The use of stained glass was rare in America prior to 1840 but became more widespread in the latter half of the 19th century despite its relatively high cost. Significant con-

(a)
stained-glass window
(a) Plymouth Church of the Pilgrims, Brooklyn, N.Y.;
designed by Louis Comfort Tiffany;

tributions to the revival of the art of fabricating stained glass were made in England by the Pre-Raphaelite studios of William Morris (1834–1896), a leader in the **Arts and Crafts movement**. In America, those at the forefront of new stained-glass techniques were the painters Louis Comfort Tiffany (1848–1933) and John La Farge (1835–1910), who independently developed a type of material variously called *opalescent glass,* *favrile glass,* or *American glass,* now often referred to as *Tiffany glass.* It is characterized by unusual combinations of colors and special effects in transparency and opaqueness, creating exaggerated color variations within the glass itself; it was much used in the late 1800s and early 1900s for decorative objects and to highlight architectural details, as, for example, by Frank Lloyd Wright in many of his works.

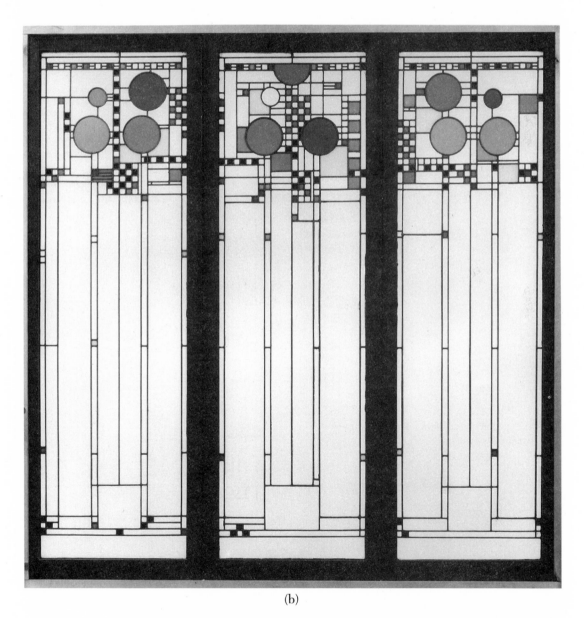

(b)

stained-glass window
(b) triptych (1912), designed by Frank Lloyd Wright, on display at
Metropolitan Museum of Art in New York City

stainless steel A high-strength, tough steel alloy, usually containing 4 to 25 percent chromium with nickel as an additional alloying element; highly resistant to corrosion and rust.

stair A series of steps, or flights of steps connected by landings, that permit passage between two or more levels or floors. For definitions and illustrations of specific types, *see* **box stair, bracketed stair, circular stair, cockle stair, cylindrical stair, dogleg stair, double-entry stair, double-L stair, double-return stair, double stair, geometrical stair, good-morning stair, halfpace stair, helical stair, hollow-newel stair, newel stair, open-newel stair, open stair, quarterpace stair, quarter-turn stair, reverse-flight stair, solid-newel stair, spiral stair, straight-flight stair, straight-run stair.**

stair bracket A decorative detail fastened to a slanting board that supports the ends of the steps in a stair; the bracket often provides additional bracing for the stair. Also called a step bracket.

staircase, stairway 1. A flight of stairs between two floors, or a series of such flights, including supports, handrails, and framework. 2. A structure containing a flight of stairs.

staircase and stair landing
Brown-Gammell House (1786), Providence, R.I.

stair flight A continuous series of steps with no intermediate landings.

stair hall A room in a home, usually of some pretentiousness, that is especially designed to contain a stair; for example, *see* **entrance hall.**

stairhead The top of a flight of stairs or a staircase.

stair landing The horizontal platform at the end of a flight of stairs or between two flights of stairs.

stair rail A bar of wood or other material that interconnects posts or balusters on a stair.

stairwell A vertical shaft that contains a staircase.

stair windows Same as **stepped windows.**

stamped-metal ceiling Same as **pressed-metal ceiling.**

stanchion 1. An upright bar, beam, or post; for example, in colonial America, a vertical iron bar across the frame of a **casement window.** 2. An isolated pillar or upright that acts as a barrier; for example, to prevent the passage of vehicles.

standing gutter A **V**-shaped gutter near the lower end of a sloped roof; one side of the **V** is formed by a long board, running parallel to the eaves, whose broad side is approximately perpendicular to the sloping surface of the roof; the roof itself acts as the other side of the **V**.

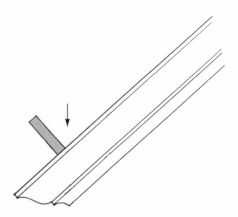

standing gutter
along ridge of roof

standing panel A panel whose longest dimension is vertical.

standing seam In metal roofing, a type of seam between adjacent sheets of material that is made by turning up the edges of two adjacent sheets and then folding them over to form a waterproof joint.

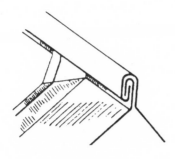

standing seam

St. Augustine house *See* **Saint Augustine house.**

Steamboat Gothic A richly ornamental **Carpenter Gothic** architecture from about the middle to the latter half of the 19th century, suggestive of the ornate and flamboyant decorations on steamboats on the Ohio and Mississippi Rivers; elaborate and sometimes imaginative use is made of **gingerbread.**

Steamboat Gothic: interior of the Mississippi steamboat *Grand Republic* (1877)

steel A very strong, hard, malleable alloy of iron having a carbon content of no more than 2 percent; distinguished from **cast iron** by its malleability and lower carbon content.

steel-frame construction Construction in which the structural supporting elements consist of some combination of steel beams, steel girders, and/or steel columns that are rigidly joined at their intersections. *See also* **skeleton-frame construction** and **skyscraper.**

steeple A tall ornamental structure, usually topped by a small **spire**; often built on a church tower or cupola. Steeples on churches in the American colonies initially followed designs taken from **pattern books** imported from England. *See also* **belfry.**

steeple

steeple house A term used by some religious faiths for a **church.**

step A stair unit that consists of one **tread** and one **riser.**

step bracket Same as **stair bracket.**

step log Same as **notched-log ladder.**

stepped arch An arch in which the **voussoirs** are cut horizontally and/or vertically so that they fit in with the masonry course above and below, forming a series of steps. *See also* **stepped voussoir.**

stepped arch

stepped-back chimney An exterior brick chimney, rectangular in cross section, sufficiently wide at the level of the hearth to enclose a very large kitchen fireplace on the interior, and then decreasing in area, in several steps, with increasing chimney height. Chimneys of this type were occasionally built primarily in Virginia and Maryland during the 17th century; they were often topped with corbeled chimney caps or decorative chimney pots. Also called an offset chimney or Tudor chimney.

stepped-back chimney
Ramsay House (1748), Alexandria, Va.

stepped gable A **gable** having a stepped edge; usually constructed of brick. Widely used by the Dutch in colonial America, but also found elsewhere; for example, stepped gables appear in Midway, the oldest house in South Carolina. Also called a corbiestep gable, corbie gable, crowfooted gable, crowstep gable.

stepped gable

stepped voussoir One of a number of **voussoirs** that are cut at their upper ends so they form a horizontal surface.

stepped voussoirs

stepped windows A series of windows, usually in a wall adjacent to a staircase, arranged in a stepped pattern that generally follows the ascent of the steps. Also called stair windows.

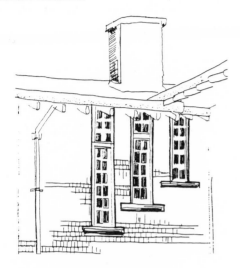

stepped windows
Pitcairn House (1906), Pasadena, Calif.

sticks-and-clay chimney, sticks-and-mud chimney, stick chimney Same as **clay-and-sticks chimney.**

Stick style An eclectic style of American domestic architecture primarily from about 1860 to 1890, mainly of wood-frame construction; usually asymmetric in both plan and section; has applied ornamentation in the form of wood boards on the exterior surfaces that is intended to express the inner structure of the building; made practical by the development of **balloon framing** in the 1830s, which significantly increased variations in types of wood construction. An outstanding example of the Stick style is the Griswold House (1863) at Newport, Rhode Island, designed by Richard Morris Hunt (1827–1895). This style was defined and given its name by the architectural historian Vincent J. Scully.

Stick-style buildings usually exhibit many of the following characteristics:

Façade and exterior wall treatments: Usually, a façade of clapboard or board-and-batten siding with structural framing materials used as exterior ornamentation; for example, wood boards prominently applied in patterns on wall surfaces with angle braces, beveled struts, studs, and **X**-braces over the exterior cladding; prominent structural corner posts. Commonly, spacious porches, decorated with simple diagonal braces or with brackets of more complex design; often, a porte cochère; occasionally, a square or rectangular tower.

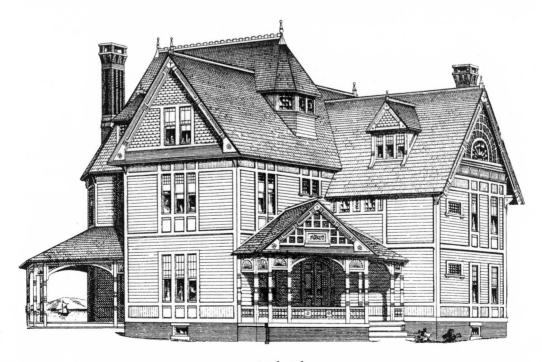

Stick style

Roof treatments: A steeply pitched gable roof, often with intersecting gables; typically, a decorative truss at the apex of the gable; cross gables; occasionally, dormers; eaves with a significant overhang, often supported by large diagonal brackets and knee braces; exposed roof trusses and rafters; corbeled chimneys. Town houses usually display vertical stickwork in this style, terminating in brackets, supporting the overhanging cornice; they usually have a flat roof.

Window treatments: Bay windows, either having a square or canted plan; casement windows or double-hung sashes. Town houses in this style often have squared bay windows.

Doorway treatments: Either single or double doors.

stickwork Wood boards applied in patterns in the horizontal, vertical, and diagonal directions, usually over the exterior wood **cladding** of a house.

stile 1. One of the vertical structural members of the framework of a door or window; *see also* **hinge stile** and **lock stile.** 2. A pair of built-up steps, facing each other; usually placed at a fence post to provide a safe means of climbing across a barbed-wire fence.

stockade A barrier consisting of a series of pointed poles, posts, or timbers, usually sharpened to a point at their upper ends, set into the ground next to each other to form an enclosure, i.e., a **palisade**. Often used for defense against Indian attacks.

stock brick In any geographical area, the type of brick that is most commonly available and that is of sufficiently good quality to use on the exterior face of a building.

stock lock Same as **box lock.**

stone Any type of rock that has been selected or processed by cutting, shaping, or sizing for use in building construction or for decorative purposes. For definitions and illustrations, *see* **brownstone, cobblestone, dimension stone, fieldstone, flagstone, freestone, granite, limestone, marble, pudding stone, sandstone, slate, soapstone.**

stone cabin A small house built of stone, typified by homes built by German-speaking colonists in Pennsylvania; usually characterized by a roof having a very steep pitch, thick stone walls, and wooden casement windows with solid shutters.

stile,2

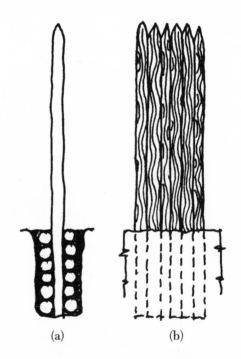

(a)   (b)

stockade: Alexander Blockhouse (1850), Coupeville, Wash.: (a) section; (b) elevation

stone-ender, stone-ender house A late-17th-century house having **post-and-girt framing**; basically, a one-room medieval-style cottage of the type described under **American Colonial architecture of early New England** but with a massive end wall built of stone; found primarily in Rhode Island, where there was an ample supply of building stone and a plentiful supply of lime for making lime mortar. The stone end wall of the house, which incorporated a chimney for a very large fireplace, usually faced north, the direction of the prevailing wind. The hearths in the earliest of these houses were of tamped earth. The house typically had a fieldstone foundation, oak flooring, oak clapboard or plank siding, a hand-split cedar-shingle roof, an impressive **chimney cap**; small casement windows containing panes of glass set diagonally in lead cames, and a **battened door** at the entry opening into a small room called the porch. Some stone-enders had a lean-to kitchen added to the rear of the house to provide increased floor space; additional space was obtained by building dormers into the roof or by setting windows into an end wall in the loft space to provide light and ventilation.

stone house A house constructed entirely of stone. Such houses were relatively rare in most areas of colonial America because of a lack of a good supply of building stone or lime mortar required in masonry construction and because houses built of wood were usually significantly cheaper and faster to build.

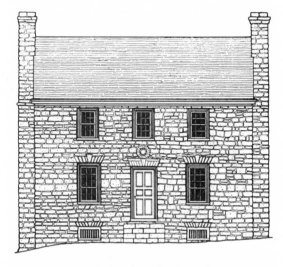

stone house (1790): Kentucky

stone medallion A term occasionally used for **date stone**.

stoop A small platform or small porch, usually up several steps from street level, at the entrance to a house, often with a bench on one side or on each side of the front door. Often found at the entrances to row houses in Atlantic coast cities in the North in the late 19th and early 20th centuries. The term is a corruption of the Dutch word *stoep*.

stone-ender
Eleazar Arnold House (1687), Lincoln, R.I.

stoop

storm cellar A sheltered area below ground level providing refuge from dangerous storms such as cyclones, hurricanes, tornados, or windstorms; usually found in regions where such storms are prevalent. Also called a cyclone cellar.

storm door An auxiliary door, sometimes with a glass panel, installed exterior to, and in the same door frame as, an entrance door to a house; improves the thermal insulation of the doorway and reduces the infiltration of outside air into the house.

storm porch An enclosed porch, or portion thereof, that protects the entrance to a house from severe weather; usually a temporary structure that is left in place only during the winter months.

storm window An auxiliary window, usually placed in the same frame as, and on the outside of, an existing window to provide additional protection against severe weather.

story 1. The space in a building between floor levels, or between a floor and the roof above. 2. A major architectural horizontal division in a building, even where no floor exists.

story-and-a-half The combination of a full story and a partial story set under a sloping roof; windows in the gable-end walls and/or dormers provide the partial story with light and ventilation, making it more livable.

stove room In a colonial American house, a term applied to any room that is heated by a stove.

straight arch Same as **flat arch.**

straight-edge gable Same as **straight-line gable.**

straight-flight stair A stair extending only in one direction, with no turns or wedged-shaped step.

straight-line gable A term descriptive of a **parapeted gable**, the face of which rises above the roof line; the edge of the parapet is a straight line that has a steep pitch with respect to the horizontally laid bricks. Found, for example, in **Dutch Colonial architecture** and **Jacobethan architecture.** Occasionally called a straight-edge gable or a parapeted end gable.

straight-run stair Same as **straight-flight stair.**

strap hinge A surface-mounted **hinge** having two leaves, one of which is fastened to the door and the other of which is secured to the door frame or door post.

story-and-a-half
Craftsman farmhouse (1909)

straight-line gable
Bronck House (1783), West Coxsackie, N.Y.

strap hinge

strapwork 1. Any type of ornament consisting of narrow fillets, or bands, that are folded, crossed, or interlaced. 2. Interlacing decorative bands found within gables; especially found in **Tudor Revival** buildings in America.

strapwork,2

straw bale house A house whose walls are constructed of bales of straw, compressed and wire-tied or string-tied into units roughly two feet by two feet by four feet (0.6 x 0.6 x 1.2m), and built up on a concrete slab as if they were oversized bricks; they are reinforced with vertical poles of wood, bamboo, or metal that pierce the bales. When the straw bales are thoroughly dry, the walls are finished with a coat of stucco or adobe plaster to promote sanitation and fire safety. The bales provide excellent thermal insulation. Houses of this construction were used in America on the Great Plains (i.e., the region between the Mississippi River and the Rocky Mountains, from Canada to Texas) dur-

ing the late 1800s in areas where other types of building materials were impossible to obtain or were in very short supply; a few are still being constructed today because they are relatively low in cost and comparatively easy to build.

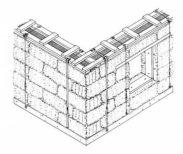

straw bale house: wall construction, showing straps and cables to provide structural strength

straw shed An extension on one side of a barn, usually at its rear, used primarily for the storage of straw; often, a two-story structure in which the upper story is used to store hay and the lower story is used to store machinery. Sometimes called a three-ended barn.

Streamline Moderne, Streamline Modern A phase of **Art Deco** that emphasizes the horizontal aspects of design, for example, by using bands of windows on the façade of the building. Usually characterized by: curved end walls, rounded corners; white or light-colored stucco walls; horizontal stainless-steel railings; flush windows, round windows, glass block. An outstanding example is the Pan-Pacific Auditorium (1938) in Los Angeles, California.

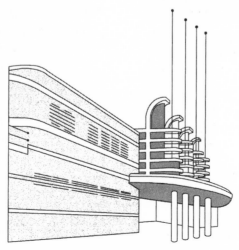

Streamline Moderne
Pan Pacific Auditorium (1938), Los Angeles, Calif.; Plummer, Wurdeman and Becket, Architects

street arch *See* **arch street.**

stretcher A brick or stone laid on its largest surface, with its length in a horizontal direction so that it is parallel to the face of the wall.

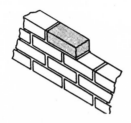

stretcher

stretcher bond Same as **running bond.**

string, stringboard In a stair, an inclined board that supports one end of the steps. Also called a stringer. *See also* **closed string, face string, finish string, open string, outer string.**

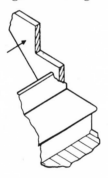

string

stringcourse Same as **belt course.**

string development Same as **ribbon development.**

struck joint 1. A horizontal masonry joint in which the mortar is sloped inward and downward from the lower edge of the upper brick, leaving a recess at the bottom of the joint. 2. Same as **scribed joint.**

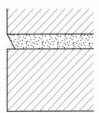

struck joint

struck molding A molding that is cut into a surface material, rather than being nailed or otherwise fastened to it.

structural clay tile A hollow masonry unit usually composed of **burnt clay**, shale, or a mixture of both.

Structuralism The referral to basic architectural forms from which architectural design and construction can be derived; Louis I. Kahn (1901–1974) was one of the early architects in America who explored and exploited this concept.

structural wall A wall capable of supporting an imposed load.

structure A combination of units deliberately constructed and interconnected so as to provide rigidity among the elements.

strut Any brace or any piece of a frame that resists thrusts in the direction of its own length; may be placed upright, diagonally, or horizontally.

strutting beam, strutting piece Same as **collar beam.**

stucco 1. An exterior finish, usually textured, formed by mixing portland cement, lime, sand, and water; often applied over wall constructions; applied over adobe to reduce the effects of erosion; Used as an interior finish, particularly in **Mission Revival** and **Colonial Revival** homes; also found in early **American Colonial architecture**, as well as in **French Vernacular architecture, International style, Prairie style, Italian Renaissance Revival, Spanish Colonial Revival, Tudor Revival.** 2. A term occasionally used in the colonial past for decorative plasterwork.

stud An upright post or support, especially one of a series of vertical structural members that act as the supporting elements in a wall or partition.

style *See* **architectural style.**

Style Moderne *See* **Art Moderne** and **Art Deco.**

stylobate Any continuous base, plinth, or pedestal, upon which a row of columns is set.

subfloor A rough floor, laid on joists, that serves as a base for the **finish floor.**

subpurlin In a roof structure, a light member of an intermediate system of beams interconnecting **purlins.**

Suffolk latch A type of **thumb latch** for doors; originally fabricated of iron wrought by hand in England and imported by the colonies. Attractive in appearance and available in many different designs, this type of latch was revived by the **Arts and Crafts movement**. Unlike the **Norfolk latch**, it has no plate behind the thumb latch to protect the door finish.

Suffolk latch

sugarhouse A building or shed, usually located in a grove of sugar maple trees, in which maple sugar is made by boiling the sap of the tree to evaporate its water content; particularly found in Vermont.

Sullivanesque A term descriptive of the architectural style and decorative designs of Louis H. Sullivan (1856–1924), in wide use in America from about 1890 to 1920. Sullivan was an important figure in the development of modern functional architecture, not only in America but also on the European continent and in Great Britain. He is known for his famous but often slightly misquoted statement that "form follows func-

tion," an assertion similar to an earlier statement by Ralph Waldo Emerson (1803–1882), which is reproduced under **Functionalism.**

Sullivan was especially noted for his **tripartite scheme** for tall buildings, which he described in "The Tall Building Artistically Considered," published in *Lippincott's* in March 1896, as follows:

> …Is it really then, a very marvelous thing, or is it rather so commonplace, so everyday, so near a thing to us that we cannot perceive that the shape, form, outward expression, design or whatever we may choose, of the tall office building should in the very nature of things follow the functions of the building, and that where the function does not change, the form does not change?…Does this not readily, clearly, and conclusively show that the lower one or two stories will take on a special character suited to the special needs, that the tiers of typical offices, having the same unchanging function, shall continue in the same unchanging form, and that as to the attic, specific and conclusive as it is in its very nature, its function shall equally be in force, in significance, in continuity, in conclusiveness of outward expression? From this results, naturally, spontaneously, unwittingly, a three-part division, not from any theory, symbol, or fancied logic. And thus the design of the tall office building takes its place with all other architectural types made when architecture, as has happened once in many years, was a living art. Witness the Gothic cathedral, the medieval fortress…and thus, when native instinct and sensibility shall govern the exercise of our beloved art; when the known law, the respected law shall be that *form ever follows function*….

Sullivanesque
decorative panel from the Gage Building (1898–1899)

summerbeam A large horizontal beam in the ceiling of an early American colonial **timber-framed house**. Summerbeams, sometimes as wide as 18 inches (46cm), were joined at their ends to **girts** by dovetail connections; they often supported the floor above or acted as a **binding beam** running in a transverse direction, connecting one post to another. After about 1750 most homes were no longer constructed with summerbeams; instead, heavier floor joists were used, thereby permitting the entire ceiling to be plastered as a single horizontal surface. Also called a summer or summertree. *See also* illustration under **timber-framed house**.

summerbeam: in ceiling of kitchen of Fairbanks House (1636), Dedham, Mass.

summerhouse A small structure, such as a pavilion, usually in a garden setting with a splendid view; a **gazebo** or **belvedere**.

summerhouse

summer kitchen A supplementary kitchen once found especially in large homes along the mid-Atlantic coast and in the South; usually located near, but detached from, the main house, and much used during hot weather to avoid overheating the house.

sunburst light A term occasionally used for a **fanlight**.

Sunday house A small house usually having a single room with a fireplace; commonly built near a house of religious worship and used only one night a week by farmers or ranchers who lived some distance away. They traded or sold produce on Saturday, stayed overnight in their Sunday houses, and attended church services on Sunday before returning to their homes. *See also* **Sabbath house**.

Sunday house: Texas (1840s)

sun disk A disk with wings, used in Egyptian antiquity as an emblem of the sun; occasionally used in America in **Egyptian Revival** architecture.

sun disk

sunk draft Around a rectangular block of stone, a margin that is sunk below the face of the stone to give the stone a raised appearance.

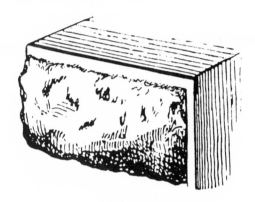

sunk draft

sunk face The face of a rectangular block of stone from which material has been removed to give the stone the appearance of a sunken panel.

sunk fence A barrier in the form of a trench; *see* **ha-ha.**

sunk gutter A **gutter** that is concealed below the surface of a sloping roof.

sunk molding A **molding** slightly recessed behind the surface on which it is located.

sunk relief A carving or other type of **relief** that does not project beyond the flat surface on which it is cut.

supercolumniation, superposition The placing of one **order** above another; for example, Ionic columns on one level of a building directly over Doric columns on the level below.

superstructure 1. Any structure built on something else, as a building on its foundation. 2. That part of a building or structure above ground level or above the level of its foundation.

sure post A vertical timber to provide added support; for example, a timber placed below a beam or **sill,1** to carry an additional load.

surround A decorative element or structure around a doorway, fireplace, or window. For example, *see* **door surround, fireplace surround, Gibbs surround, window surround.**

swag A decoration representing a festoon of flowers, garland of ribbons, folds of fabric, or the like; usually tied at, or near, each end and sagging at the middle. Also called a festoon.

swag

swallow hole A term occasionally used as a synonym for **owl hole,** even though swallow holes are usually smaller.

swan's-neck pediment A broken pediment having a sloping double **S**-shaped decorative element on each side of the pediment; somewhat suggestive of the necks of two swans facing each other; often found in the **Georgian style**. Also called a broken-scroll pediment.

swan's-neck pediment

sway brace Same as **wind brace.**

sweathouse, sweatlodge An enclosed structure (circular, oval, or rectangular in plan), usually considered sacred and widely used by many American Indian tribes, in which the men practiced ritual cleansing accompanied by prayer; also used for important social events. In the center were hot stones, carefully selected so they could be heated to a high temperature without crumbling or exploding when water was poured on them to generate steam. Most enclosures accommodated up to six men, although some had room for many more. Their construction varied, depending on the tribe, although in all of them, the doorway always faced east. Many were built of willow branches set in the ground and bent over and lashed to form a dome, as in **bent-frame construction;** this framework was then covered with hides or other material to seal it so that it was light-tight and watertight. Others had plank walls or were small versions of a **pit house** or conical forked-pole **hogan.**

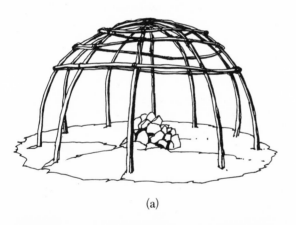

(a)

(b)

sweathouse
(a) framework; (b) in preparation for use

Swedish gambrel roof A roof that is similar to a **New England gambrel roof** or a **Dutch gambrel roof** in that there are two flat roof surfaces on each side of the central ridge of the roof, but in the Swedish roof, the upper surface is shorter and has little slope, and the lower surface is longer and has a much steeper slope than either the New England or Dutch gambrel roofs.

sweep A long pole, pivoted on a vertical post, to which a bucket is attached at one end; used to raise water from a **well.**

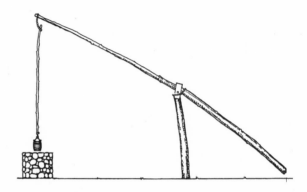

sweep: Old Oaken Bucket (1835), Scituate, Mass.

Sweitzer barn A Swiss barn; *see* **German barn.**

swinging door A door equipped with hardware that permits it to swing 90 degrees in either direction from the plane of the door frame. Also called a double-acting door.

Swiss barn *See* **German barn.**

Swiss Cottage architecture, Swiss Chalet architecture A domestic picturesque architecture patterned after its chalet prototype in Switzerland; usually a two-story house built of rough-cut lumber to enhance a rustic appearance; often a front-gabled, shingled roof of moderate pitch, occasionally with a **jerkinhead** roof; bracketed eaves having a significant overhang; exposed rafters; often, walls of board-and-batten construction; exterior porches or **integral porches**, typically with flat balusters having decorative cutouts or decorative stickwork. Popularized by Andrew Jackson Downing (1815–1852) in America in the mid-19th century, it is now rarely used.

Symmetrical Victorian style A term once occasionally used for **Gingerbread folk architecture.**

synagogue A place of assembly for Jewish worship; also called a temple. The Touro Synagogue, dedicated in 1763 in Newport, Rhode Island, was the second synagogue to be erected in America. In 1790 George Washington wrote a message to its congregation that is now inscribed on a metal tablet on one of its walls: ". . . happily the Government of the United States . . . gives to bigotry no sanction, to persecution no assistance." The architect for this building was Peter Harrison (1716–1775). Born in Yorkshire, England, of Quaker parentage, Harrison, a seaman, eloped with a Provincetown heiress in 1746, enabling him to pursue his real interests: surveying, architecture, and construction. He is said to be the first architect in America to have designed buildings erected under the supervision of others. Important buildings for which he was the architect include King's Chapel in Boston, Massachusetts, and Redwood Library and Brick Market, both in Newport, Rhode Island, but the Touro Synagogue is usually considered his finest work.

systyle *See* **intercolumniation.**

Swiss cottage architecture: a cottage designed by Andrew Jackson Downing

synagogue
The Touro Synagogue (1763), Newport, R.I.; Peter Harrison, Architect

T

tabby A concretelike material created from a mixture of **shell lime**, sand, an aggregate of seashells, and sea water, in equal proportion, which formed a dense mass when dry. When used as a building material, it was often plastered over and whitewashed. It was used primarily in Florida during the period of its settlement by Spaniards in the mid-1600s.

tabernacle 1. A large house of worship, sometimes of a temporary nature, often for an evangelical congregation. 2. A decorative niche, often topped with a canopy and housing a statue.

tabla house A primitive one-room house of frame construction sheathed with vertical rough-hewn cypress planks (*tablas*); used by early Spanish colonists in Florida in the 16th century; typically had a batten door; a gable roof thatched with palm leaves; and a hole in the roof at the ridge to permit smoke to escape from the fireplace below.

tablet A plaque, often inscribed and carved, usually affixed to a wall surface or set into the surface; sometimes used as a memorial or to commemorate a special event.

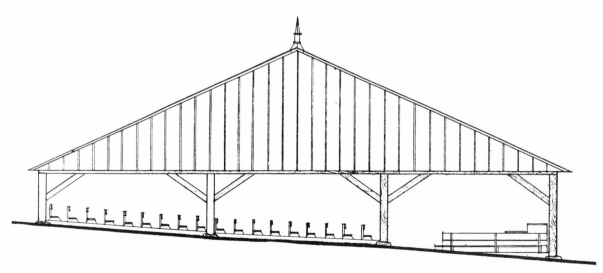

tabernacle

taenia A narrow raised band or fillet, particularly the topmost member of a Doric **architrave.**

tapeista In **Spanish Colonial architecture** of the American Southwest, a crude, rooflike structure supported by four posts; used as a somewhat protected open storage area for cornstalks, hay, or the like.

tapia An adobe-like building material consisting mainly of earth or clay in which small pebbles may be embedded; this term is also occasionally applied to **puddled adobe.**

tasolera In **Spanish Colonial architecture**, a barn to house animals or to store agricultural produce.

tavern A place where food and liquor are served for consumption on the premises. In colonial America the village tavern often served as a social center and sometimes the meeting place for discussions of town affairs and even church matters during the wintertime, because the town hall and house of worship usually were unheated. Taverns also had sleeping accommodations for travelers, so were frequently located along major roadways. Also called a public house. Compare with **saloon.**

teagle post In a **timber-framed house**, a **post** supporting one end of a **tie beam.**

teepee Same as **tipi.**

teja In **Spanish Colonial architecture**, a burnt-clay roof tile, semicircular in cross section, and usually tapered.

telescope house In colonial America, a house comprising several sections (or several additions to the original house), each of descending height, giving the building the appearance of fitting together like the components of a collapsible telescope. Compare with **continuous house.**

tenement A building having multiple housing units for rent; typically, an apartment house in the poorer section of a city, built many years earlier. Usually contains a number of ill-maintained units that sometimes barely meet minimum code requirements for safety and sanitation.

tenon The projecting end of a piece of wood, which is reduced in cross section so that it may be inserted into a corresponding mating cavity, called a **mortise**, in another piece of wood in order to form a secure joint.

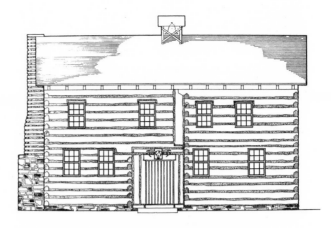

tavern
Newcomb Tavern (1796), Dayton, Ohio

telescope house

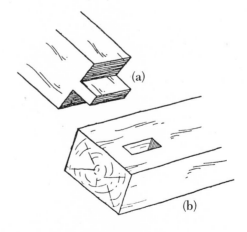

tenon
(a) tenon to fit mortise; (b) mortise

tensile-frame construction *See* **bent-frame construction.**

tepee Same as **tipi.**

terminal An ornament or decorative element at the end of an architectural member, for example, a **finial** at the tip of a spire.

terneplate Iron or steel sheet metal that is coated with an alloy of lead containing up to 20 percent tin; especially used for **pressed-metal ceilings** and for tin roofing, gutters, and leaders; usually laid on the roof in strips parallel to the rafters, the strips being joined by **standing seams.** In colonial America the use of iron terneplate was restricted to elegant brick or stone houses because of its relatively high cost.

terrace house One of a row of houses situated on an elevated, level site.

terrace roof A **roof** that has been truncated so as to form a flat horizontal surface having no ridge.

terra-cotta Clay that has been molded in shape and then burnt in a kiln at a high temperature; it is typically reddish brown in color when unglazed; when glazed, it is usually colored and used for ornamental work, such as floor tile, roof tile, and **architectural terra-cotta.** Manufactured in America since the 1850s.

Territorial style An architectural style in New Mexico from the time it became a territory of the United States in 1848 until about 1900; most popular from about 1865 to 1880; revived to some extent after 1920. Typically, a one-story house usually having a flat roof with parapets; exterior walls of adobe coated with adobe plaster or stucco, often capped with brick, to reduce erosion; an entry door commonly flanked with sidelights; brick trim around doors and windows with pedimented lintels above, sometimes with wood decorative trim suggestive of the **Greek Revival style.** Houses were sometimes built around an enclosed courtyard with rooms opening onto a covered walkway around the perimeter of the courtyard, providing a sheltered means of going from one room to another. After about 1880, pitched corrugated-metal roofs gradually replaced many of the flat roofs because they provided better protection against the weather.

terrone A building material, once used in the American Southwest, cut into rectangular units from sod in a river bottom or marsh-grass swamp and then sun-baked; similar to adobe but stronger when dry because of the added strength provided by the sod roots; used in the form of blocks.

tetrastyle A term descriptive of a **portico** having four columns in the front.

textile mill A factory in which woven fabrics are manufactured. Many early mills of this type were located in New England, where there was an abundance of water power for operating the machinery. The oldest cotton textile factory in New England was the Slater Mill (1793) in Rhode Island. Most such mills were of timber construction and in constant danger of being consumed by fire. In 1832 a significant advance in fire safety occurred with the construction of the Allendale Mill in Providence, Rhode Island. It was designed to resist fire (and to burn slowly if ignited) by the use of thick floor planking, by minimizing the number of timber beams, and by maximizing the cross-sectional area of each beam. These principles were widely applied in the years that followed, greatly improving fire safety in textile mills.

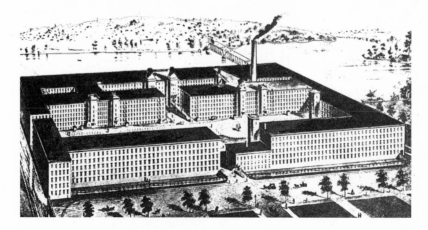

textile mill: Boott Mill (1835); one of the ten major mills in Lowell, Mass.

thatch A roof or wall covering usually made of straw, reeds, or similar material (in Spanish Colonial settlements in Florida, palmetto fronds were widely used). The thatching materials were commonly cut to a length of about three feet (0.9m), then tied in small bundles and fastened in overlapping rows to the horizontal poles or purlins on the framework to be covered. The thick bundles shed water readily and provided thermal insulation. When used as a roof covering, the slope of the thatch had to be steep enough to shed water rapidly, but not so steep as to loosen from their point of attachment and slide downward. Although thatched roofs are attractive in appearance, they are not very durable, lasting one generation at best, and they sometimes leak during steady rains. Furthermore, thatching constitutes a fire hazard in dry weather. Because of this fire-safety problem, the Plymouth Colony in Massachusetts passed a law in 1626 prohibiting its installation on roofs, although this law was not enforced. Thatched roofs were fairly common in colonies in 17th-century America, but they essentially disappeared by the beginning of the 18th century.

thatched hut *See* **palma hut.**

theater A building (or a portion thereof) or an outdoor facility for the presentation of dramatic entertainment, variety shows, motion pictures, musical comedies, stage extravaganzas, or burlesque. The first theater in New York City, the New Theater built in 1732, presented amateur performances until 1750, when a professional company from England performed Shakespeare's *Richard III*. The Park Theater (1789) was the city's first fully appointed theater. By the end of the 18th century, there were four more theaters in the city. Since then, over 1,000 theaters have been built there. Among them were the Castle Garden Theater (1839) and Tony Pastor's New 14th Street Theater (1881), where vaudeville is said to have originated. In Philadelphia the first theater was constructed in 1766; subsequently, this city became a center of theatrical entertainment in America, together with New York, Boston, and Charleston. A number of brawling Western mining towns had theaters, often called "opera houses." Piper's Opera House in Virginia City, Nevada (site of the famous Comstock Lode, which until 1886 yielded half the silver output in the entire country), was a birthplace of the American stage in the West.

theater
Castle Garden Theater (1839), New York City, where Jenny Lind made her American debut in 1850

three-bay threshing barn, three-bay barn
Same as **Yankee barn.**

three-centered arch An **arch** whose inner surface is struck from three centers, resulting in a shape approximating one-half an ellipse. Compare with **two-centered arch.**

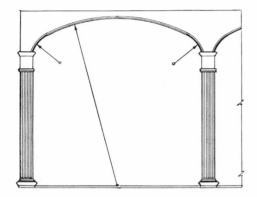

three-centered arch

three-decker In a house of worship, an unusual structure that has the clerk's desk at the bottom, the reader's desk directly above it, and the pulpit at the top. Also called a triple-decker.

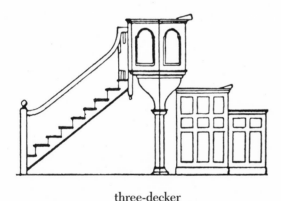

three-decker

three-ended barn *See* **straw shed.**

three-part window 1. A window having a wide rectangular sash at its center and a narrower sash on each side; all three sashes are of the same height and are in the same plane; essentially a **Palladian window** with the rounded head of the center sash lopped off at the top. Found in many **Greek Revival style** homes, this type of window was introduced in America in about 1785. Also called a tripartite window or triple window. 2. Same as **treble sash.**

three-quarter Cape house Typically, a one-and-a-half-story rectangular house of **wood-frame construction,** developed in the 1700s on Cape Cod, Massachusetts, and still found in New England and elsewhere, that has the following characteristics: a massive central chimney that serves all fireplaces; a roof covering and exterior wall covering of hand-split unpainted shingles that become gray when weathered; two windows in the façade on one side of the front door and one on the other side of the door; often, one or more windows in the end gable to provide light and ventilation in the garret. *See* **Cape Cod house.** This term is often applied to similar houses in nearby states, which are sometimes referred to as *Cape houses.* Also called a one-and-one-half-bay cottage, a house-and-a-half, or a three-quarter house.

three-quarter Cape house

three-quarter Cape house: floor plan

three-room plan A **plan** consisting of a parlor, hall, and kitchen lined up along the front of the house. The entry door, not centered on the façade, usually opened directly into the kitchen. This plan was favored by many early Dutch and German-speaking settlers in America.

threshing barn Same as **treading barn**.

threshing floor That section of a barn where wheat is separated from the chaff; in some early barns in America, an entire floor was devoted to threshing and storing hay.

threshold A strip, commonly of wood, fastened to the floor directly beneath a door, usually to cover the joint where two different floor materials or finishes meet; may also provide some protection against the transmission of air and light under the door. Also called a doorsill or saddle.

throat 1. A groove that is cut along the underside of a projecting member, such as a **belt course**, to prevent rainwater from running back across it toward the wall; also called a drip molding. 2. Same as **chimney throat**.

through lintel A **lintel** whose thickness is the same as the full thickness of the wall in which it is set.

through stone A stone that is set with its longest dimension perpendicular to a wall and whose length is equal to the thickness of the wall.

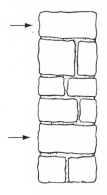

through stone

through-the-cornice wall dormer See **wall dormer.**

thumb latch A **latch** for securing a door in a closed position, usually by means of a flat bar that falls into a catch or notch when pressed by the thumb; for example, see **Norfolk latch** and **Suffolk latch.**

tide mill A mill, such as a **gristmill** or **sawmill**, operated by a waterwheel powered by tidal water confined in a reservoir after high tide. An incoming tide opens a gate, permitting tidal water to fill the reservoir; when the direction of the tide changes, the gate is closed by hand and then the outflowing tidal water turns the mill's waterwheel. Tide mills were used along the seacoast of 17th-century New England.

Tidewater cottage A one-room cottage in the Chesapeake Bay region of Virginia, after about 1630.

tie beam 1. In the **framing** of a roof, a horizontal timber connecting two opposite rafters, usually at their lower ends, to prevent them from spreading, such as a **collar beam.** 2. A **beam** that interconnects the front and rear **wall plates.**

Tiffany glass See **opalescent glass, stained glass.**

tile 1. A glazed or unglazed ceramic unit for finishing a surface; usually thin in relation to the dimensions of its face. 2. A surfacing unit of slate or of some manufactured composition. See also **clay tile, crown tile, encaustic tile, fireplace tile, mission tile, pantile, ridge tile, roofing tile, rounded tile, Spanish tile, structural clay tile.**

tile hanging Slate or tile shingles that are hung vertically or nearly vertically on a wall or roof to prevent the penetration of rainwater. Also called **weather slating.**

tile hanging: on a Second Empire–style roof

tile shingle *See* **shingle.**

timber-framed building A building having timbers as its structural elements. In colonial days these timbers were hand-hewn, prepared either at the job site or elsewhere and then reassembled at their destination. For a description of individual components in a building of this type, *see* **collar beam, girt, joist, plate, purlin, rafter, summerbeam, wind brace.**

timber-framed house In colonial America, a house in which huge posts and beams or **girts** served as major structural components. The space between structural timbers was usually filled with brick, plaster, mud, **wattle-and-daub**, or the like. The exterior of the building was usually coated with hard plaster, sheathed in weatherboarding, or covered with slates or shingles to protect against moisture and to provide increased thermal insulation.

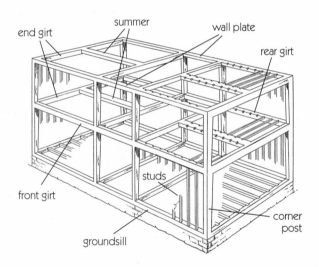

timber-framed house: illustrating framing

tin A lustrous white, soft, durable, and malleable metal having a low melting point, which is relatively unaffected by exposure to air. In America during the 19th century, a mixture of tin and lead was widely applied as plating to protect finish on iron or steel sheets used for roofing.

tin ceiling *See* **metal ceiling** and **pressed-metal ceiling.**

tin roofing A term occasionally used for sheet-metal roofing.

tipi, tepee, teepee A relatively light-weight, transportable cone-shaped dwelling primarily of American Indians of the Great Plains (i.e., the region between the Mississippi River and the Rocky Mountains, from Canada to Texas). It gave the appearance of a tilted cone because it was steeper in back than in front to provide bracing against the prevailing wind; its base was generally egg-shaped in **plan**, from 12 to 20 feet (3.6–6m) across, with the narrower end at the entrance. The framework consisted of wood poles, about 20 to 25 feet (6–7.6m) in length, fixed in the ground at their lower ends and lashed together at the top; lighter poles were set in the ground between the main poles and lashed to the main poles at the top. The framework was covered with decorated waterproof animal skins, such as buffalo hides, sewn together with sinew and secured to the ground by pegs driven through loops at the base of the cover. Stones weighed down the cover at the base, reducing drafts and keeping out small animals. A flap provided an entryway; another flap, at the peak of the cone, served as a smoke hole for the firepit on the floor below and could be adjusted from within with a long pole. The interior surface of the tipi was often lined for improved thermal insulation and to prevent the flames from the firepit from casting shadows on the outer covering. Canvas replaced animal skins after 1800. In the Sioux language, the word *tipi* means "a place to live."

Another type of tipi, used by tribes in the eastern regions of America such as the Chippewa, had a domed rather than a conical framework consisting of branches bent over, tied together, and covered by bark or animal skins sewn together with sinew to provide a waterproof covering.

tipi: of the Great Plains

tobacco barn A barn used for curing tobacco leaves, with or without the addition of heat, by hanging them from a series of horizontal poles within the barn. The leaves from this plant became a significant cash crop in colonial Virginia as early as 1612, and in other areas thereafter. The three common types of tobacco barns are designated by the curing process employed. In the earliest type, *air-cured tobacco barns*, the tobacco leaves dry naturally; barns of this type, which allow ventilation through the side walls and sometimes the roof, are especially found in Kentucky, Tennessee, Virginia, Ohio, Wisconsin, and Connecticut. In *fire-cured tobacco barns*, introduced later, the leaves are cured by the introduction of heat from a wood fire or charcoal, permitting them to retain their natural qualities for a longer period of time; such barns are especially found in western Kentucky, Tennessee, and central Virginia. *Flue-cured tobacco barns,* usually square in plan and as high as or higher than they are square, are constructed of unpainted round logs and typically have one or more attached open sheds; such barns are especially found in North Carolina and southern Virginia.

tollhouse A small building at or close to the tollgate of a highway or bridge that originally served as the residence of the toll collector.

tollhouse (1835)
National Pike, Fayette County, Pa.

tongue-and-dart molding A decorative molding consisting of a tonguelike ornament alternating with a dartlike ornament.

tongue-and-dart molding

tongue-and-groove joint A joint formed by the insertion of a continuous projecting ridge (i.e., tongue) along one side of a board into a corresponding groove in an adjacent board.

tobacco barn
for fire-cured tobacco

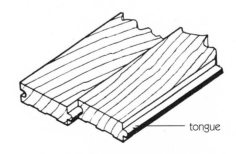

tongue-and-groove joint

tooled joint In brickwork, any joint that is formed with a tool other than a trowel; for example, a **scribed joint.** Also called a colonial joint.

top plate 1. In a building of **wood-frame construction,** the top horizontal structural member on which the rafters are seated and to which they are joined. Also called a roof plate. 2. The horizontal structural member at the top of the studs of a partition; also called a wall plate. *See* illustration under **timber-framed house.**

torreón A defensive tower used for protection against enemy attack; once found in fortified Spanish colonial communities of the Southwest, particularly in the area that is now New Mexico.

torus A projecting molding, convex in shape, forming the lowest member of a base of a column directly over the **plinth.**

tourist cabin One of a number of small separate units grouped in what were called tourist courts; found along well-traveled highways during in the first half of the 20th century; now replaced by motels.

tower A structure or building characterized by its relatively great height as compared to its horizontal dimensions. Commonly found in American architecture in the **Châteauesque style, French Eclectic architecture, Italianate style, Queen Anne style, Richardsonian Romanesque style, Second Empire style, Shingle style, Spanish Eclectic architecture, Stick style.** *See also* **shot tower** and **torreón.**

town hall A public hall or building in which town offices are located, where the town council meets, and/or where the local residents assemble for public meetings. During the colonial period, discussions of community matters were often held in the local tavern in the wintertime because most town halls were not heated.

town house 1. A comfortable, even luxurious, dwelling in an urban environment. 2. One of a series of houses constructed in an unbroken row, often having roofs that are essentially flat, separated by **party walls**; an upscale **row house.**

town plan A large-scale comprehensive map of a town or city that delineates its streets, important buildings, and other urban features in a detail compatible with the scale of the map.

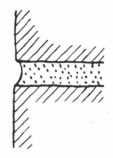

tooled joint

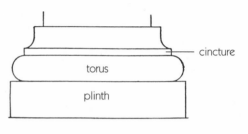

torus

tower: Allegheny Courthouse and Jail (1888), Pittsburgh, Pa.; H. H. Richardson, Architect

town planning *See* **community planning.**

T-plan The basic **floor plan** of a building having the shape of a capital letter **T**.

trabeated 1. A term descriptive of a construction using beams or lintels, following the principles of **post-and-lintel construction**, as distinguished from construction using arches and vaults. 2. Furnished with an entablature.

tracery Multicurved openwork shapes in stone or wood that create decorative patterns within a window or other openings especially found in **Gothic Revival** and **Collegiate Gothic** architecture.

trading post A store, once found in a sparsely settled or wilderness areas of America, where inhabitants could exchange products they made, grew, or trapped for goods sold by the store.

trammel In a typical early colonial American fireplace, an adjustable hook for suspending a cooking pot from a pivoted wrought-iron horizontal bar attached to one of the fireplace walls. Also called a chimney crook or fireplace crook.

transept The major transverse portion of a church whose **plan** is the shape of a cross; it is perpendicular to the long axis of the cross.

transitional style A term descriptive of the transition between two different styles, rather than an actual style, as for example, between late **Georgian style** and early **Federal style.** In America such transitions generally have occurred at different times in different parts of the country.

transom 1. A horizontal member, usually of wood or stone, that separates a door from a window, fanlight, or panel above it; sometimes called a transom bar. 2. An **operable window** hinged to the **transom,1** directly above a door. 3. A cross bar in a window frame that divides a window horizontally. *See also* **operable transom.**

transom light One of a series of small, fixed panes set above a door or window; often used, for example, in the **Georgian style** or in **Colonial Revival** architecture.

tread The horizontal surface of a step; often has a rounded edge that extends beyond the upright face of the **riser** below it.

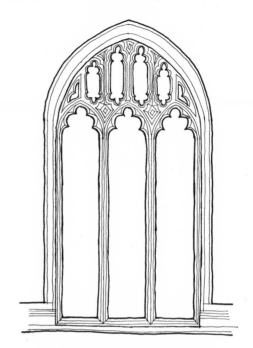

tracery: executed in cast iron

transom lights

treading barn A barn specifically constructed for threshing grain, such as the one shown in the accompanying illustration, designed by George Washington in 1792. This nearly circular barn is described in his *Building Instructions for a Barn.* Horses or oxen were led around the second floor, across layers of wheat. The grinding action of their hooves separated the wheat from the chaff; the grain fell through gaps between the narrow floorboards to the granary below. Although this type of threshing was not uncommon outdoors, Washington's contribution was to move this activity indoors, to a 16-sided barn on his estate, 52 feet (15.8m) in diameter. A full-scale model of the barn can be visited at Mount Vernon, Virginia.

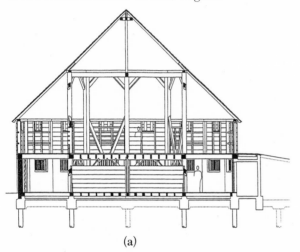

(a)

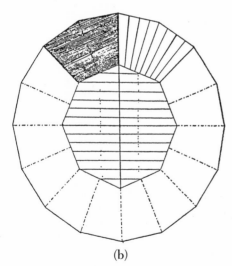

(b)

treading barn: designed by George Washington
(c. 1792) for his estate, Mt. Vernon, in Virginia;
(a) cross section through barn; (b) plan view of second
level on which the animals walked

treble sash A window having three vertically sliding **sashes**, one above the other, each of which closes a different part of the window; occasionally found in America in the late 18th and early 19th centuries in large houses having very high ceilings. Compare with **three-part window,1.**

treenail A long cylindrical pin of hardwood, usually oak or hickory, used in colonial America to secure a joint between two pieces of wood, planks, or timbers.

trefoil In an opening, a three-lobed pattern separated by cusps. *See* **foil.**

trefoil

trefoil arch A pointed arch whose inner surface is struck from three centers; the shape of the arch is determined by the position of the centers and radii of curvature; has a projecting cusp on each side.

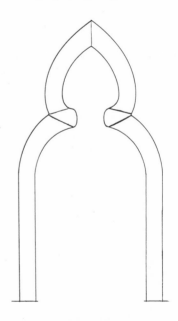

trefoil arch
St. Thomas's Episcopal Church, Glassboro, N.J.

trellis An open grating or latticework, usually of either metal or wood; often used as an arbor or a framework for supporting vines.

trellis window A **casement window**, fixed or hinged, with **glazing bars** set diagonally to suggest a trellis.

triangular arch An **arch** often formed by two large diagonal stones that mutually support each other to span an opening; found particularly in **Gothic Revival** and **High Victorian** architecture. Also called a miter arch.

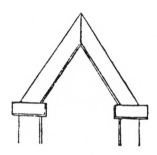

triangular arch

triangular dormer A **dormer** having a triangular gable roof. Also called a gable dormer.

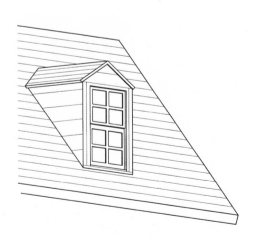

triangular dormer

triangular pediment Same as **angular pediment.**

triglyph An ornament on a vertical block in a Doric frieze that has two **V**-shaped vertical grooves (called **glyphs**) and a half-groove on each edge of the block, making a total of three grooves. Triglyphs may alternate with plain or sculptured blocks called **metopes.** Found in America, for example, in the **Greek Revival style.**

triglyph

trim 1. Decorative moldings or woodwork, exterior or interior, such as baseboards, cornices, casings, or the decorative woodwork hanging from the eaves of a **Carpenter Gothic** roof. 2. Any visible element or finishing, usually of wood or metal, that covers or protects joints, edges, ends, or openings such as doors or windows.

trim,1: in a gable

trim block Same as **corner block.**

trimmer 1. A timber that, as part of the roof framing, a wooden partition, or the like, supports a framing member that in turn supports the end of a joist, rafter, or stud. 2. In floor construction, a small horizontal beam into which the ends of the joists are framed; often named for the place of use, such as a hearth trimmer or a stair trimmer.

tripartite house In rural areas, a house that serves three functions under a single roof, for example, serving as living quarters, an area for the threshing of grain, and a stable.

tripartite scheme A type of design for a multistory commercial building often associated with the work of Louis H. Sullivan (1856–1924). The building's façade is characterized by three principal divisions: a *base,* usually consisting of the lowest two or three stories of the building; a *cap,* of one to four stories in height at the top of the building, and a *shaft,* consisting of the floors between the base and the cap. Such a building has a flat roof, projecting eaves, imposing arched or occasionally round-topped windows, vertical strips of windows separated by massive mullions, and massive arched doorways. In Sullivan's designs the decorative elements typically consist of highly ornate friezes with interwoven foliated designs in low relief (particularly in terra-cotta), which usually appear in **spandrels,1**, over entrances, and at the cornices. The verticality of such a building is emphasized by piers between the windows. *See* **Sullivanesque.**

tripartite vault A vault, covering a triangular space, which is formed by the intersection of three barrel or three conical vaults.

tripartite window, triple window 1. Same as **three-part window.** 2. Same as **treble sash.**

triple-decker Same as **three-decker.**

triplex house A house that provides living quarters for three families, each with a separate entrance; usually has three stories, with one apartment on each floor.

tripteral Having three wings or three rows of columns.

tristyle in antis A portico which has three columns between antae. *See also* **distyle in antis**.

troweled joint A **mortar joint** in a masonry wall, finished by removing excess mortar with a trowel.

tripartite scheme
Columbia Trust Company (1910), New York City;
McKim, Mead & White, Architects

truncated roof A **gable roof** or **hipped roof** whose top has been cut off, forming a flat, horizontal top surface.

truss A combination of structural members, usually in some form of triangular arrangement, that provides a rigid framework for supporting roofs, floors, and the like. *See* **king-post truss, queen-post truss.**

truss blade Same as **principal rafter.**

tuck pointing A method of treating masonry joints in which each joint is filled with brick-colored mortar; the joint is finished with a narrow groove along its center that is filled with fine hard lime or putty so that it projects slightly and is then painted white, in contrast to the brick-colored mortar around it. Thus the joint appears to be very thin. Also called tuck-and-pat pointing or tuck-joint pointing.

Tudor arch A **pointed arch** whose inner surface is struck from four centers; occasionally found in **Tudor Revival** architecture.

Tudor chimney A term occasionally used for a **stepped-back chimney.**

truncated roof: on a house with a pent roof between the first and second floor

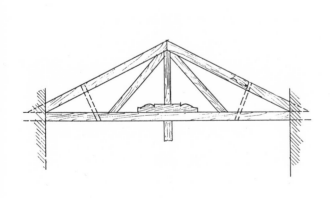

(a)

(b)

truss
(a) Mission San Francisco de Asís (1791), San Francisco, Calif.; (b) supporting roof between adobe walls, chapel of Mission San Antonio de Pala (1816), Pala, Calif.

Tudor Revival, Tudor style A mode of domestic architecture, popular in America primarily from about 1880 to 1940 and beyond; reminiscent of architecture developed in England under the Tudors (1485–1558). Compare with **Neo-Tudor, Elizabethan architecture, Jacobethan style.**

Tudor Revival homes are usually asymmetrical and exhibit a number of the following characteristics:

Façade and exterior wall treatments: Commonly clad in brick or stucco or wood and stucco; often the first story is clad in brick or stone with a contrasting material above. Commonly, **false half-timbering** consisting of boards applied over a material such as stucco on lath; usually decorated with **strapwork** surface ornamentation consisting of narrow bands that are folded, crossed, or interlaced within gables.

Roof treatments: Typically, steeply pitched gables, including cross gables, overhanging gables, or parapeted gables, with little overhang at the eaves; often bargeboards on the gables; slate or wood shingles on

Tudor Revival: (a) 19th-cent. house

the roof; tall, massive, elaborate chimneys, often of patterned brickwork or stonework; steeply pitched triangular dormers; occasionally, massive **stepped-back chimneys,** often with multiple flues and decorative chimney pots atop the chimneys.

Window treatments: Either double-hung windows or casement windows that are tall, narrow, and usually set with a number of small diamond-shaped panes or small square-shaped panes placed diagonally; usually wood or stone window frames and transoms; windows sometimes arranged in groups of three, four, or more; occasionally, oriel windows, semihexagonal bay windows, or dormer windows.

Doorway treatments: A decorative element or structure around the main entry door, often incorporating a **Tudor arch** or a round-topped arch.

Tudor Revival: (b) entrance to Hammerstein House (1921), Long Island, N.Y.;
Dwight James Baum, Architect

tufa A porous limestone used in masonry construction, usually coated with stucco; found in **Spanish Colonial architecture of the American Southwest.**

tumbled-in gable Same as **straight-line gable.**

tumbling course A sloping **course** of bricks that are set perpendicular to a **straight-line gable** in **Dutch Colonial architecture**, in imitation of a similar brick construction found in medieval houses in Flanders; such an arrangement provides a better seal against the penetration of moisture through the masonry joints than one in which all courses of bricks within the gable are laid horizontally up to the peak of the gable. Where a sloping course of bricks intersects a horizontal masonry course, a pattern of brickwork called a *mouse-tooth pattern,* said to resemble a series of teeth, is formed.

tumbling course

turned drop A hanging wood ornament, formed on a lathe or hand carved; especially found in timber-framed early colonial houses, usually suspended from a second-floor overhang, either at the corners or adjacent to the front door. Also called a drop. Compare with **pendant.**

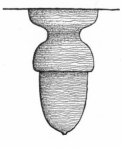

turned drop

turned work Same as **spindlework.**

turret A diminutive cylindrical tower, typically with a conical roof, usually part of a larger structure; often corbeled from one corner of the structure. *See also* illustration under **Châteauesque style.**

turret: Tiffany Residence (1885), New York City;
McKim, Mead & White, Architects

Tuscan order One of the five Classical **orders**; a simplified version of the Roman **Doric order** to which it is similar, but has fewer and bolder moldings, unfluted columns, a plain frieze, and no triglyphs; its only decorative details are moldings.

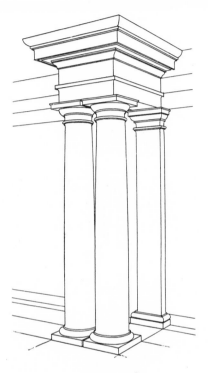

Tuscan order

Tuscan Revival A term descriptive of late-19th-century architecture based on Italian Renaissance architecture of the **Tuscan order.**

Tuscan Revival: French House, Northfield, Ohio

Tuscan Villa style A style somewhat similar to that of villas in the **Italianate style** but having a symmetrical rather than an asymmetrical plan; boxlike in shape, with a flat roof; frequently a square **belvedere** at the center of the roof; windows often round-headed.

twelve-over-twelve (12/12) A term descriptive of a double-hung window having twelve panes in the upper sash and twelve panes in the lower sash.

twelve-over-twelve (12/12) window

twin brick A double-sized **brick.**

two-and-one-half-story house The combination of a two-story house and a loft space between the ceiling of the second floor and the roof above; windows in the gable-end walls and/or dormers provide light and ventilation in the loft space, making it more livable and giving the house a usable additional half-story.

two-and-one-half-story house
in 17th-cent. Massachusetts

two-bay cottage A **Cape Cod house** having a façade with two windows on each side of the front door. Also called a full Cape house.

two-centered arch A **pointed arch** whose inner surface is struck from two centers; the shape of the arch is determined by the position of the centers of curvature and radii of curvature of the two arcs of circles that are joined. *See also* **equilateral arch.**

two-family house A two-story house having two separate living quarters, with a separate entrance for each of two families.

two-family house

two-over-two (2/2) A term descriptive of a double-hung window having two panes in the upper sash and two panes in the lower sash. *See* **pane.**

two-room plan A relatively common **floor plan** for a simple two-room dwelling in American colonial architecture of New England, the mid-Atlantic area, and the South. This plan has many variations but usually consists of an all-purpose main room (the *hall*) and an adjacent room (the *parlor*) containing the best furniture and a bed for the parents. *See* **hall-and-parlor plan.**

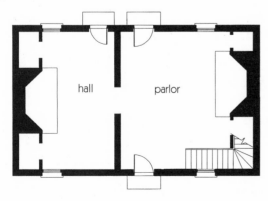

two-room plan

two-tiered porch A porch whose first and second stories are similar.

two-tiered porch

tympanum The space enclosed between the horizontal cornice of a **pediment** and the sloping sides of the pediment.

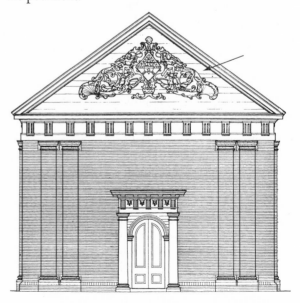

tympanum: Holden Chapel (1744),
Harvard University, Cambridge, Mass.

U

umbrá In **Spanish Colonial architecture,** a **lintel.**

umbrella roof In **French Vernacular architecture** of Louisiana, a roof having a single pitch on each side of a central ridge; the roof covers a **galerie** on each side of the house.

unburnt brick Brick, such as adobe brick, that is sun-dried rather than treated in a kiln at an elevated temperature. Compare with **burnt brick.**

uncased A term descriptive of an arch, doorway, or other opening that has no frame around it. Uncased openings are especially found, for example, in **Mission Revival and Spanish Eclectic architecture.**

uncoursed A term descriptive of masonry not laid with continuous horizontal joints.

underboarding In colonial America, boards, often about 1 inch (2.5cm) thick and as much as 18 inches (46cm) wide, that were fastened to the exterior side of the framing of a **timber-framed house;** they provided a tight surface on which to fasten a covering such as shingles. Often the boards had **tongue-and-groove joints** to provide a superior seal between adjacent boards, thereby giving additional weather protection and significantly better thermal insulation than the earlier hewn-and-pegged timber framing with **infilling** between the framing timbers.

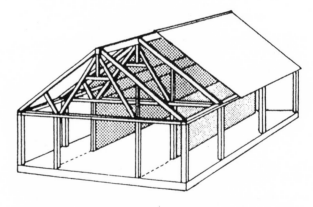

umbrella roof
an early Creole house in Louisiana; in this example, there is a *galerie* on each side of the house

uncoursed masonry: Augusta Stone Church (1749), Fort Defiance, Va.

unframed door A seldom-used synonym for **battened door.**

up-and-down sash An archaic term for a rectangular window **sash** that moves in a vertical plane; a **double-hung window.** This term was used in the early 18th century, when such windows were a novelty and first began to replace **casement windows.**

U-plan The basic **plan** of a house having a shape similar to that of the capital letter **U.**

upping block Same as **horse block.**

urban planning *See* **community planning.**

U-plan
Bandini House (1903), Pasadena, Calif.; Greene and Greene, Architects

V

valley The trough or gutter formed by the intersection of two inclined planes of a roof.

vane *See* **weather vane.**

vault 1. A structure based on the principle of the arch, often constructed of masonry, that consists of an arrangement of **arches** that form a covering over the space below; often found in America in **Collegiate Gothic** and **Gothic Revival** architecture. *See also* **barrel vault** and **groined vault**. 2. An imitation of **vault,1.** 3. A burial chamber, especially one under a church. 4. An underground chamber especially designed for the safekeeping of valuables.

vaulting rib Same as rib,2.

veneer 1. A thin sheet of wood that has been sliced, rotary-cut, or sawn from a log; often used as the top one of several layers of plywood serving as a facing, bonded to a less attractive wood or used as facing on a fire-rated material. 2. A facing of brick, stone, or other material that provides a decorative and durable surface over a structural backing, but is not load-bearing itself; for example, *see* **brick veneer.**

Venetian mode *See* **Italian Renaissance Revival.**

vault
John Russell Pope's 1919 plan for the Gymnasium Court, Yale University, New Haven, Conn.

ventilator An opening or device for providing fresh air and/or for expelling stale air. *See* **roof ventilator** and **slit ventilator.**

ventilator: on the ridge of a barn

veranda An open **porch** or balcony, usually covered, that extends along the outside of a building; usually planned for summer leisure. *See also* **piazza,** a term sometimes used as a synonym for veranda in the South.

vergeboard Same as **bargeboard.**

vermiculated work A type of masonry surface, incised with wandering, discontinuous grooves resembling worm tracks.

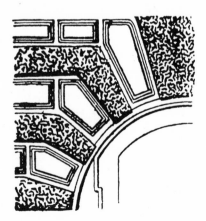

vermiculated work

vernacular architecture Architecture that makes use of common regional forms and materials at a particular place and time; sometimes includes strong ethnic influences of an immigrant population, primarily the Dutch, English, French, and Spanish in the 16th, 17th, and 18th centuries, and the German and Scandinavian immigrants in the 18th and 19th centuries. Vernacular architecture is usually modest, unassuming, and unpretentious, and often a mixture of traditional and more modern styles or a hybrid of several styles. Houses were often owner-built by people familiar with local materials, regional climatic conditions, and local building cultoms and techniques, as described under **folk architecture**. In contrast, industrial vernacular architecture has been the work of architects as well as by owner-builders; their designs often have been based on examples from pattern books, using readily-available manufactured components described in catalogs.

vertical log cabin A **log cabin** whose exterior logs are oriented vertically rather than horizontally.

vertical log cabin

vertical plank door Same as **battened door.**

vertical siding A type of exterior wall **cladding** attached to the wall in a vertical position; most often consists of wide, upright boards that have a tongue along one side edge and a groove along the opposite edge. *See also* **siding** and **tongue-and-groove joint.**

vestibule An anteroom, small foyer, or passageway between the entry door to a house and the interior rooms. *See also* **porch,1.**

vest-pocket park A miniature park that is built on a small plot of land, usually in an urban area.

Victorian architecture A loose term that sometimes covers three picturesque phases of architecture in America: *Early Victorian* (1840–1860), *High Victorian* (1860–1880), and *Late Victorian* (1880–1890 and beyond). Many architectural historians object to the use of such divisions, contending that the term *Victorian* is merely descriptive of an age that encompassed a number of specific exuberant, ornate, and highly decorative architectural styles, such as **High Victorian Italianate** (1860–1885), **High Victorian Gothic** (1860–1890), **Second Empire style** (1860–1890), **Stick style** (1860–1885), **Shingle style** (1880–1890), **Victorian Romanesque** (1870–1890), **Gingerbread folk architecture** (1870–1910), and **Queen Anne style** (1880–1910). Other architectural historians apply the adjectives *Victorian* or *High Victorian* to **Gothic Revival** and **Italianate style** to indicate their latter, more detailed, and more elaborate phases.

Victorian Gothic Same as **High Victorian Gothic**. *See also* **Gothic Revival**.

Victorian Queen Anne style *See* **Queen Anne style**.

Victorian Romanesque A term used by many architectural historians to describe architecture from about 1870 to 1900 that was an outgrowth of, and more ornate than, the **Richardsonian Romanesque style**, from which it differs in both the use of color and texture of masonry, and in being less exact in adapting **Romanesque style** forms. Found primarily in public, commercial, and to a lesser extent in residential buildings.

Victorian Romanesque architecture usually exhibits a number of the following characteristics:

Façade and exterior wall treatments: Rock-faced stone or decorative stonework, often **polychromed;** brick of different colors; terra-cotta panels in patterns, such as bands, checkerboards, and the like; semicircular arches or compound arches similar to those in the Romanesque style; polished rather than textured stone columns as supports for the arches; massive piers; pilastered arcades at ground level; occasionally, a gabled porch or pavilion.

Roof treatments: A steeply pitched roof; steeply pitched wall gables; a multicurved parapet; a **conical roof** atop a cylindrical tower.

Window treatments: Rectangular or rounded window heads framed by masonry arches.

Doorway treatments: Doors set in rounded masonry arches with **voussoirs** of more than one color; occasionally, concentric arches, set within one another, that surround the entry door.

viga In **Spanish Colonial architecture** and its derivatives in the American Southwest, a log that has been stripped of its bark and used as one of number of roof beams spanning the width of a building between opposite adobe walls; usually evenly spaced along the length of the roof to support the roof; usually round in cross section, but they are sometimes hewn square in cross section and decorated. Typically, small straight saplings, called **latias**, are laid on the vigas and covered by a matting of locally available reeds; this combination supports a thick layer of tamped earth, dried mud, or adobe that serves as the roof.

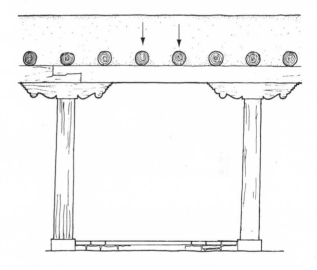

vigas
El Palacio Real de Santa Fe (1614), Santa Fe, N.M.

villa A detached suburban or country house, usually of some pretentiousness.

village green An open space or public park, usually at the center of a village, especially in colonial New England, and still found in some New England towns today. *See also* **common**.

Villa style *See* **Italianate style**.

vinette A running ornament of vine scrolls with grape clusters and leafwork.

Virginia cabin A one-room, relatively crude log cabin in the Chesapeake Bay area from the colonial period into the early 1800s; had a cabin roof and a **clay-and-sticks chimney.**

Virginia house A comparatively simple timber-framed wood house used in the South during the 17th century, originating in the Chesapeake Bay area; supported by posts sunk in the ground (as in **earthfast** construction), rather than by a foundation. The exterior walls were covered with, and the structural frame was strengthened by, a wall cladding of hand-split clapboards.

Virginia rail fence Same as **zigzag fence.**

visitá In **Spanish Colonial architecture** of the early American Southwest, same as **asistencia.**

visor roof A **pent roof,**1 that extends only along one face of a building, usually the façade; found, for example, in buildings of the **Georgian style, Mission Revival, Colonial Revival** architecture.

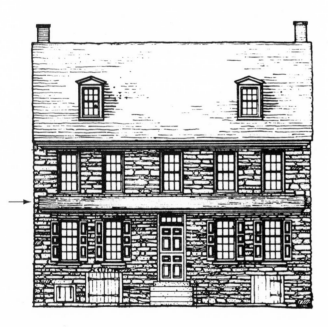

visor roof
Keyser House (1690, enlarged 1734), Philadelphia, Pa.

Vitruvian scroll A series of ornaments, having a spiral or coiled form, that are connected by a wavelike band; a common decoration in Classical architecture. Also called a wave scroll.

V-joint, V-tooled joint A recessed masonry joint, formed in mortar by the use of a **V**-shaped metal tool.

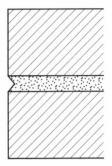

V-joint

V-notch A **notch,** in the shape of the letter **V**, cut into a log or timber near one of its ends; forms a rigid joint when mated with another appropriately notched log or timber in log-cabin or log-house construction.

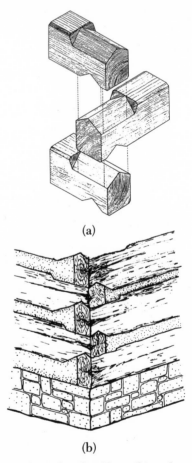

(a)

(b)

V-notch: (a) shaped ends of logs; (b) timbers with chinking between them

volute A spiral **scroll**, for example, the ornamental scroll on an Ionic capital or **console.**

voussoir One of a number of wedge-shaped masonry units that form an arch or vault.

volute (Ionic)

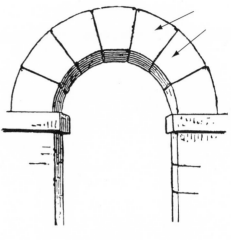

voussoirs

wagon roof Same as **barrel roof.**

wagon shed, wagon house A structure, separate from a main building, once used as a temporary shelter for horse-drawn wagons; usually had at least one open side so that the wagons could be driven directly into the shed without having to open doors. Such sheds were common in rural areas around churches before the advent of automobiles; used primarily on Sundays. Occasionally this term was used as a synonym for **coach house.**

wainscot In current usage, a decorative or protective facing, such as wood paneling, on the lower part of an interior wall or partition. In colonial America, going back as far as the early 1600s, the term commonly referred to the sheathing applied over an entire interior wall surface in either a horizontal or a vertical orientation.

wainscot cap A horizontal molding that finishes the upper edge of a **wainscot.**

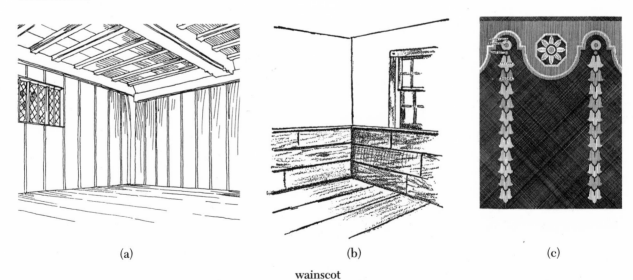

(a) (b) (c)

wainscot
(a) vertical boards used as a wainscot in a timber-framed colonial house; (b) typical low wainscot;
(c) painted wainscot in the mission church (1797–1806) at San Juan Capistrano, Calif.

walk-out basement Same as **American basement.**

wall An upright structure that serves to enclose, support, or subdivide a building, usually presenting a more or less continuous surface except where it is penetrated by openings such as doors and windows. For specific types, *see* **bearing wall, blank wall, blind wall, boarded wall, cavity wall, common wall, counterwall, curtain wall, dead wall, dry wall, gable wall, load-bearing wall, mud wall, non-load-bearing wall, party wall, retaining wall, serpentine wall, springing wall, structural wall.**

wall anchor A wrought-iron clamp on the exterior side of a brick building wall, connected to the opposite wall by a tie rod to prevent the walls from spreading apart. *Also called* **anchor.**

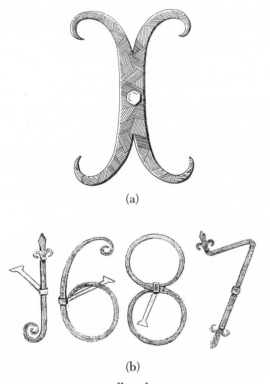

(a)

(b)

wall anchor
(a) wrought iron, of fanciful design;
(b) Dutch Tile House (1687), New Castle, Del.

wall bracket A support that is fixed to a wall to sustain the weight of an imposed load.

wall cladding A nonstructural material used as the exterior covering for the walls of a building. *See also* **cladding.**

wall dormer A **dormer** whose face is integral with the face of the wall below, breaking the line at the cornice of a building. Found, for example, in the **Châteauesque style** and **Richardsonian Romanesque style.**

wall dormer

wall gable A portion of a wall that projects above the roof line in the form of a gable.

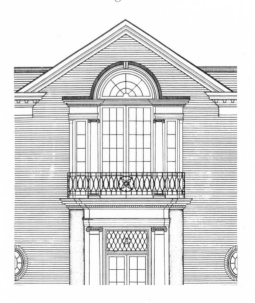

wall gable

wall garden An arrangement of plants set in the joints of a stone wall that incorporate pockets of soil for planting.

wall plate 1. A horizontal member, such as a timber, atop a wall to which it is anchored; supports the end of the ceiling beams, and supports the base end of rafters so as to distribute their loads; it also provides a surface on which to attach other structural elements. Sometimes called a false plate, raising plate, or top plate or wall piece. 2. Same as **sole plate**.

wall post A **post** that supports a **wall plate**.

wall stay Same as **anchor**.

wall tie In masonry, a type of anchorage used to secure a **facing** to the wall behind it.

warehouse A building designed for the storage of materials and merchandise. In colonial America such buildings were usually built for the storage of goods arriving by ship from abroad. Later, when river transportation developed, similar structures were required and constructed inland.

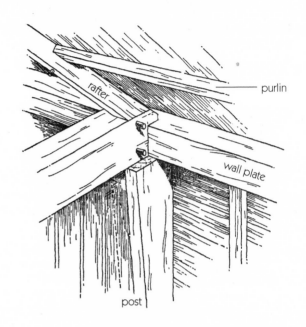

wall plate

(a)   (b)

warehouse
Patterson-Fitzgerald warehouse (late 18th cent.), Alexandria, Va.: (a) west elevation; (b) south elevation

washboard Same as **baseboard.**

wash house A **dependency** or room in a large colonial residence, plantation, or religious community where clothes and linens were washed.

waterboard An obsolete term for **water table.**

water mill A **mill** that is driven, i.e., powered, by running water, such as a stream. *See also* **tide mill.**

water pump A device for raising fresh water from a lower elevation where it is available to a higher elevation where it can be used; of utmost importance in the agricultural and commercial development of colonial America and the West; in the past, often powered by **windmills.**

watershed dormer Same as **shed dormer.**

waterspout A duct, spout, or the like, through which rainwater is discharged from a roof or gutter; for examples, *see* **gargoyle** and **canale.**

water table On a wall, an exterior horizontal ledge that is sloped so as to prevent water from running down the face of the wall below it. Water tables of molded brick were popular on buildings in America during the 18th century, as noted in **American Colonial architecture of the early South.**

water well *See* **well.**

wattle-and-daub A framework consisting of upright wood poles (*wattle*) with branches interwoven between them; then covered with plaster mixed with clay and straw (*daub*). Used, for example, in the construction of primitive structures by the earliest settlers on the Atlantic coast, and used by the padres in their buildings in the American Southwest before they were able to build more substantial missions. Wattle-and-daub was often used to fill the space between structural timbers of **timber-framed houses** in early New England, in order to provide increased thermal insulation of the structure.

wave scroll Same as **Vitruvian scroll.**

weather The portion of a wood shingle that is exposed to the elements. On colonial roofs shingles were somewhat longer than they are today, so that as much as 14 inches (36cm) of a shingle were exposed as *weather.*

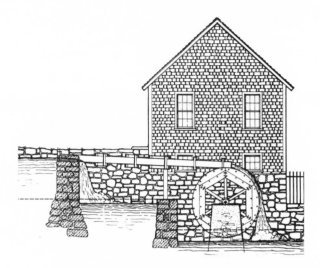

water mill: Brewster, Mass.

water table

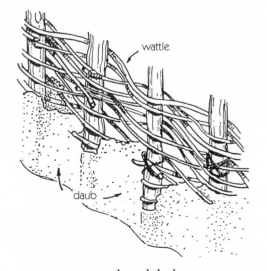

wattle-and-daub

weatherboards Horizontal boards that were commonly used as an exterior covering on early colonial timber-framed buildings to provide weather protection; used, for example, as exterior sheathing to protect the infilling between the structural timbers. The upper edges of weatherboards were commonly tapered to a thinner edge than the lower edge, so they could more easily be overlapped by weatherboards directly above them and shed water. *See also* **clapboards,** which served the same purpose but were usually not as thick as weatherboards.

weatherboards

weathercock A **weather vane** in the shape of a rooster. In very religious colonial New England, the rooster was often used as a weather vane because it was said by some to be a reminder of the perils that might befall its viewers if they denied belief in Christ.

weathercock
said to have been above a tavern (1642) in New Amsterdam that later became its *Stadt Huys* (City Hall)

weather door Same as **storm door.**

weather joint Same as **weather-struck joint.**

weather molding Same as **drip molding.**

weather slating, weather tiling Same as **tile hanging.**

weather-struck joint In brickwork, a horizontal **mortar joint** in which the mortar is sloped outward from top to bottom so as to shed water readily; formed by pressing the mortar inward at the upper edge of the joint. Also called a weather joint.

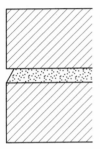

weather-struck joint

weather vane A metal plate, often decorated or in the shape of a figure or object, that rotates freely on a vertical spindle to indicate wind direction; usually located on top of a spire or on another elevated position on a building.

weather vane
hand-forged in Scotland and brought to America in 1692; first placed on spire on Old Tennent Church, Tennent, N.J., in 1751

weaving house Same as **spinning house**.

wedge coping Same as **featheredge coping**.

well A hole that is sunk into the earth to sufficient depth to reach a supply of water; often lined with brick, stones, or timber to prevent the hole from caving in.

well curb A protective structure around the top rim of a **well** to prevent objects from falling into it; also provides a mount for a mechanism for raising a water bucket.

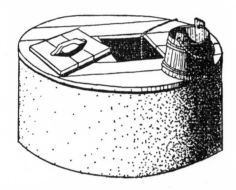

well curb

wellhole The open vertical space between walls in which a stair is a constructed.

well house A shelter for a water **well**.

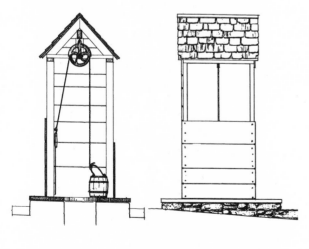

well house

western framing Same as **platform framing**.

Western Stick style An upscale version of the **Craftsman style**; one-story timber-framed residence, developed in California in 1905 and continuing until about 1920, exemplified in the work of Charles Sumner Greene (1868–1957) and his brother Henry Mather Greene (1870–1954), who practiced in Pasadena, California, and whose architectural details were carried to a high art. Compare with **Stick style**.

whaleback roof 1. Same as **ship's-bottom roof**. 2. Same as **compass roof**.

whale house In the early 18th century in New England, a small simple house having exposed rafters; especially favored by whalers of Massachusetts; a **lean-to** containing a kitchen and a small bedroom on each side of the kitchen was often added to the rear of the house. The kitchen fireplace usually backed on the principal fireplace of the dwelling.

wheat-threshing barn *See* **treading barn**.

wheel window A large circular window divided into compartments by **tracery** radiating from the center, suggesting a spokelike arrangement. Especially found in **Gothic Revival** churches.

wheel window: Hartford College, Hartford, Conn.

whitewash An impermanent coating, usually applied with a brush, on exterior walls and surfaces to give them a white appearance; usually a mixture of hydrated lime and water. In colonial days whitewash usually consisted of a mixture of ground-up chalk (*whiting*), lime, flour, glue, and water; sometimes tallow or soap was added. Also called limewash.

wicket A small door set within a larger one.

wickiup Same as **wikiup**.

widow's walk A flat roof deck or raised observation platform, sometimes having a view of the sea, situated on a house's roof, which is enclosed by a balustrade or railing; the horizontal roof surface is usually formed by truncating the top of a hipped roof. Legend has it that a widow's walk was the favorite vantage point for the wife of a ship's captain to look for the return of her husband's ship. This is open to question, however, since many old colonial homes with widow's walks are many miles from the sea. Also called a captain's walk.

wigwam A dwelling, usually housing one or two families, built by American Indians of the Northeast and the Great Lakes region; usually circular or elliptical in plan, but found in a variety of shapes. The most common type of wigwam was a domed structure having a framework of saplings set into the ground, bent over, and tied together with strips of bark. The framework was covered with an overlapping matting of locally available reeds, birch bark, or bark from other trees in the vicinity; this covering was sewn to the frame to form a watertight surface. A hole in the roof at the top of the structure provided an escape for smoke from the firepit below; an opening at the side served as an entrance. The early colonists in New England often used this term for any type of dwelling inhabited by American Indians. Compare with **tipi.** *See also* **bent-frame construction.**

wikiup A relatively small, temporary, round dwelling of the mobile Apache Indians of the American Southwest; could be reassembled relatively easily and quickly. Its lightweight framework was formed by setting a number of saplings into the ground in the shape of a circle, then bending them and lashing them together at their tops so as to form either a domed structure or a conical structure. Additional poles were placed along the sides of the framework to provide added structural strength, and the framework was covered with a thatching of reeds, grass, or the like. *See also* **bent-frame construction.**

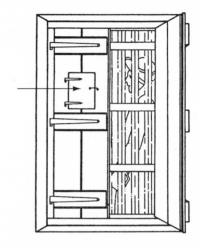

wicket

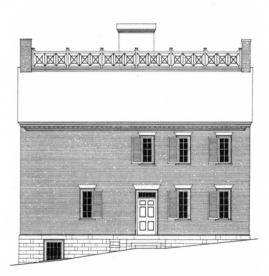

widow's walk: surrounded by balustrade,
Manchester House (1815), Washington County, Pa.

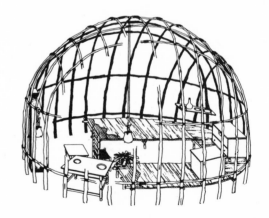

wigwam: of the Chippewas,
with outer covering removed

wind beam In a **timber-framed house**, a horizontal structural member that ties together (and stiffens) two opposite common rafters at a point usually about halfway up the rafters, as in a **collar-beam roof.**

wind brace A **brace** in a **timber-framed house** that resists thrusts in the direction of its own length and strengthens a structure or framework of a building against the wind; often a brace between a **principal rafter** and a **purlin** to provide the structure with greater rigidity. Also called a sway brace.

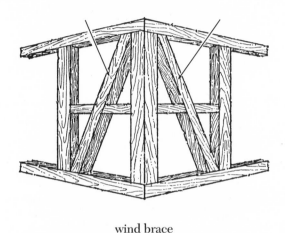

wind brace

winder A wedge-shaped step having its tread wider at its outer end than at the inner end, as steps in a **spiral stair.**

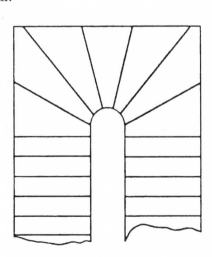

winder

windmill A large machine in which the wind acts on a number of vanes, blades, or sails, rotating them about an axis to produce mechanical power; especially used in the American colonies for grinding grain, sawing timber, and pumping water. The earliest windmills in America had four very large, slow-moving blades that were cloth-covered, similar to those used in Holland. Their speed of rotation was regulated by the amount of cloth covering the blade and by adjusting the direction of the blades with respect to the wind, adjustments that required the constant attendance of an operator. One of the earliest windmills in America was erected near Jamestown, Virginia, in 1632; by 1633 three windmills were in operation in New Amsterdam. In 1854 a patent was issued for an entirely new type of windmill, having a large number of small blades, which was self-regulating and could operate without human intervention; this feature greatly increasing its practical application. Windmills for pumping water played an especially important role in the development of the American West.

windmill (1797): Chatham, Mass.

window An opening, generally in an external wall of a building, to admit light and/or air; usually glazed. The framework in which the glass is set is called a **sash**; a flat sheet of glass, cut to fit a window, or part of a window, is called a **pane.** Because of cost, windows in most houses of the very earliest settlers in colonial America had no glass; instead, the openings were covered with oiled paper or wood shutters. In contrast, more elaborate homes had small **casement windows** containing diamond-shaped pieces of glass held together with grooved, thin lead strips called **cames**. Each of the pieces was usually no larger than four inches by six inches (10 x 15cm). By the mid-1600s, virtually all of the better houses had glazed casement windows. By 1700 many houses had as many as two windows on each side of a centrally located doorway and five front-facing windows on the floor above. Many colonial windows had fixed lights, i.e., windows that could not be opened; others were a combination of fixed lights and a single casement window that opened outward. Following their somewhat earlier introduction in England, double-hung windows appeared in colonial America early in the 1700s, a feature of the emerging Georgian style; their sashes were counterbalanced as early as the 1730s. Most casement windows in existing houses began to be replaced by double-hung windows. **Palladian windows** appeared around 1750. During the American Revolution, the lead cames in many casement windows were removed to make bullets; thus the leaded lights one now sees in many surviving colonial homes are usually replacements of the originals. Definitions and illustrations are given under entries for the following types of windows: **angled bay window, art window, awning window, band window, bay window, blank window, bow window, bull's-eye window, camber window, cant-bay window, cantilevered window, cant window, casement window, Chicago window, circle-head window, circular window, compass window, cottage window, dead window, diamond window, dormant window, dormer, double-hung window, double lancet window, drop-head window, D-window, eyebrow window, false window, flank window, French window, frieze-band window, gable window, hopper window, jalousie, lancet window, landscape window, lattice window, leaded window, lucome window, Lutheran window, operable window, oriel, oval window, Palladian window, peak-head window, pivot window, pocket-head window, ribbon window, semicircular window,**
single-hung window, sliphead window, square-headed window, stepped windows, storm window, three-part window, trellis window, wheel window. *See also* **dome light, fanlight, light, pane, skylight.**

awning window   casement window

double-hung window   hopper window

sliding window   single-hung window

window: terminology

window band Same as **ribbon window.**

window bar 1. A bar across a window to prevent ingress or egress through the opening. 2. A bar for securing a casement or window shutters. 3. Same as **muntin.** 4. Same as **glazing bar.**

window board A horizontal board on a windowsill, fitted against the bottom rail of the lower sash and between the sash frame stiles; forms a base on which the casing rests. Also called a window stool or elbow board.

window casing The finished frame surrounding a window, i.e., the visible frame.

window crown The upper termination of a window, for example, a hood or pediment; found, for example, in the **Federal style, Greek Revival style, Italianate style.** Also called a window cap.

window frame The fixed, nonoperable frame of a window designed to receive and hold the **sash** or **casement** and all its associated hardware.

window head The upper horizontal member across the frame of a window. *See also* **light** and **pane.**

window seat A seat that is built beneath a window sill.

window shutter *See* **shutter, battened shutter, boxing shutter.**

window sill The horizontal bottom member of a window frame.

window surround A decorative frame or structure on the exterior wall surface surrounding a window. Often found in 18th- and 19th-century buildings in America.

wing A subsidiary part of a building projecting from the main building structure. A building can have a wing on one side or both sides of it.

window crown
fabricated of cast iron, Town Hall, Bellevue, Neb.

window seat
Carter's Grove (1751–1753), Charles City County, Va.

wings
projecting from both sides of a colonial Virginia house
(shown in plan)

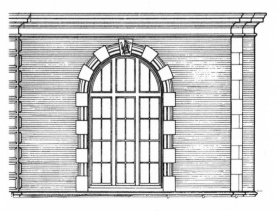

window surround
M.I.T. (1885) on Boylston Street, Boston, Mass.

winter house 1. A transportable dwelling of the Kutchin Indian tribe of interior Alaska: poles were bent to provide a domed structural framework that was then covered with tanned caribou skins, with snow piled around the base to prevent cold air from infiltrating the dwelling; the entire structure could be taken apart and transported on dog-pulled toboggans. 2. A type of **plank house.**

winter house,1

wire nail A machine-made **nail**, at first fabricated from iron wire and later from steel wire by an automatic production technique that revolutionized the manufacturing of nails. Invented abroad and first made in America in the 1850s, such nails were used extensively by the 1870s because of their low cost and ease of application over nails wrought by hand or cut from metal plates. Despite these advantages, wire nails did not entirely replace the earlier types of nails because their holding power was not as great as cut nails of corresponding size. In modern wire nails, this disadvantage has been remedied by introducing spiral flutes or saw-tooth ridges on the shank of the nail; commonly used in finishing, flooring, siding, roofing, and for general purposes in building construction.

witch door In early colonial America, a door whose lowest panels formed a capital letter **X**; thought by some to ward off evil spirits. Compare with **Christian door.**

witch door

witch's hat 1. A **conical roof** with an especially steep slope. 2. Same as **bonnet roof.**

withdrawing room An obsolete term for a **drawing room.**

withe A partition that separates two flues in the same chimney stack.

wood brick A piece of wood the size and shape of a brick; inserted in brickwork to serve as a means of attaching finishings, and the like. Also called a fixing brick or nailing brick.

wood chimney A chimney built of wood boards and plastered on its interior, usually with clay, to provide a measure of fire protection *See* **clay-and-sticks chimney.**

wood-frame construction Building construction in which exterior walls, load-bearing walls and partitions, floor and roof constructions, and their supports are all built of wood. *See* **balloon framing, platform framing, timber-framed building, timber-framed house.** Compare with **steel-frame construction.**

wood-framed house *See* **timber-framed house.**

woodgraining Simulating a wood grain by painting a surface with a translucent stain, then working the stain into suitable patterns with graining brushes, combs, and rags to produce the appearance of wood. *See also* **false woodgraining** and **faux bois.**

wood joint A **joint** formed by two boards, timbers, or sheets of wood that are held together by nails, fasteners, pegs, or the like. For specific types of wood joints, *see* **butt joint, dado joint, dovetail joint, half dovetail, half-lap joint, hewn-and-pegged joint, mortise-and-tenon joint, scarf joint, tongue-and-groove joint.**

wood lath One of many narrow strips of wood that serve as a base for plaster; usually nailed at regular intervals to **studs** or to boards in walls and ceilings. Before the early 1800s, wood lath was hand-split from larger pieces of wood. Later such strips were usually cut with circular saws, providing slats of relatively uniform width and thickness. The use of wood lath as a base for plaster is now obsolete in America, having been replaced by **metal lath.**

wood shingle A thin roofing unit of wood, usually cut from green wood and then kiln-dried, either split along the grain or cut to stock lengths, widths, and thicknesses; used as an exterior covering on sloping roofs and on side walls and applied in an overlapping fashion. Before the American Revolution, cedar, chestnut, oak, or white-pine shingles between 14 and 36 inches (35–91cm) long (much longer than present-day shingles) were commonly hand-split and were not painted. At that time, the exposed length of a shingle, called the *weather*, was usually between 8 and 16 inches (20–41cm). Wood shingles are still in use as, for example, on modern Cape Cod houses. *See* **shingle.**

woodwork Work produced by carpenters and joiners. This term is generally applied to parts of objects or structures in wood rather than to the complete structure.

worm fence Same as **zigzag fence.**

wraparound porch A full-width porch that continues around the sides of a house.

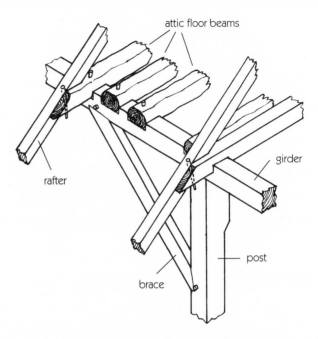

wood-frame construction

wood shingles

Wrightian An imprecise term suggestive of the work of Frank Lloyd Wright (1867–1959) and some of his followers. Unlike Henry Hobson Richardson (1838–1886), who had a style of architecture named after him, or Ludwig Mies van der Rohe (1886–1969), whose works sometimes are referred to as *Miesian,* and Louis H. Sullivan (1856–1924), whose works are sometimes referred to as *Sullivanesque,* Wright cannot be characterized by a single style of architecture. Some of his early buildings are closely associated with the work of the **Prairie School**, emphasizing a low-to-the-ground, horizontal appearance, with eaves having a considerable overhang; an example is the Glasner House in Glencoe, Illinois. These buildings are in marked contrast to later Wright designs such as the Samuel Freeman House in Los Angeles, which features the use of decorative concrete block units, or the Edgar Kaufmann House, often called "Fallingwater," cantilevered over a stream at Bear Run, Pennsylvania. *See also* **Organic architecture** and **Prairie style.**

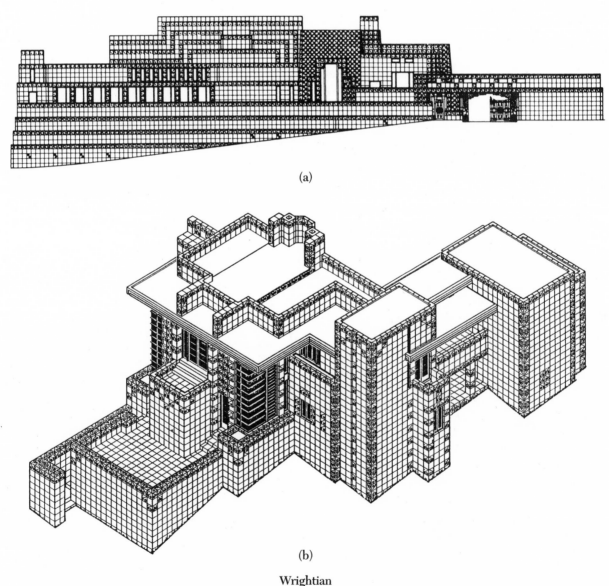

(a)

(b)

Wrightian
Frank Lloyd Wright, Architect: (a) Freeman House (west elevation);
(b) Freeman House (1924), Los Angeles, Calif. (isometric view from southeast)

Lewis Mumford, in published comments in 1925, said in a tribute to Wright:

> Safety first is an American phrase; and Safety first became the ruling word in architecture. A good building became one which in almost every particular was based on some acknowledged building. The desire to possess "old masters" did not confine itself to pictures, for the pictures needed frames and it remained for the architects to supply one. This panic for aesthetic security extended itself even to buildings which were palpably designed for use; hence the skyscraper with Renaissance facades. . . . What was the original architect to do in such a situation? Fortunately there is never a large supply of original artists. . . . The center of American architecture has been occupied by the able technicians. The periphery has been divided between the cultivated stylists and the outcasts who were neither fashionable, nor in the narrow sense "practical." In a sense, Mr. Wright is our most distinguished outcast. It is no little honor.

No longer an outcast, he is a legend.

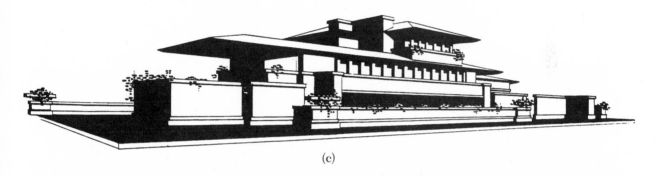

(c)

(d)

Wrightian
(c) Robie House (1909), Chicago, Ill.
(d) Edgar Kaufmann House, "Fallingwater" (1936–1937), Bear Run, Fayette County, Pa.

wrought iron A relatively pure iron that is highly malleable and so can be wrought, i.e., beaten into shape, usually by the local blacksmith, to form decorative ironwork; it is also readily forged and welded. It is valued for its corrosion resistance, its ductility, and because it is far less susceptible to rusting than cast iron, which requires painting. Compare with **cast iron.**

wrought nail An iron **nail** individually beaten into shape with a hammer, often with a head forged into a pattern that is either decorative or devised for a special-purpose nail, such as attaching a hinge to a post. The first wrought nails were imported from England and were used in building construction in America before the invention of machines for manufacturing nails. The use of wrought nails in a house is often an indication that it was built before the year 1800.

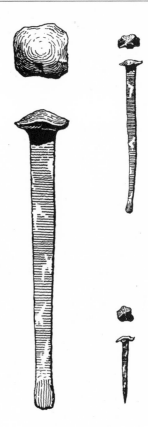

wrought nails

X, Y, Z

X-brace Any **brace** that crosses another to form the letter **X**; used, for example, in **Stick style** architecture.

Yankee barn A steeply pitched, timber-framed, side-gabled wood barn of **post-and-lintel construction**, often with a gambrel roof; usually with no **forebay.** Typically built against a hillside, with animals housed at ground level, adjacent to the barnyard; similar to a **bank barn**. Found from New England to the eastern Midwest.

zaguán In **Spanish Colonial architecture** of the American Southwest, a massive wooden gate that was often sheltered and wide enough to permit wagons, coaches, or carts to enter a courtyard (**placita**) of a **casa del rancho**; usually provided with a heavy bar that could be slid into position to prevent the gate from being opened. Pedestrians entered the courtyard either through a small door adjacent to the *zaguán* or through a small door set into the *zaguán* itself.

zambullo door In early **Spanish Colonial architecture,** primarily in New Mexico, a wood door hung on wood pintle hinges.

zapata In **Spanish Colonial architecture** of the American Southwest, a horizontal piece of wood, atop a post, that provides greater bearing area to support the load on the post imposed from above; usually carved; similar to a **bolster,1** but usually more highly decorated.

zaguán

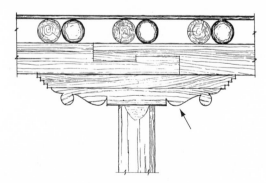

zapata
El Palacio Real de Santa Fe (1614), Santa Fe, N.M.

Z-braced battened door A **battened door** held together by two horizontal boards that are joined by a diagonal board; suggestive of the letter **Z**.

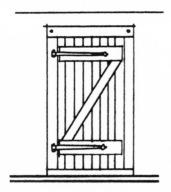

Z-braced battened door

zigzag fence A fence constructed of split rails that, in **plan**, alternate in direction, usually at a wide angle of about 120 degrees. Such a fence is simple to build. At the intersection between the two stacks of rails, uprights are sometimes driven into the ground and lashed to the fence to improve its stability.

zigzag fence

Zigzag Moderne *See* **Art Moderne.**

zinc A metallic element used in sheet form as a roofing material in America as early as the 1820s, especially in New York City; usually laid with **standing seams.** From about 1830 onward, used as a coating on iron to form galvanized iron, which has the important property of resisting rust.

zoophorus A horizontal band bearing carved figures of animals or persons, especially the sculptured frieze in Classical architecture in the **Ionic order.**